NORMANDY:
THE REAL STORY

NORMANDY:
THE REAL STORY

How Ordinary Allied Soldiers
Defeated Hitler

BRIG. GEN. DENIS WHITAKER,

DSO & Bar, CM, ED, CD, Officer Legion of Honor (Fr),
Commander of the Crown (Blg), DMSc (honoras causa)

SHELAGH WHITAKER

WITH
TERRY COPP

PRESIDIO
PRESS

BALLANTINE BOOKS • NEW YORK

A Presidio Press Book
Published by The Random House Publishing Group

www.presidiopress.com

A Library of Congress Control Number can be obtained from the publisher upon request.

ISBN 0-345-45907-5

Book design by Joseph Rutt

Manufactured in the United States of America

First Edition: May 2004

2 4 6 8 10 9 7 5 3 1

TO DENNY

Acknowledgments

The subtitle of this book mirrors its theme: *How Ordinary Allied Soldiers Defeated Hitler*. It is the thoughts and deeds of these warriors of Normandy that we now present. They were far from ordinary, these young soldiers and airmen; they gave up their youth and lives to fight for freedom. Scores of these veterans of six nations were generous in sharing with us their personal experiences, their diaries, letters, and photographs, giving us unconditional permission to use them. The many references in our endnotes at the back of this book to these interviews and personal archives are a reflection of their value. We are very grateful for the confidence and support of these men. The authors take full responsibility for any errors or omissions.

The authors gratefully acknowledge the support of the Ontario Arts Council. We thank the National Archives, the National Archives of Canada, the Public Record Office in the UK, the Royal Hamilton Light Infantry, the Royal Canadian Military Institute, the Eisenhower Center for American Studies (Metropolitan College, University of New Orleans), and the Laurier Centre for Military Strategic and Disarmament Studies, for their generous permissions for the use of their documents and photographs.

We especially single out the historians of the Laurier Centre, Mike Bechthold, John Maker, and Karen Priestman, the indexer of this book, for their invaluable research, guidance, and assistance.

We walked the battlefields of Normandy with much help and encouragement. Of great value—and fun—were the days we spent clambering over battle sites with the fine young scholarship students of the Canadian Battlefields Foundation. For each of the past ten years the Foundation has awarded scholarships to twelve senior university students for two intensive weeks studying the battle sites of the wars of the twentieth century.

We had a fascinating day reliving the St. Lambert battle through the eyes of men who grew up in that area, assembled and coordinated with the help of a scholar of the battle, Colonel Jacques van Dijke of Rotterdam. We thank Ms. Pierre Grandvalet, Fank, Margerie, Madeleine, Huille, and Masson for their *témoinages* and hospitality.

In Argentan we met M. Poulain; in Chambois, M. Chambart; in Thury Harcourt, Abbé Launay (formerly padre of Tournai-sur-Dives); in Falaise, M. Digueres and M. James; in Mortain, M. Langlois and M. Buisson; in Paris, M. Eddy Florintin.

Our research on the Polish military was greatly assisted by Krzysztof (Chris) Szydlowski, vice president of the 1st Polish Armoured Association of Canada, who introduced us to veterans of those days; and by Alicja Altenberger, executive editor of *The Life of Polonia*, a Quarterly Publication of the Polish American Congress of Eastern Massachusetts, Boston.

We appreciate the thoughtfulness and professionalism of our agents, Linda McKnight, Westwood Creative Artists of Toronto, and Milly Marmur of New York City, and of our editor at Presidio Press, Ron Doering. The excellent maps are the work of Paul Kelly, gecko graphics inc. Kirsten Sheffield created the wonderful portraits of the soldiers of Normandy.

We are grateful to Linda Risacher Copp, Professor Ian Shaw, Bill Baggs, Ken Turnbull, and Martie Whitaker for their critiques and technical advice. During the lengthy process of producing five books of military history, our families have stood by us with unwavering love and understanding. Thank you.

Contents

Normandy Key Maps

A The Normandy Bridgehead, July 24, 1944 (map on page xiv–xv)

B Breakout in the Bocage (map on page 80)

British Breakout: Operation *Bluecoat* (map on page 92)

C Mortain Counter-Attack (map on page 110)

D Operation *Totalize* (map on page 134)

E Operation *Tractable* (map on page 182)

F Trun-Chambois Gap: August 18 (map on page 226)

G Victory in Normandy (map on pages 258–59)

H Closing the Gap: August 21 (map on page 290)

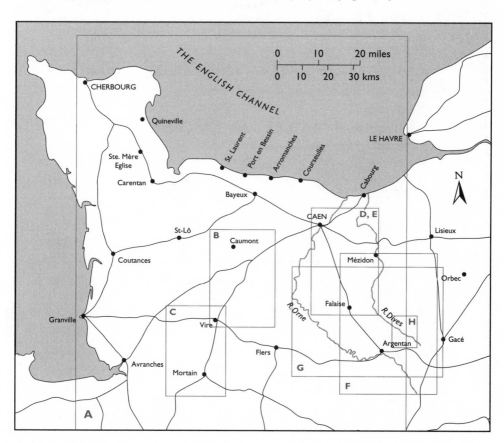

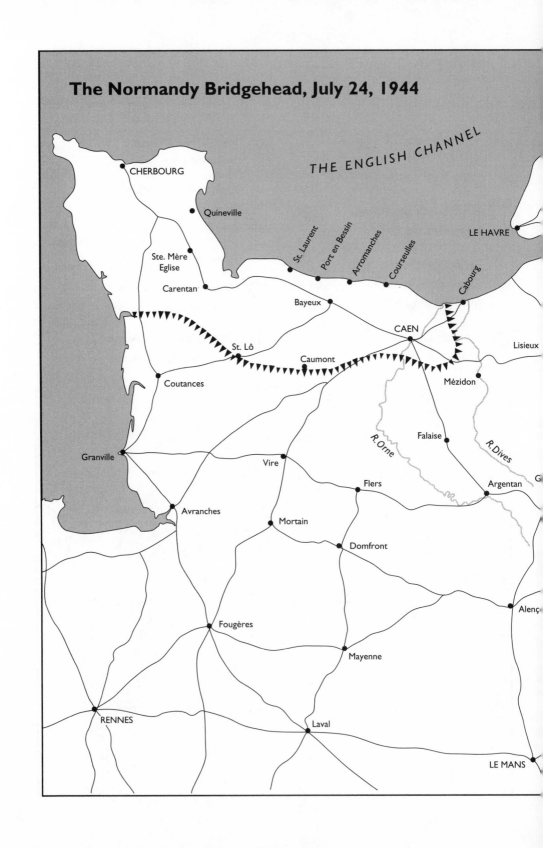

The Normandy Bridgehead, July 24, 1944

THE ENGLISH CHANNEL

CHERBOURG

Quineville

Ste. Mère
Eglise

Carentan

St. Laurent

Port en Bessin

Arromanches

Courseulles

LE HAVRE

Cabourg

Bayeux

CAEN

Lisieux

St. Lô

Caumont

Coutances

Mézidon

R. Orne

Falaise

R. Dives

Granville

Vire

Flers

Argentan

Avranches

Mortain

Domfront

Alenç

Fougères

Mayenne

RENNES

Laval

LE MANS

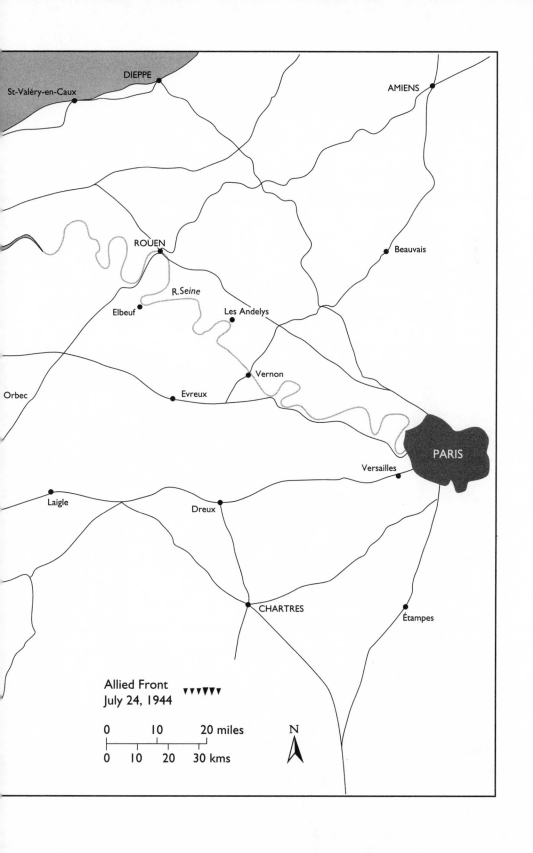

St-Valéry-en-Caux

DIEPPE

AMIENS

Beauvais

ROUEN

R. *Seine*

Elbeuf

Les Andelys

Vernon

Orbec

Evreux

PARIS

Versailles

Laigle

Dreux

CHARTRES

Étampes

Allied Front
July 24, 1944 ▼▼▼▼▼▼

0   10   20 miles

0   10   20   30 kms

N

Preface

Helping to research a book when one of the authors is an authentic war hero and the other an experienced journalist and writer is a sobering experience for an academic historian. Denis Whitaker led one of the most consistently effective battalions in the Allied armies and won two DSOs [Distinguished Service Orders] in close combat with the enemy.

A soldier's soldier, he knew battle from the sharp end and from the planner's perspective. Denis was always ready to question official explanations, especially when offered by generals or historians who lacked direct experience of combat.

The limitations of allied armor, the strength of German reverse slope defenses, the problems of combat in *bocage*like country were all challenges that he had met and mastered on the battlefield.

Denis's skepticism was reinforced by his wife Shelagh's training and instincts as a journalist. Shelagh wanted clear, comprehensible answers to basic questions. The writer's job, she argued, was to clarify issues — not to add complexity and confusion.

As we collaborated on our research of the Normandy campaign, two factors became paramount: It was the soldiers who won the battle, and it was their commanders who very nearly lost it.

The land troops and the supporting airmen destroyed two large, well-equipped German armies in just seventy-six days. They accomplished this despite faulty leadership, inferior equipment, and bad command decisions.

The allied armies were commanded by men whose inflated reputations are hard to understand. Montgomery may have been the master of the set-piece battle, but after the American breakout at St. Lô he proved unable to manage a fluid battle. His failure to reinforce the Canadians on the north side of the Falaise Pocket, or to order the Americans to close from the south allowed tens of thousands of enemy soldiers to escape to fight another day.

Montgomery was not the only one to endanger the soldiers' victory in Normandy. Eisenhower's passive behavior throughout the campaign suggests that he had not yet acquired the attributes of a great commander. Bradley's role in stopping Patton at Argentan and failing to insist that his aggressive army commander keep enough divisions in position to close the trap raises serious questions about his qualifications to command an army group in 1944.

The Allies also suffered from a high proportion of corps and divisional commanders who were not up to their job. Generals like the American Joe Collins, the British Richard O'Connor, and the Canadian Guy Simonds stand out because so many others failed to innovate or inspire.

The Normandy campaign was a learning experience for everyone, and many of the lessons were put to good use for the balance of the war, but this should not be allowed to disguise the command failures that made a great victory less decisive than it could have been.

—Terry Copp

PART I

JULY:

THE
NORMANDY
STALEMATE

CHAPTER 1

Operation *Fortitude*

D + 44: *July 20, 1944*

"Make peace, you fools! What else can you do?" Field Marshal
Gerd von Rundstedt bellowed to his army chiefs and slammed
down the receiver.[1]

This disloyal outburst by Adolf Hitler's commander in chief of many years
fanned the paranoia of the Führer. It also unleashed a desperate, if futile,
response from a rebellious hard core of senior staff officers of the German
Wehrmacht who had lost confidence in Hitler and his Nazi henchmen.

What else could they do? Rundstedt asked. The answer was clear: as-
sassinate the man who was destroying their Fatherland.

At 12:30 P.M. on July 20, 1944, Colonel Count Claus von Staffenberg
entered the conference room at the Führer's headquarters, "Wolfschanze,"
in Rastenburg, East Prussia. The stern military stance of this *Wehrmacht*
aristocrat gave no quarter to his disabilities: the patch on one eye, the
sleeve neatly pinned over an amputated arm, the remaining hand with just
three fingers.

Von Staffenberg formally greeted the Führer and took a seat nearby,
carefully lowering his heavy briefcase to the floor under the solid wooden
map table. Abruptly he left, explaining that he had to make a telephone
call before presenting his brief. An officer by chance moved the case to the
far side of the table from Hitler's seat. Moments later, an explosion rocked
the room.

It was a near miss. *Wehrmacht* General Walter Warlimont described
the map room as a "scene of stampede and destruction. There was nothing but wounded men groaning, the acrid smell of burning, and charred
fragments of maps and papers fluttering in the wind."[2] Although injured,

Hitler survived and was able to address his Nazi supporters by radio within a few hours. He quickly squashed the uprising and executed hundreds of suspected perpetrators.

Hitler later had killed hundreds of people he suspected of plotting against him. The assassination attempt verified his conviction of untrustworthiness of the *Wehrmacht*. It verified, too, his certainty of his own destiny. Stand fast remained his orders to all divisions.

It would be the death knell for close to a hundred thousand German soldiers in the next four weeks.

Rundstedt's latest audacity gave Hitler the opportunity to fire the veteran army chief. He now took direct control of his western armies, appointing only loyal Nazi officers to all-important commands.

Many of Hitler's senior commanders also disagreed with their leader, but dared not defy him in case they, too, were accused of plotting against him. However, Rundstedt's replacement, sixty-one-year-old Field Marshal Günther Hans von Kluge, frankly warned Hitler that the tide of battle was turning against them.

"*Der kluge Hans*," or "Clever Hans," as he was, not always with admiration, nicknamed, quoted from the now-doomed Field Marshal Rommel's situation report (sitrep) of July 15: "We have lost 97,000 men, including 2,360 officers. We have received up till now 10,000 men as replacements."

As well, the newly appointed Commander in Chief West reminded Hitler that constant allied air strikes were crippling their rail lines, resulting in a severe loss of arms and equipment, especially radio equipment, artillery, cannon, and machine guns. "The enemy are daily providing new forces and masses of materials for the front; the enemy supply lines are not challenged by the *Luftwaffe* and enemy pressure is continually increasing. The German reserves are dwindling.

"The moment is fast approaching when this overtaxed front line is bound to break up," Kluge reported.[3]

Hitler insisted that he would not, under any circumstances, consider withdrawal.

Fortunately for the Allies, the Führer continued to be convinced that Lieutenant General Bernard Montgomery was planning a massive attack

120 miles east of Caen at the Pas de Calais, with a fresh US army under Lieutenant General George Patton. This illusion of a further attack by the mythical *Armée Gruppe* Patton at the Pas de Calais continued to immobilize still more German divisions east of the River Seine. Hitler still stubbornly held the entire Fifteenth German Army in the northeast sector of France against such an attack.

But there was a mystery. *Where was Patton?* Was he still held in disgrace after his clash with his superiors in Sicily, the infamous slapping incident when he accused a soldier of malingering? Or was he, as the *Wehrmacht* spies insisted, waiting in the wings in Kent?

And *when* would *Armée Gruppe* Patton launch that main allied assault on the Pas de Calais?

Adolf Hitler would have been surprised to learn that on D-plus-44 the elusive Lieutenant General George Patton was sitting in a Normandy orchard in the warm July sunshine, munching an apple and venting his frustrations to his headquarters staff. "My destiny in this war," he grumbled, "is to sit here on my ass and watch the cider apples grow."[4] The only response was the energetic tail-wagging of Patton's white English bull terrier, Willie, a canny pooch whose original owner had been shot down over Germany.

Patton had arrived secretly in France on July 6. For two weeks since, the irascible tank commander had been languishing at Nehou, a rural village in the interior of the Cotentin Peninsula. As he had only a paper army, a minuscule, tented Third Army headquarters, and no orders, his frustration grew and festered. It seemed that while everyone else was doing the fighting, taking center stage, George Patton was left waiting in the wings. It was not a role he accepted easily. At fifty-nine years of age, he was afraid a younger man would take over his command. Slightly tongue-in-cheek, Patton had offered the Supreme Allied Commander General Dwight D. Eisenhower (his West Point junior by six years) one thousand dollars for each week by which Ike would hasten his operational command.[5]

In the winter months prior to D-Day, Ike had assigned command of the Third US Army to Patton. But the army could not become operational in Normandy until the First US Army achieved its breakout at Avranches, at the base of the Cherbourg Peninsula. Meanwhile, elements of Third

US Army were gradually and surreptitiously being moved into Nehou. Patton had been unable to resist jumping the gun to make his unauthorized appearance there.

His impatience stemmed from the fact that by the third week of July he seemed not much closer to fulfilling his command. For six weeks the Americans and British had been mired in a desperate and costly battle of attrition while struggling to get through the twenty-mile-deep belt of swamp and hedgerow country: the *bocage*.

For Patton, the breakout of Third Army was tantalizingly close.

Eisenhower had issued a media ban concerning Patton for security purposes, so there was no general knowledge of his appointment as commander of the Third Army in Normandy. Press interviews and quotes were forbidden. This was particularly hard on a man who so relished publicity. The media loved Patton; he was invariably good copy. Eisenhower, who was his boss and close friend, said he had a "genius for explosive statements."[6] In truth, he shot from the mouth with the same flair as he carried his famed ivory-handled pistols: indiscreetly and for effect.

Patton's impulsive "Top Secret" arrival on July 6 was a case in point: a crowd of soldiers cheering "Georgie!" met him, along with an inquisitive press, who had somehow deduced his plans. They pestered him with questions.

The performance was typical of the Patton paradox: he was feared by the troops yet adored by them; admired by his commanders and associates as a skilled tank strategist but in constant hot water with them. He was the most quoted of all the allied generals but, under an official press secrecy ban, was unquotable.

Eisenhower was unsure of his army commander. The entire world knew Patton was in disgrace, and very nearly fired, for slapping a shell-shocked soldier in a hospital ward in Sicily. How far, Eisenhower wondered, could he be trusted again?

All things considered, there never was a less suitable candidate to be the focus of a top secret conspiracy whose success depended almost entirely on Patton's prime shortcoming: discretion. Hatched by British intelligence as one of World War II's most elaborate deceptions, Operation *Fortitude* was launched.

Fortitude was the brainchild of XX (Twenty) Committee. In 1942, British intelligence became aware of reports being passed to Berlin, allegedly by a German agent in Portugal. The reports, full of inaccuracies and absurdities, intrigued the committee sufficiently that they tracked down the author, one Juan Pujol Garcia, a twenty-nine-year-old Spaniard of a good family. Garcia, it transpired, loathed the German regime and had been feeding German intelligence gross misinformation under the guise of serving as a German agent. His research resources were almost as ludicrous as the reports that stemmed from them: "a map of the United Kingdom, a *Blue Guide* [travel book] to England, a Portuguese study of the British Fleet and an Anglo-French dictionary of military terms."

Working from Lisbon, Garcia had for the previous ten months been concocting reports of troop movements of nonexistent British regiments, the sailing of imaginary convoys, and lurid details of drunken orgies of Glasgow dockworkers.[7] XX Committee lost no time in recruiting this enterprising young Spaniard as a double agent and relocating him to Great Britain. "Garbo" was born.

The objective of XX Committee was not only to pass misinformation convincingly to the enemy, but also to persuade the *Abwehr* (German foreign and counterintelligence) to eventually act on it. This was the challenge the XX Committee faced in the months leading up to the 1944 invasion of France. It was pointless to cover up the fact that an assault was being planned; the massing of troops, tanks, and landing craft would make that obvious. Their intention, therefore, became one of deceiving the enemy as to the time, strength, and location of the attack.

As plans for the D-Day invasion took shape, it became apparent to the Allies that they would have enormous difficulties landing a small force on the open beaches of the Normandy coast against a large force of well-entrenched defenders. The Germans had to be convinced somehow that the main thrust of the D-Day landing would take place elsewhere—far enough down the coast that enemy divisions would be misdirected to a benign area. Thus would the strength of the German defenders against the actual invaders be reduced.

Enter "Garbo." Comfortably settled in England by his new employers, and cheerfully banking the generous Deutchmarks of his old ones, he set about convincing the *Abwehr* that a nonexistent First US Army Group (FUSAG) was massing in strength in Kent, in southeastern England. This army would form the main invasion force, striking at the Pas de Calais after General Montgomery's secondary 21st Army Group had established a lodgment farther west in France.

Described by the dean of British intelligence, Michael Howard, as "perhaps the most complex and successful deception operation in the entire history of the war," *Fortitude* established its credibility with the *Abwehr* through an intricate weave of lies and half-truths, laced with just enough facts to make the deception plausible. To command this mythical army group, the XX Committee made the inspired selection of Lieutenant General George Patton, who was deemed "temporarily unemployable" following his disgraceful loss of temper in Sicily. The committee relied on his notorious exhibitionism to attract attention to the force.[8]

FUSAG had (notionally) two real armies under its command—the First Canadian Army and the Third US Army—with a feigned headquarters established in eastern England for this imaginary force of 150,000 men. To reinforce the fiction, a radio network was set up to handle their busy administrative and operational functions. XX Committee arranged that all of Montgomery's 21st Army Group signals to his armies in France, emanating from Portsmouth, be rerouted via Dover. The Royal Air Force (RAF) cooperated by flying twice as many air missions and dropping twice as many bombs over the Pas de Calais as it did over Normandy.

"Garbo" worked with extreme dedication for two years to establish the deception. He flooded German intelligence with manufactured data. Writing with secret ink, and hiding his communications under innocent messages written with real ink, he wrote no fewer than 315 letters, each averaging two thousand words, in the first year. Via shortwave radio, he sent five or six transmissions each day—twelve hundred in all—dedicated to persuading the *Abwehr* to divert some of their divisions to the Pas de Calais. He had built up an imaginary network of more than two dozen agents that fed him information from across Britain. His favorite invented team was "Donny, Dick and Derrick."[9]

In the months leading up to D-Day, the XX Committee spared no effort to convince the German High Command of its "invasion plan." To his credit, Patton tried to go along with the scheme. He obediently spent some time at the bogus army headquarters in Kent, where, in fact, components of his Third Army divisions were being trained for a landing—but not for the contrived assault that Hitler determinedly believed would be laid on by *Armée Gruppe* Patton from Dover to the Pas de Calais, a mere twenty miles across the English Channel.

At 0300 hours on June 6, 1944—D-Day—"Garbo" sent an urgent dispatch to his control in Madrid that the invasion was imminent. The message, of course, was carefully timed to be just too late to have any value.

There was no response from the Germans, and it wasn't until 0608 hours that he finally got through. Later that day "Garbo" complained, with mock indignation, to his German control about their lack of efficiency. "This makes me question your seriousness and sense of responsibility," he told them sternly. "I therefore demand a clarification immediately as to what has occurred." The next morning, after a "sleepless" night, he made contact again. "I am very disgusted as in this struggle for life and death I cannot accept excuses or negligence," he berated his unfortunate employers. "Were it not for my ideals and faith I would abandon this work as having proved myself a failure."[10]

The German agent apologized profusely: "I wish to stress in the clearest terms that your work over the last few weeks has made it possible for our command to be completely forewarned and prepared."[11]

Throughout the next few weeks, "Garbo" continued his extraordinary charade, and German intelligence continued to believe that an American army was at Dover, ready to launch a second invasion. By Hitler's direct order, the German Fifteenth Army—whose fifteen *Panzer* and infantry divisions were urgently needed by his armies fighting for their lives on the Normandy beaches—was still positioned north of the River Seine, awaiting an invasion that would never come. Even Rommel, the astute field marshal, "expected a second landing on both sides of the [Seine] river." An extract from his weekly report read: "In England, another 67 formations are standing to, of which 57 at the very least can be employed for a large-scale operation."[12]

Problems arose, however, when the irrepressible Patton's surreptitious visits to his actual army headquarters in France began to draw attention. It seemed just a matter of time before the media leaked Patton's movements. The planners dreaded the moment when the Germans realized they had been the victims of a hoax. "When the moment came," American historian Carlo D'Este wrote, "there would be a massive and immediate enemy reinforcement of Normandy."[13]

It was imperative that a new front for Operation *Fortitude* be devised.

Again, XX Committee went to work, persuading the highly regarded US Lieutenant General Lesley McNair in Washington to assume nominal command of the bogus army. They reckoned that McNair, chief of the Army Ground Forces, had the credibility to convince the Germans that he was replacing the once-again "demoted" perennial bad boy, Patton.

The greatest hoax of World War II continued to be played out. *Armée*

Gruppe McNair was frequently referred to as an invasion force in German intelligence well into August, and fifteen German divisions enjoyed peaceful seaside postings during June and July at the Pas de Calais.[14]

As for "Garbo," a grateful *Abwehr* agent informed him in July that the "Führer had been graciously pleased to bestow on him the Order of the Iron Cross, Class II."[15]

CHAPTER 2

Le Bocage

Normandy: D-Plus-44

*A young German lieutenant, Hans-Heinrich Dibbern, climbed to
the steeple of a village church in Normandy hoping to locate his
platoon. Instead, he found his destiny. From the top he could see
the coast. "I could see nothing but masses of matériel and
weapons—it was such an experience for me. I thought, "The war is
lost. We don't stand a chance."*[1]

After five weeks of desperate and costly fighting, the allied forces were still
penned in the anteroom of Normandy. Access to the broad Norman plains
remained firmly blocked by the weight of firepower of a desperate enemy.

The original 176,000 allied invaders had now burgeoned into a multi-
national force of more than one million men, all still contained within
that narrow stretch of land some fifty miles long backing onto the English
Channel. The deepest penetration inland was twenty-five to thirty miles;
in many places it was a mere five or six.

What overwhelmed and dismayed Lieutenant Dibbern was the spec-
tacle of the largest assembly of matériel in the history of modern warfare.
Crammed helter-skelter along the coast were tanks, armored vehicles, fuel
drums, weapons, ammunition, materials for bridging and for building
airstrips, barrels of food, of water, and of medical supplies for the troops.
And it was growing by the day. Traffic jams of immense proportions were
the norm.

After the fall of Cherbourg on June 26, the Americans had turned the
full weight of their army south. As they penetrated the enemy-held territory, they found the battleground to be as formidable as the enemy. The
area between the US sector on the coast south to St. Lô—the area the Allies had to penetrate if they were to achieve a breakout—was twenty miles
of dense, hilly hedgerow country. This was the *bocage*.

The Germans were ready for them. The Seventh Army's SS General

Paul Hausser felt secure that in reinforcing his infantry battalions with just two armored divisions—*Panzer Lehr* and 2d SS *Panzer*—he could control the advancing American army. He knew that the *bocage* would present some of the most difficult fighting terrain in France. His troops and defenses had been skillfully prepared.

There was never a land more evil for men to fight over than the *bocage.*

The Normandy farmers had done their work diligently over the centuries to enclose their small patches of green pasture and apple orchard, and protect their livestock. A single twelve-mile tract might have as many as four thousand of these small enclosed fields, each surrounded on four sides by imposing, impenetrable hedgerows.

Steep high banks, their soil compacted by centuries of rain and sun, and thick with roots, rose like ridges on a monstrous waffle around each tiny field. Tall, thickly entwined hedges surmounted each bank. Their branches could reach as high as twenty feet, forming a canopy over the narrow, sunken lanes that hugged the perimeters of the fields. Sharp ditches on both sides made the roads too narrow for military vehicles to navigate and too deep for man to traverse.

Typically, each enclosure had just one entrance. It was at these narrow openings that the Germans set up killing zones. Mortars and rockets were their weapons of choice. The 81mm mortar needed a crew of just two men. A small-weapons pit was easy to camouflage, and if two or three alternative positions were dug, the crew could fire off a dozen rounds, then move swiftly away before allied countermortar batteries could locate them.

Troops or tanks attacking through these gaps were caught in the cross fire of the *bur-rup bur-rup* of Schmeissers and MG 2 machine guns, capable of firing twelve hundred rounds a minute. American troops would face the well-camouflaged and securely dug-in 88mm antitank guns. The vaunted 88 could destroy the thinly armored allied Sherman tanks almost at will. Designed as an antiaircraft gun, to be manned by the *Luftwaffe* (and still under its command), it was without rival as an antitank weapon and also as an antipersonnel gun used in a ground role.

The Nebelwerfer, a six-barreled heavy mortar, was capable of inflicting terrible wounds. With its long range it could be sited on reverse slopes a long distance from the forward lines. The mortar was fired in groups of six rockets, the first screaming out its message, to be joined in rapid succession by the others. The effect was "a spine-chilling inharmonious screech," terrifying because the soldier on the ground was convinced the rocket was heading straight for him. One lieutenant described his lasting memories of a "whining, whistling, groaning, earsplitting roar that I mistook for dive-bombing aircraft. The noise was followed by exploding bombs all around us."[2] That soldier was lucky. When you can hear the noise, the bomb is not dangerously close. Not hearing the bomb had deadly consequences.

Allied troops called the Nebelwerfer the "Moaning Minnie" because of the eerie sound it made. The French called it *la vache*—the cow. In either language it spelled death to anyone above ground. No allied nation had weaponry anything like it.

German snipers had every advantage in the *bocage*. Some even tied themselves in branches of trees so as to have full use of their arms, picking off the GIs with ease. German antitank and antipersonnel mines shattered the American troops. Booby traps, even using lifeless German or allied soldiers, were rigged with explosives.

US war correspondent Ernie Pyle filed this account of German tactics in the *bocage*:

> The Germans dig deep trenches behind hedgerows and cover them with timber, so that it is almost impossible for artillery to get at them. Sometimes they will prop up machine guns with strings attached so they can fire [on fixed lines] over the hedge without getting out of their holes. They even cut out a section of the hedgerow and hide a big gun or tank in it, covering it with brush. Also they tunnel under the hedgerows from the back to make the opening on the forward side just large enough to stick a machine gun through.[3]

Each of these thousands of fields must be attacked, one by one. The Allies had no conception of the ruggedness of the country, nor had they the appropriate equipment or special training to assure them hope of success in this close-quarter fighting.

The unhappy reality was that the allied planners had focused so single-mindedly on the massive problems of landing two armies on the D-Day beaches that they hadn't really thought beyond it. Montgomery's assumption had been that the Germans would immediately withdraw beyond the Seine.

No one considered that the enemy would set up his secondary defensive lines so close to the beaches. The allied troops were trained exhaustively for an amphibious assault, but not for the deadly ground to follow. The planners had not factored in the enormous difficulties of being the aggressors in *bocage* warfare, where the large-scale armored operations they had trained for just didn't work.

Certainly they should have been familiar with *bocage* country. Field Marshal Alan Brooke (professional head of the British army and General Montgomery's boss) had vacationed there often; Patton had spent his honeymoon in the region. Tactics and weaponry had to be improvised as the allied troops advanced, but as American historian Russell Weigley summed up, "It was too bad that these revelations had to wait upon experience."[4]

It was a well-known fact before D-Day that the Sherman tanks were handicapped by the height of their sixteen-foot turrets, clearly visible as they poked up among the branches of apple trees. German tank guns could shoot off the turrets—and tank commanders standing in them—at will. So, asked tanker Ken Tout, "why did we have months of training on the Salisbury Plain? Why not in the craggy terrain and orchards of Herfordshire or Wales?"[5]

Lieutenant Sydney Jary, a platoon commander who fought in the *bocage*, reflected that "too little time had been spent training the [infantry] in stimulating their imagination, initiative and individual resourcefulness." If the armor and artillery weren't there to back them up, he noted, the infantrymen felt alone and helpless. They had never been encouraged to "probe, draw conclusions, infiltrate and exploit weakness in the enemy's dispositions."[6]

Not so the Germans. Private Adolf Rogosch of the German 353d Infantry Division was seventeen years old when he was thrust into *bocage* fighting. After months of practice in Brittany, he could rely on his own skills and not be dependent on other combat units.

> We knew that if the American attack came, we'd probably be cut off from one another. So we learned to fight as individuals.
>   Our division was being trained for the close combat that was

sure to occur because of the hedgerows—specialized training. So we dug in among the hedges. Coming within thirty yards of the enemy was what we meant by close combat. We trained rather hard almost every day, throwing hand grenades and so forth.[7]

The Allies tried to give themselves some protection by laying on heavy-artillery barrages designed to keep the defenders' heads down. In this way they hoped to rush the enemy position at the last moment. But the Germans were canny, at this stage of the battle. They nullified the effect with devastating counterbarrages of their own.

"They could do nothing," Private Adolf Rogosch scoffed. "We had figured out the tactics of the Americans. When the Americans pulled back, we pushed forward and threw them into the open. And when they came back, we hit them again. We caused them heavy losses there, because they had to come out always . . . toward us. They could not deploy their tanks because of all the hedges."[8]

The German soldiers had poor opinions of the caliber of the allied infantry and tankers' equipment. They had been assured that the American GIs and the Canadian foot soldiers were rank amateurs, that the British were worn down, that their weaponry was crude.

The massive German tanks and self-propelled guns, dug in and well concealed, were ideally suited to fighting in that terrain. In any tank firefight—the Sherman nose to nose with a Panther—it was clearly no contest. The Panthers were almost immune to frontal attack. Shells glanced off their sloping armor, "like Ping-Pong balls! Goddam fucking Ping-Pong balls!" one frustrated American tanker screamed over the radio net.[9] With turrets closed, the German *Panzers* could survive anything except a direct hit from allied artillery.

The Allies were hopelessly outgunned by the German Mark IV, Mark V (Panther) and Mark VI (Tiger) tanks and by their 75mm and 88mm antitank guns. These guns had a high velocity and penetrating power, and could knock out a Sherman tank at two thousand yards. The Sherman's gun—also 75mm but without the penetrating power—could only pierce German frontal armor at *two hundred* yards.

The one advantage the Allies had was that the Shermans were produced in huge numbers. They had to be. The general expectation was to lose three to five Shermans for every German tank destroyed. But whereas allied losses, however immense, could be replaced in a day, the Germans got few replacements. They depended on their efficient workshops located just behind the front lines to "cannibalize and cobble together" refurbished armor overnight.[10]

The *Wehrmacht* troops had little respect for the Shermans. "Swiss cheese!" they would sneer, or "Ronson lighters"—references to how vulnerable they were to being pierced by shells and how swiftly they torched. The tanks powered by gasoline caught fire more quickly than those with diesel. Just a flick and then . . .[11]

Tankers trapped in what they themselves called "mobile crematoriums" had just two escape hatches in the event they were hit and their tank began to "brew." But escape was not always possible. The body of the tank's commander could obstruct the turret hatch, or the gun could block the opening. The floor's escape hatch might not yield if the tank was stuck in soft soil.

The enemy knew these medium tanks were incapable of cutting through the dense *bocage* hedges and steep banks, and that they would not be able to negotiate the narrow, rutted farm lanes that zigzagged around the fields.

Any attempts by the Allies to go around the end of the hedgerow met with almost inevitable annihilation by mines, by the *Panzerfaust* (a portable, throwaway, one-shot gun), by the German bazooka, or by the lethal antitank guns.

The German infantry also had by far the most effective short-range antitank weapons. The *Panzerfaust* could knock out a Sherman at fifty yards. It was probably the best-conceived weapon of its type in any army. Lurking in woods and hedgerows, German infantry armed with this weapon exacted a heavy toll on any tanks that strayed from the immediate protection of the riflemen.

The Americans were forced to fight "from field to field, from hedgerow to hedgerow, measuring the progress of their advance in yards. Over it all a steady rain was to pour, and the odors of the Normandy soil were to mingle with the smell of decaying flesh."[12]

CHAPTER 3

Stalemate

As the allied campaign continued on through July, there was growing talk in the United States and the United Kingdom of stalemate. It conjured up the horrors of the battle of attrition in France in World War I. Americans and Britons shuddered at memories of the dreadful toll in the 1917 deadlock.

Since the American First Army had turned its energies away from Cherbourg and moved south, it had advanced just twenty-four miles in twenty-eight days with heavy losses. The British VIII Corps on their left had gained just over six miles in twelve days. It seemed an impossible task for the Allies to force their way through the dense maze of banks and hedges. The *bocage* still remained essentially an infantry battle: "dogged doughboy fighting at its worst," as Eisenhower described it.[1] The casualties—90 percent of them infantry—attested to this. Second Lieutenant J. Kussman, of the US 115th Infantry, 29th Division noted: "Advances were made one hedgerow at a time." He cited a single day, July 9, when in progressing just two hedgerows, they had suffered eight casualties: "one officer and seven men in our company. We were held up by German paratroop fire, rifle, automatic weapons and 88s and quite a few mortars."[2]

The American and British press exacerbated Monty's problems. Normandy abounded with newspaper and broadcast journalists from the US, Britain, and Canada. Someone quipped that "practically every newspaper in the US sent a correspondent except the *Dog World*."[3] The media was

not only overabundant—it was frustrated. The D-Day landings had provided the action for dynamic articles, with the pace and sizzle that sold
newspapers and delighted editors. Now the correspondents found this war
of attrition, with gains (or losses) of a few hundred yards, pretty dull stuff.

Frontline troops read in same-day or day-old English newspapers or
heard in live BBC broadcasts detailed accounts of every action—often in-
furiatingly dismal. Yet when Monty did give battle reports to the media, it
was with a bravado that exaggerated the British and Canadian successes.

The Americans smoldered. Here they were (they thought) doing most
of the work and suffering the bulk of the casualties while the British were
getting all the credit.

"Now comes the trouble," Montgomery's boss, Field Marshal Alan
Brooke noted in his diary. "The Press chip in and we hear that the British
are doing nothing and suffering no casualties whilst the Americans are
bearing all the brunt of the war."[4]

A groundswell of antagonism arose among a small but vocal band of
British and American officers from SHAEF (Supreme Headquarters Allied Expeditionary Force). Thus influenced, Eisenhower complained to
British Prime Minister Winston Churchill that Montgomery's tentative-
ness was stalling the war effort. Brooke was able to defuse the crisis, but he
could not solve the controversy.

There was really nothing General Montgomery and US General
Omar Bradley, commander of the US First Army, could do to counter the
accusations. Had the British 21st Army Group revealed the exact numbers
of troops of both nations in combat it would have been evident that in fact
percentage-wise there was little difference. Of 591,000 British and Canadians on the ground, 49,000 or 8.29 percent were casualties by July 26.
The US, from a fighting strength of 770,000, had sustained 73,000 or 9.5
percent casualties.[5]

But this was intelligence that would only help the enemy.

The high British casualties worried Montgomery for another reason.
He was running out of manpower for his British regiments. And there were
no replacements. Within a few weeks he would be forced to disband one
entire division in order to resupply the others with reinforcements.

So severe had the casualties been through the war, especially among
junior officers, that Britain had turned to Canada for help. In 1943, Canadian officers were asked to volunteer to fill the shortfall of lieutenants with
British battalions. Six hundred and seventy-three Canadians volunteered

as "Canloan" officers. They served in almost every British division and fought in every major battle in Northwest Europe. Many of them took reductions in rank to do so.[6]

It was the media that stirred up the tank-design controversy. A CBS broadcast by correspondent Edward Murrow had members of Congress on their feet posing passionate questions: "How can we send our boys to war with such inferior equipment?"[7]

In hindsight, Eisenhower's response of immediately initiating an investigation appears more political than practical. He had known for some time that Sherman guns were ineffective against German armor. But Eisenhower's boss, US Army chief of staff General George C. Marshall, had deliberately chosen quantity over quality and size. The Sherman, at thirty-two tons, was lighter and therefore faster than the *Wehrmacht's* forty-three-ton Panther and the fifty-six-ton Tiger. And tanks, he proclaimed, should not fight other tanks. Theirs was a breakout role.[8]

The men in the *bocage* found little comfort in that philosophy as they struggled frantically out of a flaming Sherman tank after being hit at long range.

In Britain there was a similar commotion. Major Martin Lindsay of the Gordon Highlanders noted in his battle diary that "[Labor MP Richard] Stokes has raised the matter time and again in Parliament and always been snubbed."[9]

In a savage attack against the government, Stokes was contemptuous: "We are just as far behind the Germans as we were in 1940 . . . this is a disgraceful state of affairs." Parliament's mocking response, recorded officially by Hansard, was mocking laughter.

"It is all very well for the honorable members to laugh," Stokes rejoined, "but these men are dying." He quoted from a letter sent him by a tank crewman from Normandy, suggesting that the Secretary of State for War should go out and fight "with one of these ruddy things." The government's only response was to censure Stokes for using rude language in the House.

British historian Max Hastings, who chronicled this encounter, wrote "the government lied systematically, until the very end of the war, about the Allies' tragic failure to produce tanks capable of matching those of the Germans."[10] Another English journalist despaired, "One can only hope the scandal of British tank manufacture will come out."[11]

In Normandy, even Montgomery finally forbade his senior commanders from speaking of it. We have the right tank, he assured them—but in the wrong place. Just wait until the breakout, when the little Sherman can show off its speed and maneuverability.

How do you, as a commander, convince citizen-soldiers—many of them teenagers and unblooded in war—that they should plunge blindly into a battle they have little or no hope of winning? How can you maintain their confidence in their leaders who seem to be constantly ordering them into no-win situations?

This was one of General Bernard Montgomery's dilemmas on D-plus-50.

Monty could hardly reassure his British and Canadian troops that their seemingly futile attempts to break through the German line at Caen, with so many men killed and wounded, were in reality achieving exactly what he had planned and hoped for.

Seven German *Panzer* divisions had been pinned down on the Caen front for almost two months. Only two opposed the Americans who—thus helped—were on the brink of a momentous breakout. As Eisenhower himself wrote to Monty on July 28, "Am delighted that your basic plan has begun brilliantly to unfold with General Bradley's initial success."[12]

Montgomery urged the 21st Army Group army commanders that "along the whole front now held by the First Canadian and Second British Armies it was essential that the enemy be attacked to the greatest degree possible."

In the same directive he admitted candidly that while the Anglo-Canadians must persist in fighting and thus incurring heavy casualties, they had little possibility of success. "[The enemy] is so strong [south of Caen] that any large-scale operations by us in that area are definitely unlikely to succeed."[13]

Indeed, in late July Monty made no pretense to his senior army commanders Lieutenant General Miles Dempsey and Lieutenant General Harry Crerar that their mission was merely as a decoy to lure *Panzer* divisions from the American front. They accepted their roles—but it was a tough sell to the young volunteers and recruits at the sharp end. His chief of intelligence Brigadier Bill Williams brutally summed up the dilemma of Montgomery's waning credibility: "He'd got to be overconfident in order to get the people to be willing to be killed."[14]

It was on the Caen front that the British and Canadian troops were not only struggling against much of the fiercest opposition, at an enormous sacrifice of lives, but they—and Monty—were getting nothing but biting criticism in return. SHAEF (Supreme Headquarters Allied Expeditionary Forces) commanders, the media, and, later, historians all denounced the British and Canadians for their "slow, feeble performance."[15] Sadly, though, the criticism—unwarranted and without justification—has been perpetuated to this day by historians. That the forces at Caen persisted in operations where they were "definitely unlikely to succeed" is a huge tribute to the citizen soldiers of both nations.

Reflecting the sometimes-negative press coverage they had been receiving, a Canadian war diary noted wryly: "The enemy is not giving ground as easily as one would gather from reading the London papers."[16]

Not in jest an NCO of the 6th Battalion King's Own Scottish Borderers asked his CO, Lieutenant Colonel Charles Richardson, "If it was the high command's intention to wipe out all the British and finish the war with the Americans?"[17]

It all seemed hopeless. Fifty days and nights of little sleep, wretched weather, and constant fear were taking their toll. As the men saw their buddies horribly maimed or killed they wondered . . . would it be their turn next?

"There was no escape—except being buried or taken out on a stretcher," one young corporal said.[18] Men going into an attack would have the unnerving experience of seeing white crosses piled up, ready for use, and ambulances lined up waiting. Makeshift graves were everywhere.

A young private soldier in the Durham Light Infantry spoke for many, when he said, "I thought that if by some fluke I survived and went back to England there would be no young men walking about at all because they were all being killed and wounded in Normandy."[19]

CHAPTER 4

Hitler's War Within

The failed attempt on Hitler's life had exacerbated the long-established bitter rivalry and resentment between Hitler's personally controlled National Socialist police force—the *Waffen* SS—and the conventional German *Wehrmacht* commanded by the German High Command (*Oberkommando der Wehrmacht* or OKW). It was now causing conflict within the German forces in Normandy.

This rivalry was felt even down to the frontline forces. Hitler pampered all of his SS divisions with their choice of the best weapons and recruits. *Wehrmacht* soldiers often resented and feared the young elitists for their arrogance and ruthlessness. While envying them their fine equipment and preferential treatment, some tried to distance themselves from the taint of Nazism. "The infantry was nonpolitical," one *Wehrmacht* lieutenant insisted. "We did not get along with the Nazis."[1]

The *Wehrmacht* commanders were furious when Hitler gave SS General Paul Hausser command of Seventh Army and its SS divisions—the first SS general officer to head up a German army. They were the only ones Hitler really trusted, and they returned his loyalty.

By D-plus-44, the Germans had two armies totaling seven hundred thousand men—some forty-three divisions—to block the advance of 1.5 million allied troops. Of these forty-three divisions, ten were powerful tank (*Panzer*) divisions, on whom the Germans placed all hopes of a successful defense.

Operation *Fortitude* had successfully subtracted one of those armies—the Fifteenth, whose seventeen fresh and well-trained German infantry divisions were sorely needed at the front—by contriving a synthetic allied force believed to be poised for an attack over one hundred miles to the east. And Montgomery had equal success in diverting seven of the nine mighty *Panzer* divisions of Seventh Army to remain entrenched in the Caen sector, convincing Hitler that the British and Canadian attacks through Caen were the main thrust.

The remaining armored divisions—the powerful *Panzer Lehr* and the 2d SS *Panzer*—opposed the Americans in the *bocage* battle. But as British historian John Keegan points out, this in a sense also played into allied hands. Lacking the infantry divisions Hitler was so stubbornly sidelining east of the Seine, the *Panzers* had to sacrifice their highly specialized riflemen and irreplaceable tanks in small-scale hedgerow fighting that was inappropriate to their counterattack role.[2]

On July 20, the SS heard via a radio broadcast of the attempted assassination of Adolf Hitler. The seventeen-year-olds of the *Hitlerjugend* Division, the 12th SS, were especially bewildered and angered by the news. This was the ultimate betrayal of their leader. How could the army attempt a coup against their supreme military leadership while the SS were themselves involved in a bitter defensive fight to the death?

"We considered those who had taken part in it as traitors," a signaler said. "They were pulling out just when the going was getting tough. It was sabotage, changing sides like that. The Führer was 'The Man' to us until the end."[3]

The division had been in action since June 7, 1944—the day after D-Day. For forty-four days and forty-four nights the Hitler Youth struggled ceaselessly to keep the allied forces from breaking out beyond Caen, holding on to their defensive positions despite everything the enemy had thrown against them. They believed in the Führer's destiny.

The Nazi party had created the Hitler Youth to provide a steady supply of young *soldaten* committed to the cause of the Third Reich. On Hitler's forty-seventh birthday, April 20, 1936, he enrolled all ten-year-old Aryan German boys in the *Jungvolk* movement. The "Class of 1926," as they became known, numbering some eight hundred thousand strong, became new members of the *Hitlerjugend* (HJ). They swore the oath that they repeated on the same date every year, promising "To do my duty at all times in love and faithfulness to help the Führer."[4]

At first the youth camps stressed competitive sports and the unquestioning discipline and obedience that is derived from athletics, paving the way to a gradual inculcation of the principles of Nazism. The lads learned to despise Jews and communists, to focus their loyalty on the state rather than on family and church, and above all, to dedicate their lives to the Nazi credo that war was noble.

The Class of '26 became the brainwashed fanatics of the thirties.

By early 1939 Hitler was demanding compulsory membership in the *Hitlerjugend* for all boys between the ages of ten and eighteen. In this way he recruited over one million new candidates to fill his demands for youth "slim and strong, swift as greyhounds, tough as leather and hard as Krupp steel."[5]

After the outbreak of war, German youth between the ages of sixteen and eighteen received intensive training in weapons and basic tactics in special instruction camps under officers from the Führer's personal security guard, the First SS *Leibstandarte-Adolf Hitler* (*LAH*). The black-uniformed *LAH* were battle-hardened troops who had fought a war without mercy on the eastern front. The teenage graduates of these camps—tens of thousands—would join Hitler's elite units, especially the *Waffen* SS.

But a separate Hitler Youth Division was drawn from the best of the class of 1926. Sixteen thousand seventeen-year-olds, selected from among the most physically fit, reported for duty. Adopting their trademark camouflage suit, the boys were flung into specialized combat training in tanks, artillery, antitank and machine guns, trucks and motorcycles, engineering, mine-laying, and reconnaissance.

About all they missed, compared to older recruits, were visits to the local pub or the local brothel. Relationships with girls were prohibited for those under eighteen. The "Baby Division," as some later dubbed it, was given sweets instead.

Some babies.

The *Hitlerjugend* were too young to shave, to drink beer, or to make love to their girlfriends—but not too young to murder. In a single generation, Hitler had created a killing machine: the meanest, toughest fighting unit Germany had ever produced.

When the *Hitlerjugend* troops—now numbering 20,540—were en

route to Normandy in the spring of 1944, members of the French Resistance made a brave but futile effort to derail their ninety-car transport train in Ascq (near Lille). The SS commander in charge immediately had the local French males between the ages of seventeen and fifty rounded up. In *L'Affaire d'Ascq*, as the tragedy is known, the 12th SS executed at least seventy-seven Frenchmen.[6]

In Caen, *SS Standartenführer* (SS Colonel) Kurt Meyer was given command of the *Hitlerjugend*. At thirty-three, Meyer was the youngest divisional commander in the German or any other army in Normandy.[7] His unorthodox battle tactics, daring motorcycle feats (which had resulted in no fewer than eighteen fractures and four concussions), and his swaggering demeanor (a rumpled camouflage suit being his habitual garb) all endeared him to the teenagers of the *Hitlerjugend*. They called him "*Panzermeyer*." He ordered reckless attacks, sacrificing hundreds of men and precious Panther tanks in fruitless efforts to destroy the allied bridgehead.

Twenty-one-year-old Gerhard Lemcke, a *Hitlerjugend* commander, justified the fanatical fighting. "One is told 'soldiers are murderers.' But that wasn't what it was about; it was about trying to weaken our enemy so that we would not be pushed back quickly. It was simplest to say 'Führer's orders,' and then no one was allowed to question it."[8]

In a bitter confrontation with Canadian troops, their frustration at not succeeding in driving the Allies off the Normandy beaches led the Hitler Youth into an orgy of violence, murdering Canadian wounded. Their officers were even more reprehensible. They not only killed in the heat of battle frenzy; they conducted the mass murder of scores of Canadian prisoners of war in cold blood. In one incident they led forty-five prisoners into the walled garden of the *Abbaye d'Ardenne*, where Meyer had his headquarters, and systematically put a bullet in the back of each young head.[9]

Before the invasion of Normandy, German troops posted there had enjoyed a peaceful and pleasant occupation, with bountiful food from the lush farming regions. Lieutenant Hans-Heinrich Dibbern remembers the friendly reception from the French populace at large: "The French lived quietly with us. The women did our laundry, the farmers gave us food when we needed it, or sold us cider. It was an excellent relationship."[10]

A 2d *Panzer* Division corporal recounted how "the farmers still had everything—milk, butter, eggs. The pastor's wife made a big meal for us—cooking eggs in a pan and so forth. She told us, 'My son is a guest worker in Germany. I do not know where he is. I have no news from him. But I hope that a German mother gives him something like I now offer to you.' "[11]

Wenzel Borgert, a twenty-two-year-old lieutenant in the 116th *Panzer* Division, was one of the millions drafted into the German army. When he was posted to Normandy he went to great pains to explain to the French villagers that despite the similarity of dress—the black uniform and the skull emblem on his uniform—he was not SS. "We were Catholics [so we] went to church with them. Suddenly we were no longer Nazis; we were German soldiers."

He got a special kick when the Americans started calling them "Jerries" instead of "Nazis."[12]

Although the Germans introduced universal conscription in 1933, they claimed, untruthfully, that many of the *Wehrmacht* and SS soldiers signed up on their own. "Naturally, my entire class registered as 'volunteers.' There was no other category," Corporal Friedrich Bertenrath, a signaler with the 2d *Panzer* Division, said sardonically.[13]

"[Some] were not asked as to whether they wanted to join an SS Division. [They] were given the SS uniform to put on and told where to go," confirmed Infantry Private Adolf Rogosch, 353d Infantry Division.[14] Some of the troops—Polish, Alsacians, Russian, and even Korean—had been captured by the Germans and forced into service. Ten thousand troops were anti-Soviet "volunteers"—Russians, Georgians, Cossacks, Turcomans, Tartars, and Caucasians—who were fighting in the German army in Normandy under the badges of their respective countries, but in German uniform.[15] They were treated apart, even as far as having separate casualty lists and pay books in their national currencies. (The Polish volunteers fighting in Normandy with their Canadian and British Allies kept spare uniforms handy in case a captured enemy soldier turned out to be a fellow Pole who would be able to rejoin his countrymen.)

With the D-Day landings, a new realism was setting in for German troops. A 21st Army Group intelligence report stated at the time that only 5 percent of German POWs believed in the possibility of ultimate victory.[16] Increasingly, many of the *Wehrmacht* troops like Corporal Bertenrath were becoming disenchanted with the war. Earlier they had been, in the words of one of their generals, "doped by propaganda," into believing in the might of Hitler's forces.[17]

"German propaganda? We believed it all. We knew nothing else," Wenzel Borgert said bitterly. "We were the dogs of war, fighting on the front, so we didn't hear much of anything."[18]

"In our unit, we would never abandon each other," Corporal Bertenrath concurred. "We had fought in Russia together. We were comrades, and always came to the rescue. We protected our comrades so they could go home to their wives, children, and parents. That was our motivation. The idea that we would conquer the world had fallen long ago.[19]

"We were trained to believe that the final victory would be ours," Günter Materne, an artillery officer said. "But during the fighting, many of us came to have a certain scepticism. The American weapon superiority was so great, I told my second-in-command that we'd be knocked back to the Siegfried Line. But of course we had to be very careful about saying this; one could be court-martialed for being a defeatist."

"The worst part was seeing comrades, with whom I had been for a long time, suddenly dying from some enemy action. I thought, 'Man, is it worth this costly price in human life to go on? Is it not incredible?' But of course one did not say this out loud."[20]

Walter Padberg admitted that: "as officers we were expected to do our duty. One cannot desert; one cannot simply throw away one's grenades. One can only . . . survive by doing one's duty. Duty, honor and custom: that's how we came out of this shitty war."[21]

"[At first] we were quite confident that we could throw the enemy back into the sea," Major Helmut Ritgen of *Panzer Lehr* Division said. "We learned on the third day that this was a dream. Rommel did not include the naval guns in his evaluation. If you have ever heard the detonation of a big naval gun — this is an unforgettable experience. It was impossible to fight a new war with just the ground forces alone. You can't do without a navy and an air force."[22]

Perhaps because of their own shortages, the enormous amount of matériel that flooded the allied beachhead awed the Germans: "We had never seen the way a rich man fights the war," 12th SS *Hitlerjugend* commander Gerhard Lemcke observed bitterly. "The Americans could fire day and night; they had an unlimited supply of shells."[23]

Morale remained high in the SS divisions. Though they had not been able to drive the Allies back into the sea, they had at least kept them from surging out of the beachhead. Even after weeks of mortal combat, of heavy casualties and growing shortages of reinforcements and ammunition, their confidence was unshaken. Their optimism was helped by the belief that Hitler's miracle weapons would destroy the enemy. The V-1 rocket was first launched a few weeks after D-Day. German soldiers were told of the horror of tens of thousands of Londoners, helpless as they watched the pilotless aircraft silently dive to the ground, killing and maiming helpless civilians.

Letters from home reported that the round-the-clock RAF bombing had eased, as the Allies concentrated their bombing in support of the invasion. The general German populace, like its forces on the western front, had little idea of the seriousness of Hitler's plight.

But in the *Wehrmacht*, confidence was wavering.

"In June we thought we still had a chance," Major Ritgen of the *Panzer Lehr* Division explained. "Then came the rockets." Ritgen was referring to missiles fired by fighter-bombers of the allied tactical air forces (Typhoons and P-47 Thunderbolts) whose relentless attacks brought daytime movement by German troops almost to a standstill.

"We were constantly attacked by *Jabos* [*Jäger Bomber* or fighter-bombers] during our march," recorded Private Herbert Meier. "Those who brought the ammunition forward lived a dangerous life. [Quite] a few were blown into the air along with their cargo."[24] German infantry companies, lacking motorized equipment or fuel, often marched all night or even bicycled twenty or thirty miles with full packs, not even stopping to rest or eat. Their transport was largely horse-drawn. Arriving at the front line they would be flung immediately into battle.

Günter Materne, an artillery lieutenant, still shudders at the recollection:

The march toward Caen was already a catastrophe. We could only march at night because of air superiority. The worst part was, sometimes the aerial observers would drop Christmas trees (clusters of lights), which would light up the area. They photographed us, our march direction, how many vehicles and of what type. Then they were prepared for their next day's bombing attack.[25]

That knowledge of enemy troop positions could also be attributed to the huge advantage the Allies had in intelligence: Ultra. The code breakers at Bletchley Park, north of London, could read many of the German signals transmitted through their Enigma machines—a coding system the Germans thought could never be broken. The Allies were able to intercept and decipher this German wireless communication. The resulting decodes were entrusted to a small handpicked group of senior military personnel and heads of state. In the Battle of Normandy, only the senior commanders and their key staff officers were cleared for the Ultra secret.

On the ground, however, soldiers cared nothing about strategy. Life, day to day, was about survival. The old adage that war is hell took on new meaning. An infantryman's world, German or allied, became a deep, cold, muddy trench. He ate and slept and cowered there like some four-legged creature with shells crashing around him without letup. The most terrifying times were when he was ordered to emerge from his trench and charge, gun at the ready, into a solid curtain of fire. He might exchange a quip with a buddy one moment—then witness his unspeakable mutilation the next.

PART II

THE
SOLDIERS:
BATTLEFIELD
LIFE

CHAPTER 5

Bless 'Em All

The meadow stretches as far as the eye can see. In a moment of sanity—the last moment before the battle begins, or before you are hit by an enemy's bullet—you might think: It's like the one at home, back of the farm. Looking around you see hundreds or even thousands of guys like yourself, moving up on the attack. Young, fit men in their twenties. Toughened by training, hardened to their mission to kill. Or be killed. Some of the tough ones are smooth-faced lads in their teens.

It could be a college rally or a high school track meet. It could be harvesttime back home or the outpouring of shop workers, like yourself, from the local factory.

But this is war, and you are attacking your enemy. Your objective is to reach the enemy positions on the hill beyond that meadow and kill its defenders.

Most times, you are too terrified to think nostalgically of the green meadows of home. But you sure as hell will often think: "Oh God, I wish I were there." Or maybe you're anguishing, can I do this? Can I make myself go across that field and up that slope and take that objective? What kind of hell is waiting for me beyond its crest? Can I help my buddies? And not let them see how scared I am? And a fervent P.S.—Please let me do my job well, or I'll never again believe in myself.

Your insides scream, "Oh God, I'm too young." You look around for a leader, a sergeant, a lieutenant, or a captain to carve the way for you.

The first shots are fired, and the cacophony of war takes over. You hear your own artillery shells shrieking overhead as you move forward. Your guns offer a temporary canopy of safety. You hope their fire will keep the enemies' heads down long enough for you to move up and overrun their position. You know you have to stay as close as you dare under the umbrella of fire because that's your only hope of survival. Machine guns are cracking nearby; mortar bombs whistle overhead, making a nightmarish sound.

The enemy wakes up; now you're sure to get it. German shells are landing all around you, cratering massive holes in the ground. But it's the ones you don't hear that kill; death comes silently with mortars' direct hits. German 88s scream by. Snipers are shooting at you from ahead and to the right and left. Shrapnel shells explode, piercing young bodies with lethal bits of fiery metal. MG42s firing twenty rounds per second make a harsh *brrrrp* noise. Now there's the sinister ghostly moan as the aptly named "Moanin' Minnie" fires its six bombs in succession.

These are the sounds of battle, and soldiers have to identify each one and recognize those that signal immediate danger to him. "Uncertainty means delay," American Lieutenant Paul Boesch noted, "and sometimes the difference of a split second is all that separates life from death."[1]

Then there are the final sounds of battle: the screams of men wounded, gutted, limbs amputated by the shells . . . suffering, dying.

You know that no matter what your age, your rank, your training, or your nationality—friend or foe—once a shell or bomb or bullet hits you, you become just another body on the field . . . a body screaming in pain, calling desperately for stretcher bearers to get you out of this hellhole . . . calling for your mother or your God.

Help came swiftly on the battlefield. At the cry of "Medic" or "Aid Man," men trained in emergency rescue, moving up in the wake of the infantry attack, appeared in minutes. They would examine the wound, apply sulfa powder, bandage the soldier up, and call for stretcher bearers. Driving their jeep ambulances through the turmoil of fire, ducking sniper cross fire and enemy shells, these men braved the battlefield to rescue the fallen soldier. It was not required, but many battalion padres made a point of going out with them to help bring in the wounded. Thirty-year-old Honorary Captain Padre Jock Anderson of the Highland Light Infantry could not bring himself to abandon those young men:

Those fellows, they were lying out there wounded and they were being mortared. And shelled. A lot of them just had a leg wound but they were unable to move and they were being killed. I thought, hey, I've got to get those poor devils out of there. I made all kinds of trips and brought them out. I had shell dressings, morphine and ether, but often I had no time to give first aid. When they're being shelled and mortared you just grab them and shove them on a stretcher and off you go.

No one ever talks about these ordinary stretcher bearers, but they were utterly fantastic. Many were volunteers.[2]

Some were conscientious objectors, who refused to carry arms but worked magnificently to save lives: The Americans initially dubbed them "Conchies," but dropped the rather uncomplimentary epithet when they saw the work of these men under fire. The 90th Infantry Division dispersed its band when it left England and assigned band members to medical support. Bass fiddle and sax players, now litter bearers, did such "good, solid work they were awarded a unit citation."[3]

Dr. Art Stevenson recalled that, on occasion, the stretcher bearers would crawl out on their bellies to the battlefield, heave the wounded man on their shoulders, and crawl back to the Regimental Aid Post or the Field Surgical Unit. "These guys were—man!—they were just great. They didn't scare at all," Stevenson recalls.[4] The ambulance centers themselves were under constant shelling, and they soon learned to carry five hundred sandbags, routinely, to protect their huts. But the drivers, moving out under that identical torrent of fire, had no such protection, and their casualties were on a par with the infantrymen they were rescuing.

Jeeps fitted with stretchers brought out serious cases. "The jeeps were just going in, getting their casualties, and going like a bat out of hell," one medic described. "It wasn't the best way to drive with casualties, but it was either do that or get them there dead. The jeeps suffered a lot, coming in with four flat tires and holes through them from shrapnel."[5] Sometimes the German mortaring was so intense that it just wasn't possible to drive the ambulance jeep into the bomb-pounded battleground. A field ambulance war diary noted that:

During a night action, cases unable to walk or crawl are often not picked up until morning. This applies especially to casualties occurring in the standing wheat, or where our troops had passed on and had not been able to notify stretcher-bearers of the location of the wounded.[6]

One stretcher bearer, Corporal Wes Burrows, volunteered for the job after he was given the sack for overzealous pre-D-Day "research" in the pubs. In Normandy, Burrows transferred his energies into driving a stretcher-jeep onto shell-covered fields to pick up casualties.

I got out two hundred wounded, easy, and sometimes I'd help out others as they ran into problems too—like, with another company that couldn't get the casualties out, I'd go and get them. It got a little hairy at times. I lost four jeeps from mortar and shellfire and once a mine blew it up.

You knew the job had to be done. There were chaps to be picked up. You got a little scared maybe when you were on your own going out there, but at the time that you were taking them back you had it in your head to get them out as fast as you could. Those mortars—the faster you'd drive, the closer they'd keep coming; you'd swear they were just trying to catch you. I had the Red Cross flag, but it was drawing fire. I took the flag down.

Burrows's bravery was rewarded with the Military Medal. On his way home, after his five years overseas, he had a pretty good feeling: "I thought I had been some help. I had no other training to do anything else." But on the troop ship, rifle drill was called, and Burrows, clumsily wrestling with the gun bolt, was hauled up by a sergeant major. "What do you think you're doing! Hold your head up! What a pitiful sight you are!" "I guess there were some people who thought I wasn't much of a soldier without a gun," Burrows concluded sadly.[7]

On occasion, one side or the other would ask for a truce. Lieutenant Harold Leinbaugh, US 28th Infantry Division, described one such instance when two wounded GIs were left hanging in barbed wire:

A private in the American lines began waving a white handkerchief, and then dared to stand upright. The Germans halted their fire, and one of their officers . . . agreed to allow the recovery of the wounded. Soldiers on both sides stood up in their holes, stretched to relieve cramped muscles, and then, as the truce ended with the evacuation of the injured, returned to earth and to the battle.[8]

These truces were sometimes organized between antagonists at company or even platoon level. The distant artillery or even a belligerent SS nearby could take aim at the medic doing the rescue mission, despite his wearing the traditional white bib with large Red Cross.

In fact, many padres and medics shunned carrying the Red Cross banners on their jeeps, or armbands on their uniforms. It attracted too much enemy fire.

"Sometimes the German would respect the Red Cross and sometimes he would show such utter disregard for it that he would actually concentrate on the stretcher bearers and ambulances," Captain Cliff Chadderton wrote, recounting with some bitterness a tragic incident. Their stretcher bearers had been working since dusk bringing in his wounded. "As night set in—but while there was still enough light to distinguish the Red Cross—the Germans swept the field with bullets. The driver was killed and the stretcher-bearer died of his wounds. Both had been murdered while doing their duty under the protection of the International Red Cross."[9]

An officer who had been taken prisoner noted a phenomenon that had been blatantly obvious to many allied troops throughout the Normandy campaign: the enemy misuse of the Red Cross. A favorite SS trick was to camouflage troop-carrying or weapon-carrying transport with a large Red Cross. They knew the Allies would never target them.

"There were Red Cross signs everywhere—on German staff cars, and even on their ammunition vehicles."[10] The airmen were furious to discover that some able-bodied German troops were being brought out in ambulances.

Flight Lieutenant Cecil Brown, a renowned Spitfire pilot, quickly improvised a solution:

> We would send one pilot down, not firing, just to make a simulated attack on an ambulance. When the back doors opened and troops started to bail out, the rest of us would come down behind and let them have it. They didn't do that very long because we massacred those [fake] ambulances.[11]

Dead soldiers were brought off the field as quickly as possible. Occasionally the Germans booby-trapped the dead or even the unconscious wounded. If the bodies had lain there overlong, there was the added danger to the padres that the corpses had been booby-trapped by the Germans. Padre Anderson recalls:

> I used to carry in my jeep a long anchor and a long rope. I would hitch it on to the casualty's belt and then my driver and I would go back to my jeep and pull. If nothing happened, then we knew it wasn't booby-trapped. But any body that was left out for any length of time posed a risk.[12]

Few Germans made attempts to rescue their dead comrades. The corpses lay sprawled grotesquely around their trenches, the agony of death lining their faces and locking their bones in a horrible rigidity.

Later, when the frenzy of battle abated, the chaplains would go back to the battlefield to bury the dead. Rifles stuck into the ground beside the body, butt ends protruding to the skies, were sentinels to the mournful landscape. It was an ordeal that the chaplains never got used to, which left them shaken for hours.

They took shovels, dug burial places, and conducted private, very meaningful services for each. The dog tags and personal items were brought back, some to send to their families, and the perishables to distribute to their mates.

There were times when it was not possible to recover the fallen. A Scottish trooper summed up this anguish: "This last forty hours we have been asked to accomplish three tasks not normally asked of human beings. First, to face appalling wounds, burning and possible fearful death at fifty yards range; second, to destroy other human beings; and third, to leave our own dead unburied."[13]

At the aid stations, close to the front, medical officers dealt with those casualties too severely wounded to be moved. The surgeons would be confronted with complex surgical problems and conduct intricate surgery in the crudest of facilities. They would often operate with shells bursting or snipers firing around them, rain lashing through the tent flaps and lights flickering from unreliable generators. Their supplies of medicines depended on the courage and determination of the transport men braving enemy fire to bring them forward. Despite these difficulties they became so slick at their jobs that casualties were known to reach the Casualty Clearing Station one-half an hour after being wounded.

The US 51st Field Hospital Unit, which dealt with "nontransportable" casualties (those wounded between the neck and the groin), developed a system of leapfrogging the doctors and nurses forward as each frontline casualty station filled up, so "the Medical Corps was able to provide continuous, effective care during our advance across Europe."[14]

Dr. Art Stevenson remembers:

> I was the first medical officer these wounded guys [of my battalion] would see, the only doctor out there. . . . I had to deal with first-stage resuscitation, keeping their blood pressure up with fluids, and quickly getting them back to the advanced field dressing station or the casualty clearing station [CCS] by ambulance where we could get medication into them. I did all the emergency surgical stuff, even a few amputations because of bleeding. We didn't have any blood. What we had to use was not even good plasma.[15]

One of the incoming casualties, Captain John Redden, was brought in with serious bullet wounds. A tag "condition poor" was pinned on him at the regimental aid post. "I passed out, to be awakened by an MO who had known me as a kid. He looked at the card that said 'condition poor,' called out 'silly bastard!' and wrote 'condition good.' It probably saved my life."[16]

Redden was experiencing the "triage" approach to combat medicine, which essentially sorted out casualties according to the seriousness of their injuries. Treatment priority was given to those with the less severe wounds. The badly wounded who could be saved were rushed to the hospital; those with lighter wounds were stabilized by medics and transferred later to CCS. The hopeless one, men like Redden with "condition poor" tags, received immediate painkillers but were last in line for treatment.[17]

The surgeons had a grueling schedule—eighteen hours in the operating room, then eighteen hours off and eighteen hours back on. In the first seven weeks of the Normandy battle, allied doctors used eighteen thousand pints of blood, fifteen thousand pints of plasma, and twenty-four hundred mega units of penicillin, the wonder drug of World War II.[17]

It was tough, grisly, heartrending work.

Major Don Campbell, MD, describes his role at CCS:

We were a fully operating hospital with full surgical, X-ray and blood bank facilities for as many as 200 patients. Our staff was small: eight nurses, two surgeons, three physicians and a medical blood bank specialist—with more surgical teams available as we needed them. There were two casualty stations side by each. One would be receiving and assessing all the emergencies and the other would be operating. Then we'd switch.

There were so many shattered arms and legs from land mines. A man would step on a mine and blow his foot off. So then we had to amputate. The army public-health manual mandated what they called an "operating pit," which was just a hole in the ground 6 by 6 by 9 feet. We filled it—just with arms and legs. Then we had to dig another one. That's how busy we were.[18]

Shrapnel from shell, gunshot, and mortar wounds accounted for many injured lads. Blast wounds saw men brought in concussed but without a mark on their bodies. It was discovered that by getting too close to a mortar explosion, the soldier could be knocked out, lung-damaged, or killed.

One man was admitted, his right foot thickly bandaged. He'd stepped on a Schü-mine.

"It's a mess," he said bitterly to the surgeon. "Try to save as much as you can. Got a boy ten years old. Hate like hell to have him see the old man on crutches with one leg. God! If I could only walk down that gangplank."

The surgeon stared at a mass of torn tissue and fractured bones. He was right . . . it *was* a mess. But there might be a chance of saving the foot . . . at least until he walked down that gangplank. Hours of repairing tissue and resetting bone followed. In the morning, the reward was seeing the toes, pink and warm. And the soldier weeping silently. "There is no joy to compare to that."[19]

A soldier whom medics had found on the field, barely alive, was saved by a bizarre medical approach: "Wasps [were] swarming on the bloody flesh of his leg, maggots already emerging." The medic said, 'Best chance is bandage the wasps [and] maggots all into the leg—provide some leeching.' "[20]

One casualty, speaking for many, called the nurses "angels of mercy." Regaining consciousness in a field hospital near Bayeux, with one eye reduced to pulp and his head and mouth pierced by a large hunk of jagged shrapnel, Lieutenant Barney Danson saw a nursing sister "in a blue uniform with gold accoutrements and a flowing white veil," comforting him with offers of food and water—to him, she was an angel.[21]

American women serving with the Army Nurse Corps (ANC) rolled up their pant legs and waded ashore on the Normandy beaches and were catapulted immediately into around-the-clock, mind-numbing efforts to keep shattered young bodies alive. One nurse, Lieutenant Aileen Hogan, recalled the challenges of making the penicillin rounds—sixty patients to a tent—especially at night. "Not a glimmer of light anywhere . . . the tents just a vague silhouette against the darkness, ropes and tent pins a constant menace, syringes and precious medications balanced precariously on one arm."

In volunteering for the ANC these women braved the contempt and mud slinging of civilians in America who viewed the work of women in nurses' uniform lewdly. They soon earned the highest respect and became the vanguard for an eventual ANC force in Europe numbering 17,345.[22]

Nursing Officer Brenda McBryde of the 75th British General Hospital, recalled her first view of the Resuscitation Department where she would spend so many hours of each day in the coming weeks. The whole medical facility was under canvas, dug in to a depth of about eighteen inches. It was floored with a heavy tarpaulin groundsheet, slippery with muddy water oozing in during the rains.

Trestles supported the stretchers of wounded as they arrived by ambulance. Here the men were given intensive treatment for shock until they were sufficiently restored to undergo surgery.

At the entrance to Resuscitation was a crudely erected treatment area. Trays of instruments, syringes, and sterilizers were laid out on trestle tables covered by sheets. Shelves were improvised from upended wooden boxes. Large, wooden chests contained transfusion apparatuses.

McBryde felt keenly the tragedy of war as she recorded the names and units of the casualties into the Admission Book, so many from famous British regiments: men of the Staffordshire Yeomanry, Wiltshire, Dorsets, Green Howards, East Yorks, the Northumbrians, and Somersets.

"Most of their proud uniforms, stiff with blood and caked in mud, had to be cut from them. We sliced the tough boots with razors to release shattered feet." McBryde mused, "Hard-won stripes and pips and crowns, sewn on by proud mums and wives and girlfriends . . . it was all the same now. The field incinerator smoked all night."

The stream of wounded seemed never to end. The tent became so cramped that there was barely room to put a foot down or kneel between the stretchers.

> The surgeon kept up a running commentary. "Stomach here: Put him in number one. Quarter of morphia, Sister. Straight away. Two pints of blood, one of plasma . . ." Gunshot, mortar blast, mines, incendiaries. Limbs, eyes, abdomen, chest. He chewed his pencil. Who had priority? Of all these desperately wounded men, whose need was the most urgent?[23]

But as one surgeon expressed it, they all had to learn to "turn off the emotional taps"—the only way they could handle shattered and torn bodies day after day. They soon became war-wise veterans.

> We saw tragic sights from which we were never to be free: men with heads shattered and grey, dirty brains oozing out from the jagged margins of skull bones. Youngsters with holes in their chests fighting for air and breathing with a ghastly sucking noise. Soldiers with intestines draining faeces onto their belly walls and with their guts churned into a bloody mess by high explosives. Legs that were dead and stinking—but still wore muddy shoes . . .
>
> Operating floors that had to be scrubbed with Lysol to rid the theatre of the stench of dead flesh. Red blood that flowed and spilled over while life held on by the slender thread of time. Boys who came to you with a smile and died on the operating table. Boys who lived long enough for you to learn their name and then were carried away in trucks piled high with the dead.
>
> We learned to work with heavy guns rocking and blasting the

thin walls of our tent. We learned to keep our tent ropes slack so that anti-aircraft fragments would rain down harmlessly and bounce off the canvas.[24]

As the casualty rates mounted, so did the strain on the medical personnel. Fortunately, rigorous preinvasion training in Britain had hardened them to some extent to primitive life in field conditions in tents. A basic training course had taught them the use of small arms and vehicle training, first aid and basic survival. This was known as the DDPP course: doctors, dentists, padres, and paymasters—a curious mixture.

Medical orderlies practiced pitching large hospital tents (thirty feet by fifteen feet) in all kinds of weather, and in the blackest of nights, in as fast a time as possible and without the use of flashlights. They had to lug in a nine-hundred-pound generator and be able to repair and service it, so it could supply power to 120 electric bulbs. They rehearsed sterilizing instruments in the dark.

The nursing sisters in particular found the British field training out in the open to be an exhilarating experience and a pleasant change from routine duties indoors. One nurse recalled that "training was strenuous, but time could generally be found for relaxation. We marched over the moors all day, and we marched to the pubs at night."[25]

All nurses had been issued battle dress and field kits. But a problem arose over nursing sisters wearing the large packs. One account relates wryly that "it was found that the position of the supporting straps over the chest had not been designed with the female anatomy in mind. A decision to try discarding the pack in favour of hand luggage produced an assortment of suitcases of varied size, shape and colour purchased by the nurses. When one bag burst during an exercise, spilling its contents across the muddy path, the reviewing commander said in disgust, "I can only liken this to the retreat from Moscow!"[26]

In addition to American, British, and Canadian troops, the hospitals treated several other nationalities. "We were very impressed with the Poles. They were a great gang," Dr. Stevenson reported. "But we had trouble with quite a few German prisoners. We treated them as we did our own, but they were all scared stiff. They took far more narcotics than our boys took. They were quite chickenhearted, I would say."[27]

One German was far from chickenhearted. For two days he had clung to his post, sniping at his enemy, holding his ruptured belly with guts spilling out all the while. When they brought him in he was still defiantly wearing his jacket with its SS insignia. The orderly tried to give him a transfusion. "No! No English blood!" he snarled, and spat at the orderly.[28]

The twenty-nine-year-old commanding officer of the Royal Hamilton Light Infantry (RHLI), Lieutenant Colonel Denis Whitaker, coauthor of this book, was wounded in the Normandy fighting. The RHLI, in a defensive position, had been continually mortared and shelled by the enemy for three days and three nights. No one had any sleep. Finally, the demolition platoon fashioned Whitaker a small dugout (using several grenades), large and deep enough to hold his camp cot. They covered it with a sheet of galvanized iron and soil. In went the cot; in went the officer, stretching his full length on a cot for the first time in three nights.

Two sounds followed each other in minutes: "Ahhh," said the relaxing CO. And shortly after, *Whaaaam!* A shell came directly through the roof into the trench, exploding in Whitaker's face and knocking him unconscious. He was taken to a CCS, where the shrapnel gashes in his face were repaired. After several days he was air-evacuated to England. His eyes were bandaged tight for three weeks. He learned to knit, to keep his mind from dwelling on the possibility of being blind for the rest of his life. Happily, he was one of the 93 percent of Normandy's wounded who recovered. Whitaker rejoined his battalion in France six weeks later.

Evacuation to English hospitals was smoothly managed by sea or air in a few days. The postoperative abdominal cases had to be retained a little longer; they found that if they moved an abdominal injury right away, they didn't survive.

In the early days of the Normandy battle, the majority of evacuations took place in Landing Ship Tanks (LSTs). As soon as an LST had unloaded the tanks they brought in from England to Normandy, the medical party would let down folding stretcher racks, fitted in tiers along the ship's sides, to accommodate 350 stretcher cases.

An operating room was set up in its stern. Amphibian vessels could bring as many as twenty-five casualties right into the bowels of the ship, where treatment would begin immediately. In this way the wounded men reached hospitals in the United Kingdom in the best possible condition, very different from the mud-covered and bloodstained casualties that had landed in England after the Dieppe raid in 1942.

An impressed surgeon in England noted that the Normandy casualties "were in good heart; their dressings were immaculate and it was difficult to believe that the careful notes which accompanied them had been made out on a shell-torn beach."[29] By early August this was streamlined. Besides sea evacuation (in somewhat more comfortable hospital ships), six air flights a day, each carrying twenty passengers, had been organized.

In the United Kingdom the allied soldier had access to the best medical treatment, superior by any standard. On top of the basic work of general surgeons and physicians, there were specialists, and even special centers, for chest surgery, neurosurgery, dermatology, ENT surgery, ophthalmology, orthopedics, and venereology.

But by now, after two months in Normandy, the hospital staffs were worn-out. In the crowded hospital tents, doctors, nursing sisters, and orderlies had been working long, exhausting shifts, often sixteen hours in every twenty-four. And to make matters worse, after the incessant rains of July, the August weather had became hot and sultry. This dry spell created clouds of dust that penetrated their clothes, inflamed their eyes, and permeated their skin and even their food. Mosquitoes and wasps increased their relentless attacks. Water was scarce. Much of the water supply had been sabotaged by the Germans, or polluted by decaying corpses of farm animals. Until the engineers repaired it, everyone was down to a tight ration transported under dangerous conditions by Service Corps personnel.

"I have never worked so hard in my life," Nurse Hogan remembers. "I can't call it nursing. The boys get in, get emergency treatment . . . and are out again. It is beyond words."[30]

CHAPTER 6

Everybody Breaks . . . Sometime

Fear, exhaustion, and misery—these are the three main ingredients that cause combat stress. Yet they are also the common ingredients of every battle. It's the intensity and mix of these three factors that determine whether at a given moment a man will be simply scared, bone tired, and depressed—because that is the state of all men in battle—or over the edge and out of control.

This type of casualty was becoming increasingly prevalent among troops who had been in action for weeks on end, constantly under fire, constantly facing death and seeing their buddies blown to bloody bits. As the war intensified, one in every four nonfatal casualties was attributed to this condition.[1]

"Everybody breaks; nobody can say that they were never scared," Padre Jock Anderson of the Highland Light Infantry maintains. It was manifested in many different ways:

> Some go completely wacky. I remember them bringing in one lad, and he couldn't move a muscle. He just lay there; you couldn't get through to him. I asked, "What'll happen to him?" And they said, "Oh, when he gets back to where he is safe he is likely to just snap out of it."
>
> And then there was another officer, he just took to his heels

and ran and ran and ran until he got all the way down to the beach and then collapsed.

"I broke once," Padre Anderson admitted. "The greatest thing is that it lets you see that everybody else has a breaking point, too." The padre's collapse came in Normandy after the battle of Buron, when 262 of his infantry were wounded and 62 killed. The sheer ordeal of helping take 262 wounded men off the battlefield created a genuine exhaustion. The stress of losing so many of his boys overcame him. "I couldn't control myself; I started to cry." The time-honored remedy—an injection that knocked a man out for twenty-four hours—was all it took to bring the personable chaplain back on his feet. But later, when he saw men in a similar agony, he found he could deal with them with deeper concern.[2]

Australian journalist Alan Wood wrote movingly of young soldiers who confronted fear—and won.

> Theirs is not always the courage of men who know no fear, but sometimes the courage of men who overcome it. A few short weeks ago, most . . . had never seen action. Many of them are young, many of them inexperienced. I think of a dispatch rider, only nineteen; he joined up when he was sixteen.
>
> The strain and terror of the battle told more and more on the faces of some of these men as they came back. One or two seemed at times almost to have reached the breaking point. Sometimes they would come in sobbing. But they would rest a little, nerve themselves afresh, and then always go back into battle again.[3]

As the Normandy campaign settled into grinding battles of attrition, the incidence of combat exhaustion escalated in direct ratio to the incidence of battle failure. It reached crisis proportions in July, during the stalemate, when the lack of progress and the high casualties induced a feeling of futility in the men.

Speaking of this, British historian David French wrote,

> Morale [is] the willingness of soldiers to fight rather than absent themselves from the battlefield. [It was] most fragile in infantry battalions, because infantrymen were exposed to the most dis-

comfort and maximum danger on the battlefield. It was probably strongest in those battalions which, through luck, were able to retain a cadre of officers and NCOs who were known to their men and who took a personal interest in their welfare.[4]

A historian describes a sad incident when a fine, once-proud battalion in 3d British Division whose morale, just briefly, had crumbled. Their leaders, the "old sweats," had fought one too many battles, seen one too many friends killed or maimed, had been themselves wounded once too often. A Spandau opened up, and they went to ground. The young reinforcements, new to the grim realities of fighting, simply followed their leaders' example. A similar episode was documented in another battalion when, at the height of battle, the reinforcements saw officers they respected and depended on gravely wounded. They panicked.[5]

The greatest number of NP [neuropsychiatric] casualties occurred when the troops were very tired, very static, dug in, and under heavy counterattack. The large numbers of reported battle exhaustion in American troops during the miserable fighting in the *bocage* dropped sharply with Patton's dramatic breakout at the end of July. By contrast the number of Canadian casualties in the August slog to Falaise led to an increase in cases of battle fatigue.

"The fear is there." Private Adolf Rogosch learned this fundamental philosophy of killing as a seventeen-year-old German infantry private fighting for his life in Normandy. "Everyone was afraid when they got close. No one can say that they were unafraid. [It's] either me or you. The fastest one was the winner."[6]

Fatigue was the biggest single threat to troop morale; sound leadership was its most vital stimulus. As long as there is hope, even just a glimmer, a man will usually accept the risks, if he is well led. Soldiers eyed their commanders warily. Will he get us killed? they wondered.

Denis Whitaker was commanding officer (CO) of the Royal Hamilton Light Infantry. "I believed that the men were concerned with two things: survival and success. If a CO demonstrated understanding of the task and consideration of the men who would achieve it, and if he had then developed a sound plan, he would win the confidence of the officers and, through them, of the troops.

The morale in my battalion was high; I think success brought a good deal of that about. We had seen others fail where we had succeeded. And our officers were strong; that made quite a difference. Through their own qualities of leadership, they could instill confidence in the other ranks.

One of my corporals described leadership more simply: "When you climb out of that slit trench . . . if you were to look around and find that you didn't have an officer, boy, that would have a tremendous effect on you psychologically."[7]

Captain Charlie Mackay, carrier platoon commander in the same battalion, recalls their successful fight to seize Verrières Ridge:

At that point we didn't know what battle fatigue was all about. We were told to capture that ridge and we did it; we were the only regiment in the division that got to our objective and held it.

The next few days we were under mortar and shell fire the whole time. I got a call to bring up three medics. When I got these three guys—one major and two captains—they said they were psychiatrists and they wanted to know what caused battle fatigue. They were going to spend two days in the front lines with us. I took these officers one at a time under heavy fire up to battalion headquarters. The next morning the phone rang, and I was told these fellows had changed their minds. They didn't think they needed to spend two days here. They wanted to leave right away. These guys found out about battle fatigue; they found out in the first half hour what caused it.[8]

Or maybe they realized they were looking in the wrong place? The battalion was pumped up with the justifiable pride of having pulled off a victory when no one else had been able to do it. Battle fatigue? Those men were too elated to be NP candidates.

A Canadian officer who had been in action fifty-four days noted this in his diary:

. . . hardly a day with respite from shelling, bombing, attacks, and the ordinary daily discomforts of living in slit trenches and eating when the exigencies of the service permitted.

Normandy will always be a blur to me. Dust, heat and worst of all the dead guys. I only look at their boots. I do not want to see the shoulder flash or the face. Having been with the battalion since the start, I might know the guy too well. What else? Oh yes, goddamn dysentery. That with lack of sleep and tiredness. How the jeez could we function; but apparently we did.[9]

That "goddamn dysentery" was a violent form of diarrhea known as "Normandy Stomach." With its gut-wrenching cramps and cold sweats it was becoming a major factor, compromising optimal combat effectiveness in the hot August weather.

Hives was another. The troops blamed the recurrence of hives and dysentery on the food. The medics disagreed. They attributed these minor symptoms to mosquitoes—attacking the men sleeping in the open in slit trenches—and to the soldiers' gorging on those sweets in their rations!

"About half the boys in the section have got hives. They are a damned nuisance; they make you itch like hell. The medic tells us that we are eating too many sweets when we are not used to them," one soldier wrote to his mother.[10]

"I am well bitten by mosquitoes," a signaler reported home. "They make attacks on me during the night. I got up last night and my left eye was swollen, both the backs of my hands and my right cheek were swollen and [I had] a nice egg over my right eye."[11]

Lice drove the men nuts. They were German hand-me-downs, picked up when men used slit trenches and dugouts abandoned by the enemy. "Everybody is having to scratch continuously," another rifleman complained.[12]

But it was utter tiredness that most debilitated the soldiers of Normandy. One diary described the agony of sleep deprivation—virtually a nonstop, weeks-long jet lag in today's vernacular—that brought "hard lines of fatigue" on the faces of the young soldiers.

Night after night passed without sleep and day after day was spent with no more rest than was afforded by the odd cat-nap. Men fell asleep as they drove carriers along a road, as they plodded in single file with their sections, or as they huddled in slit trenches under bombardment. Weariness built up until it laid its hand upon the very spirit. Men went for days on end in a sort of dazed mental stupor, in which they could not remember the events of an hour before, and in which they were utterly incapable of speculating upon the future.[13]

"I'm smoking far too many cigarettes to keep awake," a British trooper scrawled in his diary. "Between sixty and eighty a twenty-four [*sic*] hour day; my mouth and throat are like a kipper. God how tired we were! I took my boots and socks off for the first time . . . in twelve days."[14]

At some point—to keep his sanity—every man had to develop a philosophy toward killing and being killed. Perhaps hardest to bear was seeing your closest friends brutally shattered. Do you learn to hate the enemy and relish his death? Or do you pity him?

"Most people seem able to accept casualties," a British trooper wrote, "but for my part I can never overlook the tragedy that each one means to some far away, stricken home. The sadness of it all is always with me."[15]

A more resigned soldier eyed the fact of war: "We no longer think or talk of our comrades who have been killed—killing is our life and our past life is unreal."[16]

It is said that some airmen expressed their antipathy to their enemy by peeing in a bottle and dropping same when they flew over Germany. Captain Cliff Chadderton remembers an incident when his men watched an RAF bomber flying over an enemy position down the line.

The watchers could see the bombs leave the planes' bellies and arc toward the earth. Seconds later the burst would scatter earth and other objects high into the air.

Joe Sakolinski, who came from behind a store counter in Brandon to join the Rifles in 1940, was . . . a lance-corporal and had done much good work in the preceding month, so that his companions looked upon him with pride and respect.

Joe watched the bombing with relish: "It sure does my heart good to see those bastards getting a 'treatment' like that." The exhilaration of seeing their enemy disintegrate under the weight of these bombs spread through them like an intoxicant. They gave vent to suppressed feelings, running to and fro to get a better 'seat' and gesticulating wildly. "Jeez, my morale has gone up a hundred percent," one corporal said gleefully.[17]

But other men felt no joy in destroying his enemy. As British Trooper

Hewison wrote sadly in his diary, "There's ordinary blokes on each side with no desire to kill each other, yet here we are."[18]

Or as Flight Lieutenant Duke Warren mused, "We didn't feel an overpowering hate of the Germans, but rather an intense dislike and revulsion at what Germany was doing. One killed Germans to win the war."[19]

In all the allied armies, the emphasis was on returning battle-fatigue cases back to the front quickly. The US Army pioneered the importance of forward psychiatry. They'd come a long way from the crude face-slapping techniques in Sicily in 1943 by General George Patton, who, still unrepentant in August 1944, made a snide reference in his diary to "warwearies—a new name for cowardice."[20] His biographer, historian Carlo D'Este, explains that "Patton was simply unable to understand that soldiers have different breaking points. He thought all soldiers had to live up to a high standard. And in Patton's mind bravery was the highest virtue that a soldier could have, and cowardice was the deadliest sin."[21]

Exhaustion cases were kept at their aid stations for up to seventy-two hours. The first twenty-four hours focused on rest, usually under light sedation. In the second twenty-four-hour period, the men got hot food, showers, and clean clothes. On the morning of the third day, they had a personal interview with the psychiatrist.

The US 29th Infantry Division documents the three directions to which each man must now be sent: immediate return to duty; enrollment in the training program (where confidence is built up by short refreshers in such essentials as battle drill and weapon training); or reclassification as unfit for further combat duty.

The newest conscripts had the biggest problems. According to the document, "The biggest fault we find upon arrival here is the disregard of orders. They have not had obedience to orders sufficiently emphasized. Such disregard may easily result, on the battle line, in useless casualties."[22]

As American historian Stephen Ambrose notes, three-quarters of them return to their foxholes.[23]

German soldiers became similarly disturbed by feelings of futility as the Normandy campaign advanced. The penalty for desertion was the death sentence, yet many German soldiers did lay down their arms. In their landmark study on battle exhaustion, military historians Terry Copp and Bill McAndrew wrote that, in Normandy in late July and August, many Germans surrendered "in a condition suggesting complete physical exhaustion and serious nervous fatigue."[24]

There were instances of desertion in allied ranks. David French writes: "The typical deserter, 'exhaustion' case or victim of a self-inflicted wound was an other-rank infantryman who had recently joined an infantry battalion as a reinforcement or a veteran soldier who was asked to take part in one battle too many."[25]

CHAPTER 7

Cheers

As the weeks of anguished fighting went on, it became increasingly important to keep up the soldiers' morale. The comforting reminders of home—warm meals, clean clothes, family letters, and, above all else, peaceful rest—took top priorities as morale boosters to the troops.

Food, plain though it was, was amply supplied, if tedious. British and Canadian frontline men were issued "Compo Rations" boxes, each containing enough food for seven men for two days (or fourteen men for one day). They usually contained an assortment of M and V (tinned meat and vegetables), dried fruit, biscuits, and pudding, different each time. "Finding you've been given the one with the can of peaches is like winning a lottery," one officer noted.[1] As well, coffee and milk in powdered form, candy, cigarettes, and toilet paper were included. The British added "compo tea"—cubes containing a dried premix of tea, milk, and sugar.

But the Americans had the best, as one Canadian soldier noted in disgust: "Them buggers know how to do things. You seen their fuckin' K-rations? They get Spam and beef stew and coffee . . . We get jeezly bully beef and tea! Shee-it!"[2]

K-rations actually came in three varieties: breakfast, lunch, and dinner. The former comprised some compressed cereal, an egg-and-meat mixture in a tiny can, a fruit bar, chewing gum, water purification tablets, and toilet paper. Four cigarettes were included in the dinner packet, plus a sort of nonmelting chocolate bar. War journalist Andy Rooney once swapped his K-ration package with a French family for one of the best meals of his life: "half a loaf of small, crusty bread, a piece of Camembert cheese, and a bottle of unlabeled red wine."[3]

Bartering for food went on everywhere, sometimes in a very lopsided way that reflected the extraordinary needs of both parties. The bargain of a lifetime: two boxes of matches in exchange for one chicken. Many others swapped compo-ration edibles for fresh Norman eggs, butter, or milk. A Middlesex officer saw an elderly Frenchwoman standing in the doorway of her cottage munching an undoubtedly bartered army hard tack biscuit. "*Les gateaux anglais sont magnifiques,*" she said to him.[4]

Highland Light Infantry Padre Jock Anderson was probably the only man ever to swap a jeep for one dozen eggs. Anderson, who had "liberated" a German car for his own use, learned that anyone caught operating an enemy vehicle would be put on charge. He went to a Frenchman's farm. "I'll give you this car for one dozen eggs," he offered. "The farmer said that was a deal if we would help him hide it up in his loft. So we hauled the thing up, covered it with hay and we got our dozen eggs."[5]

Liberating food, or "living off the land" as it was euphemistically called, was common practice. Company commanders learned to look the other way when the heady aroma of *ragoût de poulet* wafting from behind a barn soon replaced the squawking of a chicken. One platoon caught a rabbit and boiled it up with freshly dug vegetables for rabbit stew that night. Unfortunately, the wretched animal proved to be a "granddaddy," and was taking its time getting tender when the troops were abruptly moved forward. "Our rabbit stew went into battle," they reported, with two soldiers securely balancing the pot's handle on a stick.[6]

When Lieutenant General Sir Brian Horrocks took command of the British XXX Corps in Normandy, he was startled to find himself also commanding a barnyard of chickens and cows. There were so many stray cows and so much poultry wandering loose in bomb-shattered Normandy, that XXX Corps troops who had been farmers before going to war were put in charge of collecting them for a kind of mobile farm. "We were thus able to supply our casualty clearing station with fresh eggs, milk and meat," Horrocks noted with satisfaction.[7]

Sergeant Perry "Cock" Kelly of the US 743d Tank Battalion seemingly thought that a cup of good old American coffee was worth risking his life for.

"When mail call included a sister's present of real coffee, Cock treated it as the treasure it was, but discovered nothing was stowed in his new tank in which to prepare it. He spied a nearby bombed out farmhouse and set off, trudging across the open field between tank and farmstead."

On his way back, Cock came under mortar fire. Tucking the newly found coffeepot against his chest "he broke into a run propelled by fear, zigzagging, ducking, and turning as exploding mortar shells stalked their elusive target. Corrected for distance, each shell measured Cock's progress across the field. With each explosion that rained stones, the pot was hugged even tighter until he reached the safety of the trees protecting the tank."

As he blissfully sipped his hard-won brew the next morning, the intrepid sergeant realized how close a call it had been: the backs of his legs were tattooed with shell splinters.[8]

Letters home revealed how the men rated their daily fare. Of 5,219 examined by the censors, only one complained of poor food:

> . . . Food is getting better every day. Fresh meat every day is more than we ever expected when we left England.
>   . . . All our food is canned and it is monotonous. It's good and wholesome and well cooked and served, but one would appreciate a change to fresh meat and vegetables.
>   . . . The only hardships are lack of fresh vegetables and meat, also bread. We've been living on Compo rations for quite a while now. They're quite good and miles ahead of the last war.[9]

Fiery Calvados—it being after all a Norman product—was easier to come by than coffee. French hard cider, too, could be liberated from almost any farm cellar. Cases of wine were sometimes looted from the looters—the Germans had stashed away large quantities of fine French vintages during their years of occupation. Seasoned frontline commanders found that a steady diet of cider with the occasional shot of Calvados kept them awake on long night watches.[10] A tot of rum, and even occasional bottles of beer, were issued, especially before a battle. (Curiously, soldiers were given a tot of rum *before* they went into battle; aircrew were given theirs *after* a raid.)

Increasingly, though, as the humid weather set in, water became the most important thing of all. "Men can fight without food, but not without water," wrote the *Wyvern News*—a chatty frontline newsletter for men of the British 43 Division:

> British infantry who have tramped and fought in the choking dust that has often lain over the roads and battle areas will tell you that the next best thing to the old pub at home is the "Water Point" on the Normandy roadside—the mobile water pumping and purifying unit which provides the only safe water supply for the troops in the forward areas.
>
> There have been days in Normandy when the unending convoys, and the rumbling tank squadrons on the move, have covered the roadside hedges and the fields alongside with a thick layer of dust. Through it all have come the marching troops—appearing like workers in a flour mill.
>
> A team of four men established one water point for 43rd Wessex infantrymen within three-quarters of a mile of the German positions, providing 58,000 gallons of water a day while under constant fire from "Oscar"—their flippant term for the enemy mortar.
>
> "There's 'Old Faithful,'" a corporal of London-Irish extraction boasted of their purifying plant. "Oscar knocked her about a bit—she's like a sponge. We plugged the shrapnel holes with bits of rag and wood. She's taken more bashings than I'd like to take—and she's still grinning."[11]

Understandably, to men whose skin has been embedded with dust and grime for days or weeks at a time, mobile baths and laundries brought up to "A" echelon, not far behind the front, were enormous morale boosters. The Ordnance Corps, a seldom-recognized service arm that brought up all supplies, provided these. One private wrote home happily, "We went for a complete change of clothes and a shower. We went in one end of the tent dirty as a coal bin and came out the other end looking like a new recruit in his first uniform. We felt 100 percent better afterward."[12] Even on the front lines, the men were encouraged to wash and shave. "The platoon seldom went unshaven," a British officer in 43 Wessex observed. "Never once did I have to reprimand a man for uncleanliness." However, proximity to enemy lines did make for primitive toilet arrangements. "Newspapers and food cans were our resort."[13]

The outgoing mail from the front was censored for security reasons. But the censors also noted factors in the letters—gripes or elation—that could influence a soldier's morale. They read time and again how widely the men appreciated the Postal Corps, who braved enemy fire to deliver news from home to the front. Allied troops got letters from mothers, wives, and friends with incredible speed. Mail arrived from the UK in two to three days. ("What a lovely letter is yours of the 26th. And here it is the 28th!") From the US and Canada it took six to nine days. ("Our mail from home is coming first rate, which sure is a blessing. Out here a letter is a million times more precious than gold.")[14]

Private Bill Grant wondered at some of the strange things people from home would send. "The other day I received from my old Scout leader a book called *Rovering to Success.* The book cautioned me to eschew tobacco, strong drink, loose women and bad language—suggestions not too relevant to my present situation."[15]

The paperback book—a neophyte industry in the United States before the war—found its niche in wartime supplying reading material to combat troops. A group of publishers organized as the Council on Books in Wartime spearheaded the idea. Servicemen had access, free, to thousands of titles produced in the curious but practical shirt-pocket size of four-by-five-and-one-half inches. At the height of the operation forty titles were produced each month. The publishers accepted minimal royalties (one-half cent per copy) on the condition that civilians not have access to any of the millions of copies distributed in war zones, and that the whole issue be pulped at the end of the war.

The popular Spielberg concept of invasion troops crossing the channel in white-knuckled terror is somewhat dispelled by the reality of men swapping back and forth pages torn from an Ernest Hemingway or Mark Twain novel.

Penguin pocket books, that exactly fit the battledress pocket and cost only sixpence, gained enormous popularity with British servicemen.[16]

No matter how tough the campaign, how imminent the battle, there came a time when it was imperative to give the men a respite, however brief, from the anguish of war. An effort was made to take every unit out of combat periodically to specially set up rest centers. "Out of the line at rest at last! Really out, after fifty-four days and I've worn pyjamas for two nights running and have been in bed ALL night long! It's marvellous. The men are like kids out of school and the officers much the same."[17]

The troops were also given a few hours of fun by stars of the entertainment world. No prima donnas here; they sacrificed comfort for comforting. The YMCA and the Salvation Army produced glitzy Hollywood and London show personalities like Lana Turner and Edward G. Robinson. George Formby held a concert for five thousand men ("a bit vulgar," one British officer confided to his diary) and films shown on the mobile cinema were a popular feature—even reruns.

"You should see our theater here," a soldier raved to his mom. "The only place in one piece that was large enough was the stable and in no time we had it all set up with about 50 chairs and the show was on."[18]

American troops got a kick out of the Red Cross "donut wagons" driven to the front by US volunteers. The 305th Engineer Combat Unit noted that "at Argentan the Red Cross Clubmobile visited the battalion with hot coffee and donuts and music. Four real American girls attended it. These were the first American girls any of us had seen since our arrival in France. It was a real treat to see a petite mademoiselle who spoke English! Here we saw a movie for the first time, 10 years old, but enjoyed by all."[19]

But for others, just sitting quietly under an apple tree without the incessant thunder of artillery was restorative. Lance Corporal Ken Tout described an evening when Scottish troopers—their tanks laagered for the night in a lull of battle—found solace tuning in to a BBC wavelength to listen to the Promenade Concert from London.

> Into a five-man tank a dozen of us push and squeeze as though playing at sardines. Outside, another batch of Moaning Minnies screams and thunders down. Somebody closes the turret hatches. There are not enough headsets to go round. We could, of course, spread ourselves around several tanks with ample supplies of headsets. But that would not be such fun. It would not be in the spirit of the Proms.[20]

Frontline journalism came of age in World War II. The allied countries had columnists and radio commentators whose professionalism and skill, often under fire, has seldom been matched. The USA had Ernest Hemingway (writing for Colliers), Ernie Pyle, and Bill Mauldin, creator of

"Willie and Joe." Canadian war correspondents like Ralph Allen, Greg Clark, Charles Lynch, Wally Rayburn, Ross Munro, and Fred Griffin, and radio commentators like Matthew Halton, had equal expertise, as did British writers and news commentators such as Alan Moorhead, Chester Wilmot, and Richard Dimbleby.

Troops received hometown newspapers with amazing efficiency. But they weren't always good for morale. The men followed the course of the war with a discerning eye, and sometimes disagreed with the wartime journalists' interpretation—especially if it had been focused on their particular battlefield. These resentments were alleviated to a large extent by the publications of the American and Canadian army newspapers. Richard Malone, founder of the *Maple Leaf*, bet (and won) a case of whiskey with his American counterpart that his *Maple Leaf* Canadian newspaper, published in Normandy, would roll off the presses in Caen before the Yanks could produce the *Stars and Stripes* in Cherbourg: "Each time I saw the RAF bombs dropping on Caen, I prayed that they would miss the little newspaper plant," Malone recounted to the authors with a grin.[21]

The wire services of the three countries cooperated fully with each other. But reporters, under pressure from hometown editors to produce dynamic articles, occasionally got carried away. The unfolding saga of a young Canadian lad who stumbled into international—if momentary—greatness in the press illustrates the zealousness of stateside editors to develop a story.

It began with a small item filed by war correspondent Bill Wilson that was picked up by international media. A follow-up query to the Defense Department in Ottawa triggered this immediate cable to Canadian Press Camp in Normandy:

> Aug 22/44: US newsreel editors all much interested story today of Pte Earl McAllister, Canadian who according to Wilson BUP War Correspondent single handed captured 150 enemy near Trun thus outstripping Sergeant York. Stop. Suggest something special by Army Film Unit if rushed will make feature spot all news reels stop advise soonest if anything done or can be so may be prepared for film getting special play.

Back came the reply next day: "Trying to obtain material. Will advise if successful."

And then another query from an anxious editor: "Is story now confirmed?"

While the search was on for the young man, McAllister—unit still unknown—was going about his war, innocently unaware of the furor. But the newsmen wouldn't let go. They wanted that story even if they had to exaggerate or even stage it: "Reels scream for story even re-enactment of Private Earl McAllister of Hamilton capturing 160 [sic] armed Germans near Trun. This exceeds Sgt York's record."

On August 25 the reply finally came: "McAllister prisoner story exaggerated but we are tracing him and will obtain some coverage." The outcome was this article published in New York by *Time* magazine:

Hamilton's York. Canada At War, Sept 5, 1944

Last week Canada had its own Sergeant York—Pvt. Earl ("Scotty") McAllister. 21 and 5 ft. 3.

Scotty left his furniture factory job in Hamilton, Ont. two years ago, joined the R.C.A.F. Sidetracked from pilot training, first because of his small size, then because of an ear defect, he finally joined the army as a private.

In Normandy, reported United Pressman William Wilson, Scotty was driving down a road when six Germans crossed in front of him. He fired. The Germans surrendered. Then some French resistance fighters told him there were more Germans in a nearby woods, asked him to send a tank. Said McAllister, "Tank, hell!" He walked to the woods alone, fired a few bursts from his Sten gun. Eighty-five fully-armed Germans emerged, threw down their arms. Then some Frenchmen told him that there was a Nazi tank farther down the road. It turned out to be an armored car escorted by 60 to 70 German soldiers. Scotty jumped into the armored car, ordered the Germans to surrender. They did.

Total catch, some 160 Germans, as compared with Sergeant York's bag of 132 Germans captured, a score killed, in one memorable day of World War I.

Said Scotty's mother (who has two other sons in the service): "It was just like we figured. We thought he had too much courage for his size. When he went away we said, 'Either he comes back a hero or he doesn't come back at all.' "[22]

No one was more thrilled than the parents of a twenty-one-year-old Canadian from Hamilton, Ontario, to see a hero's write-up, photo and all, in *Time* magazine. Scotty McAllister, a "hitherto anonymous Argyll," in truth became, briefly, the hero of his battalion by "bagging" one hundred (though not 160) POWs at St. Lambert-sur-Dives.

His buddies' pride and the spirit of comradeship that were engendered at the front were perhaps the greatest morale boosters of all.

Sadly, his mother's prophecy was not fulfilled. Scotty *did* become a hero; but he never came back. Promoted to the rank of sergeant, he fought "gallantly" until he was killed in action in Germany.

PART III

AMERICAN BREAKTHROUGH

CHAPTER 8

Those Guys, They Got Some Ingenuity!

Desperation brings solutions.

The resourcefulness of tankers in the field finally provided lifesaving answers to the challenges of the *bocage*.

Nineteen-year-old Edward Gianelloni, a medic with the US 3rd Battalion Medical Section, was impressed to see "a tank coming down the road that had a bulldozer blade welded on the front of it. . . . Those guys, they've got some ingenuity. The Germans started running after they saw this tank coming after them."[1]

Soon, tankers from all allied countries were welding tracks from knocked-out tanks and pieces of steel from the hulls of landing craft on the bodies of their Shermans to add armored protection.

Sergeant Curtis Culin, a twenty-nine-year-old former cab driver from Chicago, demonstrated the resourcefulness and mechanical ability of so many young Americans. He came up with an ingenious device for cutting through hedgerows to confound the *Wehrmacht's bocage* defense tactics.

Culin borrowed the idea from the burrowing antics of a rhinoceros. He collected steel blades from abandoned beach defenses and welded them to the front of his tank, enabling the Sherman to cut through the thick hedgerows. This was an instant success and a huge morale booster to the troops. Impressed, the division gave immediate priority to producing as many "Rhino tanks" as possible, and the Sherman's effectiveness was restored.[2]

As they encountered the hazards of armored combat in the *bocage*, other American and British tankers became equally innovative. Captain John McCoy of the US 743d Tank Battalion rammed holes in the banks, then stuffed them with dynamite charges to blast his way through.

Flame-throwing Crocodile tanks, some of the "Funnies" inspired by the tragedy on the Dieppe beaches in 1942 and devised by the British 79th Division, were brought in. These fired a thick black liquid into the hedges that was quickly ignited into a fire that could not be extinguished. This flushed out many terrorized enemy infantry, as did the white phosphorus "snow" that was used with equally frightening effect.

Another chronic problem that had dogged the armor—communication between tank and infantryman—was solved by American improvisation. The rifleman's job was to protect the armor by warning its crew of impending danger. The only way he could do this was to hammer on the tank with his rifle butt or entrenching tool—all the while being ripe pickings for a German sniper. Alternatively, the tank commander had to stick his head out the turret to hear the message—equally appetizing for the sniper. The Americans, as historian Stephen Ambrose noted, were "learning by doing." In this case, trial and error led them to the solution of installing an interphone box on the tank into which the infantryman could plug a radio handset. The handset's long cord enabled him to crouch for cover as he communicated any dangers to the men in the tank.[3]

Sergeant Edward Welch of Watts, Oklahoma, who used to work in oil fields, invented a gadget that cleaned rust out of a rifle barrel in a matter of seconds, whereas it used to take a man twenty minutes.[4]

Unspeakable weather made conditions in the *bocage* area between the coast and St. Lô even more unbearable. France was having the wettest July in forty years. The troops—allied and foe—lived like moles in deep, mud-filled holes, never dry, never clean.

A soldier would lower himself gingerly (or on occasion dive) into what often seemed a tomb of slop: six feet long, four feet deep, dug with his trenching tool while mortar and artillery shells exploded around him and snipers' bullets searched for their mark. The trenches became sweltering or sodden prisons as the sun burned or the rain poured down on them.

It was only at night that they could stir. Food came in fourteen-man packs that were collected at night. One infantryman remembers: "We tossed the tins from one trench to another, counted out the cigarettes and candy, and looked thoughtfully at the sheets of toilet paper also provided, hoping that it would be only in the dark that the urge came to use it."[5]

Despite the truckloads of chlorinated water hauled up to the troops each day, dysentery became the inevitable by-product of a countryside littered with thousands of dead cows and horses. "One could never get used to that appalling sweet sickly stench," Alan Moorhead wrote. "There was only one thing worse—the sweet smell of dead men."[6]

Mosquitoes buzzed around in huge swarms taking "sadistic delight in sinking the teeth into skin, veins, cheeks, ears, arms, and ankles, out of sheer rabid animosity towards mankind. No escape with darkness and no escape with daylight."[7]

British soldiers on the Americans' eastern flank shared the miseries of the *bocage*. The *Yorkshire Pud*, a newssheet published at the front for the 7th Battalion, The Duke of Wellington's Regiment, which normally ran headlines about enemy actions, was provoked enough to run this banner: "Battalion . . . attacked by hordes of mosquitoes."[8]

One Scottish officer tried incinerating them: "Every time you get out of your dug-out it gets full of mosquitoes, and once more I had to go through the drill of burning them up with a torch of paper; then, after singeing my eyebrows and almost setting my bedding alight, I closed the trap-door and went round again with a torch, swatting a few hardy survivors."[9] "They delight in catching us on the latrine," lamented one corporal, who attributed increasing illness to the pests. "They are enough to drive a man mad."[10]

Wasps were the perennial French summer plague. Sometimes they were so vicious that a soldier could not open his mouth to take a bite of food without being stung by a wasp—or swallowing the wretched insect (occasionally washing it down with a hasty gulp of compo tea, tasting sour from the fumes of a Tommy Cooker).

The bad weather in July brought another element of ill fortune for the Allies: no air support. Because of persistent rain and fog, one US Marauder unit—323d Group—had seventeen straight missions scrubbed. Others fared little better. Fifty percent of all missions for all planes in England and France were washed out.[11]

German Lieutenant Walter Padberg crouched behind a hedgerow, wondering where the Americans were and why they were silent. He cautiously peered through the brush but could see nothing. So he decided it was time to get a good look. He leapt over the hedge and landed almost directly upon the Americans' front line. "I had landed with my legs spread and in a panic the American lying there shot through my legs. I jumped back over the hedge and allowed us both to recover from the shock." Padberg received the Close Combat Medal for what he sardonically called his "greatest heroic deed. It was given to those who had stared the enemy in the eyes."[12]

A platoon of American infantry lads—"Doughboys" or "Dogfaces" as some GIs preferred to be called—retaliated with a strange and frightening ruse. A snake had slithered into their slit. They caught it with a forked stick and tossed it into a German MG nest. "Immediately there were screams and a great commotion," Private Kenneth Russell chortled. "Very shortly there were three or four hand grenades lobbed over the hedge." The Germans were routed.[13]

Bocage fighting had no shortcuts, "no dramatic charges across open fields," as war correspondent Ernie Pyle put it. The men soon learned it was to be a

> slow and cautious business, and there's nothing very dashing about it. They go in tiny groups, a squad or less, moving yards apart and sticking close to the hedgerows on either side of the field. They creep a few yards, squat, wait, then creep again.
>
> This hedgerow business is a series of little skirmishes . . . thousands and thousands of little skirmishes. No single one of them is very big. But add them all up over the days and weeks and you've got a man sized war, with thousands on both sides being killed.[14]

Hitler's order to Hausser's Seventh Army to "hold fast" was causing grave casualties to the German defenders as well. They were developing respect for the determined Tommies and Doughboys. Their price for delaying the allied advance was described by their own corps commander as "one tremendous bloodbath, such as I have never seen in eleven years of war."[15] By D-plus-44, eighty thousand of the seven hundred thousand *Wehrmacht* soldiers committed to battle on D-Day had become prisoners of war, and the same number had been killed or wounded.[16] "It was the same on both sides," German Private Adolf Rogosch said. "Because the

Americans were also only nineteen or twenty years old, the same as us. It was a 'munitions battle,' with fifteen hours of continuous shelling a day. The banging was everywhere. We thought the world was going to end."[17]

Allied casualties were now over the hundred thousand mark. The *bocage* alone had claimed eleven thousand American casualties.[18] Using pain relief as a yardstick for the agonies of *bocage* combat, the divisions' medics reckoned that they injected an average thirty-two grains of morphine per hedgerow.[19] The 29th Division's rifle companies were close to one hundred percent replacements.[20]

It seemed as though the agonizing weeks, overcoming one wretched hedgerow only to be met by another and another, would never end. Would they ever get through this hellhole?

But suddenly they did. Before dawn on July 17, Major General Charles Gerhardt's US 29th Division broke through to the outskirts of St. Lô and seized the high ground, gazing in wonder and relief at the objective so long denied.

One final hurdle for the 29th Division lay ahead: the battle to seize the fiercely defended city of St. Lô. But for the division, the Battle of the Hedgerows was over.

CHAPTER 9

The Clay Pigeons of St. Lô

The *bocage* had claimed victims enough from among the D-Day invaders. Sorely underestimating the potential infantry casualties in subsequent fighting, the allied planners had to scramble to find instant frontline replacements for the infantrymen who had fallen. US "Repple Depple" reinforcement depots were churning out soldiers who had to be rushed into battle.

It is never easy to assimilate new men, especially during heavy fighting. Many of them never made it past St. Lô. Noted First Sergeant Thomas "Tops" Kirkman of the 119th Infantry:

> We had a crack outfit when we came over the Channel. We'd been together for two years. We'd worked together in England, trained together; we were good. But since we came to France, it'd been a steady drain. We'd been shot up pretty bad. We'd lost a lot of swell men.
>
> Now we get replacements who show no signs of that training. We get clerks and mechanics and cooks who have suddenly become riflemen. Why, I remember in a group that recently arrived—I asked for somebody to handle a machine gun, and not one of them spoke out. None of them had ever handled one. Finally, one of them said, "'Hell, Lieutenant, I'll fire the damn thing."

Look at the list of NCOs. Most of them are privates with
stripes. We have to have somebody in those jobs. That's why they
were upped [promoted].

And now we go in with a bunch of replacements who haven't
had a chance to learn north from south, or whose arches have
fallen after the first five-mile hike. The new noncoms rattle
around in the old ones' shoes.[1]

Seasoned combat soldiers felt it was tough enough just staying alive
and doing their jobs without having to nursemaid these new reinforcements. American infantry captain Harold Leinbaugh described a platoon,
newly arrived at the front, that had been tossed together in a training center: "They were close-shaven, clear-eyed, and wearing clean uniforms.
They seemed totally out of place, an alien cast which had wandered onto
the wrong stage.

"They were ordered to take out an enemy post. The new captain led
his platoon straight across the field toward the objective. The Germans let
them get in close. When they opened fire, every one of the GIs was killed.

"We were as mad at the new outfit as we were at the Germans—
maybe more so," Leinbaugh remembered. "We kept calling them dumb
bastards. Twelve good men were dead. This sort of thing couldn't have
happened to us; we knew better."[2]

Knowing better didn't always save lives. Historian Max Hastings tells a
grisly story of a major in the US 9th Division who was walking with his
closest friend across an orchard near St. Lô when hit by a TOT (Time On
Target: an artillery shoot carefully synchronized to concentrate the fire of
an entire battery or regiment at a precise moment). "Suddenly everything
was exploding. There was blood all over me and a helmet on the ground
with a head inside it." It was his friend's. And another account: "Three 2nd
lieutenants had just joined us, straight from the beach and Fort Benning.
I had told them to sit down and wait to be assigned to companies. They
were dead, along with six others killed and 33 wounded in a shoot that
lasted only a matter of seconds."[3]

Like the three ill-fated lieutenants, many of the reinforcements became casualties before they even met their unit buddies. A corporal from
transport reflected on the times he would drive the replacements up to the
front line, and often pick up some of the same men, dead, that evening.
"Those lads are so inexperienced, the cost will not only be their own lives

but the lives of many of the older fellows who will try to guide and protect them. The sun never set on those poor buggers . . . No one even got to know their names, what they looked like, their likes and dislikes.

" 'Johnny . . . which one was that?' they'd ask."[4]

But survival also depended on experience, on developing the kinds of intuitive sense that is not taught at Fort Benning or any other battle school. The American resourcefulness that produced inventions like the Rhino tank also, in time, created battle-smart cunning that became instinctively imprinted in the GI's mind. So he survived by surviving. Many didn't.

At St. Lô two massive air-cum–ground breakout attacks were being simultaneously planned on two separate battlegrounds by commanding generals of two different countries. One, American, would be a brilliant success; the other, the British Operation *Goodwood*, would see 5,537 British and Canadian soldiers and almost two hundred tanks become casualties in a single day.[5] When the normally mild-tempered Eisenhower was informed that it had taken more than seven thousand tons of bombs for the British to gain seven miles, he commented bitterly: "The Allies can hardly hope to go through France paying a price of a thousand tons of bombs per mile."[6]

While Monty was taking the heat for a flawed operation, US General Omar Bradley had his eye on an attack to break out of the *bocage* bottleneck. It would be of the same immense scale as *Goodwood*. But he wasn't going to repeat Montgomery's mistakes. The Anglo-Canadian attack on July 18 was launched against Germans well entrenched in a ridge that dominated the battleground. Bradley was determined that his forces first gain high, firm ground from which to launch his assault. The terrain that Bradley coveted lay beyond the dead-straight road running east–west from St. Lô to Périers, well clear of the despised hedgerows, with wide-open countryside and plenty of maneuverability for his armor: "Where you would not be hung up by swamps or river crossings," he explained to his staff. . . . Where you could use maximum troops."[7]

Bradley considered that another of Monty's mistakes was in delaying the armored attack for several hours after the bombing, giving the enemy Tigers, Panthers, mortars, and 88mms time to recover.

Finally, while both operations depended on softening the enemy with massive saturation bombing by the RAF, Bradley decided he could avoid the extensive cratering that stopped Montgomery's advance by employing smaller, hundred-pound fragmentation bombs.

By July 17 American forces had reached the outskirts of St. Lô. General Gerhardt's shattered 29th Division struggled manfully, but the enemy garrison holding the town and surrounding hills refused to yield. In a battle that inflicted carnage reminiscent of World War I, Lieutenant General Eugen Meindl's elite II Parachute Corps gave ground only gradually, house by house. But with almost 100 percent casualties already incurred in the *bocage* fighting, the doughboys lacked the manpower to drive off the counterattacking enemy. The 29th Infantry Division had lost three thousand men, killed, wounded, or taken prisoner. The 35th Infantry Division casualties numbered two thousand.[8]

The CO of 29th Division's 115th Infantry observed, "The town was being held by the artillery, really, as the infantrymen were [so depleted] they were little more than guards for the observation posts." The GIs thus earned the sobriquet of "Clay Pigeons of St. Lô."[9]

General Patton is quoted as remarking, circa World War I, "the poorer the infantry, the more artillery it needs."[10] The bloodbath in the *bocage* battle might have induced him to amend the statement to "the *fewer* the infantry, the more artillery it needs."

First Lieutenant John Williams of the 117th Infantry illustrated case in point. "The advance was held up for four or five hours by a well-positioned enemy line on the south side of the steep ravine. Every time the two assault companies attempted to cross the stream at the bottom of this ravine, heavy automatic fire would cut loose." The clay pigeons were becoming, in Williams's words, "dead ducks." Relief only came when the 92d Chemical Battalion moved up, firing its mortars at extreme range to smother the enemy position.[11]

Weather permitting, the allied airmen were also becoming skilled in identifying enemy targets and radioing their positions in the *bocage* to ground artillery. A captured German report confirms that:

> The enemy overcomes the difficulty of hedgerow country by employment of artillery air observers. They fly over the battle zone in regular reliefs and their reconnaissance is followed by strong, short bursts of fire with considerable ammunition expenditure. In sectors where there are only a few AA guns these planes sweep down to a low level in order to direct the fire to picked targets.

The report goes on to note that "artillery is distinguished by accuracy of fire and maneuverability. Employment of fire and phosphorus bombs as well as HE ammunition . . . has been frequently observed [causing] stomach trouble and headaches."[12]

The "clay pigeons" at St. Lô—the *bocage* survivors and the new replacements—were so diminished in numbers that, as Patton had observed, they had to depend either on the artillery or on their own fierce courage to capture the town.

"Gerhardt was a tough old buzzard," recalled Andy Rooney of *60 Minutes* fame, then a *Stars and Stripes* warco (war correspondent) who had just interviewed the 29th Division's commanding general. "[He] gave the major commanding 3rd Battalion of his 116th Infantry Regiment a Patton-like command to 'take St. Lô if you have to expend the whole battalion.' "[13]

The major, Thomas Howie, was in peacetime an English teacher whose natural skills at command had earned him profound respect from his men. At dawn, Howie and his men had crept undetected through the early morning mist to reinforce an isolated battalion less than one thousand yards from St. Lô. The 116th was fully living up to its epithet as the "Stonewall Brigade" of Civil War fame.

Ordered now to move his unit to the eastern edge of the town, and despite his own exhaustion and that of his men, Howie had responded without hesitation, "Will do." He assembled his officers and grimly told them his plan: a predawn surprise attack directly on the defenders' positions using commando tactics: bayonets and hand grenades. The meeting broke up, but before the men could get back to their companies a German mortar barrage pounded the site.

"Major Howie turned to take a last look to be sure all his men had their heads down," one of his officers reported. A shell exploded a few yards away; a fragment struck the major in the back and pierced his lung. "He said, My God, I'm hit. As he fell I caught him. He was dead in two minutes."[14]

Before his distraught men could initiate the raid Howie had planned, Meindl's paratroopers followed up the bombardment with a strong counterattack. Without help, the undermanned battalion faced near destruction. The "Clay Pigeons" looked to the skies, and were saved by one more American improvisation—this time, from the air. Their quick call brought down a devastating strike of Thunderbolt fighter-bombers from Major General Pete Quesada's Ninth Tac Air Command directly on the attackers.

With its long-range capabilities and sturdiness, the P-47 Thunderbolt had first made its mark in the European Theater of War as a high-altitude bomber escort. Then in late '43 the Rolls Royce Merlin-powered P-51 Mustangs arrived. They were first used for ground attack but when they began to fly combat missions in early 1944, they proved that they could do it all: they could fly the distance to Berlin and back; they could fly faster and outdogfight the German fighters. Thus Herman Goering's famous comment: "When I saw Mustangs over Berlin in March 1944, I knew the jig was up."[15]

By 1944, the P-47 and the Mustang had switched roles. But it was a tough sell to the young pilots. The P-47 Thunderbolt was the largest, most heavily armed single-engine fighter in the American arsenal. Initially, its appearance led many pilots to dismiss the design as ungainly and ill suited for a fighter role against nimble *Luftwaffe* aircraft, such as the ME-109 and FW 190.

One US Spitfire pilot (formerly from the Eagle Squadron) and now from 8th Fighter Command described his initial disgust with the size of his newly assigned craft:

It was huge: the wing tip of the P-47 came higher than the cockpit of the Spitfire. When we strapped into a Spitfire we felt snug and part of the aircraft; the Thunderbolt cockpit, on the other hand, was so large that we felt if we slipped off the Goddamned seat we would break a leg! We were horrified at the thought of going to war in such a machine: we had enough trouble with the Focke Wulfs 190s in our nimble Spitfire Vs; now this lumbering seven-ton monster seemed infinitely worse.

However, the pilots soon came to appreciate the P-47. Its sturdy construction and air-cooled radial engine enabled the Thunderbolt to absorb severe battle damage and keep flying. P-47s often came back from combat shot full of holes, their wings and control surfaces in tatters. On one occasion a Thunderbolt pilot, Lieutenant Chetwood, hit a steel pole after strafing a train over Occupied France. The collision sliced four feet off one of his wings—yet he was able to fly back safely to his base in England.[16]

"The P-47's stability comes at a price," another pilot reflected. "This aircraft hates to maneuver. Turning ability is an oxymoron with the Thunderbolt, and half loops are an adventure."[17] Another said sarcastically, "It sure as hell can't climb; it had better know how to dive." It did, in spades.

The Thunderbolt came into its own as a ground-pounder and, because of this, it flew more than twice as many sorties as the Mustang. When its eight .50-caliber Brownings were combined with rockets and bombs, the P-47 was a powerful ground-attack machine.

They affectionately nicknamed the P-47 the "Jug," short for Juggernaut (and not, as one flyer commented, a commentary about its bloated, pug-nosed appearance). Fighter planes took on the personalities of the pilots, who were allowed to name and paint the noses of their planes ("nose art") in any way they wanted. They went to town with the most garish colors they could dream up and the rudest or catchiest names.[18]

Larry Blumer, assigned to 393 Fighter Squadron, 367th Fighter Group, named his "Scrap Iron IV," and became one of the few fighter pilots to become an "ace-in-a-day," meaning he shot down five planes in a single day.[19]

At St. Lô, the German paratroopers' first sight was of these mammoth, garishly painted single-engine fighter-bombers, diving straight down at them at over six hundred miles an hour, their eight machine guns blazing, their rockets—ten harnessed under the wings of each plane—unleashing total destruction. To the Germans, *Jabos* was another word for terror.

Ninth Tactical Air's Major General Pete Quesada led the way for allied air-to-ground communication by being the first to dynamically link up armored and infantry combat forces to pilots of the Thunderbolt fighter-bombers—the *Jabos* the Germans dreaded and the "Jugs" the Yanks welcomed. Before Quesada's intervention, just a few weeks earlier, soldiers under attack had to channel requests for air support via the time-consuming and not-always-successful route of contacting rear echelon staff, who would then pass the message—often just a map reference—forward to air controllers.

That's nuts, Quesada said. He placed skilled Forward Air Controllers (often pilots who had completed their required missions) in radio-equipped tanks right up in the infantry and armored front lines, where communication could be immediate. The ground controller would adapt the coordinates on his map and radio the encircling fighter-bombers, briefing the pilots in the air on specific information about the target, such as a detailed description of landmarks, roads, villages, and woods. These air liaison specialists were thus able to "talk" the Thunderbolt fighter-bomber pilots onto their targets in an instant.

Three squadrons of P-47s were attached to each military unit. One hovered over the column constantly. A second was on five-minute alert at their nearby air base to replace the ones in close support when their ammunition or gas ran low. The third, at the base on half hour alert, was refueling and reloading. After carrying out the attack, with their rockets used up, the pilots either returned to base just a few minutes away to refuel or reload aircraft, or looked for another target of opportunity—a potential hazard to the ground forces they were protecting. The pilots could also warn the tankers of any dangers ahead.

The RAF, flying Typhoons, had been using a very effective tactic of "Cab Rank," in which a group of orbiting aircraft was directed onto a specific target. "We'd circle overhead—just like a bunch of taxicabs circling the Regent Palace Hotel in London," Flight Lieutenant Baggs explained, "and that's how it got its name. The RAF passed this technique of "Cab Rank" on to their American allies. The AAF called it "Rover Control." The FCU [Forward Control Unit] ground specialist was "Rover Joe."[20]

The pilots put in long days hovering like hawks over the forward combat troops, diving at every likely enemy target, landing and taking off when their ammunition was expended, giving incomparable support to the infantry and tank men on the ground.

Reprieved by P-47s from the enemy counterattack, Major Howie's battalion stormed the town. Meindl's paratroops opened fire from a cemetery and the two sides fought bitterly, with bullets ricocheting off the headstones. On one occasion, riflemen used a bulldozer to bury three German soldiers who refused to surrender their position.[21] Rhino tanks took up the fight, driving the paratroopers back. After a tough battle, the doughboys of the 29th took St. Lô.

Later that day, Technician Fourth Grade Andy Rooney walked down the hill into St. Lô's town square, now pulverized into a huge mound of rubble. "I saw . . . ten or fifteen soldiers lifting a flag-draped body laid out on a wooden door up the heap of stone and mortar that had been the side of the church . . . the highest point in town. It was their leader, Tom Howie."

General Gerhardt, not really such a "tough old buzzard" after all, had ordered the body of Major Thomas Howie, draped in the Stars and Stripes, to rest on the rubble of the cathedral in St. Lô. By honoring Howie he could remind his men of the perseverance and courage of all those who had given their lives at St. Lô.[22]

"Soldiers at war do not display much emotion," Rooney wrote. "Placing Howie's body there was an unusual thing for them to have done and they were emotional about it."[23]

Many of the men, and even some of the few French citizens left in the near-demolished town, placed flowers on the tomb, remembering that five thousand young Americans had been the casualties of that conquest.

But thanks to "The Major of St. Lô," as *Life* magazine extolled him, and his fellow "Clay Pigeons," General Bradley would have his high ground: where he would not be hung up by swamps or river crossings . . . where he could use maximum troops . . . where he could finally break out into the broad plains of Normandy and Brittany.

CHAPTER 10

Cobra

In the early hours of Monday, July 24, Lieutenant General Fritz Bayerlein, commander of *Panzer Lehr* Division, received puzzling reports. For three days, troops of his division and the Second SS had been deployed in depth opposing the American positions on the St. Lô–Périers road, anticipating their inevitable attack. Luckily, they had been favored by overcast skies — a reprieve from the relentless attacks by fighter-bombers.

But now, unaccountably, the American units were pulling back from their hard-won positions along the line of advance. This was not a known tactic by General Bradley. *What next?*

At midday, Bayerlein heard the steady drum of heavy aircraft. The already gloomy skies darkened as a wave of one hundred American planes flew overhead. Inexplicably, they turned harmlessly away. Then another wave . . . also turned away. Then a third. It was the aircraft in this last flight that finally released their bombs, not on his positions but — incredibly — on their own troops.

In the American sector, the 30th Infantry Division troops were equally puzzled. They had been told that the attack had been called off because of bad flying weather. So why were the Flying Fortresses coming in on their positions? Some cheered, seeing them as friendly allies. But many never had any chance to react at all to this dreadful miscue — except in horror. In seconds, thousands of tons of explosives were falling around them. When it was over, 27 young soldiers lay dead and 131 were badly wounded.

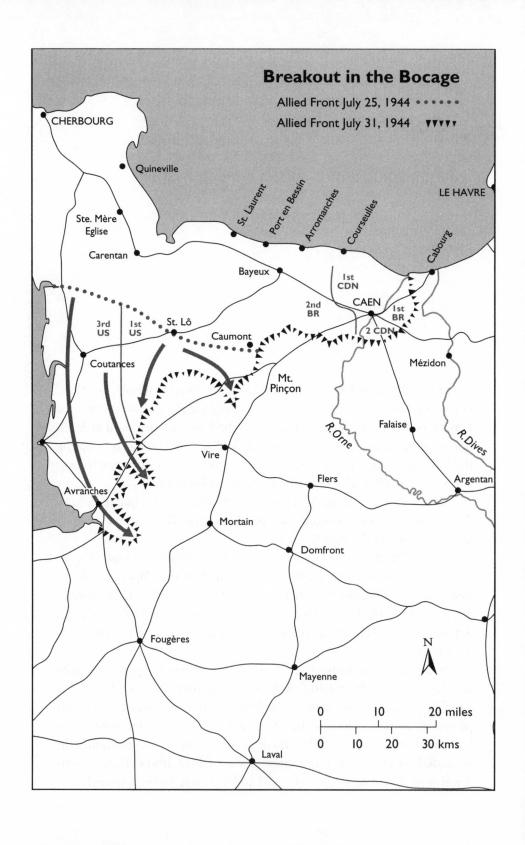

Breakout in the Bocage

Allied Front July 25, 1944 ••••••
Allied Front July 31, 1944 ▼▼▼▼▼

CHERBOURG

• Quineville

LE HAVRE

St. Laurent
Port en Bessin
Arromanches
Courseulles
Cabourg

Ste. Mère
Eglise

Carentan

Bayeux

1st
CDN

CAEN

1st
BR

3rd
US

1st
US

St. Lô

Caumont

2nd
BR

2 CDN

Mézidon

Coutances

Mt.
Pinçon

R.Orne

Falaise

R.Dives

Vire

Argentan

Avranches

Flers

Mortain

Domfront

Fougères

Mayenne

N

0		10		20 miles
0	10	20		30 kms

Laval

Operation *Cobra*, General Omar Bradley's long-planned attack to open the way for Patton's Third Army, had misfired badly. Bradley had been twice betrayed. Although his hastily radioed cancellation of the raid was received in England before the aircraft took off, somehow the message was never relayed to the first three hundred craft. The second deception was even more blatant. The commanders of the US Eighth Air Force had coolly disregarded Bradley's specific request that the bombers approach the bomb line—that dead-straight mile-long St. Lô–Périers road—on a parallel course to the line.

I'll keep my men safely back fifteen hundred yards north of the road, he had explained. You drop your bombs on the three-mile designated zone south of the road. That way, no one will get hurt.

Bradley had probably imagined he would have the same cooperation from Eighth Air Force as he had with General Quesada's Ninth Tactical Air Command. When he delivered this request in person at the Allied Expeditionary Air Force base in Britain, he believed he had been assured of their cooperation. Now, "shocked and angered at the breach of good faith," he learned that they had no intention of complying with his plan. To protect the aircraft from flak they directed the bombers to cross the road at right angles, flying directly over the American positions before releasing their bombs.[1]

The casualties on that first aborted attack put Bradley in a quandary. The enemy had now been alerted to the pending assault; they would be swarming the American lines within hours when they understood its failure. It was essential that he remount the aerial and ground attacks as swiftly as possible to counter such German moves.

The entire allied strategy now focused on *Cobra*'s success. The British and Canadians were to continue launching attacks to hold the bulk of the *Panzer* divisions east of the Orne while First Army took this great gamble to break out of the *bocage*. Bradley had no alternative; he had to risk a repeat of casualties caused by short bombing.

The next day, Tuesday, July 25, the sun finally did come out and 2,246 aircraft—1,500 heavy bombers, 396 mediums, and 350 fighter-bombers—revved their engines in English airstrips for the cross-Channel flight. At 1100 hours the first wave came with "a gigantic faraway surge of doomlike sound . . . in a constant procession," journalist Ernie Pyle wrote.

I thought it would never end . . .
From then on for an hour and a half that had in it the agonies

of centuries, the bombs came down. A wall of smoke and dust erected by them grew high in the sky. It filtered along the ground back through our own orchards. It sifted around us and into our noses. The bright day grew slowly dark from it.[2]

An observer, press correspondent A. J. Liebling, watched the barrage from artillery headquarters, an upstairs window of a Normandy farmhouse. "Some of the men, watching the bombardment from the sloping ground under my window, rolled on the grass with unsportsmanlike glee. Their emotion was crude but understandable. 'The more bombs we drop, the less fight there'll be left in them.' "[3]

An adjutant somberly handed General Bradley a message. "They've done it again."[4]

The bombardiers, barely able to see the Périers–St. Lô road due to dust from earlier waves of bombing, experienced difficulty in spotting targets and judging release points. "Short bombings" hit all three US assaulting divisions, the 30th, 9th, and 4th Infantry, killing 111 soldiers and wounding 490.

To the onlookers, the bombs seemed to hit indiscriminately: your turn, my turn . . . one to the Allies, one to the enemy. With one exception the entire command group of one regiment of the US 9th Infantry Division was killed. On the other side, the entire command group of one *Panzer* grenadier regiment was also killed.

In all, sixteen thousand tons of bombs were dropped. Almost a quarter of the bomb load hit Major General Bayerlein's *Panzer Lehr* Division, killing close to one thousand men. Von Kluge sent his staff officer with an urgent message for the *Panzer Lehr* commander: Hold the line at all costs.

Bayerlein's anguished reply:

Out in front every one is holding out. Every one. My grenadiers and my engineers and my tank crews—they're all holding their ground. Not a single man is leaving his post.

They are lying silent in their foxholes for they are dead. You may report to the Field Marshal that the *Panzer Lehr* Division is annihilated.[5]

He would say later, "My front lines looked like the face of the moon. At least 70 percent of my troops were out of action—dead, wounded, crazed or numbed."[6]

The French civilians, fortunately, had by then fled the area to escape the mutilation of their gentle Norman homeland. One tragic American casualty was Chief of Army Ground Forces, Lieutenant General Lesley McNair, who had done so much to organize and train the Army prior to its deployment overseas. Just a short while before, this man had given up his identity and his chances of taking a frontline command to help maintain the myth of *Armée Gruppe* McNair—the American army supposedly still in England, poised for a major invasion on the Pas de Calais.

General McNair was killed while observing the bombing raid. To perpetuate the charade of *Armée Gruppe* McNair, the ever-vigilant XX Committee arranged for a secret burial in the field, and informed his wife merely, and in every sense accurately, that he was a casualty of war.

In the wake of their terror and destruction, the survivors of the three spearhead infantry divisions—on paper designated to "surge ahead"—collected their wounded and dead and turned south with heavy hearts to launch the attack. A massive American artillery barrage of 522 guns, coupled with the inevitable cratering by bombs, had devastated much of the enemy territory. The riflemen picked their way through the grisly debris of rubble and corpses.

Despite the saturation bombing, scattered groups of enemy soldiers fought hard. Troops of the 9th Division's 60th Infantry Regiment, under attack but still shaken from the experiences earlier in the day, were astonished to see an old friend limping toward them. Matt Urban had come home.

Earlier that same Tuesday morning, July 25, Captain Matt Louis Urban (shortened from Urbanowicz) had been lying in an English hospital bed, recovering from multiple wounds incurred at Normandy. He woke up to the news that 9th Division was back in action at St. Lô.

Matt Urban had been troubleshooting most of his life. Born in 1919 of Polish-American parents in Buffalo, New York, a bright and personable lad, a star athlete in high school, Urban had a shining future. The single obstacle that faced the lad, and hundreds of thousands more young men in the United States, was the Great Depression. Thirty million men were out of work—but Urban wasn't prepared to be one of them.

He solved this, as he was to overcome so many obstacles in his life, by confrontation. First he enrolled at Cornell University; then he found and juggled the time for several part-time jobs to pay for his tuition and living expenses. A university degree and ROTC (Reserve Officers Training Corps) experience earned him a captaincy as company commander in the 2d Battalion, 60th Infantry Regiment of the 9th Infantry Division when the unit was shipped out to the United Kingdom.

Learning of the attack while still in his hospital bed, Urban confronted this new challenge.

My company's in trouble, he thought. They need battle-tested leaders. I've got to get back to them.

It wouldn't be the first time Urban had gone to the rescue of his lads. A week after D-Day his company had been pinned down by heavy enemy small-arms and tank fire and was in danger of being wiped out. Urban grabbed his bazooka and took off. Ducking and weaving under a continuous barrage of fire he ran through the hedgerow terrain to the German tank positions and destroyed both tanks. "Later that same day," his citation described,

> still in the attack, Captain Urban was wounded in the leg by direct fire from a 37mm tank-gun. He refused evacuation and continued to lead his company until they moved into defensive positions for the night. At 0500 hours the next day, Captain Urban, though badly wounded, directed his company in another attack. One hour later he was again wounded. Suffering from two wounds, one serious, he was evacuated to England.[7]

At 1130 hours that same morning, hitchhiking his way back, Urban reached Second Battalion Command Post. He found that his company had jumped off just half an hour earlier, at 1100 hours, in the first attack of *Cobra*. He made his way forward to retake command and found his men held up by strong enemy opposition. Two of their supporting tanks had been destroyed and another, intact but with no tank commander or gunner, wasn't moving.

> He located a lieutenant in charge of the support tanks and directed a plan of attack to eliminate the enemy strongpoint. The lieutenant and a sergeant were immediately killed by the heavy enemy fire when they tried to mount the tank.

With enemy bullets ricocheting from the tank, Captain Urban ordered the tank forward and, completely exposed to the enemy fire, manned the machine gun and placed devastating fire on the enemy. His action, in the face of enemy fire, galvanized the battalion into action, and they attacked and destroyed the enemy position.[8]*

Despite gallant efforts such as this, the infantry advance was disappointingly slow. The objective, Avranches, was thirty-five miles southwest of St. Lô, at the base of the Cotentin Peninsula on the Channel coast. In a cloud of depression following the bombers' "friendly fire" disaster, ground commanders could not help but reflect that the air strike had hurt the American troops almost as much as it had the enemy.

They faced a dilemma. The *Cobra* plan had been to catapult two armored divisions in the wake of the infantry exploitation. But if the enemy had survived the bombing, they would pounce on this vulnerable force. If, however, the air raid had succeeded in knocking out substantial numbers of Germans, the First Army should commit the armor and motorized infantry as quickly as possible before the enemy had time to recover.

VII Corps commander General "Lightning Joe" Collins decided to gamble. The time has come, he told his tank commanders, to be bold.

The next morning, Wednesday, the 26th, the 2d, and the 3d Armored Divisions joined the offensive, forming Combat Commands within each unit that combined the swiftness of infantry, the accuracy of artillery with the power of tanks. It was the start of a new phase in the Battle of Normandy: armor was on the roll.

The tanks poured through narrow lanes, many of them badly cratered by the bombing. Hedgerows bordering these roads harbored pockets of German *Panzer* troops in ideal ambush position.

Units were ordered to bypass enemy strongholds, and objectives were continually redefined by field orders to redirect the combat teams. Armored infantrymen would lay engineer tape to indicate new routes. The teams would then probe carefully in the new direction. Max Hastings wrote:

---

*Captain Urban's postwar achievements are described in the final chapter of this book: Postscripts.

The tank columns were slowed by the need for "Rhinos" to spend an average of two and a half minutes cutting through each hedgerow. But delays of this order were trifling by comparison with the hours of sluggish progress under fire that had marked each battle in the bocage since D-Day.

The entire offensive was rapidly gaining momentum.[9]

At each bend of the road the leading reconnaissance jeeps would halt the advance and call for artillery fire to be placed along the portion of the road to the south that was not visible, then would push quickly on. Craters in the road slowed the rate of advance. One tank-dozer attached to this unit filled these craters until it was knocked out by enemy fire.

The engineers played a major role in the *Cobra* breakout. At the Sienne River, engineers rushed forward to erect a bridge sabotaged by the enemy and still under fire. The infantry laid on an attack at 1700 hours but met heavy enemy fire. Their progress was too slow for their commander. "The Sienne was 20 feet wide and 4 and a half deep," the report stated. Lieutenant Colonel Doan, who impatiently led the men across himself, attested to the fact, "since the river soaked his notebook in his shirt pocket.

"The attack was ordered to proceed through the night until a bridgehead had been established. Construction of the bridge began as early as 0100, even though the height on the south side was not finally secured until 0230. By 1030 it was in operation."[10]

Aware of the old adage that armored units were able to take ground but unable to hold it for any extended period of time, the combat team had been issued a very precise plan of action in the event of enemy attack. Tanks and vehicles would swiftly pull off the road and "leaguer" or coil along the hedgerows bordering the field. "Germans dug in along the hedgerows were fired on and rooted from their foxholes" by armored infantrymen who had been riding on the backs of tanks for just that purpose.

Foot troops given the task of protecting the armored flanks could not always keep up with the Lochinvarian speed of the tanks. Then it became a game of leapfrog. One unit of infantry would have marched all night, catching up with the armor before daylight. The tanks would then roll forward to their next objective, leaving a skeleton force of infantry behind to hold the position. The remainder trudged on to the next objective, repeating the sequence.

The rules of operation had been carefully thought out; and they were tough. Major William Castille described traffic control:

> Only one-way traffic would prevail. No vehicles would be allowed to return for added supplies of ammunition or gasoline, and no ambulances would be allowed to return along the route. Casualties would have to be cared for as best they could along the route of advance.

The *Cobra* planners had the foresight to order all enemy wires "including electric, telephone and all cables, cut on the advance of all units. High tension wires were severed by blasting the poles down with AT guns. As a result, nearly all German communications were shattered."[11]

Because of disrupted lines of communications, the enemy was unable to make any organized counterattack against the Americans.

It was a slick, smooth operation, and it was working. The Germans were defending staunchly—but they were not counterattacking. This was the clue, the reassurance Bradley was seeking that the air strike had emasculated the enemy. General Maurice Rose, commanding 2nd Armored, rose to the challenge of risk-taking in a way that no other tank commander in history had done: he ordered the forward combat command to strike out in a night attack.

Tanks are notoriously skittish at being caught in darkness. A single enemy with a single *Panzerfaust* could steal up in the gloom and annihilate them with one shot.

Rose's gamble worked. By Thursday, July 27, VII Corps had opened the way through to Avranches. By Friday, two new armored divisions (the 4th and 6th from US Major General Troy Middleton's VIII Corps) added double power to *Cobra's* breakout assault.

A key element that ensured the speed and success of the armor was the close support of artillery and tactical air.

"Divarty," or Divisional artillery headquarters, was as correspondent A. J. Liebling described it in *The New Yorker,*

> a small, itinerant brain trust that moves quietly with the front-line troops and calls down upon distant Germans the thunder of the division's battalions of artillery.
>
> Divarty controls the small spotter planes, usually Piper

Cubs, which serve as the Division's eyes. The pilots and observers in these craft, known to "the dough" [doughboys] as
Maytag Messerschmitts, are not Air Force men but artillery
officers. They report not only on targets and the effect of the division's artillery fire but on all enemy troop and vehicle movements.[12]

A captured German report confirms the effectiveness of these artillery
air observers: "They fly over the battle zone in regular reliefs and their reconnaissance is followed by strong, short bursts of fire with considerable
ammunition expenditure. In sectors where there are only a few AA guns
these planes sweep down to a low level in order to direct the fire to picked
targets."

The report goes on to note that "artillery is distinguished by accuracy
of fire and maneuverability. Employment of fire and phosphorus bombs as
well as high explosive ammunition . . . has been frequently observed
[causing a shell shock condition of] stomach trouble and headaches."[13]

As well as having spies in the skies, the artillery posted forward observing officers (FOOs) to remain with frontline infantry and tank units and
communicate to Divarty potential danger points as they occurred. One
pilot who was assigned this duty as a break from flying continuous air operations was to comment, "I got the hell scared out of me riding around in
a tank, much more than I ever did in an aircraft!"[14]

All of this information flowed through a complex array of radio communication and telephone lines (laid and endlessly relayed by signalers)
with one objective: to clear enemy opposition.

Because of Ninth Tac General Quesada's commitment to give strong
air support to ground troops, his system of Armored Column Control ef-
fected many dramatic rescue missions.

Combat Command "A" of 3d Armored Division described one such
effort:

The enemy at this crossroads was dug in with tanks, infantry, artillery and mortars. Lt. Col. Doan was able to contact the P-47
flight, which had been giving support throughout the day, and all
available planes were brought up to blast the enemy, which were
separated by no more than 100 yards from the infantry. About 16

P-47s came over and did an excellent job of bombing and strafing.

A tense situation developed when one plane called in to state
with apologies that he had only butterfly anti-personnel bombs to
drop.

Put 'em down real easy, the commander implored. With textbook precision the Thunderbolt dropped its bombs accurately on the enemy as
Doan's men dived safely for cover.

Another pilot is reported to have facetiously suggested to an officer
that he had better draw in his antenna, so close was his plane diving to
bomb a German tank only fifty yards to his left.[15]

On Sunday, July 30, just seven days after the first bomb spelled disaster to the American forces, a triumphant armored corps rolled into the port
of Avranches at the base of the Cotentin Peninsula. The town, situated on
a 340-foot bluff overlooking the celebrated sanctuary of Mont-Saint-
Michel, had been a military stronghold from the time of the Romans. Its
strategic importance now to the Americans was as the gateway to the ports
of Brittany and the plains of southern Normandy.

One final obstacle stood in their way before they could escape the
confinement of the Cotentin that had contained First Army since D-Day:
a single road and a single, narrow bridge (Pontaubault Bridge) linked
Avranches to the coast.

Before they could drive out in three directions across France, seven
divisions of troops and vehicles had to get through that bottleneck.

Lapping on the right flank of this narrow passage were the Atlantic
swells. On the left flank the Germans were building a strong defense. General von Kluge signaled the German 77th Infantry Division commander:
"Avranches is to be taken and held at all costs. It is the keystone of our defense. On it hinges the decision in the West."[16] For three days the determined infantry and an awakened *Luftwaffe* tried to hit and destroy the
bridge and the American troops crossing it. Initially successful, their for-
tunes reversed when the cloud base lifted and the Thunderbolts swung
into action. The bridge remained intact.

At midnight, July 31, General Patton's Third US Army took command
of the force, releasing Patton's pent-up energies. On his feet, yelling and
brandishing his revolver, Patton urged his troops headlong. One hundred

thousand men and fifteen thousand vehicles sped down the narrow passage in seventy-two hours.

Committing an entire army to a single road with a single bridge was one of the most daring offensive strikes of the war. But nothing could stop George Patton: not the enemy, not his own startled allies, not even his own capricious nature.

PART IV

AUGUST 1–16: SETTING THE TRAP

British Breakout: Operation *Bluecoat*

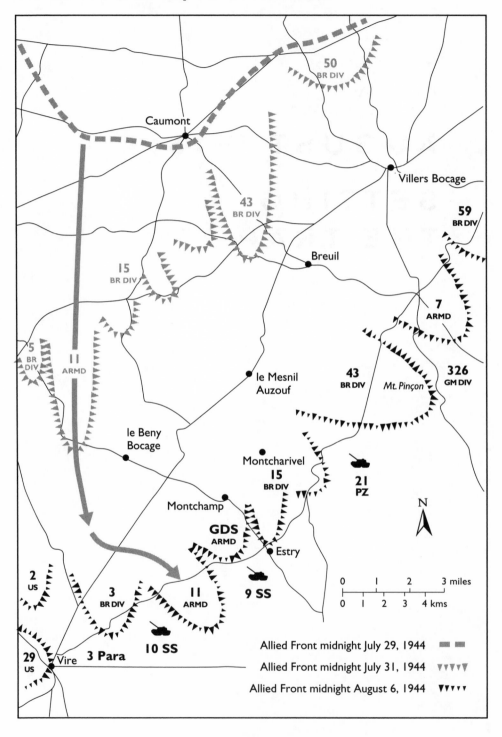

50
BR DIV

Caumont

Villers Bocage

59
BR DIV

43
BR DIV

Breuil

15
BR DIV

7
ARMD

5
BR DIV

11
ARMD

le Mesnil
Auzouf

43
BR DIV

Mt. Pinçon

326
GM DIV

le Beny
Bocage

Montcharivel

21
PZ

15
BR DIV

Montchamp

GDS
ARMD

Estry

N

2
US

3
BR DIV

11
ARMD

9 SS

0	1	2	3 miles

| 0 | 1 | 2 | 3 | 4 kms |

10 SS

29
US

Vire

3 Para

Allied Front midnight July 29, 1944

Allied Front midnight July 31, 1944

Allied Front midnight August 6, 1944

CHAPTER 11

The British Breakthrough

D-plus-56

On July 30, General Montgomery abruptly shifted almost all Second British Army troops from the Caen front west to Caumont in support of the Americans in their breakout. He was then poised to launch Operation *Bluecoat*, the most powerful British push to date. Three entire corps—some two hundred thousand men of armored and infantry divisions—were committed.

Lieutenant General Richard O'Connor's spearhead British VIII Corps drew the start position on the far right flank next to US First Army. "O'Connor is the only general who makes me nervous," Rommel is reputed to have said following O'Connor's audacious victory in the North African desert. When he was subsequently taken prisoner by a German patrol, Churchill (it is rumored) offered to swap any six Italian generals to get him back. He escaped—on the second attempt—in time to command the "White Knight" divisions of VIII Corps in Normandy.

As a British historian describes them, the infantry battalions of O'Connor's White Knights were made up predominantly of peacetime weekend soldiers. These territorial troops were "closely knit local groups: men of Scotland in regiments like the Ayrshire Yeomanry, Cameronians, and Glasgow Highlanders; men from the Welsh border counties of Shropshire, Herefordshire, and Monmouthshire; men of Wessex in the Hampshires, Wiltshires, Somerset Light Infantry, and other famous west-country regiments; there were Cockneys with the Rifle Brigade and men of the Midlands in the Northamptonshire Yeomanry.

"The years of training had turned them into professionals; but at heart they were still civilians."[1] O'Connor's lead division was the 11th Armored, commanded by Major General G. P. B. "Pip" Roberts.

In Pip Roberts, O'Connor had a man of superlatives. He was, at thirty-seven, the youngest divisional commander in the British army. He was one of the most experienced, having fought his way through the war from the rank of captain in the western desert. He was the smallest and shortest by stature, the most boyish and benign by appearance, but the toughest by performance. He led a winning team, and they knew it. "In the unblooded 11th Armored, I found everyone raring to go," Roberts observed accurately.[2]

"Step on the gas for Vire," Monty had said. Pip's similarly diminutive and tough-minded corps commander, Richard O'Connor, ordered him into what proved to be a seventy-two-hour marathon to achieve this.

Vire, the capital of *bocage* country, was a key hub for seven major roads. It also marked the junction, then unmanned, of two German armies: General Heinrich Eberbach's *Panzer* Group West and SS General Paul Hausser's Seventh Army. Vire was the home of the *andouille*, a sausage of pigs' intestines. It was *not*, as of July 30, a home to any Germans. It lay unoccupied, waiting.

Roberts stepped on the gas. His marathon began in an all-night march just to reach his start line. He wheeled his three thousand armored and transport vehicles and fifteen thousand men of his division in an incredible cross-country sweep over inferior roads, cutting across the supply lines of some ninety thousand men from two other corps. "It was a scramble, but it just worked," Roberts said in typical understatement.[3]

For Trooper John Thorpe, 2d Fife and Forfar Yeomanry, driving his tank across steep hills and valleys in pitch darkness, all the while kicking up dense dust, became a night of total misery, as his diary reveals:

July 29: It was hell trying to see and follow the tank in front of us in this sand storm in the dark. The dirt was beginning to accumulate in the corners of my eyes, but I dared not touch my eyes or face or it would have made them water and would have blinded me. A wet dew mist rose during the night and my face became encased with a thick mask.

He kept himself awake by smoking "between sixty and eighty cigarettes a day," and by lustily singing his favorite song, "As Time Goes By" . . . A *kiss is just a kiss, a sigh is just a sigh.*

The temptation to drop off to sleep through the noise, fatigue and tiredness was terrific and I could only keep awake by twisting up my ear till it hurt or singing at the top of my voice which could not be heard by anyone over the overall noise. To go off to sleep would have been to lose consciousness and perhaps our lives.[4]

The division reached the start line south of Caumont just in time to launch immediately into a heavy day's fighting in the worst of *bocage* country. Roberts had reorganized his two brigades into two forces, so each had infantry and armor as mutual support. It proved a magical formula. Riflemen went into battle clinging to tanks, "quick lift" it was called, and the attack surged forward.

Trooper Thorpe's diary continues:

July 30: We had not gone a couple of hundred yards when a number of our tanks went up on mines each side of us. Met heavy shellfire—theirs or ours? Poor bloody infantry going over like ninepins. They were advancing and there was neither cover nor the chance to dig in through heavy mortar fire.

The plan is for the infantry to lead us in this now heavy wooded area and our job is to clear away machine-gun nests.[5]

After a grueling twenty-four hours, Roberts knew they were all "yearning to call it a day as the sun went down." Instead, he received orders from an insistent corps commander—Dick O'Connor—to seize the next road.

Doggedly he ordered an exhausted and mildly protesting 4th Battalion KSLI (King's Shropshire Light Infantry) to clear a steep, heavily mined, wooded trail and then plunge single file into its depth. The Shropshires gamely set off into the moonless night on a three-mile trek. The only way they could keep their bearings was to grope for and hang on to the shoulder of the rifleman in front. Finally, they reached their crossroads objective, luckily with no enemy opposition.

Within seconds—I had just time to take my boots off and blow on my red hot feet—came another order group," KSLI Captain Clayton groaned. "This time the news was electrifying—the finding of an unguarded bridge.[6]

No one realized that five soldiers in two scout cars from the Household Cavalry (better recognized in its peacetime task of guarding Buckingham Palace) had already leapfrogged ahead, blindly unaware that they were traversing the actual boundary between two German armies. ("Though neither army had thought to guard it," Roberts added with a grin.)[7]

Soon the small band came upon an intact bridge—*the* unguarded bridge—which was the key to the capture of the ridge overlooking Vire. Lieutenant "Dickie" Powle sent three men across while he covered them in the armored car.

One of the trio describes the adventure: "After quickly dismounting, we slipped up behind a German sentry and quietly finished him off. We had to dispose of any such visitors, otherwise we were sunk as there was no hope of holding any numbers off with only two cars."[8]

The men hid, camouflaging the cars. They were at the limit of effective radio range and had lost contact. The radio operator eventually got a faint response and sent the following message:

At 10.30 hours the bridge at 63744321 is clear of enemy and still intact. I say again, at 10.30 hours the bridge at 63744321 is clear of enemy and still intact.

The regimental headquarters of the Household Cavalry picked up this faint message through the static. The map reference was plotted. It was the bridge over the Souleuvre River, five miles into enemy territory.

Wait. There must be some mistake. A repeat was requested.[9]

It was no mistake. When the message was passed to 11th Armored headquarters there was great excitement. "Cavalry Bridge" (as it was immediately dubbed by the exuberant liberators of the Household Cavalry) opened the way to Vire—and beyond.

Pip Roberts saw his chance and seized it. In seventy-two hours the 11th Armored Division had spearheaded a spectacular charge, seizing

Cavalry Bridge five miles behind the German lines. Vire was just eight miles away.[10]

On August 1, Roberts's 11th Armored was on the verge of the breakthrough Montgomery had demanded on July 30. "Throw all caution overboard; step on the gas for Vire."

Unaccountably, Monty then queered the act for Roberts. On August 1, two days after he had demanded that Pip seize Vire, he changed the boundaries to allot the task of Vire's liberation to the Americans and dashed Roberts's moment of triumph. Montgomery had established these lines to avoid any allied army colliding with its neighbor. They became, too often during the Normandy campaign, a source of rivalry and dissension among army commanders. The Germans recognized this and managed to turn inter-allied squabbling over boundary lines to their advantage on several occasions.

General Leonard Gerow, commander of US V Corps, was miffed to learn of the British success in driving a wedge deep into enemy-held territory at Vire, threatening to split Seventh Army and *Panzer* Group West.

"I don't like the British walking out front taking objectives," he complained crossly.

"What are you British doing in our sector?" echoed an indignant infantry sergeant from US 5th Division.[11]

Most troops didn't care about boundaries. Men of the British Rifle Brigade snatching a few minutes' rest watched with sympathy as the GIs plodded by down the narrow road, "quite expressionless, sallow with fatigue, one and all masticating gum and silent in their rubber studded top boots."[12] Learning that the Americans had had nothing to eat for forty-eight hours, the riflemen tossed them packets of cookies. The Yanks tossed back chewing gum.

At the rear, US and British echelon officers tossed veiled insults about whose bridge it was. Finally, after an interminable delay, the issue was resolved—amicably, in the Americans' favor. It is a reasonable speculation that Gerow's complaints, probably lodged at higher levels, influenced Montgomery's decision making. This was to have disastrous results.

The German High Command could not so easily be calmed. "The British are trying to cut us off [from the] north," signaled General Meindl frantically. "Once again we are threatened with encirclement."[13]

"The capture of Vire would have made sense, and we could have done that," a disappointed Roberts acknowledged.[14] Had this objective not been abruptly snatched from their grasp, British forces could have taken an undefended Vire "with nothing more than a skirmish."[15]

Reacting swiftly to the imminent danger, three *Panzer* divisions—9th SS, 10th SS, and 21st *Panzer* and elements of 12th SS and 116th—were ordered to plug the hole at Vire and demolish the British attackers. At dawn on August 2, over one hundred Tiger and Panther tanks were poised to attack.

By the time five divisions of American troops reached Vire on August 6 it had been heavily fortified. Over three thousand GIs of XIX Corps would be casualties in the renewed ten-day battle for an objective that could have been snapped up in a skirmish on August 1.

Pip Roberts's outstanding offensive on the right flank of the *Bluecoat* attack—a crackling twelve-mile advance through enemy lines in less than thirty-six hours—only highlighted the dismal efforts of the British XXX Corps on its left.

"Get going or get out!" was General Dempsey's final cry of frustration. Their lack of progress was so tortuous that Montgomery ruthlessly fired the XXX Corps' commander, Lieutenant General G. C. Bucknall, on the third day of the assault.

"I have ordered that General Bucknall be removed from command," Montgomery wrote peevishly. "He is nearly always 24 hours too late, and the enemy profits thereby."

Next to be sacked was the commander of the 7th Armored Division— the famed Desert Rats. "Major General Erskine is stale: he needs a rest, and a change of employment," Monty stated flatly.[16]

"I request that Major General Horrocks be appointed to command 30 Corps."[17]

In those days of frustration and lack of achievement in the *bocage* fighting of late July, Montgomery caused over one hundred officers and men in the XXX Corps to be transferred to other posts. They were all vets of fighting in North Africa, Italy, and Normandy.

In truth, *bocage* fighting *had* taken some of the starch out of the seasoned "desert warriors." Dilution of numbers, staleness, and war weariness had set in.[18] As Monty put it, "The old desert divisions are apt to look over their shoulder and wonder if it is all okay behind, or if the flanks are secure . . . 7 Armd Div is like that. They want a new general, who will drive them headlong into, and through, gaps torn in the enemy defence."[19]

They had proved themselves in vast stretches of open country in North Africa, in a desert war that stretched on for three years. Then, just a year later, on D-plus-1, they had been flung almost directly into this dangerous and strange new form of close warfare in the *bocage*.

German snipers hiding in the thick hedgerows easily picked off tank commanders accustomed in the desert to going into battle standing in their turrets.[20] But the tank commanders had no option. They had to guide the drivers whose vision was so obscured by tree branches they could not see the rest of the regiment. Their Churchill tanks, no match for the German Panthers and Tigers, became tombs for young British tank crews. They were "Tiger shy," with good reason. There were 645 enemy tanks—Tigers, Panthers, and Mark IVs—facing the British front; a mere 190 faced the US First Army. Monty's strategy was working, but at what a price.[21]

The infantry were exhausted, punch-drunk from fighting in continuous action for seven weeks. Conditions for the tankers were unspeakable. Temperatures inside the tanks soared as they crashed through *bocage* hedges and over banks. The stench of five unwashed men caged together in a hot metal box for hours combined unpalatably with the sour smell of rotting green apples that had fallen into the high turrets of the Shermans.

"We were all black and blue from the jumps we had been over," one British officer recalls of the rough terrain, "and quite a number of men, including my signal officer in my own tank, had been knocked senseless."[22]

Most of all, the men had been fighting too long. They were stale. They reckoned they'd made it through four years of fighting and now that the war was being won, they wanted to get safely home. "Why would I stick my blinking neck out and get killed when the 'effing war may be over before Christmas?" the Tommies grumbled.[23]

"Jorrocks"—Lieutenant General Brian Horrocks, the incoming commander of XXX Corps—was an old friend from the desert war. He recognized the symptoms of mass battle fatigue. The "gloss was gone," as he put it. Within days, troops became accustomed to the comfortable sight of the tall, white-haired leader casually dressed in corduroys mingling in their midst.

Horrocks first set himself the task of making a "whistle-stop tour" to his units. He explained to the frustrated and battle-weary officers and men how well the battle was really going and how close they were to breaking out of the bridgehead and swanning off across France.[24]

"He was very good, and made us feel quite cheerful," a tank wireless operator from the 4th/7th Royal Dragoon Guards said. "[Before,] we all thought that we should have to fight for every field all the way to Germany."[25]

A trooper from the 8th Hussars termed him "a very warm man, exuding confidence and determination but one who cared for the welfare and safety of his troops."[26]

The prime objective of the XXX Corps was the capture of Mount Pinçon, the steep-sided, twelve-hundred-foot hill that dominated the *Suisse Normande.* Montgomery had had his eye on this feature from the beginning. You could see for miles in every direction from its summit—and call down artillery fire at a considerable distance on all sides.

There were only two possible approach roads, each cutting through typical *bocage* fields with thick hedgerows on each side. The Germans were heavily dug in at two stone villages on the sides of the mountain, and had a full view of any attacker. It was historian John Keegan who observed "the dangers inherent of cornering first-class German formations, however worn and whatever the odds stacked against them"; this was never more true than during the battle to seize Mount Pinçon.[27]

On a swelteringly hot day on August 6, two infantry battalions from 43d Wessex Division and their supporting armor, the 13th/18th Hussars, fought their way to a small river at the base of the mountain. Casualties had cut their ranks in half. Somerset Light Infantry's 4th Battalion came under what platoon commander Lieutenant Sydney Jary described as "concentrated Spandau fire from the front and both flanks. There must have been 12 machine guns fired at one time. This devastating display of firepower stopped the battalion dead in its tracks. There was no way forward or round it and no way to retire."[28]

Their sister battalion on their right, the 5th Wiltshires, was equally pinned down by heavy fire. The commanding officer, Lieutenant Colonel "Pop" Pearson, knew that his men needed some special boost to attack the heavily defended position. Tucking a red rose in his steel helmet and swinging his walking stick, he strode calmly toward the bridge. A sniper in a tree shot him dead. But his display of courage inspired the surviving men of the battalion to swarm across the river and overrun the enemy position.

At 1800 hours an armored patrol from the 13th/18th Hussars, led by its commander Captain Denny, discovered a narrow track winding up the hill, apparently undefended. The passage was so tight that one tank following it toppled over into a disused gravel pit; another had its track blown off. The remaining seven tanks pushed steadily upward, clinging to the rim of the sheer cliff until they reached the summit. Fog settled on the heights, and the small band of tankers heard German voices all around them. The troop leader radioed to HQ that they felt "rather lonely."[29]

Later, infantry below were startled to glimpse their comrades' tanks silhouetted against the sky. How in hell did they get up there? Fourth Wiltshire soon found out when they were ordered to follow suit. Though exhausted from forty-eight hours of fighting, the battalion gamely set off in single file up the steep thorny slopes, and struggled to the top. By nightfall, Mount Pinçon had been secured, despite many casualties to the 43d Wessex. But their emblem, the golden Wyvern—a double-winged dragon with clawed feet and arrow-tipped tail—flew above its summit, restoring to the division some of its lost gloss.

If there were moments when the troops fighting in *Bluecoat* lost hope, or were discounted by their peers, there were many more times when they shone with courage.

"Basher" Bates, a Cockney corporal with the Royal Norfolk Regiment, was one such man. Basher—aka Sidney—was a product of London's East End. When Basher was asked his civilian occupation at the recruiting office, he just scratched his head, perplexed. His father was a street peddler—a "rag and bone" man, as the Cockneys termed it.

On August 6, Basher and his depleted section of five or six men of his platoon ran into a heavily defended German position. Heavy and accurate artillery and mortar fire poured down on the British. Some fifty to sixty Germans, supported by machine guns and mortars, assembled in the steep, dead ground behind a hedge opposite Bates's section. The young Cockney realized that he and his handful of men were all that stood between the Germans and his battalion headquarters. He reckoned he could better counter the enemy thrust if he could just get through that hedge and confront them.

At that moment, little "Tojo" Tomlin, an eighteen-year-old section Bren gunner from Bethnal Green, was wounded. Sidney Bates picked him up and was holding him as they made for cover. Tomlin was killed outright by a bullet through the head. He died in Bates's arms. Seeing that the situation was becoming desperate, Bates grabbed Tojo's Bren gun and charged the enemy, moving forward through a hail of bullets and splinters and firing the gun from the hip.

Basher Bates's one-man charge "repulsed a force of fanatical *Panzer* grenadiers, thereby preventing the overrunning and destruction of his unit. Corporal Bates advanced, alone, to meet and rout his enemy." Bates was badly wounded three times, in the throat and abdomen, and died two days later.

"Basher really did a job on them," his buddy Private Bill Holden remembered. "There were dead Germans all over [the] field. And I know there were more dead Germans on the other side of the hedge because I picked them up myself the next day."[30]

The Cockney corporal from London's East End was given the highest award for valor of the British Empire: a posthumous Victoria Cross.*

Montgomery's overriding mandate to all his divisions in Operation *Bluecoat* had been "push on, regardless of casualties." The order had certainly been heeded. In the last two weeks of July, the 7th Armored Division had 400 casualties and in the first week of August, 523 more.

On August 8, Trooper John Thorpe, 2d Fife and Forfar Yeomanry, wiggled his toes with relish. For the first time in twelve days, he had a chance to take off his socks and boots. "This was the battle that really won the war," he exalted to his buddies.[31]

However, a tank officer from the 7th Armored noted bitterly: "I read how we 'lost our dash' or how the infantry went to ground rather than pressing on.

"Where, I wonder, were the people who wrote this? Do they realize . . . just what the British Army went through?"[32]

---

*The Royal Norfolk Regiment won five VCs in World War II, more than any other British or Commonwealth regiment. Captain David Jamieson, who led his company in repulsing seven enemy counterattacks on the Orne, won the fourth the next day.

CHAPTER 12

Hitler's Gamble

At *Wolfschanze*, the Führer's headquarters in East Prussia, the atmosphere of the map room was electric. It was August 2, 1944, the day after Patton's breakout through the Avranches corridor. The supreme commander of the *Wehrmacht*, Adolf Hitler, was intently studying that narrow strip of land leading to the Pontaubault Bridge. He could see the danger: once across the bridge the Allies would spill out into the wide-open countryside of Normandy and Brittany.

But Hitler had a bold scheme. He ordered Field Marshal Günther Hans von Kluge, commander in chief of his armies in Normandy, to mount a counterattack against the Americans. You will immediately shift westward eight of my nine *Panzer* divisions, attack through the town of Mortain, and advance west twenty miles to Avranches, cutting off all Patton's forces from his supply line.

He assured his C-in-C that he would find Mortain only lightly defended. "The US Third Army focus is on the Pontaubault Bridge. When you retake Avranches, you will be in a position to annihilate the Third Army and drive Bradley's First Army back into the *bocage*—or into the sea.

"Avranches is the key!"

The Führer then dictated the entire battle plan. He called it Operation *Lüttich*, named for a great German victory thirty years earlier when the Kaiser broke through to the Belgian city of Liege/Lüttich. He had personally worked out every detail: the units, their positions and specific objectives—and the date of the attack: August 8, six days hence. He pointedly did not ask for advice or comment from his military commanders.

Von Kluge was astounded. If he used all the available *Panzer* strength in this one attack, the entire Normandy front could collapse. Two of his nine armored divisions were already heavily engaged in holding back the British offensive at Caumont. The 1st and 12th SS were fighting the Canadians at Caen. The 9th *Panzer* Division had not yet arrived from the south of France. The American bombing at St. Lô had shattered another division, the *Panzer Lehr*. Only remnants were left.

By the simplest of mathematics, that left only four *Panzer* divisions for Hitler's ambitious counterattack, not the eight he demanded. The alternative was to denude the Caumont front, a surefire invitation for the British to complete their breakout.

Von Kluge's own latest weekly report, sent to the High Command (OKW) on July 30, had warned Hitler that "our losses in men and matériel were so high because of the enemy's superiority in artillery and the air that it was not possible to build up a new defense front quickly."[1]

He was in fact desperate enough that he approached General Warlimont at Hitler's headquarters with an incredible demand: reinforcements delivered "by taxi, à la Paris to the Marne in 1914."[2]

"Madness!" von Kluge thought. "Does he not read his own intelligence reports? If he insists on this business, he will force the entire Seventh and Fifth Armies into a trap—100,000 men. We must withdraw our armies to the Seine before they are completely encircled and destroyed."

Von Kluge could not refuse the command. He decided the only hope was to stage the attack as quickly as possible before the Allies, who now encircled them on three sides, closed in. He dared not wait another six days until the 9th *Panzer* Division, ordered by Hitler, arrived at the front from the south of France. He would simply have to limit the counterattack force to the four *Panzer* divisions available.

Of these four, casualties had reduced two divisions, the 2d SS *Panzer Das Reich* and von Luttwitz's 2d *Panzer*, to 60 percent combat efficiency. The 3rd Division, the elite 1st SS *Leibstandarte-Adolf Hitler* Division (*LAH*), would have to be disengaged from combat near Caen and replaced by a fresh German unit (the 89th Infantry Division).

The fourth division to come under command of the XLVII *Panzer* Corps for Operation *Lüttich* was the 116th *Panzer* Division. This powerful and well-trained force was known as the *Windhund*, or Greyhound, Division because of its speed and success in Russia. Its status was almost equivalent to that of the elite SS *Panzer* Divisions of the I and II SS *Panzer* Corps, and with comparable strength. Its commander, *Generalleutnant* Gerhard Graf von Schwerin, was a skilled veteran of the eastern front and a proud and aloof *Wehrmacht* career officer, who had little use for Hitler or his SS divisions.

Count von Schwerin was, in fact, also suspected of being a major player in the assassination conspiracy. So far, he had managed to elude the Gestapo's list of traitors. His chief staff officer, Lieutenant Colonel Heinz Günther Guderian, was the son of a famous general who had "an uneasy relationship with Hitler."

The *Windhund* Division had been locked in "stubborn fighting," against General Rose's 2d Armored and 29th Infantry Division at a key point southeast of St. Lô. For three days the division had been laboring with little success in "defensive battles and reconnaissance skirmishes, under heavy air activity."[3]

It was while von Schwerin's 116th was in the middle of this brutal battle that the division abruptly came under command of XLVII Corps for Hitler's counterattack at Mortain. The commander, SS General Hans Freiherr von Funck, was a fifty-three-year-old who had risen from serving as military attaché to Spain during the Civil War to succeed Rommel as commander of 7th *Panzer* Division. To the *Wehrmacht*, this SS officer was "brutal, captious and unbeloved."[4]

Von Funck ordered von Schwerin to "disengage." Disengaging was easily ordered, but not so easily achieved midbattle, as Count von Schwerin undoubtedly told his superior officer, whom he considered "narrow-minded and obstinate."

A bitter clash between the traditional *Wehrmacht* general officer and the heavy-handed SS Nazi was inevitable. The personal animosity between these two men exploded. Von Funck accused the division of "passive resistance, cowardice and inability."[5]

Von Funck finally ordered the newly arrived 84th Infantry Division to relieve the 116th *Panzer*, and hence free them up to launch *Lüttich*. This didn't sit well with the aristocratic 116th commander, who held a poor opinion of the combat abilities of this inexperienced infantry unit. "This new division was not up to the difficult conditions of war against heavily superior armored forces; its armament and equipment were completely inadequate," von Schwerin argued. "After the first appearance of these troops, all [my] commanders of 116th *Panzer* Division were fully aware of the danger of such relief."[6]

Von Funck deceitfully transferred an entire *Panzer* battalion from the 116th as well as half of its antitank battalion to fill the shortfall of the 2d *Panzer* Division. He had already seconded its Reconnaissance Battalion.

Von Schwerin fumed. Through von Funck's meddling, his 116th *Panzer* Division had lost one-third of its armored strength—a bad beginning to a major counterattack. Inwardly he resolved to oppose the counterattack by the "passive resistance" for which he was being accused. As long as he was commander, his division would not be sacrificed in Operation *Lüttich*.[7]

Von Kluge's strategy for the Mortain counterattack depended on surprise. To achieve this there would be no preliminary artillery barrage. He had also been assured that the predicted weather conditions would ensure dense ground fog in the morning of August 7—an essential element to avoid air interference.

Two *Panzer* divisions would advance in stealth at midnight: von Luttwitz's 2d SS *Panzer*, reinforced by a combat group of the 17th SS *Panzer* Grenadier Division, would recapture the small town of Mortain, now enjoying its third day of liberation by the Americans. At the same time, the 2d *Panzer* Division would attack the village of St. Barthélémy, six miles to the north. The division was to be reinforced by von Schwerin's 116th and by a tank battalion of the 1st SS *Leibstandart–Adolf Hitler*.

An essential element was the *Luftwaffe* guarantee of substantial air support—three hundred fighters to form a protective ring around the operation.

Sunday, August 6: Von Kluge was in a panic. H-Hour was set for 2200 hours. As it neared, more crises arose. Hitler still hadn't given his final approval for Operation *Lüttich*, and persisted in holding out for a postponement until the remaining *Panzer* divisions arrived. He was even suggesting a change of command, ordering General Eberbach to replace von Funck. Von Kluge declined; it was too late to change commanders. Finally, at 1905 hours, the telephone rang: the Führer's permission to attack was granted.

A fresh problem presented itself. Initially, the 1st SS *Panzer* wired him that they had been delayed leaving the Caen front. Their second call in-

formed the already agitated commander that the 1st SS Tank Battalion—
an essential element in reinforcing the 2d *Panzer*'s spearhead attack on
Mortain—could not arrive until morning. Ironically, a British Typhoon
shot down by German antiaircraft fire had crash-landed into the leading
Panther on the road, blocking it. The entire column would have to reverse
out and find a new way around the narrow defile.

The final blow was a call from von Funck. He insisted on a two-hour
postponement of the attack because of the delays in getting his formations
prepared. H-Hour was changed to midnight—2400 hours.

Hans von Kluge feared that the bottom was falling out of his operation. His battle plan was compromised; his general officers were feuding.
There was pressure on him to fire one of his most capable commanders,
von Schwerin.

The bottom was about to fall out of his life, too. He could not help
wondering if in trying to placate Hitler by launching this flawed operation
he had raised a question mark of his own loyalty. *Der kluge Hans*—"Clever
Hans"—so careful to keep his political balance, may have gotten a bit too
clever for his own safety. He suspected, as well, that the Americans might
well be on to his surprise attack.

He turned flatly to his son, Lieutenant Colonel Klaus von Kluge, chief
of staff of XLVII *Panzer* Corps: "Our Intelligence has intercepted enemy
signals. The Allies may have recognized our intentions and discerned our
army regroupings. The pressure of superior forces compels us to launch
the attack.

"It is now or never."[8]

What he couldn't realize was that the Allies had the use of Ultra's top
secret radio intercepts and knew exactly what the enemy was doing. In this
case, the first radio communications the Germans made pertaining to the
raid were on August 6, that very morning. By the time Ultra decoded the
transmissions at Bletchley Park in England, then translated and relayed
them through to General Bradley's US First Army headquarters, it was
thirty-eight minutes past midnight.[9]

Bradley dared not expose Ultra's security by openly revealing this information immediately to the 30th US Division commanders who would
be in the brunt of the attack. However, within twenty-four hours he managed to divert five infantry and two armored divisions and redirect them toward the sector of the enemy offensive. He also asked for full allied air
support for the next morning.[10]

But the 30th Division combat troops at the sharp end had no warning at all. Had the attack jumped off at 2200 hours as originally planned, they could have been completely overrun and surely annihilated.

That crashed British Typhoon pilot who so stalled the advance of the powerful 1st SS tanks did his allied friends a very large service: He gave them a two-hour reprieve.[11]

Shortly after midnight on August 7, two *Panzer* divisions—two of the eight Hitler had originally proposed—milled about in the confusion of the start line. Jumping off with whatever units they could assemble at short notice, the 2d *Panzer* and 2d SS *Panzer* Divisions launched Operation *Lüttich*.

The *Suisse Normande* terrain made the going perilous. Dense thickets of trees masked sharp drops and gullies. Narrow, winding lanes made navigation treacherous, despite the clear light of a full moon.

One hundred and twenty tanks, each carrying infantry and engineers, advanced cautiously in single file to avoid alerting the enemy with the noise of crashing trees. The tank commander headed the file on foot, leading his tank at a steady walking pace and using only pinpoint light. His skill determined their safety.

The 2d *Panzer* troops advanced on the northern flanks in two columns. At 0100 hours, its Reconnaissance Battalion crossed a small river, the Sée. Ahead they could see the shrouded outline of Hill 314, the sheer outcropping of tree-covered high ground standing like a sentinel blocking the approaches to the small town. A thick fog rolled off the river.

Maintaining silence, the Reconnaissance Battalion stealthily skirted the hill on the north side, bypassing an enemy roadblock. They were so close they could hear English voices in their foxholes. They pushed on another eight miles until daybreak, almost reaching their objective of Le Mesnil-Adelée before enemy resistance stopped them. Avranches was within reach, a mere twelve miles farther on.

In their wake, the remaining 2d *Panzer* column, proceeding without resistance, confidently approached St. Barthélémy, three miles north of Mortain.

One more such push and Patton's army would be cut off.

"Bad weather is what we need, *Herr General*," von Luttwitz's chief of operations said softly. Indeed, the thick fog was a sure guarantee that dawn would not bring the rocket-firing fighter aircraft.[12]

Meanwhile, the lead 2d SS Division, reinforced by 17th SS *Panzer* Grenadiers, started out just over a mile east of Mortain. In less than an hour the *Panzergrenadier* infantry troops—five hundred men, faces blackened, rifles poised—poured furtively down the main street of the town.

Operation *Lüttich*—Hitler's gamble—was on.

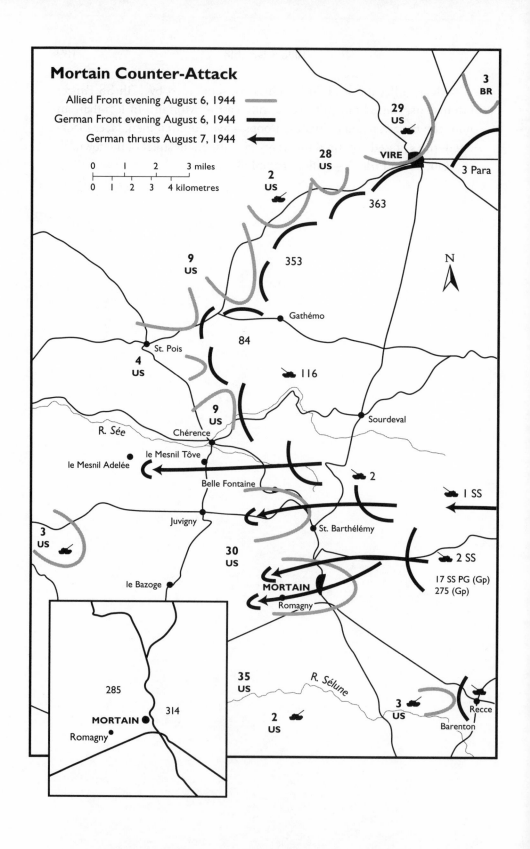

Mortain Counter-Attack

Allied Front evening August 6, 1944 ▬▬▬

German Front evening August 6, 1944 ▬▬▬

German thrusts August 7, 1944 ◀▬▬

```
0    1    2    3 miles
0  1  2  3  4 kilometres
```

N

3 BR

29 US

28 US

2 US

VIRE

363

3 Para

353

9 US

Gathémo

84

St. Pois

4 US

116

R. Sée

9 US

Chérence

Sourdeval

le Mesnil Tôve

le Mesnil Adelée

2

Belle Fontaine

1 SS

Juvigny

St. Barthélémy

3 US

2 SS

30 US

17 SS PG (Gp)
275 (Gp)

le Bazoge

MORTAIN

Romagny

35 US

R. Sélune

3 US

Recce

285

314

2 US

Barenton

MORTAIN

Romagny

CHAPTER 13

The Battle of Mortain

After the grim forty-nine-day battle through the *bocage* and the traumatic loss of life caused by friendly bombing in Operation *Cobra*, the 30th US Infantry Division, "Old Hickory," was relishing some hard-won rest and relaxation.

On August 1, a Tuesday, the troops had their first baths since D-Day. Fresh laundry and replacements of tattered shirts and worn boots boosted morale—as did grub that didn't come out of a tin, and jokes that didn't emerge from the black humor of the foxholes. Attractive American girls serving coffee and donuts from the Red Cross clubmobiles gave snatches of stateside memories.

On Friday, a USO show featuring Edward G. Robinson entertained the troops, though possibly the film with Lucille Ball and June Allyson wowed them even more. The 30th US Division commander, Major General Leland Hobbs, for once mellowing his loud, gruff-talking manner, commended the men for their fine efforts in fighting their way through the *bocage*. The US First Army had finally escaped the confining Cotentin Peninsula. Hobbs liked to win.

Twelve hundred reinforcements—many of them ill-trained—had been hurriedly moved up to replace the casualties of *Cobra* and the *bocage* battles. The newcomers barely had time to meet, much less bond, with their new comrades when the next battle order came through.

But first the division, old sweats and new, young replacements, had the heady experience of marching as liberators along the main road of the small town of Mortain, a hamlet that few of the GIs had even heard of—but all enjoyed to the hilt. The 1st US Infantry Division had actually freed the town three days earlier; the townsfolk could hardly believe their good fortune in having two liberation parades!

Diary of René Langlois (a Mortain schoolboy): Mortain, Tuesday, 3 August.

About 0700 hours we saw the first Americans. All of us, everyone in the whole district, ran out toward them, not thinking of the danger. At the same time, to announce our liberation, the bells of the Collégiale began to peal, making us believe that the nightmare was over. Or so we thought . . .[1]

In prewar days, Mortain had been a tourist's playground. Built halfway up a hillside in an attractive wooded gorge, the foaming waters of a waterfall, *La Cascade*, was the town's centerpiece attraction. An imposing rocky spur on its eastern edge rose over one thousand feet above sea level. Hill 314, as it was known, offered hikers a popular, if strenuous, Sunday clamber (ironically, French, British, and German in particular). A narrow lane curved up across a landscape of rocky outcroppings toward the summit. It passed, on the way, the twelfth-century L'Abbaye Blanche (so named because its nuns wore white homespun robes). The more adventuresome ignored the road and, instead, scaled the sheer rocky crag on the southwestern summit of Hill 314.

A dazzling view rewarded any attempt to stand perilously on the outjutting rocks behind its tiny church, *La Petite Chapelle*. Eighteen miles to the west, one could see as far as Avranches, the gateway to Brittany, and beyond it, the glistening Atlantic waters of the Bay of Mont-Saint-Michel. Due south were the flat plains of the Sélune River, bordering the province of Maine. A full turn north revealed the Norman countryside, the *bocage* terrain that tourists loved for its beauty. And soldiers despised for its deadliness.

Diary of René Langlois: Saturday, 5 August.

Americans came to see us . . . They were warmly welcomed by everyone in the district, and given cider, coffee, and, obviously, Calva [Calvados]. Which they seemed to appreciate!

On this balmy summer Sunday, August 6, elated townsfolk of Mortain finally believed they were free. They crowded the avenue, throwing flowers, laughing and cheering in the joy of being rid of the Nazis. Not a few ran up to the troops with hugs and *mercis* and always-welcome bottles of wine or the local apple liqueur, Calvados. The townspeople—some sixteen hundred souls—were grateful that their ancient buildings had emerged from four years of occupation and three days of fighting for its liberation with only a single shell hole, that harmlessly landed in the park.

Diary of René Langlois: Sunday, 6 August.

On Sunday we were sitting beside the road and passing Americans gave us whatever they had: cigarettes (in packets of three or four), chewing gum, little packets of coffee and tea, little pots of jam.[2]

Arriving in Mortain on that sunny Sunday afternoon, the three regiments of the US 30th Infantry Division headed for their assigned defensive posts: The 117th Regiment took over the defenses of the tiny village of St. Barthélémy, just north of Mortain. The 119th was in reserve nearby, and the 120th was assigned the task of defending the town of Mortain and its surrounding hills.

Colonel Hammond Birks, the commanding officer of 120th Infantry Regiment, was amazed at the carnival atmosphere of Mortain. "This town is 'wide-open,' " he exclaimed to his aide-de-camp. "The hotels are full. It should be an excellent place for a little rest and relaxation."

But his counterpart from the departing US 1st Infantry Division unit uttered a prophetic warning: "Hill 314 is the key to the whole area. In case of emergency this hill has to be held at all costs."[3]

For General Bradley and his allied commanders and for Hitler and his generals, that modest peak in the *Suisse Normande* would become the focus of tactical scrutiny. Whoever commanded its summit commanded all movement of the troops below. In short, Hitler's troops could not reach Avranches without taking and holding Hill 314. Bradley's troops could not avoid being overrun unless they held it.

Birks assigned the defense of the town of Mortain and Hill 314 to his 2d Battalion, warning that the enemy was located in strength northeast of Mortain. "If any trouble develops, it will come from that direction," Birks directed 2d Battalion's Commanding Officer, Lieutenant Colonel Eads Hardaway. "Put roadblocks on all approaches to the 2d Battalion position."

It was the intersection at L'Abbaye Blanche that concerned him the most. Four roads converged on it. The main north–south road to Mortain ran right through it. As well, three others angled into it.

"If that roadblock does not hold, the resulting gap will permit the enemy to smash through our line," Colonel Birks declared. Lieutenant Tom Andrew was put in command of a seventy-man force to hold the barricades at L'Abbaye Blanche. He had two 57mm guns from the battalion's antitank platoon, a machine gun and mortar section, and a rifle squad. To give added firepower Birks sent over Lieutenant Tom Springfield's platoon of four guns from 823rd Tank-Destroyer (TD) Battalion.[4] The fifteen-pound shells from Springfield's three-inch antitank guns were capable of penetrating three inches of armor at two thousand feet.

Lieutenant Andrew did a quick survey of his post. "There is no time to start building new defensive positions before dark," he said grimly. "We'll have to use these ones the Germans just left. They are in good natural positions."

He sited his three-inch guns on either side of the main road with two .30-caliber machine guns on each side. Then he placed a bazooka and BAR (Browning automatic rifle) team and half a squad of riflemen in former enemy dugout positions along a small hedgerow north of the railway bridge. A 57mm antitank gun covered the end of the road.

Immediately south of the railroad bridge Andrew placed riflemen and bazooka teams. He had two belts of mines laid near the bend in the road, and these were covered by the bazooka and BAR teams. Every one of his seventy men had a vital role to play.[5]

They were ready.

From his battalion headquarters at the old Grande Hotel on the main square, Lieutenant Colonel Hardaway swiftly dispatched some six hundred men from the 2d Battalion to establish defensive positions on Hill 314.

"We had to carry everything up that damn hill—guns, tripods, ammo, everything!" recalls Private John Weekly of "H" Company. "We didn't have a jeep or an ammo carrier. I was carrying the tripod for our .50-caliber machine gun. We set up in an orchard. It was a machine gunner's paradise. You could see for miles and miles. The problem was we only had minimal ammunition. We brought all we could carry, but that wasn't much."[6]

The men found that inheriting the 1st Division's hastily installed temporary defenses created a lot of problems: "They had only dug down about eighteen inches," Private George Neidhardt of "F" Company said scornfully of his predecessor's foxhole. "I went down four feet, deep enough to stand in up to my armpits."[7]

There were other snags: The phone net was unusable and had to be completely rewired. There were few large-scale maps. There had been no chance to install fortifications or minefields.[8]

Still, they reckoned there was plenty of time to correct these deficiencies: "Perhaps the battalion was suffering from a false sense of security," Lieutenant Ralph Kerley admitted.[9] Kerley, a seasoned veteran, had been wounded as a platoon commander before the St. Lô battle. He had just returned to the line to take command of "E" Company. The men worked hard at their tasks of consolidating the position, grateful for the lateness of midsummer light that let them toil away until midnight.

The Germans launched their *Panzer* attack with a heavy artillery bombardment on the town center. A number of fires broke out, forcing the civilians into shelters.

Diary of René Langlois: Sunday, 6 August.
At midnight, there was a German bombing raid. In our parents' house there were also several families. In the cellars, we were all curled up, listening to the explosions. Where would the next bomb fall?

After the bombing, which had set fire to the whole town, the people of Mortain left for the surrounding countryside. Some families went to a mine, where there were 800 people in the end. They had some problems feeding them.[10]

Amid the screech of flying mortars and the crash of exploding shells, no one heard the more ominous drumming noise of tank treads rumbling toward them. At 0125 hours, enemy small-arms fire was heard to the east of the 2d Battalion command post (CP).

It was while he was stringing telephone wire across the town streets, working by the illumination of the fires, that Sergeant Robert Bondurant happened to look up and gasp: "There they were at the other end of the street—German soldiers. Maybe thirty or more. All with burp guns. The town was full of them."

Bondurant immediately reported the crisis to Colonel Birks. "Hold the town at all costs," Birks ordered him. "Stay at your post."

He stayed.[11]

Five minutes later the full force of the enemy attack fell on the Americans. Second SS *Panzer Das Reich* Division had managed to bypass a roadblock on the southeast approaches to Mortain, enabling them to encircle the town.

Diary of René Langlois: Monday, 7 August.

On the Monday we wanted to go out quickly and beg some more from the convoys we could hear passing. But when we got to the first hedge, we realized they were German tanks going up the road.

The local policeman's wife [had been] killed. He stayed behind to watch over his wife's body during the counterattack and was reported missing. No trace was ever found of him or of her.[12]

The Americans were forced to withdraw to the high ground of Hill 314. Lieutenant Ronal Woody had just come off the hill when he spotted the enemy troops: "When the firing started I knew I had to get up to where my men were, up on top of the hill, so I went up the cliff." Woody scaled the sheer, one-thousand-foot face of the crag. "They were shooting all around me as I climbed. Somehow I made it up there. When I looked back and saw the way I'd come, I couldn't believe I had climbed it."[13]

At 0345, Hardaway signaled Birks urgently: "The Germans have taken part of Hill 314."

"Send Company 'G' to drive them off," Birks commanded him.

Minutes later, Hardaway called with an ominous message: "Enemy tanks and armored vehicles with accompanying infantry are entering Mortain in strength."

By 0700 hours he was desperate. "I've got to get out of Mortain," he pleaded.

"You get up there with your troops on Hill 314!" Birks ordered sternly.

The next call from Hardaway's HQ Company came a few hours later. With him were his executive officer, his communications officer, and a dozen men of Battalion Headquarters Company—some twenty-seven men in all.

"We tried to sneak out of town between the buildings but ran into Germans blocking any access to the hill. Then we had to duck into another building. I am cut off from Hill 314 and unable to join my troops," he signaled.

"My staff and I are hiding; my radio batteries are low."

Then—silence. Nothing more was heard. It was assumed that the commanding officer and his entire headquarters staff had been taken prisoner. (This was later confirmed by one of his staff who escaped). Command of the 2d Battalion was given to Captain Reynold Erichson.

Meanwhile, a number of other 2d Battalion men still roamed the outskirts of the town. Overrun and out of communication, the small isolated bands were striving to find their way through enemy lines to join their comrades on Hill 314. Some were killed; some managed to sneak through or to hide out in the hedgerows or barns for several days, dodging Germans.

Some, like Sergeant Robert Bondurant, were captured. The young signaler had stayed at his switchboard to the end, as ordered. The SS troops rounded up all their prisoners and forced them to sit in the middle of the road. The frightened sergeant could only think of the reported SS massacre of hundreds of French civilians in Oradour-sur-Glane.[14]

"I thought they were going to shoot us," he said. "Instead they walked us back to an aid station. Wounded were lying around everywhere, both German and American."[15]

Diary of René Langlois: Monday, 7 August.

The German counterattack was becoming fiercer, and getting nearer, and this forced us to draw further back into the country. Were we aware of what was at stake not far away? We youngsters, full of the carelessness of inexperience, slept the night without hearing too much of the noise of the battle . . .[16]

One of the last outsiders to reach the summit of Hill 314 was Captain Delmont Byrn, who was commanding "H" Company (Heavy Weapons). He located Ralph Kerley's company and was stunned by the sight of wounded men still sprawled where they had fallen: "It was my first week of combat," he said. "I was kind of shocked to see injured men lying there in the open, being hit again by shrapnel."

Erichson, now in command of 2d Battalion, had rounded up what stragglers he could, about forty, and managed to find an unguarded trail that led steeply up the hill. He quickly pulled all the companies into a communication link, established an all-round defensive position on the summit, and alerted the watches and the men positioned on the road-blocks leading to the hilltop. Dense fog rolled in, adding to the darkness of the night; visibility was nil.

Erichson took stock.

The battalion, or what was left of it, was now isolated on the summit of Hill 314. The six hundred men were surrounded on all sides by one of Germany's most elite *Panzer* divisions that even at reduced strength numbered some nine thousand men.

Its acting CO, Erichson, was a twenty-four-year-old captain, in peacetime an Iowa farmer. Three of its company commanders had never before commanded a company (Captain Delmont Byrn, Lieutenant Joe Reaser, and the irrepressible Lieutenant Ronal Woody). One, Ralph Kerley, was a hell-for-leather soldier, but noted for being unorthodox.

They had, however, as powerful tools, two forward artillery observation officers (FOOs). These FOOs were the eyes of the divisional artillery that was securely positioned several thousand yards behind them. From their hilltop observation posts, Lieutenants Robert Weiss and Charles Bartz could see all of the surrounding countryside, and thus direct and correct effective fire from the American guns against the enemy. Although telephone communication no longer existed, they still had battery-run radios with which to call down targets to the gunners from 230th Field Artillery Battalion on the flats below. Thanks to these two men, counterattack after counterattack by determined *Panzer* troops were thwarted.

The battalion could hold out—as long as the batteries lasted.

Meanwhile, less than two miles northwest of Mortain, two battalions from 117th Regiment arrived to take over the defenses of the tiny crossroads village of St. Barthélémy. French resistance had tipped off the CO of the 1st Battalion, Lieutenant Colonel Robert Frankland, that German troops were massing in the northeast. He directed two of his companies to cover roads coming in from that direction.

"A" Company seemed hardly a match for the might of the 2d *Panzer* Division. Its commander, a lieutenant, had been with "A" Company for just a week; the 3d Platoon had no officers; a sergeant commanded it. Of its strength of 135 men, 55 were replacements who had come in two days before. The company had no bazookas and no artillery support.[17]

Frankland would have been horrified to learn that the 1st SS *Panzer* Division—the powerful *Leibstandarte-Adolf Hitler* that had been stalled the previous night by the crashed British Typhoon near Caen—had now caught up with von Funck's counterattack force toward dawn. Its task was to follow and overtake 2d *Panzer*, picking up the lead for the final drive to Avranches.

Frankland's tiny force was all there was to block its advance through St. Barthélémy.

The attack came on Monday, August 7, at 0600 hours. Panther tanks from three directions poured into the little village of St. Barthélémy, overwhelming the crossroads' defenders. The tanks converged on the US 823d Tank-Destroyer Battalion's antitank and tank-destroyer guns. George Greene, a twenty-two-year-old lieutenant commanding a platoon of four guns, had joined the 823d TDs just a few days before. He barely knew even the names of the men under him. Greene and his men hung on, knocking out tank after tank, until the panthers had one by one destroyed the Americans' guns. Then he grabbed a machine gun and fired an entire belt of ammunition at the enemy, giving his men the chance to escape.

By 0700 hours, at least eight enemy tanks had fought their way into the town. Because of the thick fog that "rose and fell like a stage curtain," fighting was chaotic. Attacker and defender groped for each other, fighting blindly, viciously, often trading blows and even bayonet thrusts—a rare occurrence in World War II. Two German tanks came to within 250 yards of Colonel Birks's command post.

"The Germans rushed the positions, throwing potato mashers over the hedgerows, and some of them even jumping the hedges right into company positions," Sergeant Grady reported.[18]

Colonel Frankland still had good radio communication with his companies. "Stay in place," Frankland told them urgently. "Let the tanks break through and then get the infantry which follows." It was a tactic the Germans had so often and so effectively used against the Allies in Normandy.

The outnumbered GIs of 117th Infantry fought back with incredible tenacity and resourcefulness, and their guns and bazookas took a heavy toll on the German infantry.

The men of the hapless "A" Company were dead in the path of a column of Mark IV tanks from 2d *Panzer* Division. One tank crashed through a gap in the hedgerow directly in front of a foxhole shared by Staff Sergeant Abbie Riviere and Sergeant Grover Wright.

"Should we shoot him, Abbie, should we shoot him?" Wright asked excitedly.

But neither man had a bazooka with which to shoot the tank. Wisely, Riviere ordered his squad to withdraw, using the thick fog as cover.

Short on trained manpower or effective weapons, but long on sheer courage, the company was virtually wiped out in those first few minutes. Only one officer and twenty-seven men escaped being killed or captured.

The *Panzers* then penetrated the town and, unknowingly, surrounded Colonel Frankland's advance command post. "The colonel heard noises at the rear of the house and went to investigate," one of his staff recalled. "He got there just as two of his radiomen were being forced out the back door with their hands up. The colonel followed them out and shot the two Germans. The command group immediately escaped out the window."

A second unconfirmed report claims that the colonel also shot the commander of the tank that was attacking his headquarters. He is then said to have jumped up on the tank and started blasting away down the hatch with his .45 automatic, killing the whole crew.

Frankland's 1st Battalion and its supporting 823d Tank-Destroyer Platoon suffered heavy casualties: more than 334 men killed, wounded, or missing. One of those casualties was Lieutenant George Greene, the newcomer to battle, who made his mark on August 7. Greene was wounded and taken prisoner. In the early afternoon (he couldn't be sure of the time as a German soldier had stolen his watch), he and the other American prisoners from St. Barthélémy were loaded into trucks packed with German soldiers for a nightmare trip into German lines. Every time the convoy was strafed by Allied Typhoons, the German troops "were able to jump out of the truck and hide in the ditches. We had to stay in the trucks."[19]

The battered 117th companies stubbornly fought on. Survivors dropped back to a new defensive line on a low hill just west of St.

Barthélémy. The regimental commander, Lieutenant Colonel Walter Johnson, grabbed every man that could hold a gun—including his kitchen staff and drivers—and set up a defensive line just in front of the stone farmhouse that served as regimental HQ. A battalion from the 823d Tank-Destroyer provided fire support. The HQ name soon changed to "Château Nebelwerfer" as German artillery registered all their guns and mortars on the small house.

The Germans were fewer than four hundred yards away. They fired everything they had at the house that served as the regimental command post. Every square yard around it seemed to be hit but, amazingly, the house was untouched. Once the attack was underway Colonel Johnson refused to back down. He thought it would affect the men's morale if he changed the command post location.

That morning, before the fog could lift, the Germans attacked again, this time just with infantry. Right over the hedgerows they came. They wore stolen American uniforms, even field jackets, and carried trench knives. Close hand-to-hand fighting, even fistfights, followed for about thirty minutes.

But the obstinate defenders of St. Barthélémy, though driven out of the village, achieved their goal. They had delayed what was supposed to be the main thrust of the German attack for six vital hours until air support could arrive.

By early afternoon, the 1st SS *Panzer* Division, still sixteen miles from Avranches, had been forced to a standstill, unable to bypass the tenacious Americans. The 2d *Panzer* Division's Reconnaissance Battalion had managed to spearhead the northern column's drive, advancing six miles toward Avranches at daybreak and forcing one infantry company to abandon its vehicles and guns. A roadblock established by the reserve 119th Infantry Regiment stopped the rout. The *Panzers* were being threatened, too, by the first elements of American armored reinforcements. VII Corps commander Major General Joe Collins had rushed them up to prevent the Germans from breaking into the vital Avranches Corridor.

While 2d *Panzer* Division initially seemed to have the whip hand, they ground to a halt at nearby Mesnil-Adelée. With just twelve miles still to go they now had to wait for the remainder of 2d *Panzer* and 1st SS *Leibstandarte*, held up by the Americans in St. Barthélémy.

Those six hours bought for them by Frankland's 135 men of "A" Company had proved to be of vital importance.[20]

In that exact time span, the fog had dissipated from the River Sée. General von Luttwitz had been praying for continuing fog to provide a protective mantle from air observation over his attacking troops. Sunlight breaking through would bring the dreaded American and British air forces into the Battle of Mortain. If he could just be free from the harassing fighter-bombers (*Jabos*) for a few more hours!

He knew from past experience that when the *Jabos* attacked he had no choice but to order his foot soldiers to take cover and his armored columns to get off the roads and conceal their tanks with camouflage netting.

But brilliant noonday sun began filtering through the lifting fog, casting unwelcome shafts of light on the Mortain aggressors. Luttwitz quickly ordered his columns to take cover. It was too late. The allied gunners and airmen could now target their prey.

The "Day of the Typhoons" was at hand.

CHAPTER 14

The Lost Battalion

As the fog burned off Hill 314 in the late morning, the two FOOs, Lieutenants Weiss and Bartz, grinned broadly at each other. The view below them was an artilleryman's dream: "Columns of enemy armor and foot troops streaming (toward us) from the east and northeast."[1] The battalion's hold on the hill had become a festering sore to the enemy, as an extract from 2d *Panzer* Division war diary shows:

> 1000 hours, 7 August 44: "A battle group consisting of elements of the 17th SS *Panzer* Grenadier division has not been able to budge the stubborn American defenders on the Hill. Hill 314 provides American artillery observers with an excellent view of the entire countryside for miles around."[2]

A very effective collaboration was developing between the American infantry at L'Abbaye Blanche and the artillery FOOs atop Hill 314.

Weiss and Bartz would spot the enemy armor and infantry concentrations approaching from the east and radio their positions to the American artillery emplacements several miles to the west. They then would observe the fall of shot and when necessary correct the range and alignment. This broke up the German concentrations before they could attain full momentum.

Any vehicles or infantry getting through this hurdle then came under

the fire of the seventy-man L'Abbaye Blanche roadblock team of Lieutenants Tom Springfield's 823d Tank-Destroyers and Stewart's 57mm antitank guns.

Tom Stewart soon realized that in using the old German dug-in defense positions he was letting himself in for a lot more fire. The enemy
now demonstrated that they had full knowledge of these positions and had
targeted them for their artillery. "Whenever they opened up, our troops
would have to abandon them and take shelter in the nearest house or
barn," Stewart said. When the artillery stopped they returned to their positions. "Everything we left there such as gas masks and clothing had been
completely riddled."[3]

The Germans pounded the roadblock with everything they could lay
their hands on—flamethrowers, concussion grenades, 88mms, and nonstop artillery bombardments. Combat patrol attacked from every direction.

The 30th Division artillery, criticized as being slow at first to respond seriously to the German counterattack, now threw its vast weight of twelve
and a half field artillery battalions—some three hundred guns—at the
enemy. "Air Ops [observation posts], working out of little low-flying
Austers, were invaluable in identifying targets, especially, because of the
position of the sun, in the late afternoon," artillery commander Brigadier
General James Lewis noted. "We established a record, firing thirty artillery
concentrations (stonks) on enemy gun positions in one hour at dusk.
There was a tremendous drop in the enemy's artillery fire the next day."[4]

The allied air forces had been tipped off by General Bradley (through
Ultra) to pour on an "all-out effort." They had been watching the skies just
as anxiously as von Luttwitz had.

They decided to split the job. As soon as the fog lifted, Major General
Elwood "Pete" Quesada's US 9th US Tactical Air Force P-51 Mustangs
and P-47 Thunderbolts engaged the *Luftwaffe* over their bases near Paris.
The RAF 2d Tactical Air Force's rocket-firing Typhoons had the task of
tackling the German armor and infantry at Mortain. This cooperative effort of both tactical air forces produced the greatest concentration of
fighter-bombers yet deployed in the west. The *Luftwaffe's* promise to von

Kluge of producing three hundred fighter planes in support of Operation *Lüttich* dissolved under the impact of two hundred sorties by the Americans. As visibility cleared they swarmed the German planes as they took off, rendering the *Luftwaffe* completely impotent.

Von Kluge, expecting dogfights, got no protection at all. *Luftwaffe* Colonel von Schultz admitted apologetically, "our fighters were hard pressed by enemy fighters from the moment they took to the air. They could not reach the target area."[5]

At 1215 hours Wing Commander Charles Green, a burly South African who was something of a legend with the RAF, spearheaded the first flight of Typhoons. These would total 294 sorties by the end of the day. When he and his wingman took off from Le Fresne Camilly fighter strip, the fog still lingered, putting doubts to their chances of being able to spot enemy targets, or even being able to put back down on the airstrip after their reconnaissance. But the two men got lucky. Although the cloud base was so low they had only a split second glimpse before they pulled out of their dive, they had spotted their quarry.[6]

The German armor is already stopped on all fronts, they reported back gleefully. They're sitting ducks.

Flying out of makeshift air bases in France, not far from the D-Day beaches, the Typhoon pilots operated in teams. Planes would take off in pairs to make the fifteen-minute flight to target. Then they would attack and return to base to rearm. Thus they maintained a continuous cycle over the target from 1230 hours until dusk.

This was, as Flight Lieutenant Charles Demoulin describes, desperately dangerous. "The average survival rate for a rocket-Typhoon pilot since mass missions at low level were introduced is around seventeen operations. After that, he lives on borrowed time. Veterans stand a better chance of living than the younger ones, whose average number of ops before 'buying it' is no more than five."[7]

After an inauspicious beginning, the Typhoon had found its forte, ultimately becoming a deadly air-to-ground attack weapon. Able to outrun the German ME-109 and the FW 190, the single-seater Typhoon fighter was highly maneuverable at low level.

"The pilots learn by trial and error, on the spot," Demoulin notes. "Most casualties occur on the very first op—through lack of experience. I am sorry for these sprogs, who will probably not get past their first ten missions before 'going for a Burton.'"[8]

Flight Lieutenant Bill Baggs was no sprog. Enlisting straight out of high school in 1942, Bill was the only Canadian in 84 Group, 164 Squadron, RAF—a regular "united nations of pilots" from eleven countries that flew in support of the Canadian Army. He started flying close army support on July 14, 1944, and from that date he flew in combat for many months, with as many as three sorties a day against enemy strongpoints.

Early in July he was hit by heavy flak, an 88mm shell, resulting in nineteen holes in his aircraft. Incredibly, he got home. His early brush with death "sort of woke me up," he said. From then on Baggs flew daily in close-support sorties. "Initially, when you started flying on your tour, you didn't really see very much. You were too involved in keeping in formation with your leader. As you got more experienced you could see what was going on, on the ground.[9]

"In an attack, we would climb to about ninety-five hundred feet. That was supposedly above the light and medium flak and below the heavy flak. Then we rolled over on our backs and started a sixty-degree dive to the target, releasing our rockets at about two thousand feet."

The dives were pretty steep—so steep that sometimes the pilot would black out as he pulled out of them. "It was always nice to wake up at about ten thousand feet, not having been hit," Baggs added, grinning.

As soon as the Germans realized they'd been spotted

they let go at us with everything they've got and tracers zip past on all sides. But nothing except a lucky shot can stop a Typhoon diving at five hundred miles per hour.

We could look over our left shoulder as we climbed back up (Baggs explained) and see if a tank had been hit. Then if there wasn't too much light flak we would take additional passes with our four 20mm cannons. We in the RAF had eight rockets with sixty-pound warheads. We could fire two at a time or all of them at once in a salvo. That would be equivalent to a salvo from a light cruiser.[10]

If the Typhoon pilots had been successful in knocking out the target, the army would radio them a "strawberry"—a message of appreciation and thanks.

Flak was the main reason for the very high casualty rate of pilots. One hundred and fifty-one pilots were killed between D-Day and the end of August. "The flak could be so bad that in shows of just twenty minutes or half an hour, we would lose two or three men out of the original eight," Bill Baggs recalled.

New Zealander Desmond Scott, who at twenty-five was one of the youngest group captains, gave a vivid description of one attack:

> As I sped to the head of this mile-long column, hundreds of German troops began spilling out into the road to sprint for the open fields and hedgerows. There was no escape. Typhoons were already attacking in deadly swoops at the other end of the column and within seconds the whole stretch of the road was bursting and blazing under streams of rocket and cannon fire. Ammunition wagons exploded like multi-coloured volcanoes. A large, long-barrelled tank [probably a Tiger] standing in a field just off the road was hit by rockets and overturned into a ditch. It was an awesome sight: planes smoke, burning rockets and showers of coloured tracer.[11]

The shattering Typhoon attacks of August 7 brought overwhelming horror, destruction, and defeat to every German soldier in the eye of the attack—from the ordinary *panzergrenadier* to his army commanders.

On the receiving end of this carnage, Warner Josupeit, a German machine-gunner with 1st SS *Panzer*, remembers the terror.

> The fighter-bombers circled our tanks several times. Then one broke out of the circle, sought a target and fired. As the first pulled back into the circle of about twenty planes, a second pulled out and fired. So they continued until they had all fired. Then they left the terrible scene.
>
> A new swarm appeared in their place and fired all their rockets. Black clouds of smoke from burning oil climbed into the sky everywhere we looked. They marked the dead Panzers. Finally the Typhoons couldn't find any more Panzers so they bore down on us and chased us mercilessly. Their rockets fell with a terrible howl, and burst into big pieces of shrapnel.[12]

The staff report to General Hausser attested to the success of the Typhoon attack: "Continuation of the attack during the midday hours was made impossible because of enemy air superiority."

Lieutenant General von Gersdorff, chief of staff, Seventh German Army, echoed this. "The attack has bogged down since 1300 hours because of heavy enemy fighter-bomber operations and the failure of our own air force." He added, "OKW [German High Command] never attached enough importance to the air situation; that made the movements and the supply for the operations doubtful."[13]

Hausser himself told von Kluge at 2150 hours, "Terrific fighter-bomber attacks. Considerable tank losses. The corps have orders to continue their attacks as soon as air activity decreases."[14]

Unofficial RAF communiqués initially claimed that the Typhoons had put 162 tanks out of action with 81 destroyed and 54 seriously damaged. Three Typhoons were lost.

US historian Martin Blumenson downgrades these figures somewhat and concludes: "Of 70 enemy tanks estimated to make the original penetration, only 30 were judged to be in operation at the close of the day. On the morning of 8 August the estimate was reduced to 25 still remaining behind American lines.[15] However, further investigation also credited the US artillery with many of the 'kills.' "

The unknown factor was the skill of German tank recovery units immediately behind the front lines in salvaging the damaged armor back to repair harbors as quickly as possible after an attack.

Meanwhile, General von Funck was increasingly concerned about the northern flank of his counterattacking force. He had been forced to immobilize it at midday. He badly needed Schwerin's seventy-five tanks in action.

Von Funck blamed Count von Schwerin for not dispatching his 116th *Panzer* Division in support as ordered, charging him with refusal to engage in the battle. "He was ordered to support 2nd *Panzer and he did not. Therefore, he is the reason we failed!*"[16]

Von Schwerin was having none of this buck-passing: "How and with what should I have conducted this strong attack you wanted?" he asked sarcastically. "You've taken two-thirds of my tank strength. Then you insisted I hurriedly throw my troops, who were not ready for offensive combat, into an attack. The enemy was occupying my forward assembly area. Half of my infantry had to be employed in the rear to prevent the collapse of my lines of communication. Moreover, strong enemy with tanks and very heavy artillery cut short every attempt to attack by my advanced infantry.

"I will not allow myself or my Division be insulted," Count von Schwerin said haughtily, and strode out.[17]

Von Funck stormed furiously to von Kluge's command post. "That man must be immediately relieved of his command!" he demanded.

At 1600 hours on August 7—still Day One of the Mortain counterattack—General Hausser and von Funck fired von Schwerin from his command and replaced him with von Funck's chief of staff, Colonel Walter Reinhard. Thirty minutes later Reinhard obediently ordered the division into action. The troops almost immediately came to a standstill.

Major Heinz Günther Guderian, a senior staff officer with the *Windhund* (116th) Division at Mortain, had witnessed many successful *Panzer* attacks staged over the years by his father, the famed tank commander.

"To begin an attack with the idea that it is without hope is not a good idea," Guderian said. "We did not have this hope."[18] The Mortain counterattack had no such vestige of success and von Schwerin was too professional a *Wehrmacht* commander to send his troops into such a flawed battle.

If von Kluge had doubts about the unlikelihood of success of Operation *Lüttich* before it was launched, he surely was convinced of its folly twenty-four hours later, when he was informed that allied troops were closing in on him from three sides. General Horrocks's XXX Corps, just thirty-five miles northeast of his position, had seized Mount Pinçon, the coveted jewel of *La Suisse Normande*. Farther east, Kluge learned, First Canadian Army had launched a massive armored night attack on August 7 from Caen toward Falaise: Operation *Totalize* that kicked off at 2300 hours with more than six hundred tanks. An RAF force of one thousand planes, including heavy bombers, dropped more than five thousand tons of bombs in front of the ground troops, and 720 artillery pieces shelled the enemy. The Canadian thrust was imperiling Meyer's 12th SS *Hitlerjugend*.

Patton's Third Army threatened encirclement from the south. Major

General Haislip's XV Corps was just now rolling into the town center of Le Mans, sixty miles south. Each of these outside threats pinned down *Panzer* divisions that Kluge urgently needed at Mortain.

But Hitler insisted that he persevere with the Mortain attack—and one does not refuse the Führer, especially when one is under deep suspicion of having been a conspirator in the assassination attempt.

In truth, as General Eberbach later observed, "This would have been the right time for Field Marshal von Kluge to act against Hitler's orders to save the two armies [Seventh and Fifth]. But after July 20, he was watched in such a sharp way that it would have been especially difficult for him. The result would have simply been his substitution by a more manageable tool."[19]

The operation was to plod on for four more days, with heavy losses on both sides and few gains. By August 9, Luttwitz's 2d *Panzer* was forced to give up the ground it had won and was back to the start line, having lost thirty tanks and eight hundred men.[20] On August 10, von Kluge begged Hitler to let him transfer some of the force southeast to stem the American push on Alençon. He was ignored. Instead, he was commanded to remount the operation on August 11, with General Eberbach replacing von Funck as commander of *Panzer* Group Eberbach.[21]

Meanwhile, conditions on Hill 314 were grim.

On the first day of their isolated stand, August 7, they were bombed and strafed ten times by both friendly and enemy aircraft (a few having evidently slipped through the net) and heavily shelled. At 1507 hours two enemy tanks advanced to within 250 yards of their command post. Private Joe Shipley, a switchboard operator who had never before even fired a bazooka, grabbed one and successfully knocked out one tank, scaring off the second. "He didn't even leave his seat!" marveled one commander.[22]

The shelling of the regimental CP continued so heavily into the next day that they were finally forced to move to another location.

At 1100 hours on August 8, Acting CO, Captain Reynold Erichson, radioed a report to regimental HQ: "Need radio batteries, medical supplies, food, and ammunition. Men holding their positions. Forward observers Lieutenants Bartz and Weiss doing splendid work. Enemy has been prevented from organizing armor and infantry to effect an attack of overwhelming strength."

At 1828 hours, August 9, an SS officer accompanied by an enlisted man carrying a flag of truce issued an ultimatum to surrender to the 2d Battalion. The officer approached Lieutenant Ralph Kerley's "E" Company headquarters on Hill 314.

"You are entirely cut off and surrounded," the German said, his English stilted but impeccable. "We have captured your commanding officer [Colonel Hardaway] and many other prisoners. The position of the Americans on the Hill is hopeless. If you do not surrender before 2000 hours, we will blow you to bits."

He soon learned that you don't give Ralph Kerley ultimatums.

"Kerley was kind of a loose cannon," Captain Delmont Byrne said of the sandy-haired Texan. "He was rough, tough, unkempt, unshaven, profane, a heavy drinker, and disdainful of red tape and protocol . . . a great combat leader, utterly fearless."

Wounded men lying nearby heard the German demand. They called out to Kerley, "No, no! Don't surrender!"

"I will surrender when every one of our bullets has been fired and every one of our bayonets is sticking in a German belly," Kerley replied, stalking off angrily.

That night, the enemy struck again. They swarmed up the hill with tanks, machine-gunning the entire American front. German voices could be heard yelling, "Surrender! Surrender!" After a stiff fight, the GIs drove them off.

The exhausted defenders were forced to hold their positions in relays to beat off constant combat patrols. "One tank came within fifty yards of our observation post, fired a few rounds, called for us to surrender or die, and left," Kerley reported.

At one point, warning his men to dig in, Kerley called down artillery on his own position. The men huddled in foxholes or rock crevices. For five minutes, hundreds of shells pounded directly on top of the American headquarters, driving the enemy off.

Although they were desperately in need of food, ammunition, and medical supplies, their most urgent shortage was for fresh batteries—their lifeline. Without batteries, their FOOs would be unable to radio German positions to the artillery units below the hill, and they would be quickly overrun.

When the battery scarcity became acute, Robert Weiss would give rapid (and increasingly faint) directions to the artillery, then yank out his batteries and lay them in the sun, trying to coax one last iota of power from them.

2nd Bn Report, 10 August:

"American C-47s accompanied by fighters flew over Hill 314 and dropped food. Unfortunately at least one-half of these rations were dropped in enemy-held territory. The hungry men of Hill 314 organized patrols and went out during darkness to retrieve what rations they could, always under sniper fire."

There were nine local French farmers isolated with them on the Hill. They contributed a little milk and shared what they could. To fill out the meager diet some of the men foraged in the farmers' fields to wolf down raw carrots, potatoes, and radishes. Sergeants Kozere and Murphy of Company "C" even managed to secure some rabbits they had found in cages.

The milk was given to the wounded. Deep slit trenches were dug for these men, who endured the greatest of privation and pain without complaint. There were no doctors on Hill 314 and scarcely any medical supplies. Although the aide men worked steadily, constantly performing miracles, soldiers died.

The 230th Field Artillery attempted vainly to fire plasma, morphine, and medical supplies in 105mm shells, normally used to fire smoke or propaganda material. The priceless fluids smashed on contact; only bandages were recovered.

Morale was slipping. Exhaustion, hunger, and helplessness were taking its toll. The stench of the dead in the August heat was an ugly reminder of a fate that seemed more and more inevitable to them all.

Then there was a transformation. Anger and resolve replaced despair. The turning point was Ralph Kerley's succinct rebuff of the arrogant SS officer.

In the predawn hours of August 12, the Germans withdrew from Mortain as silently as they had come six days earlier. The Americans awoke to . . . nothing. No shells. No mortar. No enemy.

The 35th Division Quartermaster Company had loaded a truck with food, water, and medical supplies. The drivers vied to be the ones to make the run up Hill 314.

Of the seven hundred men who had reached the hill on August 7, 357 were able to walk off on August 12. Three hundred were killed or wounded.[23]

Colonel Hammond Birks, 120th Division regimental commander, hurried forward to L'Abbaye Blanche after the battle. The 823d Tank-Destroyer defenders, grown to 150 men and the company mascot—a dog appropriately named Mobile Reserve—had maintained the Abbaye road-block for six days under intensive enemy armor and infantry attacks from four roads. Owing to the effective defenses employed by Springfield and Stewart's units, the Germans' many efforts were continuously driven back.

The Americans had inflicted heavy casualties and a great deal of damage to the counterattacking Germans. Incredibly, their losses were minimal. They suffered only three killed and twenty wounded.

Lieutenant Tom Andrew said modestly, "I think we knocked out twenty-four vehicles, sir." But Birks, investigating the road, believed the number was closer to forty.

"The road was littered with knocked-out enemy armor. You won't find better testimony to the accuracy of the roadblock's fire," Colonel Birks said. "It was the best sight I had seen in the war."[24]

Birks was also there to warmly welcome the men of Hill 314 for their heroic stand as they came off the Hill. He clapped Ralph Kerley on the back. "Did you *really* give that quote to that Associated Press correspondent William Smith White, where you said you would surrender only when every one of our bayonets was sticking in a *Boche* belly?"

Kerley cleared his throat, and said, in mock apology, "No, sir. I was not quite so dramatic. What I really said was short, to the point, and very unprintable."

"That's telling the son of a bitch," Birks observed.[25]

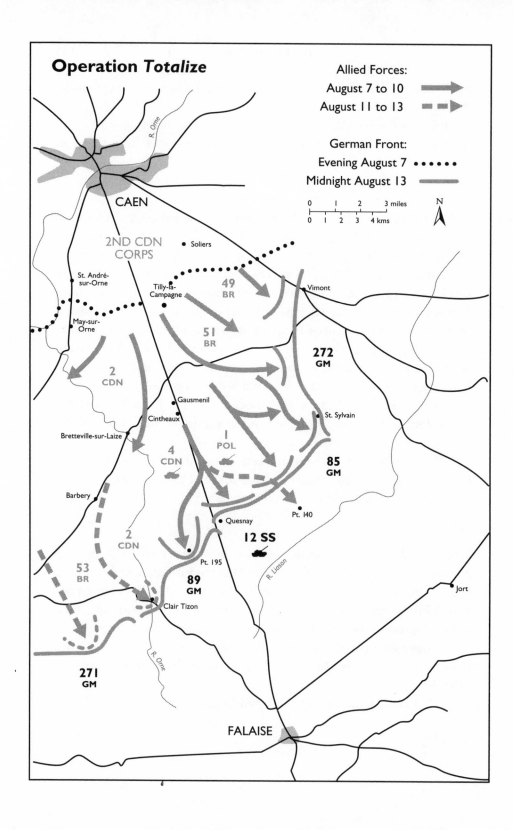

CHAPTER 15

Operation *Totalize*

Monday, August 7, 1944

While the beleaguered men of the US 2d Battalion were hanging on grimly to Mortain's Hill 314 . . . while Patton's Third Army breakout was finally materializing, and the Wiltshires, with Captain Denny's 13th/18th Hussars, were relishing their conquest of Mount Pinçon . . . II Canadian Corps, having doggedly pinned down the majority of German tank divisions on the Caen front for almost two months, was now gearing for the fight of its life.

Tank crews confined to the ruggedness of the *Suisse Normande*, or the arcane terrors of *bocage* fighting, thought often and wistfully of the kinds of terrain over which they had trained: the wide-open, gently rolling plains of the English Downs. But now, gazing south down the dead-straight Caen to Falaise road, the tankers realized that this next twenty miles were not going to be the cross-country swan they had imagined. It would prove to be "the worst possible country for allied armor . . . There were few bumps or depressions where a tank could take a hull down position and provide covering fire."[1]

The pastoral vista revealed a series of softly rising ridges, blanketed with fields of wheat, grown to August height and still unharvested in the stress of the Normandy conflict. But this undulating, open land offered the Germans endless defensive opportunities. Each of those panoramic ridges would become a battlefield, strongly held by a major enemy force guarding its approaches. The Germans could clearly see even the twitch of a

grain stalk for as far as a mile away. The numerous Norman farming villages, modest stone cottages clustered around the inevitable church, had
become a network of fortresses, heavily fortified with mines, mortar installations, and camouflaged antitank guns. The spires offered excellent
observation posts for the enemy. Thick hedges of bramble or poplar concealed *Panzerfaust* parties waiting in ambush.

Following their usual tactics, the Germans had transformed the
wheatfields into death traps. They rigged haystacks to explode, spraying
steel fragments. They erected scores of wooden tanks with dummy guns,
hulled down near the crest of a ridge to intimidate and confuse the enemy.
They booby-trapped dead bodies.[2]

In early August, Lieutenant General Guy Simonds, at the age of forty-one
Canada's youngest corps commander, was ordered to mount Operation
Totalize, a major assault that would break through the enemy lines and
open the road from Caen to Falaise.

Guy Simonds was just the man—perhaps the only man—for the job
of coming up with a winning plan for *Totalize*. He was tough, young
and smart, ruthless and intolerant of inefficiency. In a single day early in
the Normandy campaign he fired one brigadier and two lieutenant
colonels, all close friends. It was said he came in two temperatures: hot
of temperament and cold of manner.[3] In short, "the count," as he was
known, was widely admired and universally considered to be a bit of a
bastard.

To mount the operation, Simonds was given command of three infantry and two armored divisions plus two armored brigades. On paper this
was a powerful force of over a hundred thousand men. However, the infantry divisions Simonds planned to use, the 2d Canadian and 51st Highland, had lost so many men that their rifles companies were at half
strength. In reality, Simonds could employ only about five thousand infantry and three hundred tanks in the first phase of Operation *Totalize*.
While he could call upon his two full-strength armored divisions—each
with two hundred tanks and sixteen hundred infantry—to carry out Phase
II, they had just arrived in Normandy and had never been in combat.

Simonds was squaring off against Sepp Dietrich's I SS *Panzer* Corps,
including the youngest divisional commander in the German army. At
thirty-three, *Standartenführer* (Colonel) Kurt Meyer was every bit as

clever, as handsome, with blue eyes as piercing as Simonds's—and every bit as tough. Every bit the bastard.

Both protagonists knew that the final confrontation was coming. Caen had finally fallen. The next step was obvious: an allied breakout south to Falaise to link up with the Americans and drive the Germans out of Normandy.

When Hitler transferred 1st *Panzer* Division to the Operation *Lüttich* front on the night of August 5/6, he moved up the 89th Infantry Division to oppose the Canadians. This fresh German division from Fifteenth Army's reserve had been formed in Norway early in 1944 with veteran cadres from the eastern front. Transferred to France in June, it trained in the Dieppe area before crossing the Seine in late July. The division was known as the "Horseshoe Division" because of its reliance on horses for its transportation. (The soldiers had nicknamed it the "Wheelbarrow Division" because of the primitive nature of some of its equipment.)[4] The transition was slower than if it were mechanized, therefore taking several days. Daytime troop movement was severely limited by allied air superiority.

The division was "well equipped with personnel and matériel" and in common with other German pocket divisions contained a high proportion of infantry with automatic weapons, mortars, and gun batteries. Out of a total strength of twelve thousand men, seven thousand served in direct combat roles.[5]

Meyer positioned the 12th SS battle groups behind the 89th as a counterattack force, ready to pounce on Simonds's divisions when they made their move, ready to block them from their final objective, Falaise. He had an unusually large number—one hundred—of the dangerous long-range 88mm and 75mm antitank guns manned by the III *Luftwaffe* Flak Corps, and a regiment of carefully camouflaged Nebelwerfer mortars (Moaning Minnies). His proven strength lay in his Tiger and Panther tanks, which far outgunned the British Shermans.[6]

The *Hitlerjugend* commander predicted that the Allies would lay on their usual set-piece attack: a heavy preliminary artillery barrage to get the infantry troops forward, followed by an armored assault. It will be soon, he told his battle group commanders.

Back in Caen, Simonds was trying to outthink his adversary.

It won't work, the set piece, he pondered. A preliminary barrage will warn the enemy of the coming attack. Infantry advancing across those open slopes will be massacred, tanks shot up like ducks in a row. He had heard through a captured German deserter that the 1st SS and 9th SS *Panzer* had been withdrawn from the Caen front, but worried that the 1st SS might be held back in reserve. He certainly knew that his old adversary Meyer and the 12th SS were dug in, waiting.[7]

But how can he get five thousand men and three hundred tanks across open country under the eyes of a watchful and waiting enemy?

Surprise and concealment were the only answers. If he could lay on the attack at night, without alerting the Germans by a preliminary artillery barrage, and then overrun the enemy defenses in darkness before they could retaliate, he might have a chance. But how?

Moving several thousand fighting men with their tanks and equipment through unfamiliar territory at night invited chaos. With no illumination and with compass readings made unreliable by the metal of the tanks, they would be totally lost.

During the next weeks, working up to twenty hours a day, Simonds's fertile mind conjured up a hatful of tricks, many of them untried.

By bouncing the rays of huge searchlights off low clouds, sufficient light could be produced to guide his men to their objectives. On previous attempts, although successful, the technique had given the troops the uneasy feeling of being center stage under a spotlight; they had dubbed it (not with enthusiasm) "Monty's moonlight."

The attacking divisions won't be able to identify their boundaries? Bofors guns streaking green phosphorescent tracer along the flanks of the columns—another Simonds innovation—will help lead the force to its destination.

Compasses won't work inside metal tanks? Use radio beams. Give the commanders earphones that would signal a series of dots and dashes if they veered too far right or left.

Replacing the preattack artillery barrage designed to keep the enemy heads down, Simonds had an idea that 21 Army Group had never, ever tried before. "I'll get the air force to bomb the hell out of the German lines along our flanks just before we go forward," he told his sceptical staff officers. "We'll save the artillery barrage until the actual assault."

There followed an intense period of negotiation to sell the crazy, complex, Canadian plan for air support to a testy Royal Air Force. Air Chief Marshal Harris was "horrified." His bombers had never been trained to the task of close troop support at night. How could they accurately identify bomb lines in the dark without endangering the men on the ground?

Simonds had an answer for that one, too. Artillery would fire colored concentrations of smoke to indicate the targets. Pathfinder planes could then come in low, dropping markers that would be confirmed by a "bombs away" signal from the "Master Bomber."[8] (So meticulous was his planning that a special planeload of cotton wool was flown from England—enough to make a hundred thousand earplugs to avoid the dangers of blast deafness.)[9]

Another major challenge in planning this surprise attack was to figure out a way to bring the infantry forward along with the armor, securely protected from enemy small-arms fire and shell fragments. Historically, infantry's role had been to move up on foot ahead of or closely behind the tanks to protect the vulnerable armor from hazards such as enemy bazookas and antitank guns. Historically, infantry had been mowed down every time they crossed the open ground.

Everyone knew the infantry would be more effective if they had armored personnel carriers to keep them apace with the tanks. Simonds did something about it. The artillery had traded in their self-propelled guns, known to all as "Priests," for the more familiar towed twenty-five-pounders. The D-Day beach areas were cluttered with these abandoned Priests. Why not convert them into armored troop-carrying vehicles?

He called in his engineers.

In an apple orchard near Bayeux on August 2, 250 engineers from fourteen British and Canadian units of mechanical and electrical engineers converged on a field full of Priests and began the "defrocking" process to convert them into armored troop carriers.

This ad hoc Advanced Workshop Detachment was code-named "Kangaroo," and the troop carriers were named for them. (The soldiers irreverently dubbed their carriers "unfrocked priests" or "holy rollers.") The conversion entailed stripping them of their guns, welding armor plating around the gun aperture, and completely overhauling the engines.

Finding enough armor plate became the major challenge. The "Kangaroo Men" went on a spree. They cannibalized some from "W" crocks (tanks beyond repair). They raided a steel mill near Caen. The navy complained crossly that hunks of steel plating were being cut from stranded landing craft.

Each Kangaroo Man was assigned a task, to be monotonously repeated over and over on successive vehicles. Craftsman A. M. Campbell of the 2d Tank Troops Workshop concentrated solely on track tightening. As he later recalled, he worked steadily for the four days from 0400 to 2300 hours, "so busy he didn't even know what the next fellow was doing."[10]

Working these eighteen-hour stints the engineers had managed to reconstruct seventy-two troop-carrying Kangaroos, each capable of transporting a dozen men. At 2000 hours on August 5, they were declared ready for troops to practice embussing and debussing.

For the first time in the history of warfare, at least some of the five thousand attacking infantry—in this case, 10 percent—could follow close behind the tanks and disembark right on to their objectives. Some of the remaining riflemen would be carried in alternate bulletproof vehicles or by hanging on to the backs of the armor; the rest were assigned a "walking infantry" role as mop-up troops.

"A pity we did not have something like that," Private Bill Hinde, Queen's Regiment (British 7th Armored Division) noted enviously. "It would have saved a lot of lives."[11]

Finally, it was time to brief the commanders.

Ninth Brigade commander John Rockingham described the "O" (Orders) Group when Simonds unveiled his startling plan: "We were ordered to advance our tanks and troop-carrying vehicles at night. But navigation was nearly impossible in the dark. Guy said we had to use direction finders to keep the armor on direction. 'You know perfectly well you can't put compasses in tanks,' we told him, 'there's just too much metal around them.'

"But Simonds just said he'd figure a way, and he did."[12]

One 51st Highland Scottish officer, less impressed, noted, "I well recall his "O" Group before *Totalize* when the several division comds [commanders] sat in a circle under the pine trees (all being much older than GGS [Guy Simonds] and some with desert sand in their shoes) to whom he opened, 'Gentlemen we will do this attack at night with armor.' Their jaws dropped."[13]

The attack, he told them, would be centered on an unusually narrow front. Two infantry divisions and two armored brigades, packed "closer than Piccadilly Circus at rush hour" into twenty-eight tight columns, would form one enormous battering ram of men and armor to smash a hole through the German line. (It was, some remembered, a tactic that had served Napoleon well, using cavalry instead of tanks.)

Simonds went on. Furthermore, for the first time, instead of foot soldiers leading armor, the 350 tanks would head up the assault, followed by the mounted infantry. More jaws dropped.

The main north–south Caen–Falaise road would be the dividing line between the Canadians and the Scots. The 51st Highlanders with the 33d Armored Brigade would advance down the left, or east side; 2 Canadian Infantry Division and 2 Canadian Armored Brigade, with the 8th Recce Regiment, would be on the right of the road.

For the second phase of *Totalize*, at 1400 hours the same afternoon, Tuesday, August 8, the newly arrived and inexperienced 4 Canadian Armored and 1 Polish Armored Divisions would launch another massed armored assault, pushing through to Falaise. Flying Fortresses from the US Eighth Air Force would lay on a massive bombing raid to clear their way.

There had been some initial misgivings in using the Highland Division. Like the Desert Rats—and for much the same reason—the keenly honed fighting spirit of the Highlanders had dulled following their elating victories of Alamein, the Western Desert, and Sicily. Their commander inspired little confidence. Montgomery solved this.

Top Secret. Personal and Eyes Only for CIGS from Field-Marshal Montgomery:

Regret to report . . . that 51 Div is at present not, repeat not, battleworthy. It does not fight with determination and has failed in every operation it has been given to do. It cannot fight the Germans successfully. I consider the divisional commander to blame and I am removing him from command. I consider that the best man to put to 51 Div in its present state is Rennie and I have confidence he would bring it up to its former fine state.[14]

Late in July, his arm still in a sling from wounds incurred in an earlier Normandy battle, Major General Thomas Rennie was brought in to replace the hastily deposed division commander. An officer of 7th Battalion Black Watch describes the electric effect Tom Rennie had on the troops: "The morning we knew he was coming back—he was arriving at 11 A.M.— you could just *feel* the morale go up. We were back on top again. Rennie understood the Scots; he was an old friend coming back."[15]

From that moment, the 51st gradually regained its spark: "He was the most accessible and least pretentious of generals, whom every officer and man could boast as a friend," the chronicler of the Black Watch related.

> He had an impish sense of humor, and a cheerfulness which was proof against every crisis or disaster. He had a great flair for doing things the right way, and complete confidence in his own judgement, which was shared by all around him. His courage was far beyond the ordinary, but there was nothing flamboyant about him . . . There was no Jock in the Division who did not know his duffel-coated figure.[16]

Rennie made it his business to ensure that non-Scots—the English and Irish reinforcements, and the Canadian Canloan officers who came to join the Highland Division—were quickly assimilated as "instant Jocks." These honorary Scotsmen soon picked up the flavor of their adopted fighting mates: the wry humor, the verve, the clannish loyalties, and, above all, the flat-out, hell-for-leather Lochinvarian courage.

Shortly before midnight on Monday, August 7, 1,020 RAF bombers thundered overhead and the mammoth armored/motorized infantry attack was launched. A startled enemy force looking skyward saw a terrifying sight: a *son et lumière* of huge proportions. The pyrotechnics: an enormous green glow on their right, a red one on their left; a black sky splintered with brilliant streaks of green tracer fire. The ear-shattering noise: the thunder of more than one thousand heavy bombers, the crash of some 3,462 tons of bombs cratering the ground on the flanks.

At the start line, the two-mile-long column of one thousand tanks and armored vehicles of the mounted infantry simultaneously revved their engines with a collective roar that shook the earth. This huge battering ram of steel was packed so tightly together that a squadron leader of the Sherbrooke Fusiliers, Major Sydney Radley-Walters, found he could traverse the two-mile length of the column, jumping from tank to tank, with his feet never touching the ground.[17] As the tanks crossed the start line, a massive barrage of neutralizing artillery fire was unleashed, adding new agonies for the German defenders.

A German soldier with an
MG-42 machine gun

German magazine features
12th SS Hitlerjugend,
defenders of Normandy.

A menacing Tiger Tank
at close range

Cretar

Model

Simonds

Kluge

Maczek

Meyer

Kristen IOS

A German tank crew camouflages an 88mm self-propelled gun.

A dead German gunner slumped behind a Nebelwerfer

A german tank crew atop a Tiger

Nursing sisters

Troops enjoy respite from battle.

Capt. Reynold Erichson

Michael Wittman

Lt. Sydney Jary

Maj Ned Amy

Lt. Cliff Chadderton

Kurten T.O.S.

Cpl. Sidney Bates, VC

Maj. Leonard Dull

Lt. Wladyslaw Klaptocz

Capt. Bill Whiteside

Maj. S.V. Radley-Walters

Sgt. Curtis Culin

U.S. Thuderbolt

F/L Bill Baggs pictured with a Typhoon

A Typhoon of Squadron 121

Wrecked German vehicles near St. Lambert-sur-Dives

Preparation for Operation *Tractable*, August 14, 1944

"As close as we shall ever get to seeing a man win a Victoria Cross."
Major David Currie (third from left, holding pistol) at St. Lambert

German prisoners at St. Lambert

MICHAEL GUTOWSKI

Captain Jerzy Wasilewski,
Commander, 10 Polish
Mounted Rifles,
in Normandy.

The Polish Armored Division
on the move

MICHAEL GUTOWSKI

Captured German officers

Patrol hunts down snipers

GIs hunting snipers

Tanks of the U.S.
5th Armored Division

David Currie, VC

Prisoners from the 85th Infantry
Division, Operation *Tractable*

GI with German paratrooper

Falaise: Destroyed

The rubble of Argentan,
August 21, 1944

The Corridor of Death

To keep on direction, each tank commander clung desperately to the tracer fire and the faint pinpoint of light from the tank ahead, eyes smarting from the acrid smell of exhaust fumes and cordite. The drivers' vision was almost obliterated by the clouds of dust raised by the impact of the powerful bombs on rain-starved August plains. Smoke and exhaust from hundreds of heavy vehicles added to this dense fog. Often their only recourse if trouble developed was to jump down from the tank and lead it on foot.

In the ensuing confusion and chaos the tanks forged ahead blindly over uncharted rough country. They rammed their way through hedges, lurched into ditches, flushed out enemy snipers skulking in wheatfields and behind hedgerows. Incredibly, the armor led the infantry to their designated points of disembarking. The tanks reached their objectives and quickly consolidated to beat off the anticipated counterattacks.

The Germans were stunned by the devastation caused by the bombs and heavy artillery falling around them. Wheatfields had new crops now: dead bodies of animals and the torn and burned corpses of young *soldaten* dressed in field grey. Cottages and churches were hulled ruins . . . blackened haystacks and denuded tree trunks silhouetted the skyline.

The "walking infantry"—the Canadian 6th Brigade and the Scottish 152d—followed in the wake of their mounted comrades. They had the so-called mopping-up tasks, clearing out villages that the armor had been ordered to bypass. These proved to be the toughest-fought battles of all.[18]

The German defenders had fortified these positions and vowed they would never surrender them. Over the previous weeks the Canadians had been thwarted every time they tried to seize them.

In May-sur-Orne, enemy troops in this small hamlet had held out against Les Fusiliers Mont-Royal so desperately and for so long that Crocodile flame-throwing tanks had to be brought up. The terrifying jets of flaming fuel finally flushed out the defenders. Snipers in Rocquancourt held the village for six hours against the South Saskatchewans. The Queen's Own Cameron Highlanders of Winnipeg had a stiff fight at Fontenay, which they finally captured—but at what cost: the commanding officer was badly wounded; the brigade major who took his place was killed, and four senior officers wounded. Companies led by lieutenants and a sergeant major eventually wore down the German hold.

Another of these villages was Tilly-la-Campagne, a picturesque farming hamlet of grey Norman fieldstone originally defended by the fanatic 1st SS *Leibstandarte-Adolf Hitler.* The church had been reinforced into a strongpoint, its steeple giving the Germans sweeping observation of the Canadian positions. After two weeks, during which the SS fought off countless attacks, the grey stone had become smashed rubble, stained crimson with German and Canadian blood. When the SS *Panzers* were shifted to Mortain, they turned over their carefully constructed defenses to the newly arrived German 89th Infantry Division.

The job of capturing Tilly had then been given to the seasoned Highland 152d Brigade, who ordered 2d Seaforth to lay on the initial attack. No dent was made. Then a company of the 5th Seaforth was sent in as reinforcement. The fierce fighting and tragic consequence to the company was described in the Scottish history:

> Their commander, Grant Murray, was killed along with ten of his men. Captain Murray was found lying in front of the German defensive line with the dead of No. 17 Platoon round about him. They had obviously had a fierce hand-to-hand struggle with the enemy, for one or two bodies were found actually in the German line with dead Bosche beside them.[19]

Finally, a squadron of tanks from 154th Brigade attacked Tilly from the rear and after two attempts they liberated the village and captured the only survivors: one German officer and some thirty infantrymen.

By noon, after nearly twelve hours of combat, the *Totalize* force had penetrated German lines by some six or seven miles. They were on their objectives, digging in and looking forward to a hot meal. The German reaction was swift. General von Kluge radioed Hitler: "A breakthrough has occurred near Caen the like of which we have never seen."[20] This was a triple blow to the German High Command. News was filtering in that morning that the Mortain counterattack was not going well. They learned, too, that Patton's Third Army was nearing Le Mans—dangerously close to encircling them.

General Eberbach was concerned enough to rush forward to meet *Standartenführer* Kurt Meyer at 12th SS *Panzer* headquarters, just a mile or two from the approaching allied forces—an almost unheard-of act by an army commander. Meyer, aptly known as *der Schnel Meyer*—"Rapid Meyer"—informed his senior officer of the events in the early hours of the morning. When he had seen the artificially illuminated sky he realized that the long-expected attack was being launched.

As the sun rose on the waiting battlefield, the day was clear, hot, and windless. The smoke and dust still hung shroudlike, the ground mist thickened by enemy smoke shells, mortars, and artillery shell fire.[21]

Later in the morning, Meyer jumped into his scout car and drove north along the Caen–Falaise road. Through his binoculars he was stunned to view what he later described as a menacing landscape of 150 allied tanks lined up for an attack. Strangely, the force was motionless.

On his way, he encountered soldiers from the German 89th Infantry Division, retreating in disorder after a night of terror. The SS commander paused to light a cigar and strolled out in their path. Ever the showman, he challenged the deserters. So! Am I to fight the British by myself? Are you such cowards that you run away?[22]

Regrouped and reenergized, the German 89th Division was reinforced with SS-*Sturmbannführer* Hans Waldmüller's armored battle group (*Kampfgruppe*) with thirty-nine Mark IVs, in addition to Captain Michel Wittman's troop of Tigers, and *Kampfgruppe* Krause.

Meyer sent out his powerful *Kampfgruppe* (battle group) of Tigers, stressing the urgency of the situation. The legendary *Panzer* ace, thirty-year-old Captain Michel Wittman, shook hands with his commander. "Our good Michel laughed his boyish laughter and climbed into his Tiger," Meyer recounted. "Until that moment, 138 tanks had become his victims. He adjusted his throat microphone and ordered, '*Panzer Marsch!*' "[23]

As was his style, Wittman led his troop of four Tigers in a wild charge across open country. It had worked for him at Villers *Bocage* on June 10, where, in five minutes, he single-handedly destroyed twenty-five tanks and twenty-eight other tracked vehicles and self-propelled guns (SPs) of the 3d County of London Yeomanry (British 22d Armored Brigade).

This time, it would backfire. This time he was in the gunsights of "Rad" and Tom—Major Sidney Radley-Walters, commanding a Canadian squadron of Sherbrooke Fusiliers and Captain Tom Boardman, commanding a British squadron of the 1st Northamptonshire Yeomanry.

After the early-morning attack, Radley-Walters and his squadron had hulled down in a protected wooded area, waiting for the second phase of *Totalize* to start. He spotted Wittman's troop of four Tigers and their supporting force of thirty-nine Mark IVs and self-propelled guns (SPs) storming up the east side of the Caen–Falaise highway. Rad was not aware that the guns of the British squadron on the opposite side of the road were also beading in on Wittman and his squadron. It was, in fact, an ambush the like of which tankers only dream—a Tiger kill.

The Tiger was the most feared weapon in Normandy. Allied tankers were used to odds of losing five or six Shermans for every Tiger. Now the possibility of one-on-one was a dazzling concept. Neither man had any idea that their quarry was the infamous Michel Wittman—they were not even aware of the identity of the Black Knight.

Radley-Walters describes the event:

> I had moved into the little village of Gaumesnil. We got behind some bush that had a rock wall around it and we cut the rock down so we could get our tank guns over the front to be well protected. I only had two seventeen-pounder Fireflies; the rest were all 75mms—twelve altogether.
>
> When we saw the German attack coming in I just kept yelling, "Hold off! Hold off!" until they got reasonably close. We opened fire at about five hundred yards. The lead tank, the one closest to the road, was knocked out. Behind it were a couple of SPs. I personally got one of the SPs right on the Caen–Falaise road.[24]

At about the same time, Tom Boardman fired as well, but from seventeen hundred yards.

A shot struck the turret of the lead tank. The Tiger started to burn. More shots hit the next, and the next. Suddenly there was an explosion. Wittman's tank blew up in a sheet of flames. The Black Knight—the ace who in the combined Russian and Western fronts knocked out 138 tanks and self-propelled guns and disabled 132 antitank guns, this German superhero with the Knight's Cross with Oak Leaves—was dead.

There can be no conclusive proof as to which squadron, Canadian or British—or which commander, Rad or Tom—actually brewed Wittman's tank, but the results were spectacular, and to troopers who had taken a lot of beating from Tigers, no small victory.[25]

.   .   .

There was a strange hush of expectancy. With the original attacking *Totalize* force firmly on their objectives, the next wave of five thousand men—two fresh armored divisions, the 4th Canadian and 1st Polish—was assembled on the start line to initiate their part in the overall plan. These units had landed in Normandy only a few days before, and had not had an opportunity to rehearse the plan, as had the veterans spearheading the assault.

Because of the inexperience of the units, Simonds had gone to some lengths to organize protective bombing by the American 8th Air Force. This, by the plan, was to herald the second phase of *Totalize*. Simonds had ordered all units to wait while this second daylight-bombing raid was launched. The timing was precise: The launching of the armored attack would coincide with the conclusion of the bombing raid: 1355 hours.

Just a few miles south, however, Meyer was ordering his units into position to mount a counterattack. The 12th SS H-Hour was coordinated for 1230 hours.

The Allies looked up expectantly as the Pathfinders for the 678 silver American B-17 Flying Fortresses circled enemy lines, preparing to drop a directional marker to guide the American bombers to German positions. Meyer, too, spotted the Pathfinder as it flew overhead. He quickly grasped the implications and raced to his radio: "Get closer! Get closer!" he yelled to his commanders. He reckoned that if his *Panzers* remained on high ground, they would be destroyed.[26] His men obediently sped for cover nearer to the Canadian lines, safe from the bombs that now crashed uselessly onto their former positions.

The bombers came on with what one observer described as an aura of "ghastly relentlessness. The first huge flight passed directly over our farmyard and others followed . . . And then the bombs came. They began up ahead as the crackle of popcorn and almost instantly swelled into a monstrous fury of noise that seemed surely to destroy all the world ahead of us."[27]

The allied soldiers were stricken to see two groups from the US air force, each consisting of twelve planes, become directionally confused by the ground fog that lingered in the smoke-filled windless air, and mistakenly begin dropping the bombs on their own, densely packed units. Worst hit were the Poles and infantry from 3 Canadian Division, who suffered

315 casualties in all, 65 killed. The divisional commander was badly wounded. One regiment lost one hundred officers and men.

"It was a grim thing to witness just before going into battle," a Canadian regimental history relates, "To see your own people bombed by your own people. The thing that finally stopped this horrible mistake was a little Moth artillery observation plane that flew up between the bombers and the bombed."[28]

A normally hard-nosed and tough Scottish regimental sergeant major, seeing the blast kill his lads behind the lines, summed up the grief and horror in a simple sentence: "No trace of 'em. Not even a hand to shake goodbye to."[29]

In the first moments of the first battle for these wholly inexperienced Canadian and Polish divisions, they were smashed by their own aircraft. Now the stunned survivors were to be confronted by Meyer's quickly assembled counterattack, which stormed into their midst even while the air force bombs were thundering around them.

At 1335 hours, the Polish 24th Lancers, with fifty-two Sherman tanks, advanced confidently onto the battlefield to launch the second phase of *Totalize*. They could not know that the *Luftwaffe* had moved a strong battalion of 88mm guns into range, or that a vengeful *Panzer* troop was waiting, hunkered down out of sight in a gully. Guns capable of shattering a Sherman turret at two thousand yards were now waiting within two hundred yards. The German gunners, flabbergasted at their good fortune, fired shot after shot at the hapless Poles. The Lancers bravely fired back at the enemy they could not see.

In five minutes, forty tanks were in flames. The sight of men on fire, scrambling out of the blazing vehicles, was viewed in horror by their British allies, who described it as "like watching a field full of haystacks set on fire by an arsonist."[30]

The *Panzers* then turned their guns on an English troop. Their diary told the sad story:

> Our Two Troop, after inflicting losses on the enemy, disappeared into oblivion from the wireless network like a Roman legion marching into the forests of an earlier-day Germany or like an aircraft disappearing over the Antarctic. Except that [the troop] was only about three minutes walk from where we sat on the open hill-

side . . . Somewhere in those woods beyond the gully, Two Troop perished.

We counted their survivors as they trudged back from the gully, but there were not enough survivors. Count them how many times we would, the mathematics of our sadness and desperation still failed to tally with our hopes.[31]

CHAPTER 16

Take Hill 195 . . . Now!

General Simonds was gambling for high stakes in Operation *Totalize*. So far, his gamble was paying off. His night attack had taken the enemy by surprise and had propelled sixty thousand combat troops eight miles deep into enemy territory in the early hours of August 8. But the ill-fated bombing raid later on the same afternoon that was to initiate the next phase of the attack backfired. It failed to subdue the Germans and, in fact, caused heavy casualties and confusion among the unfortunate allied soldiers caught by "friendly bombs."

The 1st Polish and 4th Canadian Armored Divisions—fresh to Normandy and totally unrehearsed in the battle plan—were plunged into exactly the situation Simonds had tried so hard to forestall. They clashed head-on, with no support, against a well-entrenched and heavily armed enemy. That they managed to advance at all was a great achievement. For one infantry battalion, the Canadian Argylls, it was a superb effort, ranking in tactical brilliance and raw courage with the best in any war. For another armored unit, the British Columbia Regiment (BCR), it was a gallant effort, but one of the most disastrous of the war.

Hill 195, a gentle knoll midway between Caen and Falaise, was a green and pleasant picnic spot in peacetime. It was now a formidable obstacle in war. Guns dug into its rise could command movement from every quarter. It was the key to the capture of Falaise.

Late in the evening on the day following Operation *Totalize*, an impatient Simonds fired out an order, very succinctly, to the BCR (British Columbia Regiment): "Take Hill 195! Now!"

Lieutenant Colonel Don Worthington, the commanding officer, ordered the assault. It would be his first battle, personally, and the first for his armored regiment. He was determined to succeed.

The BCR's fifty-five tanks moved off into the darkness at 0200 hours on August 9, with their supporting infantry, the Algonquin Regiment. They were driving blindly into countryside unrelieved by any landmarks, on a complex route, with enemy on all sides of them. Encountering sporadic pockets of resistance, Colonel Worthington dropped off one squadron of tanks and one company of infantry to deal with any further attacks.

At 0650 hours they climbed the rise to what they believed was their objective and frantically dug into the gravelly hilltop before the inevitable counterattack. They radioed brigade headquarters of their successful arrival and new position. Brigade was puzzled; the fix given of the BCR position did not correlate with any map reference.

In one of war's strange, tragic misfires, Worthington had taken a wrong turn in the night and ended up four miles east of Hill 195. He was deep in enemy territory and totally surrounded by an agitated German force.

Worthington was now waiting for reinforcements to consolidate his hold—reinforcements that would never come because he was, in effect, lost.

Kurt Meyer was puzzled, too. How had the allied tanks penetrated so far into the German lines? He sent one of his lieutenants in a scout car to do a reconnaissance; the officer did not return. Clearly, he had been captured.

The situation was dangerous. This penetration by the Allies gave their gunners a clear view of the Laison Valley—Meyer's last possible defensive position north of Falaise. Furthermore, a fresh German infantry division, Lieutenant General Fiebig's 85th, was moving in momentarily and had been designated Worthington's hill as its headquarters.

Meanwhile, Worthington innocently hung on to what he still believed was his proper objective. He saw Sherman tanks approaching—relief at

last. It was a Polish squadron, but the enemy quickly drove it off. He saw
Typhoons attacking and signaled them with yellow smoke to indicate an
allied presence.

They obediently dived on the attacking enemy, but later sorties
blasted defenders and attackers alike. The Typhoon pilots had no means
of communicating with ground troops. It never occurred to them that the
tanks were part of Worthington's force.

The BCR dilemma was partially a result of the fact that the Royal Air
Force obstinately refused to establish a system where ground troops could
communicate directly with aircraft. The US Army Air Force commander,
Major General Pete Quesada, had introduced the technique to the American armored and infantry regiments the previous month with great success. But the British weren't to be budged.

Canadian historian Terry Copp recently noted that,

> if such a method had been available to 4 Canadian Armored Di-
> vision on 9 August, the Typhoons and Spitfires, which repeatedly
> bombed, rocketed and strafed friend and foe alike [around Wor-
> thington's position], would have received targeting information
> from Worthington and would have informed . . . headquarters of
> their exact location.[1]

At daybreak, Meyer's *Panzers*, recovering from the surprise of this
major penetration behind their lines, now poured every kind of retaliation
on the helpless Canadian tanks and infantry. Tigers and Panthers attacked
from every direction, inflicting huge casualties. But the Canadians refused
to give in.

One Algonquin officer recorded the grim scene as the hours spun
grimly on:

> The crash of exploding shells, the quick, lethal scream of the 88s
> going over, the cries and groans of the wounded, and the inde-
> scribable odor of burning flesh now began to have an effect on the
> defenders. Firing became wilder; men would rise out of their slits,
> stand up and curse the foe that was invisible, yet so close, and so
> inexorable. It was difficult to hold the wounded down, many of
> whom were now delirious with pain and thirst. The morphine
> supply had long since been used up, water was exhausted, and

there was little that could be done with the stricken except to hold them down out of the direct fire line.[2]

With dwindling forces and a diminishing supply of ammunition, Worthington ordered his last eight tanks to make a run for it, taking to safety as many of the wounded as they could. He covered the initial dash himself with machine-gun fire. They got out safely to Polish lines, but still the position of the isolated Canadians was not relayed to brigade.

Although suffering mortar wounds himself, Worthington now reorganized the defenses so well that they were, at least for a brief time, secure. A British officer who was in the position wrote later: "At 1830 hours a strong enemy counterattack came in. The infantry and tank crews met it with small arms and grenades. At this stage of the battle I saw one soldier, shot through the thigh and with a broken leg, still throwing grenades. Every man who was still conscious was firing some type of weapon."[3] Serious losses were inflicted on the enemy, who then withdrew.

"At about this time," the official Canadian history relates, "Lieutenant-Colonel Worthington, who had directed the fight with cool courage throughout the day, was killed by a mortar bomb. At dusk, as a final German attack was coming in, the surviving Canadians who could slipped out of the position. Most of them succeeded in making their way into the Polish lines."[4]

The British Columbia Regiment had been savaged. Forty men were killed, thirty-four were taken prisoner, and another thirty-eight were wounded. The regiment lost forty-seven tanks—almost its entire tank strength—in its first day's fighting. The Algonquin Regiment's total casualties came to 128. Lieutenant Colonel Don Hay and forty-four other Algonquin officers and men were killed or died of wounds; forty-five were taken prisoner. The rest were wounded and evacuated.

As darkness fell the whole area was lit up by the dozens of tanks on fire. In a letter to a fellow officer, Major Keith Stirling of the Algonquin Regiment described the ordeal of being captured by the Germans:

A Jerry approached holding his rifle in the air. All of us were gathered up and taken out on the road and searched . . . but not very well. We were marched down the road and then during the march I remembered the notes in my book about all the supporting arms, etc. So, as I walked, I tore page after page out and tore it to bits. I took the book out and turned it over and did the same with the other side. I did this not being able to see which side had the writing on it. I had about five maps but as they were bulky I decided to wait to get rid of them.

The prisoners had managed to carry one badly wounded soldier with them, who was finally taken to a first-aid post. The rest of the wounded were left behind by the Germans and brought in sometime later by the Allies.

Stirling described being marched about two and one-half miles to a little village and taken to a headquarters in a barn. "I managed to hide the maps under a pile of hay. We were searched and all the stuff put on a table and an Intelligence Officer went over it."

The German confiscated his watch, wallet, and other contents of his pocket.

> I was so tired I don't remember getting my stuff back from him, but the next day I had the pen and pencil set, my wallet (without any money) and a few pictures.
>
> By this time our group consisted of about twenty-five or thirty men, mostly all Algonquins but a few strangers. The Jerries gave us all a card, which if we filled [it] out would inform our relatives where we were. On this card was a Red Cross. The information they wanted on the card was correct (except for the name of the company). I advised [our group] not to fill them out, but many did.
>
> We marched all the next day to a place that used to be a racing stable. There we had our first food, a bowl of soup, since we were captured. There were a lot of prisoners in the place, including Americans and British. We stayed in this place for a few days, and then started our march across France to Germany, to POW life.[5]

Hill 195, that still-elusive knoll so essential as the gateway to Falaise, remained in enemy hands. Again Simonds's orders come through: "Take it!"

This time it was the Canadian Argyll and Sutherland Highlanders who were given the job. Commandeer any tanks or guns you need, the brigadier told commanding officer, Lieutenant Colonel Dave Stewart. Just take it.

Argyll Captain Bill Whiteside related the outcome: "Our boss, Dave Stewart—while he didn't refuse to follow orders, he changed them if he had a different idea."

"Different" was what Dave Stewart was all about. "He didn't like Brigade telling him what to do," Captain Bob Patterson of the Argylls agreed. "He was quite a guy; a good soldier. But he didn't like authority."

"He never wore a steel helmet. He just would wear his little Balmoral tam, at a cocky angle. He thought about the men, not the job, and the men loved him."

On the night of 9/10 August, Stewart put his unorthodox plan into action: no tanks, no artillery, no tracer, no bombing. Just his men. Silently.

Patterson relates: "We had an excellent scout platoon leader. He posted his men at the various junctures of the path to guide us up to the top."

"He went himself and surveyed a sort of a back-door route into Hill 195," Whiteside added. "The scouts were placed at points to keep people in line, get them through fences and that sort of thing, and company after company moved up the hill into position."

Bob Patterson:

The battalion followed the scouts perfectly up to the top in total silence. Then we surprised the Germans, got in without any casualties. The enemy counterattacked later on but they didn't make it; so we had a dominant position at the top of Hill 195 and it was successful. It was one of the best things the Argylls ever did.

Bill Whiteside:

My part was the antitank guns and I didn't have very much to do because at no time did tanks attack us. We knew where they were, because our forward company could see them. They put in an infantry attack, but we were able to mow that down. About six abortive efforts were made.

Then at about six o'clock in the morning, a funny thing happened. We'd been taking this sporadic mortar fire, not heavy but it just kept coming. Somebody said to me, "There are Germans in those trees about a quarter of a mile from here. From the trees they can see the whole of our area."

So we spun our antitank guns around and we knocked those buggers out of the trees. You could see them falling out![6]

The Argylls had outwitted the determined force of Meyer's 12th SS and Fiebig's 85th Infantry in seizing and holding this important enemy defensive position. They had penetrated two additional miles behind enemy lines.

They achieved this with the cool wit and ingenuity of one CO who cockily wore a Balmoral tam into battle, and with the verve that was becoming a trademark of these citizen-soldiers of Canada.

CHAPTER 17

Patton: Farther and Faster

Like a cork out of a bottle—one that had contained a wildly impatient Lieutenant General George Patton long enough—Third US Army burst from the Avranches Corridor.

Patton flung all three corps of his newly activated army, some 150,000 men, in three directions across France—west, south, and east. Incredibly, with over a hundred miles separating each flank, the circus master had all three rings going hell-bent toward their objectives.

He was everywhere. In his low-flying L-5 Liaison plane, he criss-crossed his battlefields, devising new routes and tactics to get farther, faster. Then, in his jeep, he screeched up to the lead troops, even leaping onto the vehicle's hood to urge the men on. He would be seen marching in the ranks, standing at a crossroads or on a bridge, waving the units through.

Patton's energy and enthusiasm were contagious. He harnessed the two skills that are inherently American: mechanization and improvisation. The media loved him. At last they had something to write about. And the tank crews loved him. Finally, he had those much-maligned American Sherman tanks doing what they did best—fighting a mobile action.

His aide, who scarcely ever left his side at this time, described him as "pushing, pulling, exhorting, cajoling, raising merry hell, and having the time of his life." He was completely unconcerned for his own personal safety. On at least one occasion he drove right through a German division. "He had an uncanny gift for sweeping men into doing things which they did not believe they were capable of doing, which they really did not want to do."[1]

The Americans swept eastward against only light opposition. Their troops were treated as heroes, riding jubilantly atop their tanks into liberated villages, being pelted with flowers and rewarded with shots of Calvados by grateful citizens. Even the Germans were in awe of Patton. Lieutenant General Fritz Bayerlein, commander-in-chief of the *Panzer Lehr* Division, had the misfortune of being in the path, first of *Cobra*'s devastation and then of the Patton cyclone. He was to observe: "The dash of Patton's army through the narrow corridor into the deep rear of an unfamiliar region belongs to the boldest ventures of the battle in France, and demonstrates in the best possible light the discipline, the aggressiveness, and the drive of the American armored force."[2]

Following in the wake of this mobile army's huge advances, the Supply Corps faced almost unprecedented challenges. Patton had thrust out in many directions, like branches on a tree, but it was through the narrow trunk of that tree that all his supplies had to flow.

"Good heavens," Winston Churchill exclaimed when he was briefed on the numbers of divisions racing through France, "how do you feed them?"[3]

He was assured that the Supply Corps did manful work each day trucking up food and fresh water and, most important of all, weapons and ammunition for 150,000 troops. They maintained two roads, the main one outgoing and a secondary one incoming. Third Army's seven hundred tanks and thousands of vehicles had to be maintained with fuel and equipment, and its artillery regiments resupplied with all manner of ammo.

Patton wasn't in the least perturbed that by flinging his divisions deep into uncharted country he had no protection on either flank. Everywhere he went he preached his gospel: "don't worry about our flanks; our tactical air force will clobber them; go where you can as fast as you can."[4] He had great faith in Major General Pete Quesada's 9th Tactical Air Force to get him out of trouble. If he outran his ground-supply channel, Quesada assured him that his B-26 Marauders could airlift two thousand tons of supplies to him daily as needed. If threatened by enemy attack, he would call down the P-47s, those much-dreaded *Jabos*.

Patton had equal confidence in the effectiveness of fighter-bomber close support. The US 367th Fighter Group noted:

> With the breakout of the ground forces from the St. Lô area, close air support of Patton's Third Army became the order of the day. First big bag came with attacks on the German Seventh Army which, to prevent being surrounded, was withdrawing eastward through the gap between Falaise and Argentan. Five convoys and 100 Tiger tanks were destroyed on one day.[5]

Patton confirmed this in his diary:

> Just east of Le Mans was one of the best examples of armor and air cooperation I have ever seen. For about two miles the road was full of enemy motor transport and armor, many of which bore the unmistakable calling card of the P-47 fighter bomber—namely, a group of 50-caliber holes in the concrete.[6]

On August 8, 1944, two events influenced a dramatic switch in allied planning. Up until that moment, the Allies had assumed that Hitler's next move would be to withdraw his forces to a new defensive line along the Seine, toward Paris. No one expected him to attack farther west, as he had at Mortain, thus putting his divisions firmly in the allied net. Certainly no one expected him to persist on keeping his troops there when the Mortain counterattack failed.

In fact, Montgomery, for one, was praying that Hitler would hang on at Mortain.

7th August 44.
    Personal for CIGS [Chief of the Imperial General Staff] from General Montgomery (Cipher one time Pad):
    If only the Germans will go on attacking at Mortain for a few more days it seems that they might not, repeat not, be able to get away.[7]

Ultra gave reassurance that the German supreme command still planned to persist in the Operation *Lüttich* counterattack and in fact drag even more forces into the pocket instead of evacuating them. A huge window of fresh opportunity opened up to the Allies: the possibility of encircling the German armies. The Canadians and British in the north were driving south on the Caen–Falaise road; the Americans were completing the encirclement, pushing north to seal the trap.

On the evening of August 8, General Dwight Eisenhower had dinner with General Omar Bradley, commander of First US Army. The supreme commander had moved the previous day from England to set up his advanced headquarters in France. He was now on direct telephone communication and an easy drive to Montgomery's and Bradley's command posts. Also, he finally had close, continual, firsthand observation of the battlefields. This was an essential first step for Ike: he had just announced that he would take overall command of all land forces from Montgomery when he fully established a headquarters in France.

On the heels of this move, Eisenhower promoted Bradley to command a newly created Twelfth US Army Group, comprising Patton's Third and Hodges's First Armies. Monty was left with the British and Canadians of the 21st Army Group. While Ike was typically vague as to who was actually in charge for the next few interim weeks, until his own overall command was fully established, the assumption taken by many historians is that, when he was on the battlefield, the supreme commander bore responsibility for major strategic decisions.[8]

Eisenhower and Bradley were impressed at the enormous numbers of German troops from the most elite *Panzer* divisions, still well behind allied lines at Mortain. They're sticking their heads into a noose, they both agreed. Let's pull the rope tight and nab them all.

A quick call to Monty's HQ brought the three men into total accord. Why not continue pressing Monty's British and Canadian divisions south to Falaise? They were making good headway in that direction. At the same time, swing Patton's and Hodges's armies up from the south to take Argentan. The two army groups could seal the trap on a line between Argentan and Falaise.

Minutes later, a delighted Patton received a telephone call from his boss. We've shortened the goal line, Bradley told him. Forget heading for the Seine; you're going to link up with Monty's forces and cut off the Germans on a line between Argentan to Falaise. Bradley gave him the go-ahead to concentrate the bulk of his armored power eastward.

Patton wasted no time in issuing his orders. Major General Wade

Haislip's XV Corps was selected to make the end run to Argentan, by way of Le Mans, Sées, and Alençon. Haislip, a stocky, balding Virginian, would carry the ball with two armored divisions (the 5th and 2d French) leading, and two infantry divisions following in a mopping-up role.

While so far these divisions had achieved their objectives on the breakout, they had not met any real opposition. So Haislip was a curious choice for such an important mission. An infantry commander of World War I vintage with little armored experience, he hadn't impressed Patton, who had grumbled that Haislip had been "sitting around the War Department in swivel chairs so long, he's muscle-bound in the ass."[9]

The corps commander's spearhead divisions were also untried in the Normandy battlefields. Bradley himself had said he wished 5th Armored Division, leading on the right, was more "battle-wise." The 2d French Armored Division (also known as *2ème* Division *Blindée*, or 2 DB), in taking the lead on the left, was an even riskier gamble. This was the vulnerable side of the spearhead, wide-open and exposed to enemy forces within striking distance. Of the two, the 2d French Armored had more experience, having fought in Africa, but its commander had a reputation for being temperamental. In Bradley's eyes, Major General Jacques Leclerc had three strikes against him. He was "notoriously undisciplined, did not speak English; and his sole ambition seemed to be to liberate Paris."[10]

Leclerc was a pseudonym for aristocrat Vicomte Jacques-Philippe de Hautecloque, changed of necessity to protect his wife and six children from Gestapo reprisals. His passion to return to—and liberate—Paris after four years of exile was to have a strong influence in the coming weeks.

XV Corps swept across the lightly defended interior of France. The French populace went wild with joy when Sherman tanks with the tricolor markings of the Free French pounded through their villages.

"General Leclerc always adapted the corps plan to suit his own type of fighting of 'liberating and celebrating.' He set a pattern of action for his division," remembers Tony Triumpho, a lieutenant in an American artillery battery with the Free French:

> He would have a meeting of his officers to set out his own battle plan. Invariably he would say, "Our objective is there but we will go on to here because I will contact my friend the mayor, or a friend in the underground, who will order a feast to be prepared for us."

     After taking an objective, there would be a splendid meal with wine and champagne.[11]

     A captain with 3d Armored Division, Thomas Cassidy, was astonished at the absence of camouflage discipline shown by 2ème Division Blindée. He described the bacchanal sight of the division at war: "I saw French soldiers spread over the fields, and spilling in and out of houses, and bivouacked *with campfires going,* and singing and feasting and wine flowing. The whole scene might have occurred in another age."[12]

Field Marshal von Kluge had always found pleasure and a certain serenity contemplating the view of the River Seine from his headquarters at Château La Roche Guyon. The château was built into chalk cliffs rising steeply above the river that wound its way from Paris to the sea.[13]

     On August 9, 1944, there was no tranquillity in his horizon. Pressure from the Allies was growing more intense as they closed in on his two German armies.

     From the west and north there was a triple pressure. The American First Army had pushed the Germans back out of Vire after a week of violent fighting. Second British Army on their left had just won the battle for the high ground at Mount Pinçon. Moreover, the Canadian breakout the previous day had brought them just eight miles north of Falaise. The German *Panzer* divisions at Mortain had been put on the defensive, told to hold on, and this they were barely doing.

     But it was over his left shoulder, southward, that von Kluge was looking most anxiously.

     Patton's XV Corps, sweeping southeast at lightning speed, had advanced an incredible one hundred miles in less than a week. Von Kluge had just been informed that the Third US Army had captured Le Mans that morning. The Americans were now fifty miles closer to Paris and the Seine than were the nearest German *Panzers*—and von Kluge's divisions at Mortain were a dangerous eighty miles into allied territory, surrounded on three sides.

     Now he had the "unpleasant and unexpected surprise" of learning that Patton was veering north toward Alençon. Clearly his aim was to cut off the German supply base centered there. His next step would be to encircle and annihilate the German Fifth and Seventh Armies.[14]

"We have no forces on hand to repel this envelopment," Lieutenant General Fritz Bayerlein informed him bleakly.[15]

The chief of staff of the Seventh Army, Lieutenant General Gersdorff, told von Kluge flat out that "judging the enemy's advance on Alençon, it was quite clear that this was to be the 'knockout blow' and the end of the army as well as the whole Western Front.

"The decision [to withdraw] is not up to me; it is in the hands of the supreme commander," Gersdorff said.[16] Hitler's "stand fast" decree after the assassination attempt was threatening the very existence of his armies.

Field Marshal von Kluge was a traditionalist, a Prussian career officer with an exemplary record through two world wars. He had commanded a battalion on the Western Front in 1914–18. Hitler appointed him to replace von Rundstedt as C-in-C West because he was more "energetic and aggressive."

Bayerlein's candid assessment of von Kluge's ability was that "Von Kluge played a more active and personal role and spent more time at the front checking on troop conditions. Personally, I thought he was a good leader of troops. But he was no armored general."[17]

Von Kluge in fact frequently spent many hours on the road traversing the routes from his headquarters to the forward lines of two armies. He privately viewed the Mortain attack, Operation *Lüttich*, merely as a means of keeping the enemy off-balance long enough to move the German armies back, preferably to the River Seine, where they could establish a new defensive line. Despite Hitler's optimistic belief that they would sweep the Allies back into the sea, von Kluge was too shrewd a soldier to think this was possible.

"We are underestimating the striking power of the American Army," he observed to an associate, theorizing that such a highly industrialized nation had the resources to rapidly improvise a good army.[18]

The Führer had flung all the blame for the failure of the Mortain counterattack on von Kluge. "Von Kluge did that deliberately," he said spitefully to General Warlimont. "He did it to show me that my orders were incapable of being performed!"[19]

Having found a scapegoat, Hitler could now justify ordering a remount of the attack that afternoon, this time under command of General Heinrich Eberbach. Von Kluge met Eberbach at his command post at Château La Roche Guyon.

"By the Führer's orders you will put together an emergency staff as

Panzergruppe Eberbach, and with a number of *Panzer* divisions mount a repetition of the counterthrust on Avranches," he instructed.

Eberbach tried to beg off. "Sir, I consider this offensive impossible and hopeless. I therefore request that someone else be put in charge."[20]

Hitler was not to be dissuaded. He had chosen Eberbach as a last-minute replacement for the ill-tempered von Funck on the eve of the first Mortain counterattack, believing the former to be more aggressive. Von Kluge had refused to make the switch then. This time he could not refuse.

But both men received a temporary reprieve. The Canadian attack the previous day, Operation *Totalize,* sabotaged the remount. Von Kluge could not afford to pull additional *Panzer* divisions from the British/Canadian front at such a critical time; even Hitler agreed.

Now the Führer was demanding a *re*-remount of the Mortain counterattack two days hence—on August 11.

"*Madness!*" thought von Kluge. Did he not understand that the main German supply base at Alençon was about to be overrun?

I have five hundred thousand troops in danger of encirclement, von Kluge thought desperately. They need fuel for their tanks, food for their bellies, and ammunition for their weapons. We must forget about Mortain and confront this new danger first. People there [at Hitler's HQ] live in another world, he mused.

Still looking over his shoulder, he saw twin threats from this latest idea of the Führer. By defying Hitler, von Kluge would be fired; then the Gestapo would question him about his role in the assassination conspiracy. By conforming, the German armies could be wiped out.

Von Kluge felt as though he, too, was in a vise. It was squeezing the breath and heart out of an old soldier.

Wheeling north from Le Mans on August 10, the US XV Corps reached Alençon the next day, capturing (as von Kluge had feared) the Seventh German Army's supply base. On Friday, August 11, Haislip ordered both armored divisions to advance north to Argentan. To this point, the German resistance had been negligible. At Sées, all that the battered 9th *Panzer* Division could muster up in the way of opposition was a company of bakers.

Patton's mood was mellow, and justifiably so. "Third Army has advanced farther and faster than any army in history," he bragged happily of his 170-mile advance.[21] So far, the French 2nd Armored Division had earned all manner of praise for their fine achievements on the drive north: "Be sure to bring along a bag of Bronze Stars for Leclerc's sons of bitches," Patton joked with his aide. On Saturday, August 12, Patton's mood was quite different.

Haislip's orders had been clear enough to each of his XV Corps divisions. Ahead of them, five miles south of Argentan, was a large forest, the Forêt d'Écouves. The Germans were notoriously skilled at using forests as defensive positions. Haislip called for an air strike to clear it. For safety's sake, 5th Armored was therefore ordered to skirt the woods on the right, using the main N158 road to Argentan. Leclerc was similarly told to bypass the road through the forest, taking the route around it on the left, or west, side.

Leclerc had other ideas. Eager to advance, he sent his troops up *all three* roads. Fortunately for his troops in the 2d French Armored, the bombing was canceled in time to avoid a tragedy. But the ensuing traffic chaos caused its own kind of fireworks.

There is possibly no traffic jam comparable to that created when one armored division (French) collides with a second one (American) at a village intersection. Thousands of troops, not understanding a word of each other's language, milled about in the village square at Sées. Scores of wildly excited just-liberated townsfolk frolicked among them while several hundred tanks and armored vehicles meshed hopelessly at the congested crossroads.

"You have no right to be here," shouted the 5th Armored Division's chief of staff.

"We're only passing through," replied the French commander haughtily.

"Argentan is our business. Our tanks need the N158," insisted the American.

"And Écouves is ours," replied Leclerc, his cold blue eyes flashing steel.[22]

Leclerc was not to be budged. Haislip roared his frustration at the Frenchman to Patton.

"Hell, Wade, don't get so upset. He's only a baby," his boss retorted.[23]

The "baby" had in fact stopped the war—or one element of it. The 5th Armored's tanks ground to a halt, its gasoline supply vehicles hopelessly entangled as the French preempted their road.

Six valuable hours were lost in this debacle—six hours that marked the difference between an enemy in total disarray and a German force once more given time to mount a defense against the American onslaught.

Late that same Saturday evening, August 12, XV Corps's General Wade Haislip, reported to Patton that he expected to capture his last objective—Argentan—the next morning. What were his further orders?

Here was a chance to cut off the German army—an opportunity too great to pass up. Without hesitating, Patton replied, "Push on slowly in the direction of Falaise" and "continue to push on slowly until [you establish contact with] our Allies."[24]

Patton then phoned his superior, General Omar Bradley, to report the sensational news. To his surprise and anger Bradley told Patton "nothing doing. Stop where you are and build up on the shoulder. The German is beginning to pull out. You'd better button up and get ready for him."[25]

Both Bradley and Patton were acting in character for their roles. As an Army Group commander, Bradley had always leaned on caution. As an Army commander, Patton always preferred action. But it was Bradley's job to consider the overall picture, and Patton's merely to pursue the immediate goals of his army. Bradley interpreted intelligence on the buildup of *Panzer* Group Eberbach as a threat to the extended American flank. He preferred "a solid shoulder at Argentan to the possibility of a broken neck at Falaise." Patton thought this cautious approach was typical Bradley and a monumental error.

Patton was also a proponent of the "rock soup" approach to orders. If he could persuade Bradley to give a little—a piece of "rock" to boil for soup—vegetables and even some meat might follow. His orders forbade an advance beyond Argentan, but who knew what might happen during a battle for the city.[26]

At 1130 hours Sunday morning, his boss, Bradley, again gave Patton the order: *Stop!* The red light infuriated him. He had within reach the closure of the gap between Argentan and Falaise—the entrapment of two German armies. And he was told to stop?

"You're kidding!" Patton exclaimed angrily.

Patton urgently called Bradley. He found him at Eisenhower's headquarters. But his pleas brought him no comfort. They knew through Ultra that the four German divisions that had done so much damage at Mortain were trying to mount a fresh attack on the American flank.

You are overextended, Bradley told his upset commander. You are wide-open to attack. There's a dangerous gap of some twenty-five to fifty miles between your Third Army at Argentan and the nearest American force; First Army is still back at Mayenne on your left flank.[27]

Eisenhower, who apparently was in the room, was to say (at the time and later in his memoirs): "I completely support Bradley."[28] And Bradley himself wrote, "Eisenhower would captain the team."[29] Clearly, as British historian Major General Essame noted, "By his very physical presence in Normandy, Eisenhower did assume direct responsibility for the decision — a responsibility the American people expected him to exercise."[30] Martin Blumenson, an American authority, agrees. "Eisenhower could have done [it]" — i.e., stopped Patton from closing the trap around the German armies.[31]

In the early hours of Sunday, August 13, 5th Armored Division approached the outskirts of Argentan. They were too late. The 116th *Panzer* Division (under new command after von Schwerin had been sacked) had taken advantage of the confusion of Saturday's traffic jam at Sées, and the ensuing six-hour delay, to infiltrate Argentan and reinforce its slender defenses. Elements of two further *Panzer* divisions arrived a few hours later. The Americans were driven back with "surprisingly heavy" losses.[32]

Despite the momentary success, von Kluge was deeply worried. His defenses at Argentan were too weak to hold out for long. His line was so thin that enemy reconnaissance units had managed to bypass the town and probe eight miles beyond Argentan, reaching a point just six miles south of Falaise. Less than fourteen miles now separated the Anglo/Canadian and American spearheads. The German encirclement was imminent.

Unaccountably, at the moment that he was staring at defeat, von Kluge received an astonishing reprieve. He was informed that the American attack had come to an "abrupt and surprising halt."[33] He would have been even more amazed if he had known that General Bradley, furious at having his standing order disobeyed and worried about the consequences, was the commander who stopped the advance.

General Patton's indignation evaporated with suspicious alacrity. Was Paris a gleam in his eye, too? The next day the mercurial commander dreamed up a new plan. Now he would drive east toward the Seine and

Paris, taking with him three of his corps away from the Argentan/Falaise Front. Bradley approved the idea, without consulting Montgomery, and by nightfall it was executed. As a military coup it was *par excellence*.

Patton's Diary, 14 August.

I flew back to see Bradley and sell him the plan. He consented.

It is really a great plan, wholly my own, and I made Bradley think he thought of it. I am very happy and elated. I got all the corps moving by 2030 so that if Monty tries to be careful, it will be too late.[34]

Moving over a dozen divisions, some 150,000 men and all their equipment and vehicles, on a whim, in less than twenty-four hours was an amazing feat. Whether or not the fact that Patton didn't get his way in closing the Argentan/Falaise Gap motivated this action has never been determined. But his gloat in his diary that he had shifted this force away without Montgomery's knowledge and moved them out of range is some indication of his pique.

Patton's Diary, 15 August.

Bradley came to me suffering from nerves. There is a rumor, which I doubt, that there are five *Panzer* divisions at Argentan, so Bradley wants me to halt my move east. I am complying with the order and by tomorrow I can probably persuade him to let me advance [farther].[35]

Patton had persuaded Bradley to change his focus of encircling the Germans at Falaise to the broader encirclement at the Seine—and, incidentally, give the Francophone Patton's ego a boost by making him the liberator of Paris.

The only question now was, could the three unproved divisions left behind—Leclerc's *2ème* Division *Blindée,* and the US 80th and 90th—manage to achieve what Patton had been blocked from doing: close the southern jaw of the trap on two German armies?

CHAPTER 18

The Scapegoat

War Diary: General Eberbach: 12 August 1944.

The whole day MG fire was heard from a short distance. Every moment the enemy might appear at the headquarters. Fighter-bombers, however, made the transfer of the headquarters impossible. The enemy was forcing its way toward Argentan.[1]

From his headquarters "Wolfschanze" in East Prussia, Hitler issued a fresh order to General Eberbach. He was to attack southwardly past Alençon immediately "as a preparation for the attack on Avranches."

Eberbach was stunned and incredulous. Has Hitler still not given up on Operation *Lüttich*, the Mortain/Avranches counterattack? Can he still think we have divisions enough to mount two counterattacks when we do not have sufficient for even one? It was as if Hitler was no longer aware of realities; his confidence in a successful assault on Mortain and Avranches still persisted.

General Heinrich Eberbach was unhappy with his orders but obedient to them. When the forward units from the 116th *Panzer* Division arrived on August 12, he sent them to engage the Allies at Sées. The outcome was described by the divisional historian as "a catastrophe." The French 2d Armored Division had virtually destroyed *Panzer*-Grenadier Regiment 156, a unit of 116th *Panzer*.[2]

War Diary: General Eberbach: 12 August.

In the night, both of the headquarters made a shift to the region of Chenedouil, 12 miles west of Argentan. This shift took six hours. The whole supply service for one and a half armies was congested on the few roads between Falaise and Argentan. The columns were able to move only in the night hours. A big number of burnt-out motor vehicles created many bottlenecks. In consequence all streets were congested and the traffic was moving merely at a walk. The loss of Alençon deprived 7th Army of its supply base. It is now entirely dependent on the 5th Army [for] gasoline and ammunition.[3]

Still, in that six hours provided him by the French traffic jam, Eberbach had been given breathing room, a chance to stiffen his defenses.

By Sunday, August 13, *Panzergruppe Eberbach*—a sorry lot of unkempt troops, their tanks chugging sluggishly on their last dregs of fuel—had straggled in piecemeal after having completed the last of their seventy-mile route march from Mortain. The retreat had begun in darkness to avoid allied air attacks, but because of the urgency of its mission, it was concluded in daylight. Their numbers were so depleted that the counterattack that Hitler had ordered against the US Third Army, and that Eberbach was attempting to mount, had to be canceled. Eberbach could use his troops only for defensive tasks, to hold the paper-thin line at Argentan.

War Diary: General Eberbach: 14 August.

I sent my last special-mission staff officer to the Army Group High Command with the following report:

"Enemy attack with a presumable strength of two *Panzer* divisions and one Infantry division. He has surprised 2 *Panzer* Division and 1st SS *Panzer* Division *Leibstandarte* causing heavy losses to them. Parts of 116 *Panzer* Division annihilated. Rest holds against heavy enemy attacks both sides Argentan. 9 *Panzer* Division has company strength.

"Owing to fighting bombers at daytime and traffic congestion at night, fuel and ammunition situation very serious. Lack of fuel caused 1st SS *Panzer* Division to blow up a number of tanks. Under flank protection a quick withdrawal from encirclement of the 7th Army imperative in order to avoid catastrophe. Success improbable."[4]

While Eberbach was imploring Hitler to authorize the withdrawal of the Seventh Army beyond Argentan, Field Marshal von Kluge was urging the Führer to withdraw all German divisions even farther, all the way back to the Seine.

Eberbach told his boss, von Kluge, far more frankly than he dared tell Hitler, that the German troops had lost the will to fight.

"The fighting morale of German troops has cracked," he said. "The German troops in the west have now to wage a war of the poor man against an enemy who has everything in abundance; who is fresh while the German soldier had already been engaged in hard fighting for five years and, moreover, during the last two years suffered only defeats.

"He feels himself betrayed. He no longer fights with the belief in victory and a reliance on his command but only from a soldier's pride and for fear of defeat."

Eberbach cited sorry examples of the depths to which the soldiers' spirits had sunk:

For the first time not only Poles and Alsacians but even single Germans deserted to the enemy. Tanks are left standing without being blown up, MGs thrown away, guns left lying, stragglers without arms are numerous. Catch lines [to intercept deserters] in the rear of the front had to be inaugurated. Even the SS were no exception. The 1st SS Panzer Division Leibstandarte had never before fought so miserably as at that time.

Perhaps, Eberbach hinted to von Kluge, this would be the right time for him to act against Hitler's order to save the two armies (the Seventh and Fifth). But he could do no more than hint. He was well aware that the Gestapo was watching von Kluge with growing suspicion.[5]

At his command post at La Roche Guyon, "*der kluge* Hans," Clever Hans, was feeling increasingly not so clever. His military training told him the Führer's demands were ridiculous. Yet, always the conciliator, he had hoped that by appeasing Hitler he could dissuade his leader from believing that he supported the assassination attempt. It hadn't worked.

He had, in Hitler's eyes, failed at Mortain and now he would be blamed for the disaster at Sées. He was the scapegoat. He had his family to worry about, too: his wife, and his son, Klaus, a lieutenant colonel and chief of staff with *Panzer Group Eberbach*.

It was imperative that he gamble. Von Kluge issued the command to withdraw from Normandy despite not having Hitler's direct orders to do so. He then set the wheels in motion. All noncombat units were to be dispatched back to the Seine: "Rear elements, repair tanks, half-tracks, artillery, antiaircraft artillery, crews without tanks and armored infantry cadres."

Now he realized it was essential that he meet with his army commanders to inform them of his actions. On August 14, he saw General Dietrich at 5th *Panzer* HQ in Bernay. Dietrich had only bad news. The Canadians had laid on a massive attack that day; Falaise would soon be in their hands.

At dawn the next day, von Kluge set out in his Porsche command car with his usual entourage, a motorcycle escort and a communications truck, to see Eberbach and Hausser. His rendezvous was at 1000 hours at Nécy, some forty miles south and midway between Argentan and Falaise. The convoy advanced perilously, with maddening slowness, over the cratered roads.

Suddenly, a P-47 aircraft attacked them. Von Kluge leapt to safety in a ditch; his communications vehicle was smashed, its crew killed. He sent his aide ahead to inform Eberbach of his delay. Alone, he tried to get back on the road. Again and again fighter-bombers attacked the imposing Porsche. Meanwhile, at Nécy, after waiting two hours, Eberbach and Hausser returned impatiently to their headquarters. Further bad news awaited them: the Americans had successfully invaded the south of France that morning.

They reported von Kluge's disappearance. We cannot reach him, they told Army Group B headquarters at La Roche Guyon. He is not on the radio net.

15 August: Adolf Hitler to General Eberbach: "Establish whereabouts of Field Marshal Kluge. Report results hourly."[6]

"The inquiries by the Supreme Command were not prompted by an anxiety for the personal fate of Kluge," Eberbach noted wryly, "but by the suspicion he might have had a meeting with American officers in order to capitulate or surrender personally."[7] Indeed, Eberbach had heard through German intelligence that the Allies were rumored to have been in contact with a German general that day. That was all Hitler needed. His suspicions were confirmed that von Kluge was implicated in the assassination conspiracy of July 20.[8]

The nightmare trip ended for Field Marshal von Kluge at midnight. Exhausted by the heat and the effort of crawling in and out of ditches, frustrated at being out of communication with his armies, he limped into Seventh Army headquarters. A new nightmare was just beginning.

By now, his twelve-hour disappearance had fueled Hitler's paranoia about the man. He was a traitor.

Within forty-eight hours, von Kluge was removed from his command in disgrace and ordered to Berlin for interrogation by the Gestapo. On his way to Berlin, he swallowed a cyanide capsule provided him by his physician son-in-law.

The pounding of heavy guns from the American sector near Argentan—and a new thundering from the north, nearby and menacing—disturbed his final moments on earth. The Canadians were closing on Falaise.

It was all over, anyway.

CHAPTER 19

Barbery Cross

On Monday, August 12, 1944, Hitler finally authorized the German retreat from the Mortain counterattack. The German forces began a slow
withdrawal toward the Falaise/Argentan Gap. The Gap was being closed
from five directions by five nations: Patton's Third Army's French 2d Armored was nearing Argentan, fifteen miles south of Falaise; the British
were squeezing the retreating enemy units from behind, forcing them
more and more tightly into the narrow escape hatch. On the ridge overlooking the Laison River Valley, the Canadians and Poles were exerting
pressure from the north and northeast. They were eight miles from Falaise.

A mere twenty-five miles separated the two jaws of the trap.

At 0500 hours on August 19, 1942, two brigades—five thousand men—
from the 2d Canadian Infantry Division had been ordered to mount a "reconnaissance in force" on German defenders in France. The objective
was a small fishing village named Dieppe. The cost was 3,367 casualties in
a single morning.

Two years later, at 0500 hours on August 12, 1944, two brigades from
the same infantry division were again ordered to mount a reconnaissance
in force on German defenders in France. The objective this time was a
small farming village named Clair Tizon, just west of the Caen–Falaise
road on the Laize River and some four miles to the south in the direction

of Falaise. On the way they were ordered to take out the tiny hamlets of Barbery and Moulines.

As the August sun beat down on the advancing foot soldiers of the Royal Hamilton Light Infantry, who had fought on the main Dieppe beach, the coincidence was hard to shrug off.

The same sweltering weather, the same scratchy wool battledress and wretchedly uncomfortable steel helmet; even the flies dive-bombing sweaty faces seemed the same. And the prebattle dread—heightened for some of the lads by recollections of that bloody day almost two years before—that was the same.

The Rileys led off the assault on Barbery. This dubious distinction was probably a spin-off from an earlier meeting with General Montgomery following the RHLI's hard-punching attack at Verrières, when it had been the only battalion in the 2d Canadian Division to seize and hold this objective. The battalion adjutant, Captain Bill Parker, was there when Montgomery congratulated the men: "He told us that we did what good infantry regiments should do: we took the ground and we held it against counterattack. Then he said that he would 'honor' us by letting us lead the next big attack."[1]

Some "honor" it turned out to be!

The Barbery attack had been designated as the II Corps' main effort that day, meaning that the Rileys would have all the resources of the 2d Division in support: the Reconnaissance Battalion's armored vehicles, a regiment of tanks, and the entire divisional artillery plus two Army Groups Royal Artillery (AGRAs).

Following behind them, the Royal Regiment of Canada and the Essex Scottish would advance in single line, each to leapfrog over the unit ahead as it achieved its set objective and consolidated. Then the 5th Brigade battalions, all with armored and artillery support, would follow, emulating this tactic until the final objective, Clair Tizon, was reached.

These single-line "advance to contact" tactics were standard infantry operations, well rehearsed in battle drills prior to D-Day. The infantry learned to plan not only the attack, but also—and just as importantly— what to do when the attack succeeded. The Germans were certain to counterattack; to prepare for this, tasks had to be assigned to the rifle companies and all its supporting arms: artillery, machine guns, armor, and engineers. The infantry also had to formulate a counter-counterattack plan.

It had seemed fairly straightforward, practicing it in England. But they had never before put it into effect in Normandy. No amount of practice could prepare you fully for an exercise under heavy enemy fire. The rules often changed.

If the attack succeeded, the assault would catapult the Canadians well behind enemy lines, taking the pressure off the British on their right and off Simonds's pending Anglo-Canadian attack, Operation *Tractable*, toward Falaise on their left.

Royal Regiment patrols confirmed that the German 271st Division was withdrawing in stages.[2] They were digging their artillery into new defensive positions on the high ground along the Laison Valley. Scout patrols described a slope with orchards and woodlands—the kind of landscape that offered the enemy every opportunity for stiff resistance.

The ground had been carpeted with land mines. The Germans were trained to booby-trap ordinary roadside articles with hand grenades and trip wires: a pump handle on a well, a doorknob on a cottage, a bottle of wine on a window ledge—even corpses on the side of the road. All were rigged to maim and kill.

Reconnaissance patrols were a battalion's eyes and ears. The scouts' prebattle sorties into and behind enemy lines detected the German dispositions—their location, strength, and weaponry—and, where possible, even the placements of the lethal obstacles.

It took a special sort of man to volunteer for the scout platoon: someone with a natural instinct to use the ground to his advantage; someone with skill, agility, and all sorts of courage. It was the elite unit of every regiment, with tasks of such priority that its commander, a lieutenant, worked directly under the battalion commanding officer.

Company Sergeant Major Charlie Martin of the Queen's Own Regiment describes his vast experiences operating in some seventy-five patrols in Normandy alone:

> Speed, timing, teamwork and sometimes physical strength were important. The ability to work together in silence was vital. For example, I'd never take along a man who had any sign of a head cold—that's what we meant by total silence. We didn't want to hear a man breathing. We had to be very closely tuned to one another, communicating in the subtlest way—quick and quiet.
>
> Some could move like a ghost. One moment he'd be there, the next moment, gone.

Then there was the danger of panic. It was necessary to train our men to "freeze." Only movement could be seen. A man frozen motionless, particularly if next to a tree, was virtually invisible. Don't flop, I'd tell them—unless the enemy opened up.

Frozen silent in the ghostly flare, black face, muffled weapon, no helmet—a helmet looks just like a helmet and can cause a rattle—there's every chance a man will not be spotted or will even look to the enemy like a stump or part of the terrain.[3]

There were three seven-man sections in a scout platoon. "Our training was very concentrated and of a special nature," Corporal Doug Shaughnessy of the RHLI recalls. "We worked in pairs mostly."

These two men, Harold Green—'Harry' to all the guys—and Shaughnessy—known as "Sandy" for the color of his hair—had been training together in the scout platoon for five months prior to D-Day, always a team.

We were given the best possible training in camouflage and concealment, marksmanship, map and compass reading, unarmed combat, all aspects about enemy rank structure, vehicles, weapons and aircraft recognition, demolition and about anything else required to survive by our own wits.

Sandy turned twenty shortly after the division landed in Normandy— "Not a boy any longer, but not quite a man either." On the eve of his last day as a teenager he found himself alone, hunkered into a hastily dug slit trench, experiencing his first heavy enemy bombardment.

I didn't sleep that night—one is more apt to be frightened of things he cannot see or a situation he cannot fully understand— but I was not alone. Somewhere out there in the dark were some six hundred other members of the RHLI who I am sure were preoccupied with their own special feelings.

Since the 2d Division's landing in Normandy in July, their scout leader, Lieutenant Hughie Hinton, had led them on any number of patrols, usually at night, to glean information on the enemy. "Military maps do not necessarily show all the detail that may be found on the ground and this was particularly true that summer in Normandy."[4] Hugh Hinton himself had spent so much time on the enemy lines the scouts kidded him that he should be drawing German rations.[5]

"Harry and I moved out quietly," Sandy Shaughnessy recalls,

> sometimes crawling on our stomachs, sometimes moving in a crouched position, but always hopeful that we would not end up in an enemy minefield or pull one of those hateful trip wires that would set off a flare or explosive charge.
>
> Listening patrols were a nasty business because you had to get as far forward of your own position as possible and remain there until early morning, then get back just before daylight. Quite often listening patrols gave the first warning of enemy attack and more often than not they were the first to be taken prisoner of war—or worse. Then, too, there was the problem of getting back through your own line in the early morning hours when everyone was on "Stand-To."

Crawling back through no-man's-land, often ducking fire from both sides, was daunting enough—worse if you couldn't get past the battalion sentry because you didn't remember the nightly password. "It was a very serious business," Shaughnessy recalls. "Many a man had been seriously injured or even killed because he forgot the password.

"It was always a double-barreled word, such as apple-pie, or orange-juice. As you approached our lines the sentry would say, 'Halt!—Apple!' You had to reply, 'Pie!' "

One night the password was 'Holy-night.' Shaughnessy, on guard duty, challenged an incoming scout: "Halt! Holy . . . ?"

The scout, Ace Bailly, "a Nova Scotian and a real character," shouted: "Holy . . . holy . . . holy shit! I forget!"[6]

Once back to the relative safety of his unit, the scout immediately starts digging his slit trench. It was often tough work, digging four or five feet down in Normandy's hard-packed clay. But it wasn't an option. No matter how exhausted he might be, he knows that a rifleman's survival often depends on how deeply he has dug his slit, and how quickly he can get into it before the mortars come crashing around him. He has learned—often by seeing his buddies killed—that his trenching shovel is almost as important for survival as his rifle, and without it a man would feel "as naked as a man in Piccadilly without his trousers," as historian John Ellis graphically described it.[7]

The French farmers had not harvested their wheat in this hot, dry summer from hell. The Rileys marched chest deep through dense, dusty wheatfields, avoiding the mined road. They were soaked in sweat, hating the chafing wool uniforms.

Major Joe Pigott's "C" Company led the advance. Joe was twenty-two years of age, "tall, magnificently handsome and put together like a strip of hard steel." The men called him "King," with a lot of respect.[8]

"He was very cool, almost lackadaisical," Private (now Colonel) John Williamson recalls. "Nothing ever seemed to bother him. He just went calmly on, doing his job to the best of ability. He was the only person of the battalion to wear body armor—the rest of us got rid of it, but it saved his life."[9]

On Pigott's left was another of the "old sweats," Major Huck Welch, commanding "B" Company. Welch, thirty-one, moved ahead as lithely as the all-star football player he had been.

They reached the crossroads village of Barbery, with nothing but the reassuring clank of the tanks breaking an almost eerie silence. The village seemed deserted; nothing stirred. At the end of the road stood a life-sized crucifix. "Quite a sight in the middle of a war," Sergeant Arthur Kelly observed to a buddy. "I hope the peace that Jesus thought He died for prevails today" was the fervent reply.[10]

They advanced a few hundred yards farther, warily eyeing the copse of woods on a small rise ahead. Abruptly the quiet was broken with the staccato drumming of machine guns and the shrieks of mortars as the woods on the left came alive with sheets of enemy fire, directly on Pigott's company.

Pigott, now under continuous fire, urged his men to attack. Lieutenant Hughie Hinton, the Rileyses' scout leader, led his section in a rush across the Barbery crossroads against the German defenses, throwing grenades and firing his Sten. He was the first to fall.

German Tiger and Panther tanks roared out of the copse, knocking out the vulnerable Shermans and spraying intense machine-gun fire on the Rileys. The Germans closed on the attackers. Bayonets and knives swung wildly. "They were fanatical devils," Pigott later recounted. "We started to have casualties right away. There was hand-to-hand fighting as these fellows came running out of their slits, firing rifles and throwing grenades."

Meanwhile, on the right flank of the attack, Welch's company had got to its assigned objective without serious opposition. "We were spread out wide on a lateral front," recalled Lieutenant Colin Gibson, platoon commander in Welch's company. "Our orders were to start digging in when we had got on the ground we were to take and then hold our position. I found some old German slit trenches and got my men in these."

Gibson made a dash for Welch's HQ to report his position:

That's when the stuff started flying. I ducked partway under a carrier when an 88mm shell from a German tank exploded near me. The blast broke my right leg; I was in pretty bad shape. A buddy got out of his trench even while we were under fire and came over and stuck the shell dressing on me and gave me a jab of morphine. It was one of the bravest acts I can remember. While he was doing that he got hit in the shoulder, and I got hit again, this time in my other leg and arm. Right after that I turned my platoon over to the senior NCO.[11]

By then the entire battalion was under "the most intensive mortaring and shelling the unit ever witnessed," as its intelligence officer later noted.[12] At 1800 hours a mortar shell smashed into battalion HQ, and five men, including the Rileys CO, were wounded.

The RHLI history recounts the final moments of the battle. "Towards twilight the enemy armor moved in for what appeared the *coup de grâce*. The [German] tank commanders had no nerves at all," Major Huck Welch reported later. "They stood exposed in their turrets looking for targets through their binoculars, their guns traversing all the time."[13]

Suddenly they stopped, made a last desultory sweep with their machine guns, and left the field of smoking hulks, the dead and wounded. The Germans pulled out to replenish their ammunition and dig in a new defensive line farther back, against what inevitably would be a renewed Canadian attack.

A survivor, Sandy Shaughnessy, recalled the next hours.

We were detailed with the padre and a couple of other guys on a burial party to the Barbery crossroads. We saw Hughie Hinton first. He had a burst of machine-gun fire in the chest. So did Billy Lister; he was just a short distance from him. It could have been from tanks with self-propelled guns in the bush beyond the crossroads or from a MG-42.

We found the others, about eighteen or twenty, all killed there. We picked up Hinton, Billy Lister, Sunday Soldo, and Eric Hughson—he had a brother with us in the battalion who was devastated.

Then Sandy picked up the next body lying sprawled across the Barbery crossroads: Harry Green, best pal and scout buddy of a lad who had just turned twenty.

It was one hell of a way to grow up fast.

The Rileys had responded valiantly to General Montgomery's challenge; they took the ground and held it. The battalion's "butcher's bill" on that sunny summer August weekend, fighting a diversionary action that barely made it into the history books, was twenty dead and one hundred wounded in one bloody afternoon.

Now these young men lay in hastily dug graves, each marked by a rifle with the despised steel helmet atop: a grisly garden.

Some honor, Monty.

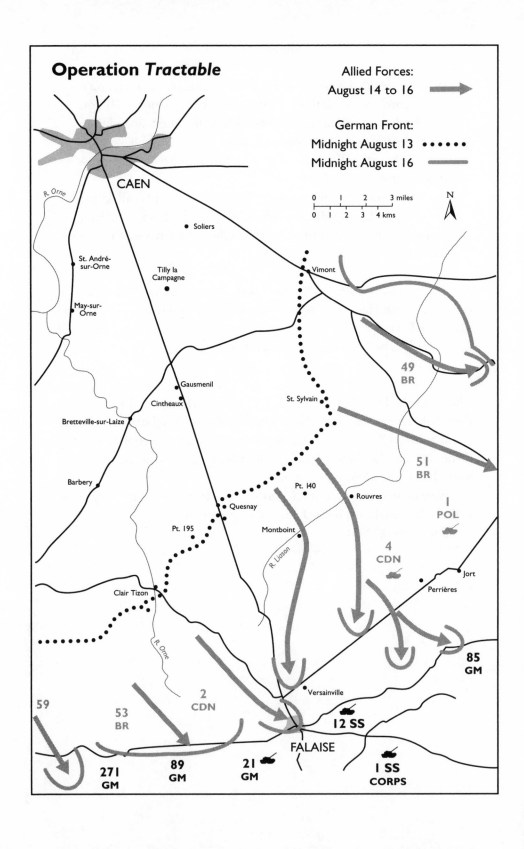

Operation *Tractable*

Allied Forces:
August 14 to 16

German Front:
Midnight August 13 ••••••
Midnight August 16 ───

0 1 2 3 miles
0 1 2 3 4 kms

N

CAEN

R. Orne

Soliers

St. André-sur-Orne

Tilly la Campagne

Vimont

May-sur-Orne

49 BR

Gausmenil

Cintheaux

St. Sylvain

Bretteville-sur-Laize

51 BR

Barbery

Pt. 140

Rouvres

1 POL

Quesnay

Pt. 195

Montboint

R. Liason

4 CDN

Jort

Perrières

Clair Tizon

R. Orne

85 GM

Versainville

59

2 CDN

53 BR

12 SS

FALAISE

271 GM

89 GM

21 GM

1 SS CORPS

CHAPTER 20

Tractable: "My God! We're Bombing Short!"

At an emergency late-evening meeting on August 13, a Canadian delegation approached Bomber Command at High Wycombe, Buckinghamshire with a startling request. General Simonds, commander of the II Canadian Corps, was launching a renewed assault to break through to Falaise at noon the next day, August 14. To ensure its success, Simonds requested RAF bomber support to knock out five key German defenses. They described the battle plan. Simonds was essentially re-creating the tactics of the successful Operation *Totalize,* employing the same immense numbers of armor and motorized infantry as a phalanx to smash through the German antitank defense ring. But this time, instead of using darkness to blind the enemy guns, he was attacking at high noon, substituting dense, man-made smoke to mask the attack. The code name: Operation *Tractable.* Bomber Command and its C-in-C, Air Chief Marshal A. T. "Bomber" Harris had serious reservations. "Our heavy bomber force has had very few daylight missions," they said. "The risk of bombing our own troops exists to a serious degree." The only way to avoid this would be to route the aircraft entirely over enemy lines—and that would put them directly in the path of enemy antiaircraft fire. "I [am] not prepared to subject my crews to this additional risk in order solely to lessen the risk of bombing our own troops. Their casualty rate is far in advance of anything suffered anywhere by our ground troops," Harris protested.[1]

Casualty figures for bomber crews had indeed been staggering. Of every hundred RAF aircrew, fifty-one had been killed on operations. Twenty-four more were either killed in crashes in England, or seriously injured, or taken prisoner. That left only twenty-four men who theoretically got home alive of the hundred who flew out in each sortie. Ten thousand aircraft had been lost.[2] Harris also expressed serious apprehension about the visibility of the targets: "There would be a tendency for smoke from the initial target to obscure the remainder," he pointed out. Following this gloomy prediction he asked two final, urgent questions: "Is there any possibility that Allied ground troops would use pyrotechnics [colored smoke signals] that could confuse the bombers?" Incredibly, the Canadians make no reference to standing orders issued pre-D-Day by Supreme Headquarters Allied Expeditionary Force (SHAEF) that yellow flares or yellow smoke would be the standard signal for forward infantry to identify themselves as friendly troops. "Absolutely not," was the reply. "Then do you enter this venture, as does Bomber Command, in full knowledge of the possible risk to our own troops?" "Absolutely."[3] With this, a quick telephone call confirmed the raid to the RAF squadron bases on standby in northern England.

At 0700 hours on August 14, some six thousand air force personnel in Yorkshire and Durham dug into a breakfast of bacon and eggs (real eggs for the aircrew, powdered for the ground crew).

Over eight hundred aircraft had been hastily designated for the operation—Halifaxes, Lancasters, and Mosquitoes. While they were being fueled and loaded with bombs, the aircrews crowded the briefing areas.

For the first time, the men learned their mission: a daylight bombing raid on five German strongpoints in support of Operation *Tractable*, a massive allied infantry/armored/air attack near Falaise.

The flight path over allied positions added extra hazards to the mission. The pilots had a very limited view of the ground. Therefore, a precise bomb line was indicated to navigators. North of it was allied, south was enemy. This addressed the very real danger of pilots' "short bombing"— dropping the bombs prematurely on their own troops.

Another safeguard was the use of Pathfinders. These aircraft would fly in ahead of the bombers, lighting "proceed with bombing" flares to guide them in over the bomb line to their targets—yellow target indicators, the briefing officers emphasized. There was no other way the aircrew could identify ground targets at eight thousand feet.

Flight time was three hours. When they reached the French coast the bombers would fly a timed run to a specified crossroads at Caen, and then continue with another timed run from that crossroads to the target. This would be the final safeguard against short bombing.

To be sure of timing the navigators were given stopwatches. The sweep of the second hand of a watch would govern the blind release of thousands of tons of bombs.

It was a daunting assignment. The airmen had only been trained for night raids. They were not trained for daylight raids or for visual recognition of targets. Nor were they used to flying in formation.

As Harris had pointed out, the turnover rate in bomber crews was very high. Few crews gained experience before they were killed. Those that did survive were veterans of harrowing tours—flying many nights a week for five solid weeks—on night raids over France and Germany. They lived with danger and with death. They watched close friends become statistics.

Flak was the universal fear. "Everybody gets hit by flak, no question," Flight Sergeant Roy Clarke, a wireless operator on the Falaise attack, noted.

When you run into flak it sounds like handfuls of gravel being thrown against a tin garage roof. Going into a target you can see the black puffs straight ahead of you. Sometimes they were so heavy you'd think you could get out and walk on top of them. Those German flak batteries were bloody good. If the flak gunners got you with a direct hit, there was no way you were going to come out of it—just boom! And that was it.

If it was predicted flak—that's when the flak guns down below got a range on you—the skipper "jinked" the aircraft by moving it slightly to starboard or port, to get away from the flak.

The scary part was when even at nighttime you could see the shape of an airplane to the right or left or above you and all the sudden you saw the thing blow up. That's what kind of shook you. Sometimes you knew whose airplane it was. It could be your own squadron, your best friend.

Another worry was collision. "With the sky filled with one thousand or so aircraft, you had to be careful. We all watched for other aircraft, even fighters."[4]

The constant stress of losing close friends, of wondering when you yourself would be killed, often created a physical twitching or stuttering known as being "flak-happy"—a condition that almost all the men endured but few gave in to.

The airmen never got used to fear; they just didn't show it. Far worse would be a transfer from action with LMF (Lack of Moral Fibre) stamped on your papers.

Flight Lieutenant Jim Llewellyn, a Welshman with No. 4 Group RAF, recalls an incident typical of the "stiff-upper-lip" air force tradition. "I was hit by flak coming back from a raid and crash-landed in a field. My rear gunner, a good friend, was killed; we were all badly shaken. When we finally made it back to base, all my CO could say was, 'Where the bloody hell have you been?' "[5]

That was a tough lesson for a twenty-one-year-old.

At midmorning on a sultry August 14, crews of over eight hundred aircraft pulled on warm boots and heavy, fleece-lined jackets or flying suits. Temperatures could dive well below zero in unheated craft at high altitudes. They butted out a last cigarette, buckled parachute straps, and prepared for takeoff.

Three hours later, the giant air armada, stretching over ten miles as far as the eye could see, crossed the French coast.

Under a relentless hot August sun, eight thousand troops from British, Canadian, and Polish brigades—many in tanks or armored vehicles— looked up to see the first of the medium bombers thundering overhead.

Troops on the start line of Operation *Tractable*, poised to launch the fight of their lives on the banks of the Laison River, could afford only a single grateful glance skyward at the eight hundred aircraft supporting their attack.

Above the din, commanders leading the tightly melded force of 250 tanks shouted as one: "Move now!" The assault was launched.

"Speed is essential," the tankmen had been warned. Accelerators were jammed to the floor and engines roared as 160 tanks all abreast plunged headlong through the fields of unmown wheat in what the First Hussars termed a "mad charge." Ninety more tanks followed in tight formation.[6]

"Follow the sun" was the next command. This was deemed the only way to keep direction in the smoke and dust churned up by armor and artillery. But the glaring sun was soon reduced to a faint pinpoint. Even that light became obscure as the gunners blasted their twenty-five-pounder smoke shells into the valley. Before long an impenetrable grey-white mist obliterated all visibility, blinding both ally and foe.

Meyer's 12th SS and 85th Infantry Division had ambushed and killed a Canadian officer carrying the operation orders the night before and were forewarned. The Germans' hastily beefed-up antitank defenses exacted a hefty toll on the allied armor. Soon the valley was checkered with flaming hulks of steel.

As the aircraft approached the coast, navigators watched for that key crossroads at Caen. At this point they carefully marked the speed and time by seconds to the target.

"We bombed by time instead of looking for a target," confirms Flying Officer Ken Fulton, who flew as navigator in the first wave of the *Tractable* raid with No. 426 Squadron. Fulton's log reflects in minutes and seconds the precision of the flight:

> Cross coast: 14:46:10 hours. Timed run from coast to road west out of Caen: 3.18 minutes. Speed 180 mph. Altitude: 8,000 ft. Timed run from Caen crossroad to target: 4.57 minutes.

As he neared the target, Fulton's aircraft ran into predicted flak from German ack-ack guns. As an experienced airman he knew too well how deadly this could be. Radar-directed predicted flak was so accurate the Germans had been known to shoot down a single plane at twenty thousand feet with one or two rounds of an 88mm. He glanced at his stopwatch. Still over a minute to go to target. The pilot, acutely aware of this danger, kept a straight and level course, unwaveringly ignoring the lethal fire exploding around him.

Fulton looked out his window. At last: the Pathfinder below was dropping yellow target indicators. Fulton activated his safety switch, a precaution that prevented the bomb-aimer from releasing his bombs prematurely. Anxiously, he watched the bombs descend and explode. The smell of cordite was strong. *200 yards from target*, he noted in his log.[7] Coming that close to a target from eight thousand feet was considered to be very accurate. He was sure the plane's photographs would confirm a good result and a positive contribution to the ground troops.

There was no time for celebration. Within a few seconds the flak became dense. Now, free of their bombs, the plane was able to maneuver to dodge the fire. The pilot corkscrewed, diving to port and climbing to starboard in a zigzag pattern to avoid being hit.

Corkscrew to 4000 feet, Fulton logged. *Small-arms fire commences. Plane receives bullet holes.*[8]

Fulton's squadron headed for home. They were lucky. As the first wave in the raid, they had clear vision—no smoke or dust. The damage they inflicted on a number of enemy strongpoints would be a huge contributor to the success of *Tractable*.

Moments later, the second wave made its approach.

Below, deep in the nearby Hautmesnil Quarry, men from the Canadian and Polish infantry and artillery regiments who were LOB (Left out of Battle) were enjoying a few hours free from war. The portable baths had been brought up, and they were reveling in the warm, sunny day and the chance to catch up on laundry and letter writing.

Nearby, Lieutenant Ken Turnbull had hunkered his platoon of machine gunners of the Toronto Scottish into a large German dugout. They had ordered up their first hot meal in days, and were idly cleaning their guns, enjoying the respite. They spotted Polish troops moving into a nearby field.

Elated at the sight of the heavy RAF bombers flying low overhead, many of the men waved and yelled at their protectors. Not one had any qualms about the accuracy of Bomber Command, which had made six previous raids without causing a single allied casualty.[9]

Following in after the first wave, Flight Lieutenant Russell Curtis, an American with No. 428 Squadron, No. 6 Group, RCAF, and Flight Sergeant Roy Clarke's craft in No. 419 Squadron, were in the next run-ins to the target area.

By then, "bomb creep"—the smoke and dust that filtered back from the earlier bombing—was obliterating the target, just as Air Chief Marshal Harris had feared. Peering through the smog the pilots saw yellow flares and believed they were the agreed signal described in their briefing. They heard the master bomber, or "master of ceremonies," as he was called, break radio silence to instruct: "bomb the yellow target indicators."

What they didn't realize was that the master bomber was giving that bombs-away order to the first wave of bombers who were at that moment successfully on target—not to the second wave craft.[10]

They also could not know that some Canadian troops, watching the huge bomb bay doors open, panicked. They rushed to light their Verey pistol flares, as they had been trained, to alert aircraft of friendly troops below—yellow flares.

"It would only take one crew to bomb short," Flight Sergeant Clarke believes. "Then the troops would start sending up the yellow Vereys and, once that started, some of the crews behind them would say, 'Oh! They've changed the target!' "

This, in fact, happened to Clarke's crew. After the bomb-aimer had dropped the bombs, the navigator went up behind the pilot. Clarke wriggled into the dome behind him. "The navigator was yelling, 'My God! We're bombing short!'

"We could see the bomb bursts going down to the yellow Verey flares, a paler color than the intense yellow of the target indicators. You could definitely see the difference. I saw it myself.

"The master bomber could see it, too," Clarke remembers. "He started screaming, and shouting 'You're bombing short, for God's sake! Don't bomb those yellows coming from the ground!' "[11]

Wing Commander Chester Hull faults the Canadian Army for the arbitrary assignment. "There were five targets all in a row along the front, and the army insisted they be bombed in a certain order, one after the other. So the smoke from the first target drifted over the others. That was one cause of the confusion."[12]

Each of the five targets had a master bomber, each on a different radio frequency. Most of the remaining pilots of the operation flying in the next waves were unaware of any problems. As ordered, they used their stopwatches to put them on target for accurate bombing.

But 10 percent of them forgot to use their watches and, hence, neglected to time the run. They depended instead on visual identification. Tragically, they dropped their lethal loads on their own troops below.

On the ground, elation turned to horror as tons of deadly bombs poured down on them relentlessly. Hundreds of troops at Hautmesnil Quarry dived for slit trenches as the attack continued. Direct hits were made on the troops and on the vehicles that were massed in the quarry prior to moving the men out that evening.

Seeking cover in the slits was probably the worst thing they could have done. When Lieutenant Turnbull saw the bombs, he thought, "Holy Jeesuz, here it comes! We're goners if we stay in this dugout."

Turnbull's quick thinking saved many lives that day.

"Get the hell out of here!" he yelled at his men. "Get to the open fields!"

"We threw everything into the carriers—our guns were dismantled and we just tossed in all the parts in a jumble—and took off for the next open field. We felt awfully vulnerable, standing there in the open, but we were lucky. I lost one sergeant, wounded in the arm, that was all."[13]

In the Polish sector, terrible carnage was experienced. In all, 397 men were casualties. One hundred and fifty were killed.

"The absurd thing was that there was no direct ground-to-air communications, which could have stopped it at once," observed the Gordon Highlanders' diarist, who experienced the same futile helplessness as bombs thundered about him.[14]

The war diary of the Royal Regiment of Canada described the terror of the men on the ground: "For more than half an hour the stunned survivors hid in what shelter they could find while this dreadful hammering beat upon the battalion. At last it stopped. Here and there men emerged from the wreckage to find the area unrecognisable."[15]

A thick pall of smoke hung over the area as the men gradually crawled out of their trenches. In anger and dismay they viewed the terrible scene. "It was the only time our morale really sank. We couldn't go anywhere to escape the bombs," Corporal John Angus McDonald remembers. McDonald was one of three brothers in the regiment. His younger brother Francis was wounded on July 19 in Caen and died the next day. (Another brother, Jim, a corporal, would be shot in the knee at Boulogne in September.) "We could see them opening the bomb bay doors. There was not a thing we could do—there's our own people trying to knock us off."[16]

The chaplain of the 2 Derbyshire Yeomanry (51st Highland Division), Major N. F. Jones, comforted what he described as "horribly shattered" Scots.[17] A British gunner, Sergeant J. G. Perry of the 15th Medium Regiment, Royal Artillery, stumbled into his base camp. His clothes were torn, his body bruised and filthy. Shakily he recounted to startled friends the story of his escape from being buried alive. Two thousand-pound bombs had exploded a hairbreadth away from him, one ten yards to his right and the other six yards on the left. By some sweet miracle he eluded death.[18]

Of the 811 aircraft, seventy-seven of the aircraft bombed "short." The majority—90 percent—performed their tasks with great skill and accuracy. As historian Terry Copp later noted, "the neutralisation of a dozen key antitank positions spelled the differences between success and failure."[19]

Clearly, the blame for the tragedy was shared two ways. Canadian Army headquarters was at fault: for not alerting Bomber Command to SHAEF's policy of using yellow flares as an infantry signal, and for arbitrarily insisting on the sequence of targets that produced "bomb creep."

"The smoke and dust were very strong factors in the erroneous bombing. It was blowing into the approach," Turnbull believes. "Even my flight commander and his group captain [flying as a passenger] got sucked into the same mistake."[20]

The risks that had been initially pointed out by Bomber Command but then ignored by the Canadian Army—sending aircrew on a mission for which they had little or no training—were being tragically realized.

Also to blame were the 10 percent of aircrew who did not follow clear orders to time their runs, using the stopwatches provided them. Unused as they were to "timed runs," a number of navigators neglected to set their watches when they reached the Caen crossroads. Because they were on a day flight, they were using a visual observation of the flares rather than a stopwatch. Then, seeing the army's yellow signal, they thought they were on target. On both sides, remorse and guilt were acknowledged.

The air personnel of the errant seventy-seven bombers were victims in a very real sense. Most of them first learned of the disaster when they returned to base for the debriefing. Sadly, forty-four of these craft were piloted by members of the Royal Canadian Air Force. Bombing their own countrymen bore an extra sting. For US Flight Lieutenant Russell Curtis, who had volunteered in the Royal Canadian Air Force, it was a devastating error.

Flight Lieutenant John Turnbull, RCAF, would normally have been flying on this mission. Luckily for him he was grounded that day. "My flight commander took the station's group captain with him; they flew in the second wave. So I only sat in on the briefing."

Turnbull was back at the base waiting to attend the debriefing of the men on their return. "They didn't know that they had bombed short until we debriefed them. They were chagrined . . . very unhappy people."[21]

Bomber Command's reaction was swift and uncompromising. "The whole squadron was put under a form of house arrest for about twenty-four hours until they got the thing straightened out," Turnbull recalls. "They had to turn in their logbooks and no one could leave the base or even use the telephone."[22]

Flying Officer Ken Fulton also attended the debriefing that broke the news to the squadron. "Every aircraft was sealed, and they took every camera out of the aircraft. In other squadrons there were a few people disciplined for bombing short. We got pictures of the target and all of our squadron was fine. There was a lot of consternation. I never did hear who did it and of course we never talked about it. It was all hushed up."[23]

Judging by the London *Daily Mail* account the next day, the hushup even included a British correspondent who actually flew on the raid. Terming it a total success, with no mention of the disaster, he wrote:

> Aerial policemen were on duty over the target areas right through the bombing to ensure that the bombs did not creep across the narrow line marking the positions of our own ground forces. They gave frequent directions over the radio to the bombers . . . They were part of an intricate organisation to ensure that the attack went right home to the mark.[24]

After the investigation, disciplinary measures taken against these crews found responsible included demotions of one or two ranks, reprimands, and "starring" them from participating in similar raids without further training.

No discipline could ever redress the terror the victims of the errant bombing endured, or the justifiable anger they felt. One gunner reported seeing men six months later, just returned to the front after lengthy treatment for battle trauma induced by the bombing in the quarry.[25]

Even forty-five years later there were scars. "I met a captain from my hometown who was in charge of the artillery unit that we bombed," Fulton remembers. "He lost quite a few men and he was still very bitter that he had been bombed by our side . . . still bitter, after all those years."[26]

But no punishment could match the hell the aircrews put themselves through after that day of bombing their own countrymen. Their lack of training was not their fault, but their carelessness was.

The pall of his reprimand continued to be keenly felt by US Flight Lieutenant Russell Curtis until a night raid over Dortmund nearly three months later. Flying through heavy antiaircraft fire he was severely wounded, incurring a compound fracture of the head.

The squadron CO tells a story of an incredible vindication:

> Having been chastised by me for bombing short at Falaise, Curtis was determined to prove that this time he had bombed where he was supposed to have. He hung on long enough to enable the bomb-aimer to drop the bombs, and then for another couple of minutes to take the picture of where the bombs hit.

Curtis then collapsed. The air bomber took over the controls although he had never previously landed an aircraft, much less a four-engine Lancaster. With the help of the remaining crew members he brought the craft home, managing an emergency landing despite having a tire, that had been hit by flak, burst on landing.

The entire crew was decorated for the feat of fulfilling their objective and returning the plane home with the pilot unconscious. Curtis received one of Great Britain's highest awards, the DSO (Distinguished Service Order). "I don't know of any other crew when all the living members were given a decoration for one incident," Hull added.[27]

It was a brave apology to the men in Hautmesnil Quarry.

CHAPTER 21

Falaise . . . at Last

The battle from Caen to Falaise had been a bitter two-week struggle, ridge by bloody ridge, mile by grudging mile, across the rolling cornfields of the Caen plain.

Simonds's Operation *Tractable*—propelling some fifteen thousand men and their armor across the Laison River under a mask of smoke—was an innovative success. In this battle of attrition, the Laison Valley victory, one of the most remarkable assault operations in the war, leapfrogged the Allies a vital five miles. They were at last within striking distance of Falaise and Trun, their objectives for so many weeks.

Just one more ridge to conquer. Just one more river to cross.

But from here on the drive to close the gap became a deadly struggle.

Despite the near annihilation of the German 85th Division on August 14, the 88mm guns of *Luftwaffe* General Pickert's III Flak Corps continued to create a curtain of formidable fire. It was virtually impossible for the Allies to advance in broad daylight across open country against an enemy with well-sited and dug-in antitank guns overlooking the battlefield. Minefields covered by the antitank weapons also slowed progress.

The enemy *Panzers* still roamed the heights as predators. At Soulangy, the Fort Garry Horse lost six tanks to the gun of a single Tiger in the space of a few minutes.[1]

With no thought now of winning, the *Wehrmacht* tactics were designed to create major delays in the allied advance. Buying time was what it was all about: time to permit von Kluge's orderly retreat to the Seine of all noncombat units; time to keep the narrowing neck of the Falaise Gap open long enough to allow the *Panzer* units still escaping from Mortain to elude the allied encirclement.

"The German habit of leaving snipers and machine-gunners as ambushers could be both tough and expensive," the Queen's Own Cameron Highlanders war diary noted. "Two or three men could hold our battalion up for hours."[2]

A German *Panzer* officer described their tactics: "We always tried to delay them and we succeeded. We erected roadblocks just from leaves, twigs of trees, flower boxes, and so forth, which we took off the houses. We put them on the road. Then we painted a sign *ACHTUNG MINEN!* [Beware of Mines]."[3] That bought the German army more time, too.

As they fell back from the River Laison, the Germans firmly entrenched a new defensive line some three miles north and northeast of Falaise. The accepted battle school wisdom dictated that the attacker must have three to five times the strength of the defender to overcome a well-dug-in defensive force.

The Allies had nothing like those numbers.

There were no easy answers. Hulks of smoldering Shermans dotting the landscape gave mute evidence of that. Allied recovery units cannibalized parts from wrecks to keep the armor going. Crews frantically welded on extra tank tracks to give added protection to Sherman tanks inadequate in this static warfare.

Although squadrons and battalions faltered at times in the face of dogged resistance, individuals shone. The skill to lead and the passion to prove victorious were never more evident.

The First Canadian Army's battalions were at half strength. Exhausted troops were fighting with determination and little hope of immediate rest. Casualties among officers created strange command situations: majors became acting commanding officers; lieutenants took over companies; and sergeants or corporals led platoons.

In battle, it is the leaders who inspire the men to fight. The Normandy fighting saw more than a dozen Canadian commanding officers killed, wounded, or replaced. In just one twenty-four-hour period, three commanders of the Governor General's Foot Guards were killed or wounded.

The 4th Armored Brigade lost three commanders to wounds; one, Brigadier Leslie Booth, was killed. The commander of the 3d Canadian Infantry Division, Major General Rod Keller, was severely wounded. This turnover of command upset the continuity of leadership style and rocked the solid confidence within the battalions.

The Glens (Stormont, Dundas, and Glengarry Highlanders) watched sullenly as the commanding officer who had led them onto the D-Day beaches, Lieutenant Colonel Ben Cunningham, was summarily dismissed from his command. Lieutenant Colonel Roger Rowley was parachuted into the job. Just turned thirty, with a major operation to launch (*Totalize*) in just three days, Rowley had some eight hundred somewhat resentful frontline soldiers with whom to forge a new relationship that could mean life or death to them all.

"They loved their commanding officer, and they were mad because he was fired," Rowley explains. "So they didn't like me. The only two people I knew when I arrived at battalion headquarters were my driver and my batman, and I brought them both with me. I had a pretty rough time there for a while, but we got along well at the end."[4]

The eighteenth-century Château d'Assy, pleasantly situated in an orchard bordering the Laison River, was the assigned objective for the Glens. It was also a fortified defensive strongpoint of the 1053d Regiment, a horse-drawn unit in Fiebig's 85th Division.

The Canadians warily crossed a shell-cratered moonscape of littered human remains and pieces of horseflesh. Shattered apple trees, now stripped of their young fruit and blackened, stood among the craters. Rowley's men swiftly cleared the château and rounded up the prisoners.

A young Glen reinforcement, new to the line, spotted a German Tiger tank that had suddenly appeared two hundred yards away. Turning to his company commander in the passenger seat of a Bren carrier, he asked excitedly, "Sir, is that one of ours?"

"If it isn't, we've had it!" the major snapped. A moment later an 88mm shell crashed into the carrier. The officer was instantly killed; the private leapt safely into a ditch amid machine-gun fire.

Rowley, up forward as usual with his lead companies, called for fire from a nearby six-pounder antitank gun, and the tank was dispatched. But the well-dug-in enemy machine-gun nests stubbornly kept the Canadians at bay. Rowley ordered the "Wasps" to attack. These flame-throwing Bren carriers could wreak fearful damage, hosing liquid fire on positions more than forty yards away.

The sight and sound of seared and screaming dead and dying victims of this deadly weapon would live long in the minds of the young soldiers.

As darkness drew in, Colonel Rowley was in a dangerous position. His left flank was wide-open, and he was out of communication with brigade headquarters. He established his command post in the château's pitch-dark wine cellar. It was a sinister place, made more eerie by the head of a dead horse plastered like some grotesque carving over its entrance. The floor was awash in wine from burst vats.

Finally, communication was restored with brigade and M10 tank-destroyers were sent up to knock out some five Tigers that had been stalking the regiment.

"We were the only guys who got there and stayed there," Rowley would say of the battalion's efforts in capturing and holding its objective. "That was one tricky battle."[5]

The achievement of bonding eight hundred fatigued and dissatisfied men into a smooth-running effective machine capable of holding off German *Panzers*—all in less than two weeks—had been one tricky feat for the thirty-year-old commander.

In this sense, the battle for Falaise became a series of outstanding acts of initiative by small groups of riflemen.

Lying in ambush on the high ground above Falaise—Hill 159—Kurt Meyer was ready to pounce on the leaderless 4th Canadian Armored Division. He observed the Canadian Grenadier Guards and the reconstituted British Columbia Regiment moving up Hill 159. He was aware, too, that the Americans had just captured Alençon and were closing in from the south. It was imperative that he hold the line as long as possible if the German Seventh Army were to have any hope of escaping the trap.[6] The terrain made his task easier: rolling wooded country studded with stone farmhouses, and ridges that could be fortified.

"Hill 159 is a boiling mountain," Meyer reported. "Shell after shell explodes around us." The *Hitlerjugend* commander, wounded in the head by a shell splinter, continued to tough it out "with a half-shaved head and a couple of stitches."[7] Meyer ordered the 3d SS Artillery Battalion to open fire. The heavy 88mm guns pinned down the Canadians. The Grenadier Guards were reduced from fifty-six to thirty-nine tanks.

Meanwhile, the Canadian Scottish Regiment was also moving toward the coveted hills above Falaise. Heavy mortar fire poured down on the Can Scots, and their supporting tanks came under intense antitank fire, driving them back.[8]

Their war diary describes the grim encounter with a 12th SS battle-group:

> All ranks of the Scottish now stepped into a molten fire bath of battle. They were tired, hungry and thirsty. These conditions made them doubly mad.
>
> The SS defenders fought back bitterly but could not stop the momentum of the [Can Scot] advance. Few prisoners were taken; the enemy preferred to die rather than give in. [German] snipers were posted along hedgerows covering each tiny field with rifles and MG-42s.
>
> B Coy [Company] slugged its way through all opposition to be the first company to consolidate on its objective, where they were counterattacked by Tiger tanks and armoured cars.[9]

A bitter action now took place. So close was the fighting that the Canadian Scottish ducked for cover underneath the hostile tanks that were milling around them through the rocks and hedges of the heights. From the midst of the chaotic violence, "B" Company yelled over the radio net for tank support. The only reply that came through to them was a BBC announcer benignly introducing the program *Music While You Work*.[10]

But if the Germans were determined, so also were the Canadian Scottish, who pushed stubbornly on despite their losses. Company Sergeant Major J. S. Grimmond won the Distinguished Conduct Medal by leading his company headquarters against two German tanks and supporting infantry.[11]

But the price was high. By 1645 hours, one company was halved to forty-six. The thirty-seven men killed and ninety-three wounded marked the most costly day of the Normandy campaign for the Can Scots.[12]

. . .

A mile or so east of that attack, the Winnipeg Rifles had similar success with an assault on the ridge. The company commander, Captain Cliff Chadderton, noted in his diary, "I gave the okay and we went up the hill after I had ordered some smoke and covering fire. We got onto the objective (four or five farm buildings) and took eighteen to thirty prisoners. Great big mystery—there were two SS *feldwebels* [sergeants] but the rest were from ordinary [*Wehrmacht*] divisions."[13] This, in fact, was more evidence of Meyer's tactic of inserting small combat groups of his 12th SS into ordinary *Wehrmacht* infantry companies to "stiffen" them.

Still further east, the 51st Highland Division provided left flank support for the Canadians. The Highlanders approached St.-Pierre-sur-Dives, a picturesque riverside village. (A lustful Scot, not understanding the French pronunciation "Deeves," chortled, "Dives! Real French dives at last!")[14] Meanwhile, 1st Polish Armored Division seized a crossing of the same river at Jort following a bitter fight.

The eastern arm of the allied encirclement was inexorably closing in toward Trun and Chambois, the Germans' escape route.

On the night of August 15, the Highland Division padre N. F. Jones wrote in his diary:

> Tuesday we eventually moved to South of St. Sylvain. We found some lovely Jerry gun sites with slit trenches. We spent quite some time digging in the half-track & then getting our own slit trenches ready. It was just as well. When night came we had a concentrated Jerry bombing all round. This was coincident with the first heavy downpour for some time. It was the most uncomfortable night I've spent for years as the rain poured into my trench. In the morning the sun came out quickly & we managed to dry out.[15]

The *Luftwaffe* maintained a rare patrol over the Falaise area that night, dropping clusters of parachute flares, a prelude to antipersonnel bombing raids. The skies would suddenly fill with a virtual blizzard: thousands of whirling white phosphorous fragments, each no larger than a bar of soap, tumbled down. US Army Lieutenant Robert Weiss recalled the horror of it: "Where the particles landed on shirts and trousers they sizzled and burned. We brushed our clothing frantically . . . If any of the stuff touched the skin; it could inflict a horrible burn, increasing in intensity as it burrowed into a man's flesh . . . Another shell. Another missile from hell. Fiery snow!"[16]

A young Canadian lieutenant, Edward Glass, a Canloan officer newly arrived in Normandy, had moved into position minutes before. He had just sent off a letter to the commanding officer of his regiment in Toronto, the 48th Highlanders, telling them of the warm welcome he had received by the affiliated British regiment, the Gordons, when he arrived ten days ago.

"The CO has insisted that I wear our regimental flash alongside their own," the lad reported proudly.[17]

Gazing skyward in astonishment Glass saw the white slivers cascading down, almost like a Canadian snowfall. Then he heard an eerie swishing noise as the shower came through the air . . . and his final sound on earth: the steady drumming as they exploded.

The Highlanders dived for their slits. Major Martin Lindsay, acting CO of the 1st Gordons, recorded the next moments. "Unfortunately 'D' Company, the last to arrive, had only dug down about eighteen inches by this time and they had twenty-three casualties. Most were only lightly wounded, but two were killed and one of them was Glass, the young Canadian officer who came to us ten days ago."[18]

It was a deadly blizzard.

On August 15, General Simonds ordered the Canadians to capture Falaise. Immediately!

The proud home of William the Conqueror was in ruins. The twelfth-century castle where he was born was perched on a high rock (or *falaise*, giving the town its name). Allied bombing and shelling had made the roads through the historic town almost impassable.

Fanatical young SS *Hitlerjugend* snipers were sheltered behind broken walls or in ruins of buildings. They knew that in savage street fighting, a single machine gun could hold up an entire battalion. This was their mission: to delay the attackers as long as possible so that other *Panzer* units could escape the Allies' net.

A German antitank gun at the gates to the town had pinned down and stopped the South Saskatchewan Regiment moving in from the west. The squadron commander of the supporting Sherbrooke Fusiliers, Major

Radley-Walters, was astonished to see a lone man running forward from the rear of the battalion. After a sprint of several hundred yards, this un-known soldier reached the forward company, dropped to the ground, and opened fire at the antitank gun, silencing it.

After that astonishing feat, without a word of command from anybody, the infantry and tanks came to life. They leapt to a renewed attack and, within minutes, were pouring into the town square.

"It was a fine example of one man moving the whole bloody battalion without a word, just through his own example," Radley-Walters notes. "That man was Lieutenant Colonel Freddie Clift, the CO of the South Saskatchewans."[19]

It was now 2300 hours, and the battalion had penetrated the town. They reached the château square, still under heavy fire and surrounded by snipers firing on all sides from the upper windows of the buildings.

Clift saw one of his company commanders shot between the eyes, the bullet exiting from behind his left ear. That decided him. "We can't stay here all night, being shot at," he told his staff. "Line the battalion up, put the forward platoons in carriers, and we'll charge straight through to the far side of the town."

The plan worked. Clift himself climbed aboard the forward carrier to direct the attack. He noted a large house on his map, laid on a hasty flank assault, and captured what turned out to be the enemy headquarters.

A brigade staff officer advised him that it would be safer to press on out of town. "That's bullshit," the doughty commander bellowed. "My boys haven't slept for thirty hours. We'll set up defenses right here."[20]

The man who had single-handedly inspired his troops to fight was clearly able to demonstrate his compassion for them.

Next morning the Cameron Highlanders of Canada broke into the town, their supporting Sherbrooke tanks having been held up by huge craters. Then it was up to Les Fusiliers Mont-Royal to mop up the last re-sistance.

The 12th SS commander, Bernhard Krause, ordered his Hitler Youth troops to withdraw. The order failed to reach a group of SS Grenadiers holed up behind the thick stone walls of the *École Supérieure*.

The band of some fifty or sixty rabid young Nazis hung on until dawn. Their NCO held a ballot to decide which two would be sent out to report to *Sturmbannfuhrer* Krause. A ballot was necessary because not one of the SS wanted to leave his comrades in this last fight.

When the Canadians stormed the fortification at 0200 hours, setting fire to the buildings and plastering the school with machine-gun fire, they found only the corpses of the defenders.

The battle for Falaise was won. But a twelve-mile gap was still open. Chambois and Trun had become the keys to sealing the trap on the escaping enemy.

PART V

AUGUST 17–21: CLOSING THE TRAP

CHAPTER 22

Command Fiasco August 16–19

When Bradley decided to halt XV Corps south of Argentan and allow Patton to advance east toward the Seine, he left three divisions behind to hold the southern jaw of the trap.

Not much was expected of this improvised force, made up of the temperamental French Armored Division, the untried 80th US Infantry Division and the 90th, thought by many to be "the single worst division in the European theater."[1]

Not much was expected but on August 16 much was demanded. Montgomery, finally convinced that substantial German forces were still west of the Argentan–Falaise road, directed the Americans to seize Trun and Chambois. They would meet the Canadians there and close the gap.

Bradley relayed the order to Patton, who appointed his chief of staff, Major General Hugh Gaffey, to command an improvised corps headquarters and coordinate the advance. Gaffey issued orders to launch a three divisional attack in the morning of August 17.

But Bradley, without even consulting Patton, sent V Corps Commander, Major General Leonard Gerow to Alençon to take over the divisions.

Not only had they been orphaned when Patton took off, but now they had two commanders from two different armies—and neither one could find them. The divisions had seemingly disappeared.

Gerow spent a frustrating night driving around in a pelting rain looking for his new command. He grizzled that "V Corps that night was composed of ten rain-soaked officers in three jeeps out searching the country-side for three divisions."[2]

Gerow finally located 90th Infantry Division and set up temporary headquarters a few hours later in the bar of the Hôtel du France in Alençon. His first act was to cancel Gaffey's battleplan.

It resulted in a "strange situation," the unit history reports. "Here were two major-generals, both charged with the command of the same divisions. Both wanted to attack immediately, but one [Gaffey] had to wait for orders from above, while the other had been given authority to act on his own."[3]

The outcome of this botch-up was that while all three units had been ready to do battle on August 17, none was now cleared to launch an attack. The situation remained "obscured," as the war diary described it, while urgent radio messages flashed back and forth between the higher commands.

The command situation was equally confused on the north side of the gap, where Montgomery also failed to take advantage of the opportunity to encircle the enemy.

On August 14 he told the Canadians that Falaise must be captured before the advance to Trun could begin. General Simonds, however, believed that "Falaise was just a name"[4] and could be left to the Canadian and British divisions advancing from the west. He believed the proper role of the II Canadian Corps was to get to Trun and Chambois as soon as possible.

Simonds had to obey orders, but he decided to send the Polish Armored Division, which was in reserve, to Trun, while the rest of his corps carried out Monty's plan to capture the high ground above Falaise. The next day, Monty transferred the 7th British Armored to First Canadian Army but instead of allowing it to reinforce the Polish thrust he insisted that the division move northeast to Lisieux—away from the fighting in the Gap.[5] This left a single understrength armored division—the inexperienced Poles—as the only force moving to close the Gap from the north on August 17.

The situation hadn't gotten any better on the south side of the Gap. Gerow decided that the French Armored Division, desperate to get to Paris first so that city could be liberated by de Gaulle's Free French, could only be used in a supporting role. This left him with the 90th and two of the three regiments of the 80th Infantry Division.

Gerow decided to commit one of the 80th Division's regiments, the 318th, to the east of Argentan with orders to bypass the town, then turn and enter it from the northeast.[6]

The 80th Division's intelligence report described the enemy defenses that they encountered on August 18:

> The city of Argentan and the high ground from north of Argentan to Le Bourg-St. Léonard was strongly held by the 728th Infantry Regiment of the 116th Panzer Division. Argentan itself was held by a G.A.F. Battalion and a detachment of about 100 SS troopers. Fourteen to fifteen Panther tanks and numerous self-propelled 20mm A.A. guns were also committed to the defense of the city and vicinity. The enemy defensive position was well protected by minefields and booby-traps and the enemy had had ample time to dig in. The Forêt de Gouffern, between Argentan and Chambois, provided cover for the enemy supply, installations and communication lines.[7]

The 80th Infantry Division had landed in France in early August, too late for Mortain and, indeed, for any fighting until its first battle assignment on August 17: to capture Argentan. The leadership skills of its commanding general, Horace McBride, were, according to General Bradley, "suspect."[8]

The men who served under "Hairless Horace," as they dubbed him, went even further: Captain Nordstrom, Battalion Intelligence Officer of the 702d Tank Battalion, rated General McBride as "nervous in combat and inept with battlefield decisions."[9]

McBride, against all military protocol and good judgment, strode onto the battlefield on August 18 and gave three direct orders over the heads of his battalion, company, and platoon commanders that resulted in the deaths of many men and the demoralization of the rest.

("Later," Nordstrom wryly noted, "he stayed in his headquarters, which improved the situation immensely.")[10]

Lieutenant (now retired Colonel) William B. "Bull" Miller gives this account of the actions of the 3d Platoon, 702d Tank Battalion on 17/18 August: "On the evening of the 17th, 'B' Company's Commander, Captain Richard E. Stover, pulled into the assembly area, drew us together and informed us to be ready to go into battle for Argentan on the 18th of August."[11]

Corporal "Buck" Weaver remembers that Staff Sergeant Frank L. "Pappy" Ream was instrumental in Captain Stover's decision to use 3d Platoon tanks first, in the upcoming attack. "Pappy" considered it an honor that his platoon was the first out of the entire 702d Tank Battalion to go into battle.[12]

The 3d Platoon diary records: "Aug 18: We are all awake under this clear French sky, it is 6:30 A.M. We eat 'K' rations for breakfast." Lieutenant Miller's 3d Platoon is preparing to move into the attack. At 8:00 A.M. the platoon leaves the bivouac area in support of 318th Infantry Regiment.

Eighty Infantry Division History: "The platoon was ordered by Brig. Gen. McBride to go across a road into a hedgerow and counter the light machine-gun fire that men from the 318th Infantry Regiment were receiving from Argentan." This order proved to be disaster for Lieutenant Miller, his platoon, and Captain Stover, the company commander.

"The platoon ran into well placed anti-tank guns and enemy tanks," the history recounts. "The platoon fought well, but under these conditions the odds were against them."[13]

Four tanks were completely destroyed and burned.

"Bull" Miller continues:

We suffered considerable casualties. My tank was the lead tank to cross the road, followed by my section—Sgt. Royce and Sgt. Marriotti. Sgt. Ream's tank did not make it; it had ditched, stuck behind the lines. Sgt. Thomas was the other tank we lost at the time. Three men killed, twelve wounded. It was a great loss to the company and the battalion as a whole, because it was our first real battle loss.

Colonel Miller argues that McBride handled the operation badly:

I . . . should not have really received a direct order to go in line, across the road and get behind the hedgerow and engage the automatic weapons. General McBride should have relayed the order to reconnoiter and support the position, and then to take up position across the road.

But I'm sure it didn't enter his mind, whether he knew how to do it, or just wanted some direct support, not knowing that there were tanks in Argentan to cover the fields that the [infantry] men were advancing over.

Incredibly, in the face of one disaster, McBride courted another. He ordered Captain Stover, commanding officer of "B" Company, to send more tanks across the same field to support the action.

"With that order," (Colonel Miller continues)

my company commander, Capt. Stover, tried to explain that it was not a position for tanks to be in, for support; that we were out-gunned and that someone from the anti-tank outfit should come in and engage the tanks. As I recall, General McBride did not lis-ten to this, and gave him [Stover] a direct order to bring the tanks up and engage them.

Stover refused to obey the order and commit his company to more car-nage. McBride relieved him of command. He was later court-martialed.

I, myself, feel that Capt. Stover was correct in the order, that he (McBride) should not tell him what to do with his remaining tanks. Lt. Wilfred Hansen, 1st Platoon Leader took over as Com-manding Officer of "B" Co., and did not specifically bring the tanks up and engage them into battle. He reconnoitered the area and at-tempted to learn what could be done with armor to support the in-fantry. This is what should have been done in the first place.[14]

Many of the men of "B" Company felt that General McBride's treat-ment of Captain Stover bordered on the criminal. Sergeant "Ole" Olson, Battalion Intelligence Sergeant, remembers seeing the good captain being led away, under arrest, in the custody of two MPs.*

---

*After Capt. Stover was convicted at his court-martial of disobeying a direct order, General Dwight D. Eisenhower, in reviewing the Stover case, reduced the sentence handed down by the court, in view of the fact that Captain Stover was acting in good faith, in trying to pre-vent the annihilation of his command and not out of any concern for himself. (NA.RG 94. WWII Operations Report. 80th Infantry Division. August 1944.)

The battle for Argentan raged on, with massive artillery and heavy losses on both sides, until the Germans were driven out (or abandoned it, as the 116th history insists) on August 20.[15] The remnants of the German *Panzers* sought refuge in the Forêt de Gouffern, where they could regroup with other tattered units and plan their escape.

The bombardments since August 13 had reduced Argentan's thirteenth-century defense bastions, its fifteenth-century Marguerite Tower and its historic buildings and old cobbled streets to mere mounds of rubble.

"Patrol after patrol of General McBride's infantry, for whom the Argentan battle was the first test . . . against well trained and well equipped enemy in force, entered the town," a specialist in this battle, Frenchman Eddy Florentin wrote.

> There was soon excitement such as we had not known for a long time . . . refugees streaming in from the country and mingling with the men in khaki . . . Cameras worked overtime to record for the rest of the world the plight of our city, which had suffered so grievously from the appalling seven-day bombardment. It had the sad privilege of being the third worst damaged city in Normandy.[16]

But gaining Argentan still did not close the trap.

CHAPTER 23

The Tough 'Ombres Gain a Soul

While the 80th Division fought for Argentan, the 90th, a Texas-Oklahoma division nicknamed the "Tough 'Ombres" was trying to regain Le Bourg-St. Léonard and the high ground overlooking Chambois and the Dives River Valley. This was a formidable challenge for a single division but it gave the 90th one last chance to prove itself in battle—or be dissolved.

According to General Bradley, "Almost from the moment of its starting attack the 90th became a 'problem' division. So exasperating was its performance that at one point the First Army Staff gave up and recommended that we break it up for replacements."[1] In those early days of fighting in Normandy, he dismissed the division as "ill-trained" and sacked its first commander after just five days of combat command, replacing him with Brigadier General Eugene Landrum, an experienced officer.

During Landrum's brief and dismal period of combat command (five weeks during which this "short, fat and uninspiring" man commanded "from an arm chair in the cellar"),[2] the 90th Division was plunged into three brutal, costly battles. Despite horrific casualties, the division held its own. They were slow, at times uneven in performance, but no more so than other divisions in First Army adapting to the agonies of war. Landrum's inability to inspire and motivate his troops was a key reason for their poor reputation.

Leadership was faulty or at best inexperienced at all command levels. Infantry regiments had lost 48 percent of their platoon leaders *each week* in the seven weeks of *bocage* fighting. A lieutenant lasted an average of two and a half weeks. They were gone before they had learned the ropes. This situation was duplicated amongst the NCOs.[3]

One regimental commander caused so much "chaos and confusion" that his aide was instructed to countermand every order he issued and, literally, "shoot him" if he persisted in his outrageous behavior.[4]

On August 1, two important changes occurred in the division: it came under Patton's Third Army, and two seasoned commanders took the helm. Brigadier General Raymond McLain was a peacetime banker from Oklahoma and longtime National Guardsman who had fought in Africa as artillery commander. His assistant divisional commander, fifty-six-year-old "Wild Bill" Weaver added his dynamic leadership. The 90th was given another chance.[5]

The pair is credited as giving the division back its soul in the German-infested woods of the Forêt d'Ecouves, the turmoil of Le Bourg–St. Léonard, and the carnage of Chambois in August 1944.[6]

The enemy confronting the 90th consisted of elements of 116th *Panzer* Division, including a fresh tank battalion borrowed from 9th *Panzer*. Major Heinz Günther Guderian recalled seeing the rookie battalion commander standing in the turret of the first *Panzer*.

> We were members of the same year group of officers [commissioned in the same year]. I subordinated the battalion [to 116th Panzer] and ordered him to immediately take up position at the southern edge of Argentan and to defend it against the approaching enemy. The battalion had not yet been in battle and brought about 25 Panthers into combat.[7]

Beefing up the depleted strength of the 116th *Panzer* became something of a scavenger hunt. Its commander, *Oberst* Müller (replacing the deposed Count von Schwerin) ran into—and promptly seconded— another *Panzer* regiment that still had a handful of tanks. He then contacted an antiaircraft regiment that moved a light battalion to Argentan in the night. Soon the division's engineers were moved up.

The 116th *Panzer*'s morale rose with a letter from von Schwerin that somehow made its way through the embattled German lines. He expressed concern about their pending entrapment and encouragement on their escape. The note was signed, "Your loyal old commander."[8]

The tattered remnants of a powerful *Panzer* division were stirring to potency again—just in time to intercept the American 90th Division.

To the Germans, here was an unexpected opportunity to capitalize on their enemy's errors. They were baffled as to why the Americans had halted in their approach when the 116th was so terribly vulnerable. But it gave the division the opportunity to keep the gap open as an escape hatch for Seventh Army and *Panzergruppe Eberbach,* and they seized it.

"Because of the inactivity of the enemy, the Division succeeded in rallying and establishing a certain defense toward the south and to keep the passage open for the units of Army Group that were fighting west of the Orne," Guderian wrote.[9]

On the afternoon of August 16, the German *Panzers* attacked US 90th Division's 359th Infantry Regiment at Le Bourg-St. Léonard with tanks and infantry.

Le Bourg was little more than a crossroads, an ordinary hamlet that was to become of extraordinarily vital importance in the coming days. A road running through the town center led down a gentle slope to the village of Chambois, three miles north. Due south for seven miles it reached Argentan.

A captured German prisoner carried a document showing some of the proposed enemy escape routes. It stressed the use of secondary roads and trails [that] led through open country.[10] Le Bourg's many small dirt lanes and trails crisscrossing into the woods and slopes of its eastern perimeter had become sought-after routes for the nineteen enemy armor and infantry divisions trying to escape. A narrow belt of dense woods between Le Bourg and Falaise to the north offered the Germans good concealment from air observation and allied attack and a safe harbor for coordinating their breakout attempts, which were now in full intensity.

Sited on the wooded ridge, citizens of Le Bourg enjoyed panoramic views of the broad Dives Valley to the north and east, where the many church steeples signaled the clusters of villages below. An officer with the US 915th Field Artillery Battalion climbed the hill and was stunned at what he saw: "It was a sight such as man seldom sees. Trucks burning, artillery bursts galore, tanks and T.D.s [tank-destroyers] firing; it was bedlam and confusion."[11]

This observation point gave the Americans a huge advantage over the fleeing enemy. On one of many such instances, the gunners responded to a report of a huge enemy column moving to the east. Artillery fire was placed on the head of the column, disabling the lead vehicle, then moved down its length, leaving it "halted and helpless" on the ground as a group of P-47s came over to strafe and bomb the remnants.[12]

Under the four-year German occupation of their pastoral homeland, the Norman townsfolk of Le Bourg had packed away their tricolor flags in secluded cupboards. On August 16, the villagers jubilantly hung out their flags to welcome the liberators—then hastily stashed them away as repeatedly in the next two days the 1st Battalion of US 359th Infantry Regiment and the German 116th *Panzer* battled furiously for possession of the town.

Le Bourg-St. Léonard became a no-man's-land. "Three times (the regiment recorded) the Americans were driven out of the town before they gained and permanently held it on the 17th of August."[13]

It was during those forty-eight hours that the 90th Division came of age.

The initial confrontation displayed a dismal repetition of the division's earlier problems, although every infantry company in Normandy had experienced the symptoms of panic at one time or another. A platoon leader, Second Lieutenant Morency Dame, took a small reconnaissance patrol of five or six men through an apple orchard and into a dense woods. They ran into strong German opposition of twenty-five to thirty men who opened fire on them.

"The sudden opposition and the fact that he was wounded slightly must have rattled Dame, for he grew excited," a fellow officer recounted shortly afterward.

> The patrol pulled back hastily, in complete confusion. The rest of the platoon, seeing this and noting the little finger of Dame's left hand gashed and spouting blood as well as seeing him with blood all over his face (probably from rubbing it with his bloody hand) got excited, too, and withdrew in poor order. They fell back, badly shaken and out of control, men going in all directions.[14]

The commanding officer of the 1st Battalion, Major Leroy Pond, sent a staff officer to take control of the panicking platoon and he quickly restored order, but the unit had lost ground to the attackers.

Pond, a twenty-seven-year-old sandy-haired schoolteacher from Arkansas, was a quiet, intense man who had risen to command the battalion in the *bocage* fighting. He had the style of leadership and verve that could turn his unit around. The men called him "Fireball." It would take all of his skill to hold this vulnerable town against a determined *Panzer* division.

He identified three major problems, the first being a shortage of maps: He had just seven maps of the region of 1/50,000 scale, and none of 1/25,000 scale. "My platoon leaders are forced to go through the ensuing action without maps," Pond worried.

He was concerned, too, that the battalion had been assigned a front of some 6,000 yards. "Normal front according to the 'book' is about 800 yards." The distances between his headquarters and the forward artillery observers and gun batteries put a strain on the wire teams that linked each position by cable. He was also troubled that his fourteen machine guns were insufficient in a front that had previously been held by fifty MGs.

Pond had positioned "A" Company to hold Le Bourg-St. Léonard with two tanks. Now he moved "B" Company in support and ordered the units to retake the town. In a "short but stiff fight" they regained their positions, but with the loss of two officers.

"We are faced with something different than the disorganized resistance encountered in the previous campaign," the normally taciturn Pond now warned his men. . . . "A desperate and well-coordinated force of two-battalion strength is fighting savagely to maintain the shoulders of the Gap through which the German 7th Army is fleeing."[15]

During the rest of the day the enemy accelerated heavy artillery concentrations on 359th Infantry, knocking out their communications by cutting the wire lines between the battalion and the artillery observation point (OP). That afternoon, a renewed German counterattack, this time with tanks, compelled "A" Company to abandon its CP [Command Post]. "The Germans ransacked everything in the lower portion of the house," Second Lieutenant Vernon Cross recounted,

> while eight men of A Company defied them in the upstairs part of the house. These men withstood a shower of German grenades and a flood of rifle bullets as the Germans called up, intending them to surrender.
>
> "Hands up, or I kill you."
>
> [Two men] took over the leadership of the group and, tossing off a "Fuck you" eventually managed to escape through a back part of the house.

> This fracas cost the company a jeep with mounted .50-caliber machine gun. The Germans . . . also rummaged rations, cigarettes and mail.[16]

The wireless operator at the forward switching central, [Technician] Tec 5 Amos Davis, urgently contacted battalion headquarters: "We are being attacked. Send help."

Major Pond sent two of the battalion wire men, Privates Schroeder and Kresinski, down the supply trail to check the wires. Both men were picked off by rifle fire before they had gone more than three hundred yards. Lieutenant Raymond Wright then took off with a squad of twenty-five men in three trucks to extricate the men and equipment.

> We found the switchboard operator, Davis, still at his board, two wounded Germans lying in the same room, one of which he had shot himself. [He told me that] a column of German reconnaissance vehicles had approached down the main road and there was an exchange of fire with the wire team. Thirty-five prisoners were taken and removed to the rear, but not before two were shot and killed by Tec 5 Heinrich Gergs, a German-speaking lineman, when he overheard them scheming to jump the guard, secure his weapons, and escape.[17]

The shortage of maps resulted in one unusual death of an American soldier, as Lieutenant Cross discovered:

> A [paymaster] officer had come up with the monthly payroll to pay the men. He went forward to determine the locations of some of the men, leaving the money with the supply sergeant. The map shortage was acute, so he had to look for the positions right on the ground. He . . . was checking around when he was killed by a direct hit from a tank in the town.[18]

At dawn on August 17, 116th *Panzer* renewed its attack against the battalion. The Germans surrounded "B" Company positions, killing its commander. The counterattack caught Major Pond in the open, on his way to personally check his forward companies. "We sure cleared out of those jeeps in one hell of a hurry . . . taking our machine guns with us," the CO later recounted. He contacted his executive officer, who assured him that a platoon of tanks was just coming up. "Make it fast!" Pond yelled. Fifteen minutes later he jumped on the turret of the lead tank and led the attack, effectively calling down fire from his mortar platoon in support.

"The enemy was broken and beaten in hand to hand fighting, but still hiding and skulking in the hedgerows and orchards," the battalion history records.[19] The day spun out with attack and counterattack, tank versus tank. Pond was on his feet directing his troops the whole time. In the heat of the action, the assistant divisional commander, "Wild Bill" Weaver— never one to miss out on the action—personally directed tanks into the fight.

"By 2217 hours the battalion, worn-out and tired, dead tired, from nearly forty-eight hours of fighting and enemy artillery, was relieved by the Second Battalion during the hours of darkness."

Their mission was completed. Men like "Fireball" Pond and "Wild Bill" Weaver—but other soldiers too: young second lieutenants, NCOs, privates, gunners, and engineers—had all looked deep and found the leadership that instilled a new sense of achievement and pride in the "Tough 'Ombres." But, *still*, the Gap was not yet closed.

CHAPTER 24

Bogeys, Bandits, and Lovable Erks

While the allied army commanders hesitated, the allied air forces seized the day, bombing, strafing, and rocketing targets lined up like rows of ducks.

When the early-morning mist lifted on August 17, pilots on a routine reconnaissance sweep rubbed their eyes in disbelief. Below, across the entire seven-mile width of the Dives Valley from Falaise on the northern rim of the trap to Le Bourg/Argentan on the south, the German Seventh Army was executing a mass exodus.

No. 35 Wing, RAF, a tactical reconnaissance wing providing intelligence information to ground forces, heralded what was to be "three days of the largest scale movement presenting such targets to Allied air power as had hitherto only been dreamed of."[1] It was a stunning sight. Thousands of trucks, armored vehicles, half-tracks, ambulances, horse-drawn carts, even soldiers on bicycles and on foot, were crammed nose to tail, three abreast, on every road and country lane that led to the east.

The final order von Kluge had given before he swallowed the cyanide capsule—the evacuation of all nonessential units—was being executed to the fullest measure. Some sixty-five thousand administrative and rear echelon noncombatant soldiers had been steadily pouring out, many making their way in horse-drawn vehicles or on foot. These included tankers with no tanks, gunners with no heavy weapons, transport drivers with no vehicles. Only active combat troops and their key headquarters staff were left behind in the trap.

For the first time, the Germans did not limit troop movement to night time. They wanted *out*—and were prepared to sacrifice untold lives to achieve this.

The retreat was on; the rout was yet to come.

The reconnaissance airmen were the eyes and ears of the army; their camera shutters clicked furiously as they cataloged the catch. As historian Christopher Evans noted:

"They kept a general watch on road and rail movement and on shipping. They flew over rivers to observe barge movement; bridging and ferrying sites; they made detailed searches of specific areas at the request of 21 Army Group to detect possible concentrations for counter-attacks. They also carried out intelligence missions in search of gun-sites, dumps, supply centres, etc., and for purposes of bomb damage assessment.

A measure of just how active reconnaissance aircraft were during the campaign is the sheer volume of photographs taken in such a short span of time: 1,481,000 prints were produced during the Normandy campaign.

These photographs were distributed widely, often down to the platoon level, providing the ground forces with up-to-date information on enemy dispositions, thereby allowing for a more informed plan of attack. Information was to come from other sources too. With fighter aircraft operating almost constantly over forward enemy positions on other missions they reported back on what they saw, supplementing the dedicated reconnaissance squadrons many times over.[2]

Thus alerted, allied fighter squadrons now based across northern France raced for the kill. Hundreds of fighter-bombers swarmed the skies: American P-47 Thunderbolts, Mustangs and Lightnings, and British and Canadian Spitfires and Typhoons.

For almost three months of the Normandy campaign, these pilots had stalked their prey. They had done incalculable damage to the enemy and to his morale, knocking out hundreds of tanks, armored vehicles, and self-propelled guns. Equally important, they had intimidated the Germans to such a degree that as the weeks of the Normandy campaign wore on, the enemy increasingly dared not risk daylight movement.

The costs to the allied air forces had been massive. The *Luftwaffe's* antiaircraft guns had shot down or damaged a large percent of the total available fighter aircraft since D-Day. Whole squadrons had been replaced. Fighter-bomber casualties were by far the highest: Typhoon losses, with 151 pilots killed, reached the 128 percent mark in the three months.[3]

In the face of statistics like that, what kinds of men would voluntarily hurtle through the skies, bearing tons of explosives in highly vulnerable craft, with hundreds of potent guns waiting below to blow them up?

Airmen had always been a little different from the other arms of military service. They wore rather spiffily tailored dress uniforms; the foot soldier rarely even got to change his socks in midbattle. In a single day the pilots' experiences could swing wildly from the terror of seeing their craft, or their friend's, explode into flames, to enjoying a cold beer, a sizzling steak for dinner, and crisp white sheets on his bed that same night. The foot soldiers had no escape from terror. They spent days and often nights at battle. Sleep, when they got any, was in sodden slits. Their dinner was K rations.

The pilots and aircrew were by now based in airstrips in France. The Jug flyers found life in Normandy to be quite different: "pup tents, squad tents, fox holes, plenty of C and K rations, pierced steel plank runways and thousands of yellow-jacket [wasps] in the jam and jelly."[4]

British airmen even had their own lingo, graphically described by air historian Hugh Halliday:

> A "gong" was a decoration, "gen" was information, "ropey" and "dicey" were adjectives for dangerous . . . If there was a "flap" on, the situation was confused or unpleasant. On a patrol one might report a "bogey" (unidentified aircraft) which could turn out to be a "bandit" (hostile aircraft). If a man had been jilted by his girl, the men would nod their heads wisely and say, "Poor old so-and-so. He was shot down in flames by his popsy." A flyer who had been killed or was reported missing had "gone west", "bought it" or "gone for a Burton." Supply officers were "gro-

cers", scientists were "boffins", the intelligence officer was referred to as "the spy" or "the Gestapo", soldiers became "pongos"
or "brown jobs", and sailors were "blue jobs".[5]

The mechanics who toiled all night to get the planes serviceable for
the next day's combat were "loveable erks." Their bosses became
"chiefies."

There was one other essential difference between air and ground troops.
The latter had to cope with just one enemy, the Germans. The airmen had
two: the Germans plus the elements—wind, rain, hail, and fog.

As air bases were hastily established on the Normandy beachhead, the
dry, hot August weather was causing a serious problem: dust. On takeoff
and landing, when the wheels touched the landing strips, a fine dust,
inches thick, rose like a cloud, infiltrating and damaging the motors and
the firing mechanisms of cannons and guns.

Allied engineers who constructed the landing strips even tried spraying the field with water or oil—to keep the dust down.[6] Ingestion of these
particles of sand and dust also had disastrous results on the cannons, causing misfiring and structural failure. "Stoppages were always a problem,"
Flight Lieutenant Bill Baggs of 164 Typhoon Squadron, RAF, said.[7]

One of the "erks"—those magnificent fighter-bomber mechanics—
made such a significant contribution to solving the problem that he became known among his peers as "The Hero of the Falaise Gap."

David Raymond Davies was a leading aircraftsman with the 123d
Rocket Projectile (RP) Wing, which operated Typhoons. His expertise was
as an armorer for the 20mm cannon. When cannon stoppage became a serious problem, someone figured out that Davies's squadron was experiencing fewer cannon stoppages than the other squadrons currently
operating from the sandy conditions of the beachhead airstrips.

Davies's grandson, Dr. Jonathan E. C. Tan, of Muncaster, England,
gives this account:

They sent a senior armament officer from the UK to investigate.
He discovered that in setting up the rounds of 20mm cannons on
his workbench, Davies had positioned the ammunition slightly in

advance of the specified settings. The consequence was that the cannons had been firing slightly faster and had thus let less sand/dust into the firing mechanisms.

When these new settings were communicated throughout the group, Dr. Tan's grandfather earned his justifiable reputation.[8]

Davies's resourcefulness was also exercised—somewhat cunningly—in speeding up the work crews charged with breaking open and unpacking urgently needed ammunition. Dr. Tan recalls:

> My grandfather and his closest comrade came up with a plan. They slipped a spurious 'letter from home' that they in fact penned into one ammunition box. The letter supposedly was from a young lady, working in a munitions factory, thinking about the boys out there. The next day, the letter was "found" with much shouting and prompting from the two partners in mischief. Never had they seen men work so fast, tearing open all the other ammunition boxes in the hope of finding further letters.[9]

Each type of aircraft had a specific role. Fighter-bombers—P-47 Thunderbolts and Typhoons—used rockets and cannons mainly against tanks and enemy strong points. The Spitfire safeguarded them from *Luft-waffe* interference, ensuring air superiority. "Spits" also did armed reconnaissance and fighter-bomber attacks against troops and trucks, or "targets of opportunity." The Spit carried two 20mm cannon and two Browning machine guns, and could also carry one 500-pound or two 250-pound bombs. The "Tiffy" had eight rockets with 60-pound warheads or two 500- or 1,000-pound bombs as well as four 20mm cannons.

Other breeds of fighter planes were P-51 Mustangs and the fast and deadly Mosquito. Their specialties were in combat missions and as night intruders, hunting down German night fighters who preyed on bombers. For one month, from just after D-Day until the RAF destroyed the launching pads, the "Mossies" intercepted Hitler's terror weapon, the lethal *V-1* "Doodlebugs" that rained so much havoc on the English in 1944, killing fifty-five hundred civilians and injuring sixteen thousand more.

A Canadian ace, Wing Commander Russ Bannock, was one of the fifty thousand Canadians in the Commonwealth Air Training Plan. He set something of a record in kills. His aircraft, a Mosquito named "Hairless

Joe," carried a long string of swastikas and *V-1* symbols to indicate his score: nineteen flying bombs destroyed, plus eleven enemy aircraft shot down. That actually makes him a double ace. His technique was uniquely North American: "I used my duck-shooting experience," he admitted. "You had to shoot from the side in a deflection shot. If you shot them from the back, the resulting explosion could knock out your aircraft, too."[10]

US 367th Fighter Group reported their "first big bag," which occurred during the Dives Valley fighting: "Five convoys and a hundred Tiger tanks were destroyed on one day."[11] They claimed that American Flying Officer Larry Blumer was one of the few fighter pilots to become an "ace-in-a-day," shooting down five enemy aircraft in fifteen minutes of aerial combat.[12]

Their fellow Spitfire airmen were confused when the Warren twins, Bruce and Douglas, checked in at one of Normandy's first operational airstrips.

"What is your name?" an airman would ask one of the twins.

"Duke," was the reply.

"Well, what's *your* name?" The other twin would be asked.

"Duke," again, was the reply.

The twins were used to the confusion about their names. It had begun in the first grade. "Our teacher, trying to explain that we were identical twins, said we were duplicates of one another," Warren said. On the playground, the word was transposed and the brothers were called, none too kindly, "Dupes." After "a bit of persuasion," the nickname was softened to "Duke." It stuck to them both.

So here, at the height of the Normandy battle, were two Dukes. Solution? "My twin was called Duke Mark I (he arrived there first). I was Duke Mark II."

But they never called each other by name; they didn't need to. Their communication was so intuitive they could finish each other's sentences.

Both men, now twenty-two years old, were skilled and experienced fighter pilots and flight commanders. Initially they flew the single-pilot Spitfires as a section of two. "It was excellent as we had complete confidence in the other's ability," Duke Mark II explained. Even when flying in different sections, they still managed to watch out for each other. But they made a pact: if one of them was shot down or killed, the other would not do anything "foolish" in rage.[13]

They both knew the risks. "Low-level attacks by their nature were dangerous," Duke Mark II recalled. "The flak was plentiful and accurate." Losses had been heavy. When hit at low altitude, there was very little time to bail out.[14]

Flight Lieutenant Roy A. Crane, a pilot in 124 Typhoon Wing, was lucky. He managed to get his parachute open.

> On the 2nd August 1944 I was shot down after twice being hit by "flak" near Falaise. I parachuted from low level into a German SS Camp and was quickly surrounded by about 20 hostile SS. I was rescued by the German Air Force gun crew, one an Oberfeld-webel, who had shot me down. Later I was taken in an open staff car with an armed motor cycle escort. We had only travelled a short distance when, passing some German tanks in a wooded val-ley, we were signalled to stop by German soldiers standing as look-outs under some trees. Much panic ensued and I was pushed by the Oberfeldwebel into a ditch. It was quickly evident we were being attacked by Typhoons which came round again and again firing their rockets and cannons. I have since established there were six Typhoons being led by my Best Man, Phil Strong, an Australian from 182 Squadron, who went out to seek revenge after hearing I had been reported killed.[15]

For the aircrews, the chase was on. The German exodus meant that their flak was lessening and the escaping Seventh Army provided endless targets of opportunity. At first the constraints of the bomb line within the valley restricted the allied tactical air forces from harassing the fleeing troops and their vehicles. Then a special arrangement with the allied armies opened up these tempting targets to an "August Bank holiday" of Spitfires, Thunderbolts, and Typhoons careening and diving wildly over the valley. For three days, operating in almost perfect flying conditions, hundreds of fighter-bombers converged on the narrow country lanes where a hapless enemy was attempting to escape in increasingly chaotic conditions. Action reached its most intensive pitch on August 18. All day long the allied tactical air forces attacked the German columns that jammed the roads, flying more than three thousand sorties that day. The possibilities of midair collision were enormous. Maintaining the aircraft under such intensive use was itself a Herculean effort. Again, the mainte-nance crews came to the rescue. One squadron describes the challenges:

"Amid the dust and noise, the 'erks' performed minor miracles of servicing and repairing. Aircraft could be refueled and repaired in eight to nine minutes; propeller changes were made in forty-five minutes; radios changed in less than ten."[16]

The air became filled with the screams of airplanes and the thunder of artillery as the Allies pounded the escaping enemy. Although the Germans clung to the shelter of wooded paths, narrow twisting lanes, and sunken hedgerows, terrible damage was inflicted on them and on the once-beautiful Dives Valley.

An officer, who was captured on August 18 but escaped two days later, described what he saw in this valley of death:

> All roads, and particularly the byways, were crowded with transport two abreast, grinding forward.
>
> Everywhere there were tanks and vehicles towing what they could. And everywhere there was the menace of the air . . . On many vehicles an air sentry rode on the mudguard. At the sound of a plane every vehicle went into the side of the road and all personnel ran for their lives. The damage was immense and flaming transport and dead horses were left in the road while the occupants pressed on, afoot . . .[17]

Duke and his twin especially felt the anguish of the animals.

> When we attacked horse-drawn transport along with staff cars and trucks, the German soldiers would hold the horses' bridles as the horses reared in fright and pain. Duke and I, having grown up on a farm with an intimate knowledge of horses, felt especially sorry for the animals because they could not understand what was happening to them.[18]

The tactical air forces were inflicting immense damage, but even they could not close the trap.

The Trun-Chambois Gap: August 18

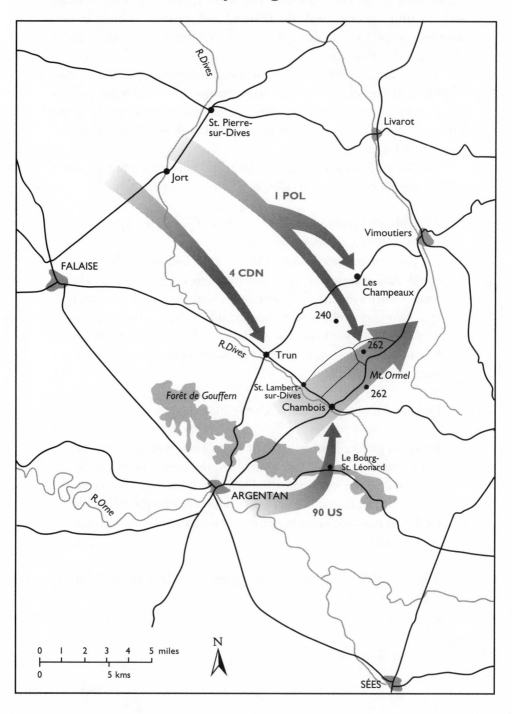

CHAPTER 25

Bloody Warsaw

By the morning of August 17, 1944, the allied senior commanders were beginning to realize just how many Germans were still trapped in the pocket. With the US 90th Division locked in battle at Le Bourg-St. Léonard, it was up to the 1st Polish Armored Division to close the gap from the north. General Simonds issued firm orders: 1st Polish Division must thrust on past Trun to Chambois to meet US 90th Division "at all costs and as quickly as possible."[1]

Fifteen thousand men from the 1st Polish Armored Division had planted their feet on French soil on August 1—the first step, they hoped, in the long road home. It had been almost five years since their ignominious retreat from their homeland in the face of advancing Nazi troops.

When the Germans attacked Poland in September 1939, the Poles mustered a military force of some million and a half men, determined, but ill equipped, to defend their country. Such a man was Michael Gutowski, a cavalry captain with the 17th Lancers and an outstanding Olympic horseman. In those early days of September 1939, Captain Gutowski twice led successful cavalry charges against the invaders, "pushing the Germans quite energetically with very bloody fighting, ninety-nine killed."

Although wounded, he dared not seek medical help. "Being in hospital meant becoming a prisoner of war," he explained. During the next weeks the Poles stubbornly fought on. Gutowski and his unit covered close to one thousand miles on horseback, caught up in numerous skirmishes and battles as they tried vainly to stem the onrush of Germans. Twice again wounded, he still managed to avoid capture.

The crisis came on October 19, 1939. "There was no place to go, no fighting left. I found civilian clothes and with a pair of horses I went back to western Poland to find my wife and children."

Gutowski discovered to his dismay that many of the prominent people of the country had been rounded up by the SS and put in concentration camps. His wife and young children, a three-year-old and a six-month-old baby, were among them. When he tried to free them, he was himself arrested.

"I have orders from the SS to shoot you tomorrow morning," the commandant informed him. At dawn the next day they came for him. To his surprise, instead of marching him out to a firing squad, they released him. "For the moment I was able to save your life," the commander, an Olympic equestrian admirer, said. "At least you won't be shot. As soon as you leave the barracks, disappear. Change your name. If the SS get their hands on you, you won't live twenty-four hours." Gutowski's reputation as an international equestrian had saved him.

He joined an underground resistance group. When he later learned that his wife and children had been released and were safe with friends he decided to leave the country, skiing over the mountains to Slovakia and Hungary. Finally, in May 1940, he reached France and joined other escapees trickling in to re-form the Polish 10th Cavalry Brigade. A month later France fell, and the Polish military were evacuated to hastily erected camps in Scotland.

Through the next four years this nucleus grew and flourished. Poles like Gutowski came from around the world, including the United States, Canada, and South America, as volunteers for the Polish army, navy, and air force. By 1944, the 1st Polish Armored Division, under the seasoned command of General Stanislaw Maczek, was ready to fight in Normandy.[2] At long last, victory was in sight.

Their determination to fight was sharpened by a crisis that by coincidence broke out in Poland on the same day as their landing in Normandy: August 1, 1944. The thirty-thousand-man Polish Home Army in Warsaw had staged a bloody uprising against the Nazi oppressors. Their objective was to liberate Warsaw from German rule and establish independent Polish control before the approaching Russians, now just twelve miles away, could impose their own Communist regime on Poland.

It was a valiant but futile effort. The Germans rushed in reinforcements, including the Hermann Goering *Panzer* Division. The Resistance captured the whole city but had ammunition for only seven days. Armed with only one thousand rifles and twenty-five thousand homemade grenades, they were trapped in the inner-city cellars, where they fought on for some weeks with little more than their bare hands and courage.[3] The Warsaw Uprising created a symbiotic and very emotional bond with the Poles liberating Normandy. Both armies were fighting the Nazis to free their homeland: the one from within the country and the other from without.

"What news of Warsaw?" was the first question Polish airmen would ask when they returned to Britain from bombing raids. Air crew and artillerymen symbolically scrawled "For Warsaw" across bombs and shells before releasing them over Germany. In France, bomb-shattered roads south of Caen bore signposts that read "Caen–Warsaw." The Normandy Poles in their slit trenches hung on to hourly BBC reports of the progress of the Warsaw Uprising.[4]

One Polish tanker remembers that

> near the command vehicle, a crowd gathered. The news was on: "This is the home service of the BBC. Here is the news." Faces looked serious—Warsaw was rising. The names of familiar districts, streets and buildings were mentioned.
>
> Warsaw was fighting.
>
> We knew what fighting meant. We knew from bitter experience what Tigers were like. And Warsaw had no 17-pounders with which to fight Tigers, had no flame-throwers to burn the Germans out of the city, had no tanks, no guns, no weapons, no ammunition . . .
>
> Faces grew grim.
>
> The broadcast was very short. It ended with the chorale 'Z dymen pozarów' [with the smoke of the conflagrations . . .]."[5]

The Home Army in Warsaw faltered, weakened by lack of ammunition. They were finally starved out of their cellars under the city and defeated. Thus sprung the tragic Polish adage, "If you take a handful of Warsaw soil and squeeze it, the blood will run from it."

Every Polish soldier in Normandy felt the anguish of Warsaw. Their hatred of the enemy deepened. Their determination to defeat the Nazis grew.

Unhappily, bad luck marred the initial efforts of the 1st Polish Armored Division in Normandy. They were now fighting under command of General Simonds's II Canadian Corps. Twice they had been victims of friendly bombing: the first on August 8, by the US Air Force, and next on August 14, when Operation *Tractable*'s ill-fated RAF bombing mission saw ninety-three Polish soldiers killed or missing. Then, during the advance to Chambois, when the 1st Polish inadvertently crossed the bomb line into enemy territory, they came under fire from strafing Spitfires. In three days, from August 16–18, 72 Polish troops were killed and 191 more were wounded by allied planes.[6]

Despite these losses, the Poles seized an important crossing over the Dives River at Jort and at Simonds's urging pushed on during the night of August 17/18 in a remarkable twenty-mile night march through enemy lines toward Chambois.

General Maczek had noted on his map an imposing summit overlooking Chambois. The contours, with twin hills each eight hundred feet high, somewhat resembled a mace or two-headed axe. On the northern "head" of the mace was a fifteenth-century stone manor house, Château Boisjos. It had witnessed a decisive conflict in the Hundred Years War. It would soon witness a battle even more bloody.

The twin hills were divided by a narrow, sunken road running northeast from Chambois to Vimoutiers—a road that would prove critical in the coming battle. Again, the road's contours reminded Maczek of a long handle of a mace. To preserve security he code-named the entire battle site "Maczuga," the Polish word for mace.[7]

It has become a name, and a battle, that the Polish even today revere. The road would come to be called the "Corridor of Death."

The soldiers' grueling cross-country route led them through the Pays d'Auge. This lush corner of Normandy had long been an attraction for tourists. Its steep hills, meandering creeks, and winding lanes bordered by dense overgrown hedges invited hikers. At the end of a day on the trails they could enjoy the local specialties of Camembert cheese, Calvados, and cider.

It was a country for tourists, not tanks. Some of the most difficult fighting terrain in France was found in this untamed land. "Surely we must be on the borders of Switzerland!" one Polish trooper exclaimed in wonder.[8]

Traversing it at night with no maps and no light was a daunting task for the Poles. One of the two armored units—2d Armored Regiment, with riflemen of the 8th Light Infantry—took a wrong turn. This surprised no one as its commander, Colonel Koszutski, was known to be so anxious to forge ahead that he was "inclined to lead with his heart, not his head."[9]

Koszutski took that order from General Simonds very literally: ". . . *at all costs and as quickly as possible.*"[10]

It was midnight; his troops were asleep on their feet after a forty-eight-hour advance; his supply trucks had not caught up with him. So keen was he to obey that he set forth immediately "without refueling and without replacing spent ammunition."[11]

His men called him the "Happy Wanderer."[12]

Wander they did, that strange dark night of August 18—straight into German lines. At the precise moment when the Polish tanks cut across the Auge hills on an east–west tangent toward Maczuga and Chambois, a motorized enemy column was struggling through the same terrain but on a different tack, from south to north.

Captain Ted Walewicz of 2d Polish Armored Regiment recalls: "It was a terrible night, I remember it well . . . dark, not pleasant, especially after a whole day of fighting. We were driving through the German lines and the enemy began coming up in front of us."[13]

The two columns, Polish and German, encountered each other at a crossroads. The German policeman with white gauntlets stopped the north–south convoy and waved the Polish tanks through, not knowing, or not wanting to know their identity.

Gutowski confirms the strange encounter. "The German traffic police ordered the Polish tanks to go first and the Germans to move aside; in the middle of the night they didn't recognize our tanks."[14]

Certainly, neither protagonist welcomed a close battle in darkness. Did they tacitly ignore each other's insignia? The Poles were later to discover that these were units of 2 SS Division, escaping the allied encirclement, ordered to regroup and rearm outside for their counterattack to save their trapped comrades.

To make the night trek even more bizarre, the French guide had misunderstood the Polish pronunciation of their objective, Chambois. "We were given the order to secure Chambois," Captain Walewicz explained. "But we were led instead to Les Champeaux. It was unbelievable.

"It was the headquarters of a German division. I know because we found in one of the houses in Les Champeaux a German staff officer's uniform."[15]

The Poles had inadvertently penetrated well behind enemy lines and had in fact stumbled on the headquarters of the 2d SS *Panzer* Division. A firefight ensued. The Poles captured an enemy command post and found two generals' uniforms and a number of suitcases filled with loot. These "various trinkets" from the fashion houses of Paris included "beautiful furs from Rochas . . . dresses made by Maggy Rouff . . . ladies' underwear, silver cutlery—everything carefully folded and beautifully packed," the division history records.[16]

General Maczek had directed half of his division to head down the valley toward Chambois to drive the Germans from the village and its surrounding area, as General Simonds had ordered.

But his experienced eye saw a flaw in the plan. That won't keep the Germans from infiltrating the line and escaping east to the Auge hills on one of the many country paths and lanes, he thought.

To counter this he ordered his remaining units—the 1st and 2d Armored Regiments and three infantry battalions—to seize the high ground of Maczuga some two miles east of Chambois and the Dives River.

The men were exhausted. They had been fighting for three days. Their all-night, twenty-mile trek had been a test of endurance. The infantry had marched or clung white-knuckled to the sides of the tanks, fearing that if they dozed off, they would tumble to the ground and perhaps be crushed. The heat inside the tanks was stifling; drivers' grips on the steering levers were weakening. They were hungry. Water was scarce.

But they hadn't come down this long road home to quit now. The next morning, August 19, Polish soldiers and their tanks attacked Hill 262 at the northern end of "the mace" and drove out the German infantry company defending this critical vantage point.

At 1240 hours the first Polish troops—2d Armored Regiment with 8th Infantry Battalion—rolled into Boisjos, the stone manor house on Hill 262. Pierre Grandvalet, a Norman farmer who lived in the manor with his wife and two young children, recalls the excitement of the liberation:

A German came to my house and asked me to give him some potatoes. He said he hadn't eaten for three days. I pointed him toward a neighbor's field. He busied himself putting the potatoes on the cooker in the kitchen and after a while he ran outside, and warned me, "The English are coming!" He left the house in a great hurry. My wife and I ran into the cellar and waited. A short while later we heard voices in the courtyard. The Polish had arrived. Next a convoy of tanks came. They were very thirsty and hot. We brought out carafes and bottles of cider. They were welcomed with great joy.[17]

By late afternoon, the 1st Armored Regiment and Lieutenant Colonel Szydlowski's 9th Infantry Battalion were digging in, using trenches recently abandoned by the Germans. Two thousand Poles with eighty-seven tanks and well-sited artillery now had firm possession of Maczuga.

One of the officers assigned to the Polish Armored at Maczuga was Pierre Sévigny, a French-Canadian artillery captain with 4th Canadian Medium Regiment. His role at Maczuga was to serve as forward observation officer (FOO).

"I trained with the Poles in Scotland," he recounted. "Since their second language was French, particularly so with the soldiers, they requested a French-speaking officer who could communicate with English-speaking senior artillery officers at Canadian Army HQ when massive fire was needed."[18]

From the high ground of Hill 262, Sévigny would be able to identify enemy positions and radio these to Canadian artillery. He had the authority to call down, in an instant, all the available corps' firepower — hundreds of guns — in whatever strength he deemed necessary to knock out the menace.

As General Maczek had shrewdly surmised, the Polish position at Maczuga commanded far-reaching views in every direction. As if in the best balcony seats, they could see across the broad valley of the Dives below them. Here and there were glimpses of the river. It seemed incredible that the blue line on their map — a river wide and steep enough to stop tanks — could be that narrow, tree-lined creek meandering through the old Norman farming villages of Chambois, St. Lambert-sur-Dives, and Trun.

The local Norman populace rated the hilltop views in their luxuriant country by the number of steeples that dotted its landscape. "On a clear day, from Mont Ormel, one could see thirty steeples in all directions," local inhabitant Robert Chombard noted recently.[19]

The Poles could use these landmarks to identify friend and foe. Four miles southwest they could make out the distinctive hundred-foot towers marking the corners of the twelfth-century fortress in Chambois. Here their comrades—Major Zgorzelski's 10th Polish Dragoons, with the 10th Mounted Rifles (the regiment in which Gutowski served) under command, were preparing to attack.

Beyond Chambois, the Forêt de Gouffern obscured the steeples of Argentan and Le Bourg-St. Léonard. But through their binoculars, they could see artillery flashes that identified the positions of the 2d French Armored and Bradley's 90th and 80th Infantry Divisions as they attempted to close the trap from the south.

Veering their gaze slightly to the west they could see the church steeples of St. Lambert and Trun, where, on this August 19, the Canadians were attacking to close the trap from the north. "From our hill there was a panoramic view of the combat zone," Sévigny recalled: "At our feet the battle raged for the possession of the villages of St. Lambert and Chambois. We could see the Shermans advancing, blazing away with their guns and machine guns. The attacking tanks and infantry exploited the folds in the ground for cover."[20]

And just two or three miles beyond St. Lambert, more steeples marked the several small farming villages clustered amid the woods and high hedges west of the Dives Valley: Tournai-sur-Dives, Villedieu les Bailleul, Meri, and Nécy. These villagers had until then been scarcely touched by war. The tawny stone of their modest barns and cottages still took on a warm amber glow in the August sunshine, in dramatic contrast with the awful, bomb-shattered heaps of grey rock strewn obscenely in the town centers of Trun, St. Lambert, and Chambois east of them. The apples in their bountiful orchards, nearing maturity, were untouched by bomb splinters, tank turrets, or treads. Their cattle grazed contentedly, plodding at will down trails that led to the nearby Dives watering holes.

It was here, in these hamlets tucked away in rural backwaters just behind the Dives, that some of the 140,000 Norman refugees fleeing eight weeks of raging battles to the north had sought sanctuary and were welcomed by their compatriots.

On August 13, celebrants of Sunday mass at Tournai-sur-Dives were distracted by an unusual clatter outside. They emerged into the sun-filled square to witness a terrifying sight: the narrow lanes of their small hamlet were jammed with German vehicles and military equipment. The German army was escaping before their very eyes. Remnants of twenty divisions of the German Seventh and Fifth Armies were seeking harbor in their village. The bountiful apple trees now had Tiger and Panther tanks securely hidden under them; those tawny stone homesteads housed *Panzer* troops foisted on reluctant farmers.

"We are caught in the middle of the battle!" Abbé Marcel Launay exclaimed to his parishioners. There were 314 townsfolk in Tournai, but their numbers had swollen as refugees from stricken towns sought refuge in the formerly peaceful village.

Launay could offer little consolation to his parishioners. The Germans must cross the Dives to break out of the allied trap, he told them. All roads leading to the river go through Tournai-sur-Dives. So our small village is a rallying point for an army in full retreat.

"They are escaping with three vehicles abreast everywhere they can," the padre noted tersely in his diary that day. "Some toward Vimoutiers, some toward Chambois. Allied planes are constantly strafing them. This afternoon, between St. Lambert and Trun (two miles) twelve German vehicles are in flames. Two of these are ammunition transports and explode for hours."

An eyewitness described the exodus: "German vehicles of all kinds, tanks, small and large trucks, motor bicycles and carts fleeing en route for Chambois. Some of the cars had lost their windows, others had no doors left . . . one had no front tires, and another had only three wheels."

Who were they, these fleeing Germans? A comrade described the hodgepodge of noncombat personnel: "Infantrymen without weapons, civilians employed by the *Wehrmacht*, workers from the Atlantic Wall, newsreel operators, buyers from ministries . . ."

The villagers didn't care who the stragglers were. They were leaving, that was the important thing. "Get going! It's your turn to run now!" one shouted gleefully at the retreating foe.

In the next few days, panicky civilians in neighboring villages reported increasing misery. By day, enemy trucks and tanks were camouflaged in increasing numbers in sheds and under apple trees awaiting the safety of dusk. "As usual," Launay wrote, "as the sun sets we hear Germans on the move." French villagers were forced to hand over food and drink. Some were ordered to drive their cattle toward the German border. In one afternoon every chicken in Villedieu was slaughtered to feed German troops.

Launay noted that: "People are sleeping where they feel the safest, some in the dry drainage ditches of the fields. In Villedieu the local prison and the quarry passages are filled with people trying to find shelter. The

Germans take advantage of this situation to pillage their homes of all items of value."

Not only did the Germans cause suffering and death to the villagers, but the Allies also created havoc. As the Americans closed in from Argentan and the Canadians and British from Falaise, the townspeople were caught in the cross fire of their guns. On the fourteenth, the padre wrote, "the Allied artillery has concentrated on Trun and Chambois which both suffer terrible damage."

At 0530 hours on August 15, the day of the Feast of the Assumption, Abbé Launay arose early and went out of the presbytery into the street. His entry in his diary that day was one of horror:

> A troop of German tanks were setting up at a nearby school. Worse, one of their soldiers had been shot. The commander declared the town of Tournai under siege. Three Frenchmen had been arrested and detained in the school basement. The SS lieutenant decreed that for every German harassed or threatened, 10 French civilians would be imprisoned.

Launay and the mayor negotiated the release of the civilians, but the German, fearing more resistance, forbade any man of the village to attend the important religious celebrations that day.

The next day, the mayor asked the SS lieutenant if he intended to fight it out in the town. He received a terse response: "We are here to fight, and we expect to fight the 'Tommies' soon."

"The villagers start preparing themselves for this outcome," the padre noted. "The civilians move their belongings into cellars and build shelters as best they can. The shelling continues unabated all day. The Germans, who are in the midst of a fighting retreat, occupy the abandoned houses and refuse to let the French civilians back into them to get some of their belongings."

Civilian casualties increased, but many doctors refused to come out because they were afraid to be on the road during the invasion. The Allies thought that if you were on the road, you must be a German. And so they strafed and killed you.

Some French risked their lives to loot the escaping Germans. Tires were removed from smashed vehicles. Their contents, often perfumes and elegant ladies' wear that the enemy himself had looted, were snatched back. Bodies were searched for watches or money. Boots were stripped from corpses.

The villagers were furious to hear the monstrous story of a farmer in a neighboring hamlet. The SS had occupied his home. His wife and four children cowered in a shed. The Germans ordered the children to fetch them water from the well. As the youngsters crossed the farmyard, an allied mortar made a direct hit, killing all four children. With his wife in hysterics and his neighbors scattered into ditches, the wretched man was left with the solitary and grisly task of burying his own four children.

On August 18 the abbé wrote:

The American artillery is stronger than ever as they smash Argentan and the Trun-Chambois road. The fleeing Germans are forced to go by Tournai: their last possible exit. But in fact, once in Tournai they are stuck in a terrible traffic jam with their comrades [escaping] from Mortain. Everybody wants to get to Chambois quickly, and with our narrow streets everybody must wait their turn, but everyone wants priority! Once in a while an officer is forced to dismount his vehicle and pull out his pistol to ensure his unit's passage.

By now, allied bombing and shelling had increased to a frenzied level. Every thirteen minutes, from 2230 to 0500 hours a shell falls in the center of town. "We are stuck in the middle of an artillery duel between the Allies and the Germans," the padre said helplessly.

"We are now at war. The battle has begun."[21]

CHAPTER 26

A Rough Start to a Tough Battle

When World War II broke out, North Americans—unlike the Poles—were very remote from the events that provoked it. However, they had their own compelling distractions. The mean, lean years of the 1930s had created a crisis of unemployment and economic despair: the Great Depression.

The continent was brought to its knees; productivity was almost halved, and one-fifth of the population became destitute. By 1933 millions were out of work. Bread lines were a common sight in most cities. Hundreds of thousands roamed the country in search of food, work, and shelter. "Brother, can you spare a dime?" went the refrain of a popular song.

A severe drought hit the Great Plains states, significantly reducing farm production. Violent wind and dust storms ravaged the southern Great Plains in what became known as the "Dust Bowl." Crops were destroyed, cars and machinery were ruined, and people and animals were harmed. Approximately eight hundred thousand people, often called "Okies," left Arkansas, Texas, Missouri, and Oklahoma during the 1930s and 1940s.[1]

In Canada's midwest, half a million—a full 5 percent of the Canadian workforce—were on relief. Drought and blight contributed to a market downslide of wheat that devastated the provinces. With few buyers, the railways began to lay off workers.

It was a cruel time for these restless young men of America and Canada. Stubbornness kept them going, steadfastly plodding through the "dirty thirties," despite the miseries of the long, dark winters of bitter cold and biting wind, and summers of intense heat and bugs so voracious you huddled indoors. Endurance had helped them stick to meanly paid jobs, shrugging off the degradation of the Depression.

From this dark outlook they rose to become what broadcaster Tom Brokaw aptly termed the "Greatest Generation." They brought those qualities of patience, tolerance, endurance, stubbornness, and raw courage to the battlefields.[2]

By 1943, after the United States declared war on Japan and Germany, there were fifteen million men and women in the armed forces. They were strongly motivated by the Japanese attack on Pearl Harbor.

Canada had its own special motivations for supporting the war effort. As a young nation, she was loyal to her mother country. In her own right, Canada abhorred the tyranny of Nazism. When Great Britain declared war on Germany following the Nazi aggression in Poland, Canada swiftly followed suit, making its own declaration of war on September 10, 1939. By 1944, 10 percent of the Canadian population was directly involved in the war effort, all as volunteers. Some soldiers fought in the Dieppe Raid in 1942, and in Sicily and Italy in 1943; but many saw their first action in Normandy on or shortly after D-Day on June 6, 1944.

However, the 4th Canadian Armored Division, like the 1st Polish Armored Division, had been kept waiting impatiently in England for close to two months after D-Day before being committed to battle. These neophyte units, with little or no previous battle experience, saw their first day of action on August 8, spearheading the second phase of Operation *Totalize*. There never was a single day of more difficult fighting than on that steaming August afternoon when two inexperienced divisions were ordered to attack in broad daylight across open country against a prewarned and strongly armed enemy.

Those who survived the cruel toll of that day became "blooded" troops, determined and skillful in the art of war. One such man was a Canadian major, David Currie.

David Currie was a seventeen-year-old lad from Saskatchewan in Canada's midwest when the Depression began, a boy of modest background who had to settle for a technical-school education although he had his sights set on university. At thirty-two, rising through years of dogged military training to the rank of major, Currie was given command of a tank squadron with the South Alberta (29th Armored Reconnaissance) Regiment. His CO would say, prophetically, "[Currie] wasn't a brilliant tactician, but he was very stubborn, and if you gave him an order to do something that was within his capabilities, he would do it—period."[3]

By August 18, 1944, the regiment had been in action only two weeks. Under Currie's unflappable leadership, his squadron was bonding into a cohesive fighting force. What each soldier hadn't known—and was in some ways afraid to find out—was how he would react under fire. It's one thing to carry out a maneuver on the English Downs; it is quite another when mortars are exploding around him and a German 88mm gun has him in its sights, as was the case in *Totalize*.

On August 18, the regiment thundered through the bomb-shattered streets of Trun, many of its houses in flames. Defeated German soldiers were still wandering down the road, trying to surrender. Currie halted his squadron at an orchard overlooking the Dives River, marveling at the dramatic sight of the German exodus across the rolling valley. Only this single six-mile ribbon of land along the Dives, running from Trun through St. Lambert-sur-Dives to Chambois, offered a way out for the retreating enemy.

> In the distance, we could see rising clouds of dust . . . we were witnessing . . . the remnants of the German forces in France trying to escape the pocket. The columns were about three to four miles from our location and seemed to consist of every type and kind of vehicle, gun, tank and horse drawn equipment that the German army possessed. The column stretched as far as we could see. It was an awe-inspiring sight, and from the distance, it appeared to be a crushing force.[4]

At 1500 hours, Currie reported in to regimental headquarters. Orders were waiting, orders filtered down from Montgomery through Crerar and Simonds to the commanders on the ground: it was "essential" to close that trap. St. Lambert was the key.[5]

"I've got a tough assignment for you," the CO said grimly. "The German withdrawal has to be stopped—now! The Allied success in Normandy depends on it. There is no time to bring the artillery into range before you launch the assault. You'll have to "go in naked" until we can move the guns forward."[6]

Both men knew that laying on an attack without close artillery support was a dangerous operation. Only the urgency of the mission could allow this risk.

Currie's squadron was understrength for the assignment. He was down to fifteen tanks from the normal nineteen, with a force of just seventy-five officers and troopers. And the infantry backup he would have under command, just one company of the Argyll and Sutherland Highlanders, was also understrength.

Normally an infantry company's fighting strength is about ninety combat troops. After the ravages of the past ten days of battle, and their stunning exploit when their commander Lieutenant Colonel Dave Stewart devised a silent night attack up the back trails of Hill 195, the Argyll infantry company was down to a depleted strength of about fifty-five all ranks. Added to Currie's fifteen-tank squadron of officers and troopers, this armored/infantry combat force that was to oppose the tens of thousands of Germans escaping through St. Lambert initially numbered a mere 130 men.

Currie and Stewart were similar characters. Together they would make a tough team, with the abilities and determination to get the job done—one way or another. There's a strong tie between armored squadrons and infantry battalions that in war can be, literally, life supporting. Tankmen are highly vulnerable to attack by enemy infiltrators armed with the lethal handheld *panzerfausts*. Their infantry pals, therefore, had a protective role to rout out opposition. On the other hand, foot soldiers badly need the protection of the fire support of powerful tank weaponry.

Tankers knew the Sherman tank was no match for the German Panther or Tiger. Their only hope of destroying them lay with nimble-footed and courageous infantrymen who could stalk the tank, get in behind it within close enough range—say, ninety yards—with just one chance to get off a shot with their PIATs before the Tiger spotted them. (The PIAT was a handheld antitank weapon, fired from a prone position, and had terrific recoil. Its firer needed strong nerves. "Even in short-range tests, it scored only 57 percent of its hits. Failure meant probable extinction."[7])

Returning to his squadron, Currie held a quick "O" Group with his four troop commanders. "The assignment given us by the colonel is to take the village of St. Lambert-sur-Dives," he told them as they grouped around a map of the area. "I reckon this will place us squarely in front of the vast array of the German forces that we have been watching most of the day."[8]

The maps and recce photos showed clusters of small stone cottages and farms hugging a dusty chalk road that connected Trun and Chambois. The road dipped sharply down to the village and wound through its modest center for less than half a mile.

The key elements were two small bridges over the Dives River—the only two escape hatches open to the columns of retreating enemy tanks and vehicles. The Dives was a meandering little stream, often obscured by stands of trees. Its steep banks, however, formed effective barriers to tanks and vehicles.

H-hour for the attack on St. Lambert was 1800 hours.

Prebattle anxiety was lessened by the practical joke of one of the troopers. As Currie recounted,

> The boys brewed tea, and made the last-minute preparations for the coming battle. Just about one minute before we pushed off, an infantry sergeant came along holding his mess tin.
>
> I was sitting on top of my tank. He asked me if I wanted a drink. I said, "Sure, what is it?" He said he didn't know and passed it along to me. I took a good healthy swallow and almost choked to death. His remarks at my antics, "Sure is hot, ain't it?" was the understatement of the year. I found out later that I had had my introduction to that fiery Normandy specialty known as Calvados.[9]

This gambit produced a rare smile from the shy major: "A small grin from Dave meant the same as hilarious laughter from another person," one of his troop leaders recalled. "Dave was always a very private individual but he was also easy-going and very matter of fact. He gave his orders clearly and distinctly and he had confidence in his abilities. Everybody in the regiment held him in high regard."[10]

At exactly 1800 hours the tanks pushed off down the long hill that led to St. Lambert. A German 88mm suddenly opened up. The lead tank was hit and although its commander and a crew member were wounded, they all managed to bail out.

Moments later, more fire: this time it was two Royal Air Force Spitfires confusing them for an enemy. The planes dived down, making one pass over Currie's headquarters squadron.

"The back end of my tank is on fire!" Currie shouted, grabbing a fire extinguisher. The Spits attacked again. This time, Currie dived for safety into the ditch beside the road. Four of his men lay wounded. His first-aid ambulance vehicle was hit and out of commission.

"The hatch on our turret was not closed," one officer recalls. "Bullets ricocheted inside the turret. My gunner had a face injury and my right arm and leg were wounded."[11]

The normally mild-mannered Currie was furious. His second-in-command Captain John Redden, "mad as hell," tried to nail one of the aircraft with his turret gun, but they were too fast. "Our CO wanted our own ack-ack troop to open fire but the padre talked him out of the idea," Redden remembers.[12]

Currie's tank crews frantically threw out yellow smoke canisters to no avail. It was "like poking a hornet's nest, they got so agitated and came back twice as bad."[13]

The frustrating aspect for the troops was the inability to communicate ground to air. As in Operation *Tractable,* yellow smoke was the recognized signal identifying the bomb line. In fact, one battalion even posted a warning to its companies that there was a likelihood of us being " 'RAF'ed' unless forward troops displayed yellow smoke."

The pilots made every effort to respect the new bomb lines that delineated friend and foe. However, the battle was so fluid that no line on a map could keep up with the ebb and flow of the troops of five allied nations on the ground. There were a number of unfortunate "friendly" strafing incidents.

General Crerar finally issued a directive to all units. He suggested that being strafed and wounded by your own aircraft was a necessary evil: "There have been a number of attacks by our own aircraft on our own tps [troops] during the last two days and particularly today. It is necessary to stress the peculiar difficulties to the Allied Air Forces caused by the convergence of US, British and Canadian armies on a common objective with air action against the enemy force within that Allied circle desirable up to the point of their surrender."

The directive emphasized the positive aspects: the damage done to scores of enemy tanks and trucks by 2d Tactical Air Force: "Tank flamers 77, smokers 42, damaged 55. Mechanical transport flamers 900, smokers

478, damaged 712." He stressed that if the Canadian units would "compare their vehicle casualties proportionately to the above they will obtain some idea of the tremendous military balance in their favor."[14] For the Albertans it was a rough beginning to a tough battle. Two of their fifteen tanks had already been disabled, and six men wounded in the initial minutes of the attack. Now they discovered a Tiger tank positioned squarely in their path, prohibiting any advance into the village. They had to get around it before they were spotted. It was then that Currie made the decision that first marked him as a man of great—of greatest—courage and determination. Ordinarily, when a commander required urgent information about the enemy, he would send out a reconnaissance patrol of men especially trained for the job. Not Currie. He made up his mind to go alone on foot into the village center that night to find a way to somehow outflank the German tank that controlled the main road into town.

As dusk settled into darkness, and rain clouds hovered threateningly over St. Lambert-sur-Dives, Major David Currie strode purposefully down the road that led into the silent village. His findings were not encouraging. The Dives River, curving through the town, would prevent them from maneuvering around the Tiger's lethal 88mm gun.

In the darkened streets of St. Lambert-sur-Dives there was an eerie hush. Not a single villager was present; not even the barking of a dog. But there were Germans entrenched in the silent cottages and hedges along the road. Currie was convinced of that.

"I could hear voices of Germans in some of the buildings, but did not run into anyone during my reconnaissance on foot," he reported back to his CO.

Let me lead the men on foot tonight to wipe out that Tiger, he urged his commander.[15]

Sit tight until morning, was the reply. Attack at first light.

There was little sleep that night at South Alberta Regiment headquarters on nearby Hill 117, where tanks and infantry harbored in an orchard one thousand yards north of St. Lambert waiting for the attack to go in. A soft rain, the first in weeks, brought the threat of cloud cover and the fear of no air support for their morning attack. Less than a mile away, an entire German army could be down there, determined to keep the escape gap open.

Inevitably the terrifying thought came to each of the 130 men peering out into the eerie silence: How can a handful of men and fifteen vastly inferior Sherman tanks stand a chance against tens of thousands of escaping enemy equipped with the awesome Tiger and Panther tanks?

Inevitably their eyes rested on the tall profile of David Currie, leaning casually on the side of a tank, gaze fixed determinedly upon the dark ridge beyond the Dives Valley.

Yet there was something in his stance. "He was so cool, it was impossible for us to get excited,"[16] one of his NCOs later recalled.

They would have been surprised to know the turmoil of his thoughts at that moment. His greatest fear, he was to say, "was the possibility that I might not measure up."

He confronted that fear. "Well, Dave," he thought, "up to now this has been a pretty good war, but this is it!"[17]

CHAPTER 27

St. Lambert Under Attack

Daybreak: Saturday, August 19

The Canadian attack went in at dawn.

The lead tank moved ahead. Currie and the Argyll company advanced on foot to support it. The Sherman got a third of the way through the village. So far, so good. Suddenly, a German armor-piercing (AP) shell slammed into it. The three crew nearest the turret of the disabled tank scrambled out as they had been trained for years. But before the driver and codriver could escape, a second AP shot smashed into the Sherman, setting it on fire. Both men were badly burned as the tank brewed.

Currie spotted the two enemy tanks creating this havoc—a Tiger and a Mark IV—a quarter of a mile down the road at the southern end of the town. Son of a bitch! He had no radio to alert the squadron. It was his rear link, Captain John Redden, who saved the day. Realizing that he'd lost communication with the commanding officer, Redden abandoned his tank and sprinted up to Currie's. He was able to pinpoint one of the German tanks, the Mark IV, in the gunsight, fired, and destroyed it. This was a first confirmed "kill" for the South Albertas. (Currie's crew got the colonel's prize—a bottle of rum.)

Meanwhile, the Argyll infantry company of sixty men had the dangerous job of clearing pockets of Germans from each house along the road. The Tiger had pulled back out of sight, but a forty-five-ton Panther had drawn up beside a cottage. It towered ominously over the riflemen, as they now had to tackle the horrific job of destroying it. Lieutenant Gil Armour asked for volunteers. The lads in Armour's platoon were used to following Gil on crazy missions; they had him pegged as "a little wild."

"A suicide squad," one private muttered, but he volunteered with the rest of them.[1] Armour climbed on top of the tank with a 36-grenade in his hand. Just as he was about to drop it in the open turret, a German officer armed with an automatic pistol thrust his head out. The two men wrestled furiously and Armour forced his adversary out of the turret. Face to sweating face, they grappled on top of the tank until the Canadian finally gave an almighty lunge and shoved the German to the ground, tumbling down as well with the effort. One of the Argyll platoon volunteers grabbed his rifle and shot the German, seriously wounding him. Moments later, Armour scrambled on top and dropped his grenade in the turret, immobilizing the Panther. A Piat was brought up to finish the kill.

By midmorning Currie could signal headquarters that the village had been cleared. Now, with just twelve tanks and some sixty infantrymen left, he faced the job of holding it against almost inevitable enemy counterattacks. He ordered Armour to consolidate his platoon on the vital southern crossroads, with three tanks in support. That left just nine tanks and some three dozen men to hold the rest of the village. These dug in facing the western edge of town, where most of the infiltrators seemed to be coming from.

During the afternoon, fighting became spasmodic, but the countryside around the town fairly seethed with small groups of Germans, some wandering aimlessly, giving themselves up without a fight. As Currie was walking back up the street, two German officers rapped hard on the window to get his attention. Currie gestured them out of the building and accepted their surrender, but not the gift they offered with it: a small puppy.

One group surrendered with about a dozen American GI prisoners who had been captured somewhere to the south. A Canadian trooper grinned to see the Yanks "going around [to] different tanks bumming smokes."[2]

Other Germans, more militant, took their toll as snipers. Captain Redden, already a hero for coordinating the attack earlier that day on the enemy tank, pushed his luck—and was taken in by an old German ploy: "Suddenly about a dozen two-ton trucks loaded with enemy troops blundered into our area," Redden described. "We used a high-explosive round to stop the lead truck, and two rounds of AP on the rear of the convoy."

Redden decided he would "be a hero by conning these bastards into giving up." A German approached waving a white flag. "I popped out waist high to talk." the Albertan said. "Another German came around the corner with a Schmeisser . . . The guy with the [white] flag ducked out of the line of fire." Redden went down, seriously wounded.[3]

German prisoners began to pour in. Currie organized them into groups, establishing a first-aid post for those that were wounded, under the direction of an English-speaking German doctor. He was too thin on the ground to spare any infantry to escort them back, so he sent them off in batches of three or four dozen, with a "watch dog" tank trained on their every move. Of 2,500 POWs, only one tried to escape. "He took off through the fields but did not get very far."

"Up to this time I had lost two officers," David Currie recounts. "During the rest of Saturday, the fighting was bitter." So far, the Albertas and Argylls had been fighting "naked," with no artillery support. Finally, three regiments of field artillery were moved into range.[4]

Captain Fred Clerkson, the regimental FOO, set up an observation post on Hill 117, the South Alberta's forward HQ. From the high point he had an incredible view of the Dives Valley. By now, the funnel of the gap through which the enemy were escaping was a mere two miles wide. He began calling down fire on the fleeing Germans: "It was an OP officer's dream," an amazed Clerkson said. "Below in the valley targets appeared one after another. Roads and fields were full of Germans moving eastward seeking a way out of the trap. The resulting carnage was terrible."[5]

Just a few miles south, American artillery also pounded the hapless escaping German troops at the Fôret de Gouffern on the southern ridge of the Dives Valley.

At St. Lambert, the situation was getting desperate. An apparently never-ending stream of enemy was wading across the Dives into the town and attacking the small band of defenders. Emboldened by their superiority of numbers, the Germans swarmed the Canadian tanks, even leaping on board to attack the troopers. Currie described those tense moments. "Our tanks were running around in circles firing at one another to keep the enemy from climbing on top of them."

Drastic measures were required. Currie requested a massive artillery concentration directly on his own position. He shouted a warning to all his men, "Get under cover!"

It came down with lethal force, crashing within fifteen yards of his position, a powerful-enough explosion to wipe out his whole squadron. This was a seldom-used tactic, only employed in desperate situations. But the Germans were out in the open; the Canadians were dug in. "We were lucky," Currie said. "We suffered no casualties from our own guns, but it had a very devastating effect on the Germans."[6]

Now the Albertas faced a new problem: their tanks were running low on fuel and ammunition. With enemy shells pounding the roads, refueling midbattle was far too risky for the three-ton trucks, each hauling more than one thousand gallons of gas and quantities of ammunition. At St. Lambert they devised a shuttle system. The trucks deposited their cargo on a hill several hundred yards behind the front line. This was picked up in smaller loads by South Alberta Regiment Crusader tanks and brought in by back roads to Currie's HQ. One by one each tank would then pull back to the headquarters to refuel and rearm. By late afternoon Currie's small band was fighting off ever-increasing German pressure from the west. Sniper and shell fire were heavy both in the town and up on Hill 117. Regimental headquarters urgently requested brigade to send reinforcements, warning "unless relief comes, Germans will move back in."[7] Yet forty infantrymen were all the reinforcements the brigade could muster to help the desperate Canadians.

At 1800 hours the token reinforcement of two companies, both gravely depleted in strength, arrived. Currie personally led the newcomers into key positions, while still under heavy enemy fire. There was only one crossing over the Dives that could sustain the weight of the German tanks and heavy vehicles: the stone bridge at St. Lambert. There were also two crossings for foot soldiers. One was a footbridge at Moissy, just southeast of the village. A second was a small bridge built to carry farm equipment at the Château de Quantité farm and mill half a mile west of the town.

With darkness falling, Currie's forces were too extended to be able to maintain strong control of all the vital crossings over the Dives. He tried. He consolidated his force into a tight defensive core in the center of the village, guns sighted on every escape route.

Nearby, at the mill at Quantité, Currie had directed his infantry to dig in near a group of farm buildings at the edge of the river. To add to the confusion, dozens of terrified villagers huddled in the barns and outbuildings of the chateau.

Two Sherman tanks supported the outpost. Disorganized bands of Germans continued their sporadic entries into St. Lambert. As night fell, Argyll Lieutenant Dunlop reported "literally hordes of Germans" crossing the river. . . . I would think between 1,500 and 2,000 prisoners of war . . . a sad-looking lot. Their uniforms were ragged and dirty. The Canadians removed all their arms—mostly grenades and revolvers—putting them into a farmer's wheelbarrow. It soon overflowed.

> To get the prisoners back to the main force, we gathered them in lots of perhaps 100 to 150, and marched them directly across the field with one of our chaps escorting. I remember we were careful to tell the escort that he must take them only to the town and then return for more since we were extremely short of help. Through the tank radio they were able to notify HQ when another flock of prisoners was coming.[8]

There would be no sleep that Saturday night for the captives—or for the weary troops that guarded them. The prisoners were herded onto a large flat field near Currie's headquarters. "That night, up on Hill 117 just above Dave," Lieutenant Danny McLeod relates, "we had a couple of tanks with headlights. The Germans were lying prostrate. We were saying, 'Don't bloody well move or we'll fire!' "[9]

Argyll Private Art Bridge never forgot the wistful tune that drifted out in the deepening twilight when one of the prisoners picked up his squeeze box and started playing "La Paloma."[10] To some of the Canadians, it was a disconcerting experience to see these Germans whom they had regarded as enemies become just ordinary men: "A couple of days ago you were fighting with them. And you start to wonder . . . if these guys have got families . . . because you start to think about your own family . . . and if you're ever going to get back. There's no hostility."[11]

Currie had sent a platoon of the newly arrived Argylls in the direction of Moissy and Chambois, to "possibly make contact with the Poles who were supposedly in Moissy, and if not there, in Chambois."[12]

In the blackness of that Saturday night, it was solely the infantry, barely more than one hundred men in total, who had to guard each woodland, each slope, each narrow farm track of the entire area surrounding the town. Guns cannot see in the dark, and tanks are helpless against enemy infiltrators.

There was no hint that, just two miles away in Chambois, officers from US 90th Infantry and 10th Polish Dragoons were at that moment shaking hands and toasting each other with Polish vodka in an historic encounter.

Only one mile away was the rustic Moissy ford. It had traditionally been a meeting place where washerwomen laid a plank from one bank to the other to carry their laden baskets of wet laundry across the Dives.[13] Now, Moissy had taken on a more sinister importance as an escape route for the German Seventh Army. In wooded hideouts a short distance away, German officers were issuing urgent whispered orders to their fleeing soldiers.

Company Sergeant Major George Mitchell remembered that night patrol through St. Lambert to Moissy as "terrifying." The men got about two miles down the road when they ran into enemy small-arms fire and grenades. "We couldn't tell where the fire was coming from so we hit the ditch. I ended up on top of an ant hill . . . the nasty little buggers bit me everywhere!"[14]

They found out later that they were on top of something hotter than an anthill: "Little did we know that we were right in the line of march of an entire [German] army trying to get out of the gap. We could have kept right on going along the same road to Chambois. Several of their group were wounded, including the major in command who, though his wounds were slight, evacuated himself out. As there were indications that they were dangerously behind enemy lines, and they had lost their leader, the men cut back cross-country, creeping through back lanes, sometimes crawling on their bellies. They made it back to St. Lambert in three hours. Had the major managed to carry out his orders, the gap could have been sealed.

"But one understrength infantry company didn't stand much chance of stopping the swarms of Germans who started moving through St. Lambert-sur-Dives and Moissy the next morning."[15]

CHAPTER 28

Vive les Americains, Vive les Polonaises

Saturday, August 19, 1944

While Canadian troops battled to seal the northern rim of the trap at St. Lambert, stern opposition from a determined 116th *Panzer* Division was thwarting American efforts to reach and close the southern jaw just three miles south at Chambois.

Chambois had been a tranquil village bordering the River Dives. Many of its citizens had fled the town during the week of intensive shelling. But not all. The baker of Chambois, who made all the bread for the three hundred people of the village, stayed on. He devised an unusual pocket of serenity for his wife, their four children, and the other youngsters still in the town. "There was a big trench where the children were put," he recalled. "We made them sing songs to the violin while the artillery raged." As shrapnel burst over their heads, the familiar notes of *"un petit moulin sur la rivière"* brought some comfort to the fearful children. Rosaries were tearfully said by children and adults.[1]

Finally, on Saturday morning August 19, 359th Infantry Regiment of 90th Division was given the green light to approach Chambois from the south, meeting enemy opposition on the way. This time it was the 2d Battalion's turn to lead the attack. Commanding Officer Major Leonard Dull had orders to block the roads and cover the village by fire only.

An hour later there was a shift in orders. Dull was instructed to occupy Chambois. Now the village was to become a battlefield. This "snafu," as Dull later called it, caused a major delay while he reorganized his battalion and disengaged his men from the firefight with the enemy outside the town. In midafternoon he sent patrols into Chambois, and at about 1730 hours elements from two companies waded across the shallow waters of the Dives south of Chambois and managed to penetrate the village.[2]

At about the same time, Major Zgorzelski's 10th Polish Dragoons were advancing on Chambois from the north, preceded by its reconnaissance regiment, the 10th Mounted Rifles.

"We advanced to the top of a hill just south of Chambois," Captain Michael Gutowski of the 10th Mounted Rifles reported. "There was a ravine in front of me and buildings of the village beyond it. Suddenly we came under fire from *Panzerfausts.*"

Gutowski sent a foot patrol to investigate. They radioed back anxiously: "The valley is black with Germans!" Gutowski ordered his squadron to dismount and attack on foot—an unusual and highly dangerous tactic for an armored reconnaissance unit.

"My squadron had sixteen tanks left, each with three men. We attacked with machine guns and hand grenades; there was nobody else to support us." The small band engaged bravely in a fierce firefight for some thirty minutes, capturing and killing many Germans.[3]

At 1630 hours, the forward observation officer, Captain Sévigny, viewed the Polish action from the heights of Château Boisjos. He reported that the lead troops had passed from his sight as they reached the orchards and hedged enclosures on the outskirts of Chambois itself. Zgorzelski's 10th Dragoons, and 10th Mounted Rifle were herding along a great number of German prisoners as they entered the village.

Second Lieutenant Karcz, a troop leader with 10th Dragoons, described the scene as they entered the town: "The place was on fire. The roads leading to it and the side streets were jammed with German armor already alight or smoldering, enemy corpses and a host of wounded soldiers. No civilians were to be seen." From every orchard, ditch, and house they collected prisoners until their numbers grew enormously. As they approached the Dives River they came under a hail of bullets from the houses; a Polish grenade silenced this.[4]

Elements from Major Dull's 2d Battalion, by chance approaching the town at about the same time (but from the south), were equally overawed by the scene of destruction.

Captain Gaskins, a company commanding officer of the US 2d Battalion, reported that it was the first time he ever had living proof of the old phrase "rivers of blood—blood was actually running in sizable streams in the gutters." Houses were burning, the stench of dead and burned flesh was almost unbearable; there was an unbelievable clutter of dead Germans, horses, and vehicles. Ammunition exploding all around the place made him think briefly, "It was just like a Fourth of July!"[5]

Suddenly, Lieutenant Karcz's second-in-command shouted news of the approach of enemy infantry attacking across the fields. Before they could open fire, they were able to identify from their helmets that these were American infantry.

"An American captain ran toward me and, still running, caught hold of me and lifted me in the air as if I had been a child," Lieutenant Karcz remembered.[6]

This encounter between a 10th Dragoon squadron and a patrol from Major Dull's 2d Battalion, 359th Infantry Regiment, was a historic moment: the first time American and Polish troops had ever met on a battlefield.

The 90th Infantry Division historian reported another such encounter in an after battle report: "Major Booth, the Regimental S3, met the Polish commanding officer who, although he spoke English, said when asked his name, 'Here, give me a book and pencil. You'll never be able to pronounce it anyway, so I'll write it down.' He was Major Zgorzelski of 10th Polish Dragoons."[7]

Zgorzelski scrawled his name and unit on a scrap of paper torn from a notebook: Captain Laughlin Waters, commanding "G" Company, 359th Infantry, reciprocated.[8] These two allies appropriately commemorated the occasion in a toast with Polish vodka (from a bottle fortuitously liberated from a German officer's jeep). Elbows bent in quick succession to a lusty round of drinks and many "*Vive les Americains and Vive les Polonaises.*"

> This meeting on the Chambois/Mont Ormel road, although one of several "first" contacts reported, seems to be the one nearest to the "first," the 90th Infantry Division historian noted. Several others took place almost simultaneously however, so the point is debatable. As it turned out, the Polish unit was a flying column which had shot ahead of its main body and was almost completely out of supplies when it met the Americans.[9]

After this first contact by the advance units of two divisions, both brought up their forces quickly. The Dragoons handed over some two thousand German prisoners to the Americans, explaining that their resources were too limited to keep POWs. The new allies then worked out a mutual plan for defense of the town.

The Poles had seriously outstripped their supply lines. They had not been resupplied since their amazing twenty-mile night march three days earlier. Just prior to their exodus they had lost half of their petrol stores and a great deal of their ammunition to RAF bombing during Operation *Tractable*. Now the division was cut off both from its own units at Maczuga and from all of their other allies, excepting this one tenuous and, so far, unproductive link with US troops.

"Our position is very flimsy," Captain Gutowski emphasized to the Americans. "We are out of food. We have no water, no gasoline, and no ammunition. Some tanks have no more than five or ten shells left. For machine guns there is maybe ten minutes' firing left." He asked the Americans for help.[10]

"Major Dull contacted his higher echelon and informed them of the situation," the battalion history records. "I had one hell of a time convincing the higher authorities of the actual conditions," Dull confirmed.

> The Poles did not have enough gas left in their vehicles to allow them to go the few miles south to Le Bourg-St. Léonard. Finally, after urgent negotiation up and down the chain of command, the American First Army, through V Corps, supplied the Poles with 4,000 gallons of gasoline, 140,000 rounds of machine-gun ammunition and 189 rounds of 75mm ammunition for the guns of the tanks.[11]

The 1st Polish Armored Division history applauded the generosity of the Americans. "[They] shared with us their rations, ammunition, gasoline, and were very generous with their cigarettes. It will be difficult to forget the supply officer, Major Miller, who, being short of working hands, helped personally to load ammunition boxes on our trucks."[12]

But all of this negotiation took time—too much time. In the waiting period, both units were too thin on the ground to develop a solid barrier against a determined enemy. They had no resources to extend their line that single mile north to the small village of Moissy, as per General Simonds's orders, where a small ford offered the enemy a shallow crossing over the Dives.

In fact, it was on that same evening that the Canadian Argylls probed south from St. Lambert-sur-Dives as far as Moissy. Had the Canadians or the Poles been able to reach out that extra mile or two, the trap enclosing the German army would have been at least technically snapped shut.

Although they were, like the South Albertas and Argylls down the road at St. Lambert, celebrating the formal closing of the Falaise/Chambois Gap, in truth the allied defenders on the Dives, with their limited troops, were finding it hopeless in the rough, hilly, and wooded terrain to block even small groups from filtering through their lines.

They had no knowledge that this misgiving would be put to a test within a few hours. A massed enemy breakout, heralding twenty-four hours of violent conflict, was planned for dawn the next day.

CHAPTER 29

Trapped!

Saturday night, August 19, 1944

Oberstgruppenführer Paul Hausser sat at the edge of a ditch, studying a map.

Even in this rude setting, the sixty-three-year-old SS general maintained his demeanor: back ramrod-straight, uniform impeccable, black patch neatly adjusted on the eye lost on the Russian front, expression as aloof as ever.[1]

He ignored his staff, hurriedly setting up a new command post—an old stone quarry near the village of Villedieu les Bailleul. He seemed unconcerned that his new CP was a mere two miles west of the allied positions on the Dives and could be overrun at any time.

He took no notice of the August sun, just now setting on this nineteenth day of the month. He had seen seventy-four suns go down over Normandy since the D-Day invasion.

The task that absorbed his attention now was how to extricate over one hundred thousand men from almost certain capture or death as the allied trap closed around them. The encirclement was obviously complete. The intention to keep the "bottleneck" open was outdated.[2]

General Hausser had just returned after personally visiting on foot the headquarters of each of his four corps threatened with encirclement. With them, he explored a means of organized escape.

It was true that for the past two or three days continuous columns of German troops and even some equipment had been pouring east across

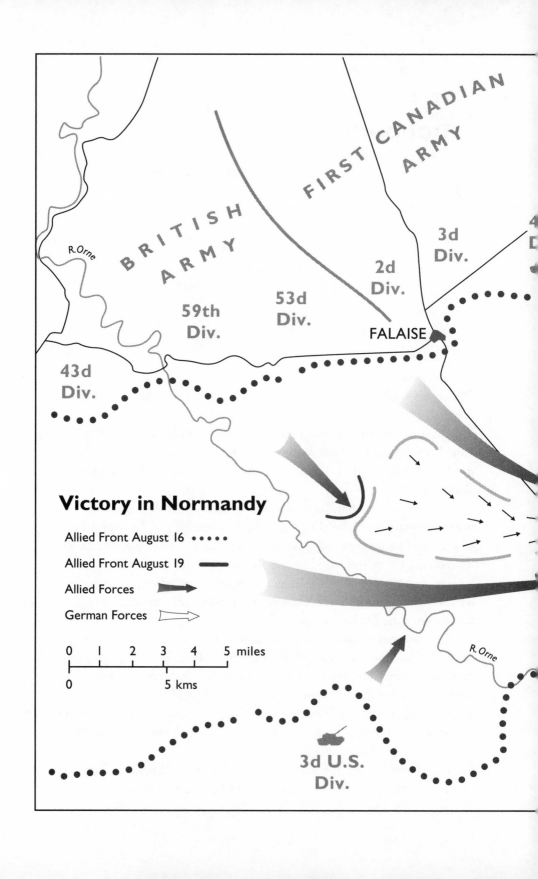

FIRST CANADIAN ARMY

BRITISH ARMY

R.Orne

3d Div.

2d Div.

53d Div.

59th Div.

FALAISE

43d Div.

Victory in Normandy

Allied Front August 16 ••••••

Allied Front August 19 ▬▬

Allied Forces ➡

German Forces ⇨

0   1   2   3   4   5 miles

0   5 kms

R.Orne

3d U.S. Div.

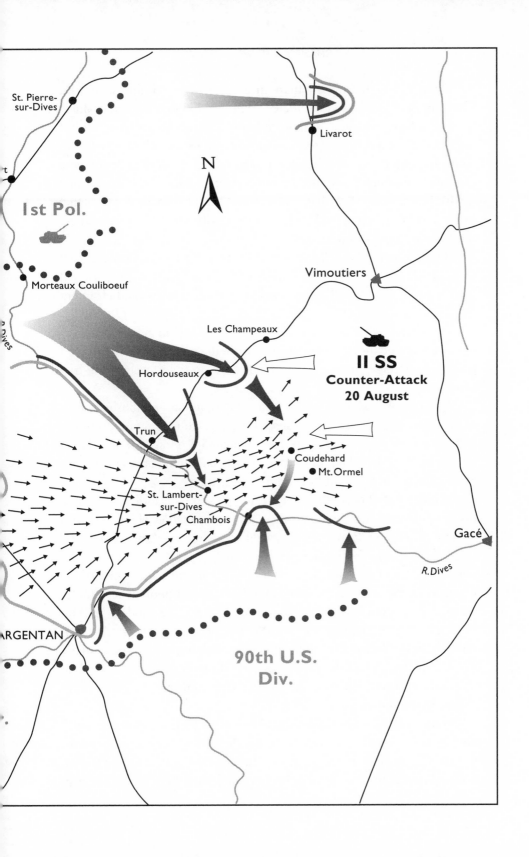

St. Pierre-
sur-Dives

1st Pol.

Morteaux Couliboeuf

R. Dives

N

Livarot

Vimoutiers

Les Champeaux

Hordouseaux

II SS
Counter-Attack
20 August

Trun

Coudehard

Mt. Ormel

St. Lambert-
sur-Dives

Chambois

Gacé

R. Dives

ARGENTAN

90th U.S.
Div.

the Dives Valley, finding sanctuary in the ruggedness of the Auge hills. They were part of the exodus initiated on August 14 by General von Kluge. In all, five *Panzer* divisions and two infantry divisions had managed to get most of their rear-echelon troops safely out before the Allies closed in to create the entrapment. Supply troops and a large mass of matériel were also saved, although few of their vehicles, being mainly horse-drawn, had survived the passage. They had followed the secondary roads and trails that led from villages west of the Dives River to crossings at St. Lambert and on-ward toward Mont Ormel.[3]

It was while following this escape route that they had been intercepted by the Poles during the previous night's trek. The German escapees had "courteously" waved the Poles through, not wanting to reveal their intentions.

Incredibly, although allied troops were closing in on them, small groups still found they could elude capture in the myriad wooded hills and paths. The terrain, to their relief, made it impossible to close the trap completely.

A reconnaissance unit of 21st *Panzer* Division, now established north of Les Champeaux, had been assigned the task "to reconnoiter from the east unoccupied points of sortie to the encircled troops."[4] These battle groups, probing the allied lines, enabled the clandestine passage of senior commanders and their staffs in and out of the trap.

Hausser's chief of staff, General Rudolph von Gersdorff, was making his way independently through the gap to attend a high-level meeting with General Model (replacing the disgraced von Kluge) at Army Group "B" Headquarters at La Roche Guyon. He brought a grim description of the plight of some of the miserable troops caught in the trap: "Things look black inside the pocket," he said. "Hundreds upon hundreds of vehicles [have] been put out of action by enemy fire. Untended wounded (and) innumerable dead characterize a battlefield in a manner rarely seen throughout the entire war."[5] The allied air offensive and the particularly heavy artillery fire had destroyed the bulk of the army vehicles. Lack of fuel and ammunition had already made it imperative for the Germans to destroy many of their guns.[6]

Von Gersdorff informed General Model that their situation was bleak on the American front. The enemy had broken through at Chambois, threatening to close the trap from the south. Recent Canadian penetrations into Trun and St. Lambert threatened the northern rim of the gap.

British XXX Corps and 53d Welsh Division are squeezing us from behind like a limp tube of toothpaste, he told them. To keep the British from baying at our heels we have sown thick minefields and employed other delaying tactics such as booby traps.

Von Gersdorff was in an agitated state when he stealthily made his way back into the pocket to report to Hausser, dodging intense artillery fire. Von Gersdorff was shaken to learn that in his absence Welsh troops had attacked Hausser's Seventh Army command post at Nécy (four miles south of Falaise), reportedly wiping out the entire Seventh Army staff. The rumor proved to be untrue; the staff had escaped, but the Germans had lost most of their vehicles and radio equipment under intense British and Canadian artillery fire.[7]

Later, at an orders group with senior commanders, von Gersdorff reviewed the bleak facts. It was a sorry handful of men who huddled in a farmhouse, sitting on two benches around a worn wooden kitchen table. A flickering candle etched the battle weariness of their faces.

Attending the "O" Group were the commanders of 84th Infantry Corps (Lieutenant General Elfeldt) and 12th SS *Hitlerjugend* Division, (SS Colonel Kurt Meyer). As well, there were several senior staff members: Major Hubert Meyer (12th SS), Lieutenant Colonel Heinz Günther Guderian (116th *Panzer* Division), and Colonel Klaus von Kluge (*Panzergroup Eberbach*). Von Kluge had just learned of the suicide of his father, disgraced by Hitler.

Colonel Guderian described the emergency measures he had employed in recent days to try to hold that critical line against the Americans. His 116th *Panzer* and units from XLVII *Panzer* Corps had rushed whatever battle-fit groups they could muster to the front.

Initially, he told them, his force was so ill equipped that he had not had much hope of success against Patton's powerful forces: "We fought with very few tanks." Luckily, Guderian ran into a detachment of another division, whose commander was a friend. "I told him, you fight here [with me]!"

But when 116th *Panzer* sent an urgent demand to Army HQ for reinforcements from 1st SS *Panzer* Division, the *Wehrmacht* was furious to discover that—without even consulting them—some combat units of the 1st SS had already been moved out of the pocket.

"Probably acting on orders received through SS channels," von Gersdorff grumbled.[8] It was this underhanded and debilitating power struggle

between the *Wehrmacht* and the SS that continued unabatedly to under-
mine them, despite the crisis.

The German *Panzers* had put up stiff resistance, trying to stem the
American force. Suddenly, Guderian was astonished to find the pressure
exerted by the Americans abruptly relaxed. Incredibly, to the Germans,
the allied commanding generals Bradley and Montgomery seemed to
have lost interest in entrapping them.

He couldn't know that Patton's precipitous departure for the Seine on
August 14 had left just three inexperienced divisions holding the southern
edge of the trap, and these had been temporarily halted for lack of a commander.

"If the [Americans] had attacked without stopping, we were blown
up," he reported. "There is no doubt. They could have met the English
and Canadians coming from the north without difficulty."[9]

The 116th had gained some time, but now the Americans had driven
them out of Le Bourg-St. Léonard and had closed on Chambois.

One of Guderian's officers, Walter Kaspers, an adjutant in the 116th
Antitank Division, described his unit's feelings of pending catastrophe:
"The British pushed from one side and Patton from the other. We could
not hold, and were pushed closer and closer together. This is not a nice
feeling, to be so concentrated. The artillery grew more and more intense,
and we had less and less room."

Kaspers noted that three-quarters of the division was horse drawn.
"That was terrible for us. The horse-drawn part could not get away because
it moved too slowly. Patton was much faster."[10]

Von Gersdorff stressed the urgency of coordinating a massed breakout
out of the trap. Our strongest combat troops are still caught behind the
lines, he told them.

There is one note of hope, he added. Throughout the fighting in Normandy in the past months, Seventh Army strategists have observed that the
enemy is most vulnerable at the junction, or "seam" of their lines. Remember Vire, he said. Remember Argentan. Every time the Anglo-
Americans try to fight on adjoining battle lines, they seem to have
time-wasting disputes. We capitalized on them then; we will again. "Here
again the seam between the Twenty-first Army Group and Twelfth US
Army Group seems to [play] the part of guardian angel to us."

The army chief pointed out that another encouraging factor was the
outside support they could expect. General Model has masterminded a

carefully coordinated attack plan to withdraw our units that were still trapped west of the Dives River, he told them. The breakout will take place eastward across the Dives between Trun and Chambois.[11]

Escaping the pocket was to be a two-prong operation. Dual forces would attack. One, Hausser's Seventh Army, would break *out* of the encirclement. The other, the II SS *Panzer* Corps would break *in* to support the escaping troops.

Operating from Army HQ near Paris, Model had spirited II SS *Panzer* Corps out of the pocket two days before. Its orders reflected the desperation of the German plight. The Corps (comprising the 9th SS and 2d SS *Panzer* Divisions) were "to march during the day regardless of losses . . . from enemy fighter-bombers."[12]

General Bittrich, the commanding general of the II SS *Panzer* Corps, had reassembled the corps near Vimoutiers, a market town five miles north of Maczuga. His job was to launch a major counterattack back into the pocket and hold it open long enough for the armies to escape the trap.

Bittrich had hoped to launch the attack on August 18. He was getting a lot of pressure from the trapped Seventh Army commanders to move as quickly as possible, before the Allies became aware of the plan: "The withdrawal of the 11th SS *Panzer* Corps cannot for long remain concealed," von Gersdorff warned him.[13]

However, shortages of fuel and ammunition had delayed the assault. General Model was attempting to airlift petrol. General Bittrich now hoped the expected refueling would allow him to launch the 2d SS and 9th SS counterattack force at 1000 hours Sunday morning.

The job of breaking out of the trap was organized in two stages. First was Lieutenant General Eugen Meindl's advance force of two thousand paratroopers and infantry.

"The entire movement is to be conducted as a surprise attack," they were told. This was laid out as a precise—but wildly unorthodox—military operation. The breakout itself was "only men."

No artillery pieces could be taken other than the few self-propelled or mobile antitank guns they still possessed. All troops were ordered to expend ammunition the day before the breakout, then destroy their guns. They would have to take advantage of any small undefended gap in the four-mile stretch of river for their flight. The 21st *Panzer* Division's reconnaissance units patrolling the enemy positions along the Dives had identified these soft spots.

General von Gersdorff shocked the orders group by declaring that the only support for the paratroopers would be the headquarters staff of 84th Infantry Division. Staff officers acting as support troops? Unheard of!

Meindl's paratroopers would advance stealthily on foot through the night to St. Lambert-sur-Dives. Their orders were to steal through the allied lines in a wedge formation, "using Indian tactics," without firing. They would set their course by compass and regroup at Coudehard, near Mont Ormel, linking up with the incoming II SS Corps. Ammunition, food, and water would await them. They were then to wheel in their tracks and attack back against the Americans, Canadians, and Poles they had just eluded.

Next, with the paratroopers safely out, Kurt Meyer and his 12th SS *Hitlerjugend* would follow in the breakout. The Hitler Youth Division was now a sorry lot, virtually dissolved as a fighting force. Of the ten thousand teenage fanatics who had marched into Normandy at the onset of the invasion, only one hundred were left.[14] Their last two Tigers were committed for the expected fighting after dawn.[15] Then, at 0800 hours, the main German force would launch a massive breakout onslaught, with tanks, vehicles, and the majority of the besieged German troops. By sheer weight of numbers, screaming *Sieg Heil* and brandishing revolvers, tens of thousands of the desperate infantry would surge in a mad charge across the Dives at St. Lambert and on to Hill 262. *Panzer Group Eberbach*, along with Lieutenant General Heinrich von Luttwitz's 2d *Panzer* Division, would lead this attack. Von Luttwitz, a rotund, monocled Silesian officer of stern *Wehrmacht* tradition, insisted that he was taking no chances with his fifteen remaining tanks. They were all he had left of the 120 with which he had arrived in Normandy. He told his *Panzer* commanders that the tanks and armored vehicles had no chance of getting through roads clogged with corpses in the dark: "On the route leading into St. Lambert-sur-Dives from Bailleul where my division was collected, a colossal number of shot-up horses and vehicles lay mixed together with dead soldiers in large heaps which hourly [grow] higher and higher."[16]

The two forces—one attacking out and the other attacking back in—would link up in the high ground at Coudehard, a village in the hills of Maczuga, where the paratroopers would join in the battle to save their comrades.

Many of the *Wehrmacht* troops waiting to attack despaired of ever escaping; a great many were ready to surrender. Filthy, starved, and half-crazed by the incessant shelling and strafing by the dreaded *Jabos*, one corporal wrote to his family: "Nothing to eat for two days. There is no leadership left. I don't want to fight anymore, it is so useless. Our future looks hopeless . . . most likely we will be taken prisoner."[17]

Some of them were forced to continue with a pistol to their heads—an SS pistol.

Not so for Hitler's tough and dedicated Nazi paratroopers under Meindl's command: "Their mood was excellent; I had seen nothing but glowing eyes the whole day through."[18]

The paratroop commander was contemptuous of those German soldiers who had given up hope. The first thing he had done had been to establish a circle with a radius of one thousand yards around his command post to keep out his own soldiers "so as not to be betrayed by the troops gone completely wild." It was only in such a situation, he said bitterly, that "one finds out who is really the soldier and who is only a military . . . *who belongs to the brave and who to the bosses and cowards and even traitors!*" [his emphasis].

He deeply resented the favoritism shown the SS divisions of the II SS *Panzer* Corps. Why had they been sent ahead out of the encirclement? Clearly the army thought so little of the elite paratroopers that they left them in the trap to face possible annihilation: "We were good enough to be left inside the ring!" he said sarcastically. "I put a black mark in my mind against the commander in chief."[19]

There were only three bridges across the Dives that could handle the weight of tanks, General von Gersdorff reminded them: at Trun, Chambois, and St. Lambert. "A rumor reached us that Trun had been cut off by British troops," he said, piling on the harsh news. "Chambois [is] impassable because of the heavy enemy artillery fire."[20]

Of the three, only one—the bridge by the church at St. Lambert—was still open. St. Lambert, Hausser believed, was ideal for the breakthrough. "The commander in chief has therefore decided to order a breakthrough from the pocket at the weakest spot in the enemy's enveloping ring, namely on both sides of St. Lambert-sur-Dives."

"Our crossing stands or falls at St. Lambert."[21]

The Poles at Maczuga, the Americans and Poles at Chambois, and the Canadians at Trun and St. Lambert were directly in the path of this desperate German force.

CHAPTER 30

The Breakout

Dawn, Sunday, August 20

At 2230 hours the first patrols glided forward like shadows into the dark night.[1]

Thus began the Seventh Army's mass breakout, a bold attempt to funnel some sixty-five thousand men through a corridor less than four miles wide.

At 2315 hours Lieutenant General Eugen Meindl led two thousand paratroopers across the Dives Valley as spearhead units in the escape. Almost immediately Meindl's group came under direct fire from allied tanks. "We lost time whenever a star shell lit up the landscape," he noted. "We had to lie low until it got dark again." The group soon fragmented into handfuls of combat units.

They crept through innumerable hawthorn hedges covered with barbed wire and dodged around some tanks at the roadside, arriving at the river Dives about 0030 hours . . . looking for a fordable spot . . . south of the mill.[2]

The troops were ordered to maintain strict silence. No cigarettes, no torches, and no firing unless fired upon. When the artillery opened up, the Germans dived into ditches. Slowly, sometimes crawling, sometimes sprinting from cover to cover, they neared the River Dives.

It was a nasty job getting the whole crew across the stream without lights, noiselessly . . . The eastern bank was covered with black-berry trailers and was steep into the bargain and the enemy tanks were standing just behind the bushes.

As the Germans edged closer to the enemy tank positions they felt safer. They won't fire on their own comrades, Meindl whispered to his men.

By now the intensity of the fire had caused a number of casualties. Meindl's band—reduced to just fifteen men and a first lieutenant—was crawling cautiously around Hill 117 where the South Alberta tanks were massed. So fluid were the Canadian and German lines at that point that when the paratroopers heard an enemy tank rolling toward them they turned to Meindl in confusion.

" 'A German tank?' his lieutenant whispered hopefully. 'That's no German tank!' [Meindl] snapped back."[3]

Suddenly other tanks opened fire. The Germans froze; they were so close they could hear the Canadian crews talking by radio to one another.

There was no time to be lost if we hoped to get past the tanks while it was still dark. I stole around three tanks . . . but suddenly we were discovered by one that we hadn't seen in front of us. Its crew opened fire at us at a distance of thirty yards.

I threw myself flat on my face with a few of the others in a potato field. As the tank fire flew about a yard over my head I crept and crept along with my people, inch by inch along a deeper fur-row in the field—eastward.

Cautiously bypassing that hazard, Meindl and his band clambered over a fence into a garden. "The buildings had a deserted look . . . only a dog barked . . . a tank was firing away . . .

"We had no time to lose. It was now about four o'clock in the morning and a glimmer of dawn was to be seen in the east. It would soon be light enough for the enemy to take potshots at us. Forward then . . . east and northeast.

We had to plunge up to the neck for the second time in that cursed stream again. We were covered with scratches and our clothing was torn to ribbons. At about 0430 hours I heard the sound of tanks again. A soft light rain began to fall and enveloped us in its folds. It was very welcome to us."

Meindl's objective was the little village of Coudehard on the slopes of Hill 262, the southern head of the Polish Maczuga. Food and water would be waiting at the rallying point. Here they could regroup and rearm the men. Here, too, on this high point, they expected to rendezvous with II SS *Panzer* Corps breaking in from the east to launch the attack.

To their bitter disappointment, enemy tanks had taken over this vital tactical position: "In a minute we made out that the tank crews were talking Polish to one another. Now we had to lie low without a sound. I gave a sign to this effect. We lay there for at least an hour and a half under the eyes of the British tanks with Polish crews, not daring to move a finger. By this time it was at least 0730 hours."

Meindl, peering ahead, anxiously watched for tanks from II SS *Panzer* Corps rescuers that were coming "from outside."[4]

Back in the woods at Seventh Army's command post, Colonel Kurt Meyer paced anxiously by the stony quarry. With his 12th SS *Hitlerjungend*, he was still deep in enemy territory behind the Dives. Meyer's assignment was to stay put until he received word of the paratroopers' breakout. The distant roar of battle sounds gave them no clue. Had Meindl got through?

Finally, at 0200 hours, the Hitler Youth decided to strike out on their own.

There was a "solemn farewell" to their comrades in the division they were leaving. They would break out later with the motorized group. Each man wondered, "Would we ever see each other again?"[5]

In single file the small group filed down the footpath leading east. Trailing behind Meyer was the unfortunate Lieutenant General Otto Elfeldt—the corps commander (LXXXIV) without a corps—soon to be separated from the group and captured by the Poles at Chambois. Meyer and his chief of staff, Major Hubert Meyer, pressed on until they spied the village sign poking up from the rubble: "*St. Lambert.*"

At last! They crept along the far banks of the Dives, crossing at the Château de Quantité. Enemy tanks and artillery fired at them.

They heard Canadian voices. This was the enemy with whom they had been in almost continuous direct confrontation since the invasion over two months before. It galled them not to attack their arch foe. They dared not. The Canadians would be swift in reprisals for the mass murder of sixty-eight Canadian prisoners of war in cold blood, captured earlier by the *Hitlerjugend*.[6]

On the far side of the Dives they still had three miles to go to reach the heights of Coudehard. Stragglers, most without weapons, wanted to join them: "*Panzer* Meyer accepted only those who were still armed or managed to find weapons," his chief of staff recorded.

Pistol in hand, blood oozing from a head wound, Kurt Meyer led his group, now swollen to two hundred men, across the fire-swept country. He had been stationed in the area before the invasion. "I know every tree and bush," he reassured them.[7] They advanced from hedge to hedge . . . sometimes crawling stealthily, sometimes running, leaping over ditches filled with their own dead. "Out! That was their one thought. Out of this inferno."[8]

On the pastures and in the ditches thousands of dead and wounded Germans lay abandoned, caught by enemy fire. They also saw groups of soldiers who had thrown away their weapons and were waving white flags attached to sticks, indicating their willingness to surrender. Meyer was appalled: "A disgraceful, never-before-seen picture."[9]

Completely worn-out, the men had still to clamber up the wooded trails of the steeply ascending hill to reach their designated rallying point. Here they would regroup their own forces and rendezvous with II SS *Panzer* Corps, now supposedly attacking from outside.

A third unit, General Mahlmann's 353d Infantry Division, had forded the river at Moissy and also escaped in the direction of Hill 262 at Mount Ormel.

There were many other isolated bands of soldiers stumbling about in the dark, body-strewn no-man's-land that was once a tranquil Norman valley. The hills were alive with such Germans—many exhausted, disoriented, and weak with wounds. "You wouldn't know the name of the man next to you; you might not even know what regiment he was from," one German survivor later remembered.[10]

Some were determined to escape; others were recruited into a counterattack force, sometimes at gunpoint. A few—Meindl's paratroopers and Meyer's *Hitlerjugend*—continued to fight hard.

In the confusion of the breakout, antitank officer Walter Kaspers had the frightening experience of being left behind by his unit. He made his way out alone:

> I knew the direction to go in because I carried a small compass. This helped me—as well as the hedges which gave me cover. One could only see about fifty yards. So I made my way like an Indian through the hedges. It is no fine feeling if you are alone and on foot. There were many wounded and quite a few dead. One of my good friends lay there, as well as other fine men.
>
> I wandered into a wood and watched an SS division launch a counterattack. Then I became dog tired. I came to a small farmhouse. I asked the girl if I could sleep in the barn. I pointed to the east and said that I was heading that way. She told me not to worry about the Resistance and allowed me to stay and even brought me a jug of milk and a few pieces of white bread.[11]

Lieutenant Walter Padberg, staff officer of Grenadier Regiment 959, recalled the total confusion as he struggled out of the trap: "There was no battle line anymore, everything was mixed up. Communication had ended; I did not know where the regimental commander was; I did not know any of the people around me. Everything was chaos. Allied artillery and airplanes were everywhere."

Padberg, with a group of twenty or thirty men, found an armored assault vehicle. It had gasoline but no munitions. They drove through the Polish position on the hills, luckily escaping being mortared.

"When we made it out of the pocket," Padberg recounted sardonically,

> we were of the opinion that we had left hell behind us. We climbed out of the armored car. There stood a colonel. "Line up!" he began to bellow. "Everyone is now under my command! We are going to launch a counterattack!" We were a pile of twenty or thirty men. I had a pistol and nothing else. Unfortunately, I had to go behind a bush to relieve myself and missed joining the group behind the colonel.[12]

Günter Materne, a battery officer with the 363d Artillery Regiment, also recalled the difficulties of the retreat.

Sometimes we had to go to farmhouses, many of which were abandoned; sometimes we ran across trucks whose contents were spread out over the ground. Everything was in chaos from the bombing attacks: burned-out vehicles, dead horses. We were living off the land.

We helped the wounded as much as we could, as did the medics. But it was terrible for those lying there in pain. It was terrible to see men lying there in the throes of death, screaming. They cried "Mama! Take me with you, don't leave me here! I have a wife and child at home. I'm bleeding to death!"[13]

Just five miles east, at Vimoutiers, II SS *Panzer* Corps finally received the airdrop of gas that would allow them to launch their counterattack into the allied lines.

Trapped between the German rescuers coming at them from outside the trap and the escaping Germans now clambering up the rough Auge hills toward them were two Polish armored regiments, frantically digging in at Château Boisjos and Maczuga.

In the darkness of that long night, Major David Currie and his men could hear and even sometimes glimpse shadowy bands of Germans crossing the river and heading north through the town.

With less than one hundred infantrymen to cover this broad stretch of infiltrated country where tens of thousands of Germans were slipping past them, there was little they could do except wait: wait for reinforcements and wait for dawn.

CHAPTER 31

Black Sunday

Sunday, August 20, 1944

At 0800 hours, as the fog lifted on a brilliant Sunday morning, warriors from six nations joined battle at the River Dives.

The Texas-Oklahomans of the US 90th Division, fresh from their victories at Le Bourg-St. Léonard and Chambois, reached the Dives with a growing sense of pride in the transformation of their unit. The division had not only been given back its soul by General McLain, but it also had found leaders at all levels. Now they could finally live up to their division's proud World War I sobriquet "Tough 'Ombres."

The Poles—expatriates like Michael Gutowski, still anguishing for their Warsaw brothers in arms—bore ever-growing hatred in their hearts for the Nazi oppressors and ever-increasing determination to defeat them.

Canadians such as Major David Currie were sustained by the deep confidence of men who had just the previous day found their answer. They truly *had* measured up.

Bemused by the magnitude of their artillery fire, and by the uniqueness of it—when ever had the artillery fired in two opposite directions at once?—allied gunners began to realize that this was essentially a fire war and their contributions would be the decisive factors.

So, too, did American, British, and Canadian airmen, taking off from bases just minutes from the battlefield, swooping again and again across the Dives Valley, have the certain knowledge that their skills were key contributors in the coming battle.

The English, Welsh, and Scottish troops who had seen so many thousands of their men fall in the seventy-five days of unrelenting and deadly fighting to reach this last battle of Normandy, could now only look on, their numbers so sadly depleted.

The French? With what emotion did they watch their country being torn apart, their countrymen mowed down by shells and bombs, while they dreamed only of Paris?

And the Class of '26? Could they, and the thousands of other tattered but still proud remnants of Hitler's elite SS, *Panzers*, and paratroops — could they still believe in their destiny?

With daylight came the German horde, descending like a tidal wave — huge, unstoppable rollers of desperate men. Earlier, the paratroopers had crept by in darkness, small handfuls at a time, crawling on their bellies past night-blinded Canadian tanks. Now this second force descended by the thousands in strident fury.

"As they marched out, the men were singing," Lieutenant Colonel Max Anger, a member of the SS *Panzer Kampfgruppen*, remembered of the start line. "The mood was good. It was a rare picture."

At Tournai-sur-Dives, still west of St. Lambert, the unit ran into a huge traffic jam. Colonel Anger felt that the *Wehrmacht* was for once showing them real respect. "For the first time, after all these many campaigns (he said with pride) I heard the call, 'SS to the front!' "[1]

Reaching St. Lambert, von Luttwitz's 2d *Panzer* Division, with fifteen tanks and various armored and horse-drawn vehicles, led the charge across the stone bridge. Screaming their *Sieg Heils* and brandishing fists, they stormed the Dives. Infantry and columns of vehicles followed in their wake.

As the fog lifted, allied artillery opened up in "a storm such as I had never before experienced," Luttwitz would long remember. Many of the horses pulling vehicles balked under the hail of fire, wheeling in frantic circles until they were shot up and blocked the narrow roads. "Towering pillars of smoke rose incessantly from petrol tanks as they were hit," he wrote. "Ammunition exploded, riderless horses stampeded, some of them badly wounded." Men, horses, and vehicles tumbled from the bridge and lay "jumbled together in grotesque heaps."[2]

What started as an orderly attack collapsed into a confused shambles. Success in escaping the closing allied ring now depended on the individual initiative of each unit commander, on unit morale and the will to fight, and on pure chance—the good fortune, for example, of finding an undefended crossing or a shallow ford.[3]

In the next five hours of "embittered close-in fighting" the battle for Chambois and St. Lambert raged as wave after wave of Germans battered the defenders.[4]

At Chambois, startled Americans from the 90th Division's 359th Infantry and their Polish allies were at first overrun by a horde. "The Americans . . . defending the crossroads were to experience the most agonizing hours of the war," wrote Major Zgorzelski.[5]

A series of strong enemy counterattacks swept 2d Battalion lines in the next hours, as their historian describes:

> At 0700, Germans in considerable numbers, estimated to be remnants of two panzer divisions, attacked from the west. Their attack was in such strength that, when it hit the K Company positions, the latter broke and folded back into F Company, leaving a gap between the two companies. Before the gap could be filled six German tanks piled on through this gap, followed by several hundred infantrymen. Three of the tanks were knocked out almost immediately but the others [with infantry] succeeded in getting into the town and occupied several buildings.

An hour later the US antitank and bazooka platoons destroyed the infiltrating armor, taking three hundred prisoners.

At 1000 hours another large German column showed up, this time veering south and east of Chambois and severing connections between the battalion command post and the town. The adjutant rounded up all available personnel, "from truck drivers to clerk-typists," and broke up the attack. In the early afternoon the Germans tried yet another assault through American lines. "Five tanks came into the area and fired pell-mell for about an hour." Again the bazookas came to the rescue.[6]

During one of these counterattacks a young machine gunner, Sergeant John Hawk, set a benchmark for personal initiative and courage when he stalked and finally directed fire on two enemy tanks. His citation for America's highest award, the Congressional Medal of Honor, reads:

Two of our tank destroyers were brought up. Their shots were ineffective because of the terrain until Sgt. Hawk, despite his
wound, boldly climbed to an exposed position on a knoll where,
unmoved by fusillades from the enemy, he became a human aim-
ing stake for the destroyers. Realizing that his shouted fire directions could not be heard above the noise of battle, he ran back to
the destroyers through a concentration of bullets and shrapnel to
correct the range. He returned to his exposed position, repeating
this performance until 2 of the tanks were knocked out and a third
driven off. Still at great risk, he continued to direct the destroyers'
fire into the Germans' wooded position until the enemy came out
and surrendered. Sgt. Hawk's fearless initiative and heroic conduct, even while suffering from a painful wound, was in large
measure responsible for crushing 2 desperate attempts of the
enemy to escape from the Falaise Pocket and for taking more than
500 prisoners.[7]

The 359th Regimental history relates the sorry outcome of the lives of
some of the eighty men from the US 80th Infantry Division, who had been
captured while attacking Argentan on August 17. Only thirty managed to
get free. For the rest:

For three days, they had lived as best they could on shrubs and
roots. They said that was about what most of the German troops
who had taken them prisoner had to eat. But when the German
force attempted to escape to the east they forced the remaining
fifty Americans to ride on the German tanks in the hope that seeing these Americans, our forces in Chambois would hold their
fire. Most of the men lost in this action were killed by fire from
our own weapons when the men of the 359th refused to take the
bait. Under the constant confusion of this chaotic battle, it is very
doubtful that the troops in Chambois were able to spot or to recognize the American prisoners in German vehicles.[8]

The Americans were unlucky. During the breakout the Germans usually had no time or inclination for prisoners; they disarmed them and continued on their way. "We did not even know what to do with them,"
recalled General von Gersdorff.[9]

Meanwhile, back at St. Lambert, Major Currie's small force, now down to 120 troopers and infantrymen and just five tanks, was fighting desperately to hold off another huge swarm of thousands of enemy infantry. It was "like trying to stop a buffalo stampede," one officer said. "They went around us, they went over us and they went under us."[10] Currie was forced to pull back from the south end of the village, consolidating his slender resources to the eastern edge to keep from being totally wiped out.

General von Luttwitz managed to establish a command post of sorts in the village church and round up a few "energetic officers" who kept a narrow escape hatch open for a few hours. Panicky SS troops, banded into fragmented combat groups, fought their way through the town.

At the Château de Quantité, Lieutenant Don Stewart was just starting to shave behind his tank when someone yelled that the Germans were attacking.[11] Two platoons of infantry—one Argyll and one Lincoln—were dug in at the mill with two South Alberta tanks in support. This small band of thirty men was dead in the path of one massed attack, probably the 12th SS led by Kurt Meyer.

Lieutenant Arkle Dunlop and his platoon of sixteen men at the mill, facing overwhelming odds, had three of their number killed by the onslaught. Private Stan "Red" Roberts, so named for his blaze of hair, had been guarding a number of prisoners at the river. He was shot through the head by a German soldier who suddenly appeared at the top of the bank on the enemy side.[12]

"We've got orders to pull out or we were going to get slaughtered!" Dunlop yelled to his platoon. They started backing out, herding the prisoners before them. With their two tanks shielding them, they headed across the open fields to St. Lambert.

"Lieutenant Stewart reversed his tank all the way so he could use his firepower on the Germans who were coming up over the hills at us," Dunlop recalled. "He accidentally backed over one of my guys who had been hit. Seeing a fellow backed over lengthways by a tank is terrible."[13]

German troops set up a machine gun on the top of a knoll with a full sweep of the area the Lincs had to cross. "We began playing the old game of 'leapfrog' by which each of us would run perhaps twenty or thirty yards, then dive flat on the ground. Someone in a different sector would then get up and run his stretch and do the same thing. By doing this we were fortunate in getting out with a minimum number of casualties." When Lieutenant Stewart's guns jammed, he started firing his pistol at the Germans. "He actually got one in the head before being wounded himself."[14]

The situation at regimental headquarters was getting out of hand. The Albertas moved their tanks to better fire positions and began to mow down the advancing enemy. But there were just not enough infantrymen.

Four times in the early hours of the morning, their commanding officer had radioed brigade for more infantry backup. Now he sent a final warning: "*Unless support arrives [we] may be pushed out of position.*"[15]

Even this dire forecast did not result in any additional manpower being sent forward. Meanwhile, Major Nash and his South Albertans had dug in on their hilltop position. They were surrounded. The enemy was fairly swarming under the cover of the thick woods on all sides. They had no infantry support at all. "[They] were all around us and we kept up random fire and threw hand grenades into the hedges and ditches in an effort to drive them off," Trooper John Neff recalls.[16]

The chatter they could hear on the wireless from the Americans, just a few miles to the south, frustrated the crews. Nash felt like cutting in and yelling for help, "When are you coming over, Yanks?" but he had to maintain wireless silence.[17]

John Neff remembers the viciousness of one close attack:

> I was standing on the back deck of our tank with a Sten gun and Major George Evans's tank was no more than twenty feet away from mine. I could hear movement about his tank and it sounded to me as if someone was pouring petrol over it. Suddenly, there was the flash of a grenade explosion and George's tank just went up in a sheet of flame. I could see a couple of jerries duck under the major's tank.[18]

The assault had been coordinated to hit the allied "soft spots" along the river, preidentified by German reconnaissance patrols: Trun, Chambois, Moissy, St. Lambert. By sheer weight of numbers the Germans punched isolated holes through the fragile allied lines, sweeping aside determined units posted at the crossings. At Trun, the Canadians staved off successive assaults by frenzied attackers.

David Currie was grimly hanging on to his squadron position, assaulted now from two sides. At one point he used his command tank to knock out a Tiger and his rifle to deal with snipers who had infiltrated so close to his headquarters that they were "pinging bullets off the top of the tank." The day took its terrible toll on his officers. "In the early hours, two tank commanding officers were wounded in the head by small-arms fire," Currie recalls. "A little later one of my tank officers was on the ground when he was wounded by shell fire—he died from his wounds."

Only a quirk of fate kept Currie from being the next officer killed. He and Major Ivan Martin, who had been a dynamo throughout the battle, were talking to a German doctor who was trying to get help for his wounded. Lieutenant Al Dalphe was translating. Currie was called to his tank to speak to the CO on the radio. "I had just climbed into the tank when in came an 88mm HE shell and both officers [were] killed by the shell." This meant that at this stage, all the South Alberta officers were out of action—five wounded and two killed.[19]

Currie was on his feet most of the time during the three days and nights of battle. He made a point of visiting the men often. This boosted their morale more than anything, giving them "the feeling of being a part of a team that could accomplish anything . . . he kept us in the picture at all times.[20] After his visits to our weapon pits, my men felt that nothing would force them off the position. Just to go up and talk to him was enough to give us confidence," one sergeant said. "Without his example I do not believe we could have held out. He didn't give a damn how close the Jerries were, and he always had the same every-day expression, just as if we were on a scheme."[21]

Things looked pretty hopeless. "We didn't think we were going to live," another said. A visit and a few words from Dave became a lifeline to his crews.

Currie's soldiers had been collecting several thousand prisoners during the battle, some of whom were wounded. During a lull in the fighting, a young soldier, who himself had been taken prisoner the previous day, turned up with two medical half-tracks and about seventy-five enemy walking wounded whom he had captured. In a stone barn used as a temporary medical aid post, wounded Germans and Canadians were tended by a captured English-speaking German doctor and two German soldiers who had been born in America.[22]

"The Germans occasionally would send in a medic with a white flag and request that the artillery and other fire be stopped. Then he would return to his lines and lead in a flock of prisoners and walking wounded," the 90th Division diary recorded.[23]

The gunners and fighter-bombers, meanwhile, were playing key roles in the battle. Long lines of enemy trucks, tanks, wagons, carts, and other vehicles could be seen approaching from the west. The tank gunners would pick off the lead and tail vehicle and then systematically shoot up the whole convoy.[24]

> At one time [the history noted] about seventeen battalions of 90 Division artillery were firing simultaneously near Chambois. For four straight days . . . [the division artillery] delivered murderous fire . . . causing untold destruction and lowering the German morale to and below the breaking point; unquestionably the artillery was largely responsible for the resulting mass surrender. [In that period] the division took over 13,000 prisoners, killed or wounded 8000 Germans and destroyed 1800 horses, freeing 1000 more.[25]

"The fighting had reached a very dramatic stage," a Canadian field regimental history noted. "Enemy targets involved switches of over 300 degrees. It was not uncommon to see the regiment engaging targets in one direction, with medium artillery nearby, firing in the opposite direction."[26]

One last, large attack was broken up by artillery at dusk. The remaining German troops lacked the will to continue and many thousands surrendered. The fight had gone out of the enemy.

St. Lambert was in flames. Nine Shermans were still smoldering. The blazing trucks lit up the ruins where the enemy soldiers "fired, crawled, set fires, and crawled," in the words of journalist Herbert Fairlie Wood. "The flames were so intense that the night was as hot as the midday August sun."[27]

One of Currie's men asked permission to go to the Dives Valley where hundreds of wounded horses were thrashing about in agony. It took over a thousand rounds to put the wretched animals out of their misery.

The battle of St. Lambert had been, as Currie had prophesied from the beginning, "a fight to the finish."[28] The obstinate stand of the Americans and Canadians had funneled the enemy into a corridor of death. The guns and the aircraft did the rest.

Alan Moorhead cabled the London *Daily Express:*

If I were to be allowed just one more dispatch from this front, this would be it: We have begun to see the end of Germany here in this village of Saint-Lambert today.[29]

CHAPTER 32

Maczuga: The Polish Agony

Sunday, August 20.

Dawn broke over the troubled hills of Maczuga. General Meindl and his band of paratroopers had crouched, motionless, waiting for a Polish patrol to move on. The voices faded. A *Panzer* rearguard reconnaissance battalion loomed up, passed, and reported: "Nothing behind us." Meindl woke the men of his escort, commandeered two tanks, and set out along the Vimoutiers road. It was 0500 hours.

Two hours later the parachute commander entered the lines of II SS *Panzer* Corps near Vimoutiers as it was assembling troops to mount the rescue attack from outside the trap. Nearly three thousand of Meindl's men had managed to reach the rallying point. General Mahlmann's 353d Infantry Division arrived at about the same time.

At 1000 hours Sunday morning, General Eberbach's break-in force of two *Panzer* divisions—2d SS and 9th SS—attacked Maczuga from the east. For once, the weather favored the German attack. Allied planes were grounded for most of the day.

"Both divisions had together 20 tanks," General Eberbach recorded. "One of the divisions possessed only one battalion of infantry, the other had two. At first, the advance made good progress. It came, however, to a stop at a range of hills. In the afternoon, the range of hills was taken. After that the advance made practically no more progress."[1]

Meanwhile, von Luttwitz's 2d *Panzer* Division was spearheading the avalanche that swept through St. Lambert, leaving in its wake thousands of shattered German bodies and vehicles. It picked up new impetus as it plunged headlong eastward toward the Polish hilltop fortress at Boisjos.

The tenth-century manor towered some eight hundred feet above the eastern rise of the Polish "mace," Maczuga. From its turret the entire Dives River Valley could be seen, now a ghastly panorama of smoke and fire and death. Corporal Edward Podyma of the 1st Polish Armored Division marveled that "from Trun, stretching before us in a cloud of dust in the midst of the explosions, we saw thousands and thousands of Germans. It was such an extraordinary sight. We didn't realize there were so many Germans in Normandy."[2]

Boisjos had become a fortress for the beleaguered Polish—two thousand men and eighty-seven tanks holding out against the combined strengths of a German SS Corps and two thousand paratroopers.

It was clear to the Germans escaping from the west—as well as those attacking from the east—that the Poles on Maczuga held the critical position astride the main roads eastward from the Dives. They blocked the exit routes. The Poles were now surrounded by the German forces and had been subjected to constant German artillery shelling and armored attack for the past twenty-four hours from both forces.

In the Coudehard hills, the southern Maczuga, von Luttwitz's Second *Panzer* Division was regrouping. There the division encountered 1st Polish Armored Regiment and Lieutenant Colonel Szydlowski's 9th Infantry Battalion. There was bloody hand-to-hand fighting throughout the night. The only option for the Poles was to consolidate with Koszutski's 2d Armored forces at Boisjos. This opened a passage for some of the Germans escaping across the Coudehard hills, but strengthened the Polish position at the château.

The Poles were isolated on their hilltop fortress, with no hope of outside help. The nearest allied unit that could have intervened was the one with secret orders to stay uninvolved. Colonel de Langlade's tactical group, on loan to 90th US Infantry Division by General LeClerc's *2ème Division Blindée*, was at Ommeél, barely two miles south of Maczuga. He had eighty Sherman tanks—and strict orders from General LeClerc to remain "passive" and keep his unit free to proceed to Paris. The political imperative overcame the military one: It was essential that Paris be liberated by the Free French forces rather than by the communist partisans. Defying direct orders from 90 Division, de Langlade coolly withdrew behind the Dives, leaving the road between Chambois and Maczuga open for German forces to attack the Poles.[3]

Even their comrades—the 10th Polish Dragoons and 24 Lancers now fighting in Chambois—were cut off and unable to help. The Canadians in 4th Armored and 3d Infantry Divisions had their hands full at St. Lambert and Trun; the Canadian Army Reconnaissance unit, the 12th Manitoba Dragoons, was nearby, but essential for protecting the northeast flank. The fighter-bombers that had governed the skies through the turmoil of the past three days were grounded by bad weather.

Artillery support, then, was all the Poles had—all there was to prevent them from being overrun and massacred. This became the task of Captain Pierre Sévigny, the French-Canadian artillery captain attached to the Polish Armored as Forward Observation Officer. Sévigny had his driver, Corporal Podyma, position his observation post—a Sherman tank—on the perimeter of Hill 262.

Equipped with two radio sets, he and the other Polish FOOs had been able to call down artillery fire from Polish and Canadian divisional and regimental guns to ward off enemy infiltration. His firepower was enormous.

> I had four medium regiments, two hundred guns at least. Their hundred-pound shells were very effective. There was one time I fired a Victor target with all available guns and also I fired all sorts of Mike targets (employing all 16 regimental guns).[4]

A Victor Target was a massive and rarely used concentration of fire that called for a bombardment of four thousand shells, some fifty tons of high explosives.[5]

All the Polish defenses were pointed toward the west, to where the enemy was escaping across the Dives. Eberbach's SS attack from the east took them completely by surprise. All day, the SS and Meindl's paratroopers kept up relentless pressure from two directions. They killed and wounded almost a third of the defending Polish forces and knocked out dozens of their Sherman tanks.[6]

"They were coming wave after wave," Captain Ted Walewicz recalled. "Our machine guns were so hot, they were just exploding. It was a very vicious fight. I lost my tank.—I think an 88mm gun hit it. The Germans tried everything they could to break through. There were many occasions of hand-to-hand fighting. Hill 262 had a lot of shrubs and trees, so the Germans could come quite close."[7]

Lieutenant Colonel Koszutski, the "Happy Wanderer" of Les Champeaux, assembled his officers from the 2d Polish Armored Regiment and their supporting 8th Light Infantry and stressed the seriousness of their position. We are entirely cut off, he told them. With this new assault by the 2d SS *Panzer* Division from outside the gap, we are surrounded by enemy attacking simultaneously from all sides. Our American, Polish, and Canadian allies at St. Lambert and Chambois are fighting for their lives on the Dives. Supplies of ammunition and petrol are dwindling. No supply trucks have managed to break through the encircling German line.

Sévigny recalls: "[The CO] said to me in French, 'Can you surround the hill with fire from your guns?' I replied in the affirmative. We shook hands and each went back to his post. I directed [registered] my guns on four targets where I expected an enemy attack. In this way they could fire later as required and with accuracy."[8]

That night there was little sleep for the exhausted Poles. "Everyone was on the alert. Our tank crews had been in action for over seventy hours and hardly left their vehicles. The fatigue element was beginning to create a serious problem," Commander Czarnecki, chief of staff, Polish 10th Armored Cavalry Brigade reported.

German infiltration was unnerving. The Polish troopers remember "shadows emerging from in front of our posts and disappearing into the moonless night."[9] To Sévigny, "that was the worst part."

Pierre Grandvalet, a Norman farmer living in the manor with his pregnant wife and two young children, six and eight years of age, spent that long night huddled on some hay in the basement. Sleep was impossible. "The wounded kept pouring in. Everyone was in anguish." As day broke they heard machine-gun and submachine-gun fire, which seemed heavier than the previous day.[10]

A soldier ran in. "Fire! Everyone to the caves!"

Grandvalet and his wife ran upstairs to get necessities to keep the children warm in the cold underground passages. When they returned the children—left for a moment in the care of their workman—had vanished. They rushed outside to the courtyard in panic.

"The yard was a raging inferno," Grandvalet recalled. "Amid all this fire there were Bren carriers coming and going at top speed. There were bullets ricocheting all over the place on the walls."

As Pierre and his wife tore across the courtyard toward the barn—where the underground passages were concealed—their Flanders sheepdog tried to follow them. Pierre remembered how upset the children had been the day before when the dog had been wounded. Then, the medics had taken a minute from tending the wounded to bandage him up. Now he turned to warn the animal again, but the terrified dog clung to his masters. He was killed two paces behind them.

The Polish troops had set up a command post in the barn. Desperate, Pierre asked a soldier there to take his wife to cover while he tried to locate their children. They've disappeared! he cried. They're not in the underground passage!

> My wife was [talking] with this soldier. He told her he was a Catholic priest, that the children were surely in heaven, and that she must be strong and resigned. She kept crying, "Let me go! I want to find my children!" In the end, I came up to my wife and the soldier who was still holding her, to tell her I had found the children sheltering in the underground passage.
>
> We both went off to join them, accompanied by unceasing machine-gun fire. We went past the body of a German soldier who had just been killed and whose head had been run over by a vehicle which had flattened it in an awful way.[11]

As Sunday morning broke, the attacks on the Poles at Maczuga intensified. "Fortunately, our dominating position ruled out any surprise attack," Sévigny said. "We kept firing without stopping till the machine guns and rifles were red hot! In the end the enemy retreated. But now he was threatening [from] the right: Careful! I gave hurried orders to my signaller. The shells fell; the Huns retreated in disarray."

Conditions at the Boisjos fortress were becoming grim. The commander had been hit in the chest by shrapnel. Their rations were used up; there was barely a half a bottle of water left per man; ammunition was running low. The men had been fighting for seventy-two hours without respite. They had some three hundred German prisoners, and almost no manpower to guard them. They disarmed them, sat them in a field, and assigned a sergeant, Frank Lisowski, to guard them. Lisowski couldn't help but wonder what would happen if the POWs decided to overrun him and take off.[12]

They had sent an urgent appeal for supplies. A flight of American Dakotas flew over, dropping their load of ammunition, food, and water. Stricken, they watched them overshoot by five miles. Captain Walewicz has never understood why the Germans didn't catch on to the desperate plight of the Poles:

> What surprises me is that the Germans never figured out that be-
> cause they were dropping ammunition and food we were in a bad
> way. We had nothing to defend ourselves.[13]

That Sunday night, the Grandvalet family was reunited but still in great danger. From their shelter they could see the soldiers seven or eight yards away, hurling grenades and firing at the Germans infiltrating through the trees in the thicket that encircled Boisjos on that side.

"Seeing the state of my wife, who was expecting a baby, a soldier took off his helmet, put a biscuit in it, and it was passed on from hand-to-hand to her. Being unable to eat anything, she wanted to refuse it, but the soldier next to her told her: 'Take it to please the soldier over there who is waiting for his helmet, and is at extra risk of getting wounded.' "

At dusk, the order came to return to the manor as the Germans might come and throw grenades down into the underground passages. They heard someone using a pickaxe close by; German soldiers were digging foxholes, preparing to attack the next morning.

> We saw on the faces of these brave Poles an immense fatigue and
> an immense determination. I asked one of these men, who spoke
> French, whether the Germans would manage to gain a foothold
> on Boisjos; he told me that as long as there was one Pole still alive,
> no Hun would set foot in the place, but he also told me that they
> were down to mere rifles for fighting against tanks.
>
>   Grandvalet recalls that night as one of the most disturbed.
> Nobody could even think of sleep; fear and dread had taken com-
> plete control.

"In the yard, everywhere, there were German prisoners who this time had lost their arrogance," he said.

The house and the buildings were full of wounded Poles and Germans, nearly three hundred of them. They were being attended to and operated on all over the place. There was a Polish soldier standing leaning against the wall who had had his jaw shot off. It was frightening; you could see the suffering in the way he looked at you.

On the threshold of my home, they cut off a Pole's leg without an anaesthetic; in his pain, the man bit into the blanket on which he was lying. He was then carried into the kitchen.

My wife, who was beside the wounded man, and seeing him in such a bad way, went to fetch the surgeon and told him how the wounded man was. "I know," he answered her helplessly, his medical supplies long gone. "He's going to bleed to death." My wife offered to give some blood. "You can't give blood, Madam, in your condition." So she said "My husband will be willing to give some then."

"So would I, Madam, but I have nothing to do it with." And the wounded man died a few hours later.

In the yard the Poles were treating an SS soldier with a broken leg. When they finished they ripped off his decorations, including the Iron Cross, and threw them in his face, saying, "Dirty SS!"[14]

A German prisoner looked on. He was thirteen years old. "By nightfall, on the Sunday evening," Sévigny relates,

the commander assembled his officers: out of sixty, only four were still in a condition to fight, three lieutenants and myself. The others, including the commander, had been more or less seriously wounded.

Stretched out on a pallet and suffering terribly, the Polish major found enough strength to sit up and give us his instructions. I shall never forget his words: "Gentlemen," he said, "everything is lost. I do not think the Canadians can come to our rescue. We are down to one hundred and ten fit men [from the original fifteen hundred]. No more supplies, very little ammunition, five shells per gun and fifty rounds per man! That's not very much . . . you must fight all the same! As you know, it is useless surrendering to the SS! I thank you: you have fought a good fight! Good luck, gentlemen, tonight we shall die for Poland and for civilization!"[15]

With these words the Pole handed over his command to the Canadian, Captain Sévigny.

The Corridor of Death

Monday, August 21

A cold steady drizzle fell on the men of the Dives Valley on Monday morning.

At Maczuga, Pierre Sévigny awoke around 0400. He turned on his radio and heard Strauss waltzes, played by a London orchestra, drift softly across the night. With a sudden pang he listened to the voices and laughter of the dancers. "Over there, a whole world is enjoying itself!" he mused. "I thought back to the days when I too had no experience of war . . . I saw my parents again . . . so worried since they had known me to be on the continent . . . feelings shared by thousands of families throughout the world, whose prayers all had a single purpose: to ask God to protect their sons who were in the furnace."

At dawn the shelling started up again with great violence. On the slope of Boisjos a terrible hand-to-hand battle was raging. Soldiers used whatever weapons they could seize: rifles, machine guns, knives. Pierre Sévigny remembers, "Amidst all the noise and shouts, we thought we could hear men calling 'Mother!' before they died."

The Germans tried one, last, desperate suicidal counterattack.

"Suddenly to our left we heard the noise of numerous tanks on the move. The Canadians at last!" Sévigny thought. The Poles sent up identifying green flares. Nothing! They suddenly realized that those were German tanks heading toward them.

"Soon sixteen enormous German Tiger type tanks appeared." Sévigny

Closing the Gap: August 21

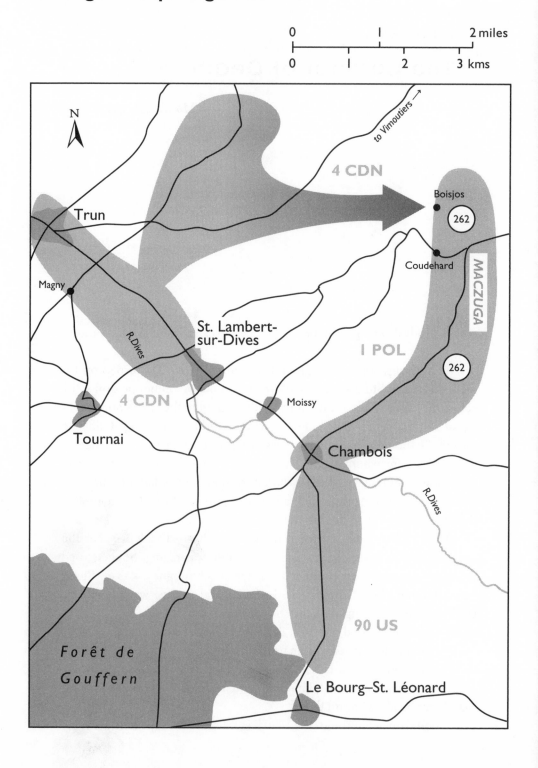

and the remnants of the Polish unit, now down to just twelve tanks, took a desperate gamble; they launched an attack against the enemy. Within three minutes, six of the Polish tanks were destroyed, for just one German one.

He realized their only real hope was the artillery he had previously registered on the German positions. Crouching in a foxhole, he gave his signaler orders over a portable radio for him to relay these positions on to the Canadian gunners.

"I waited. Had I studied my map properly? Did I indicate the place correctly? Would the guns be able to fire in time? The steel monsters were still moving forward, with all their guns firing. I could see their machine guns blazing: their 88s were whistling over my head."

Sévigny was baffled: Why weren't his guns responding to his orders?

The first tank was only 500 yards away . . . 400, 300, 250, 200! It was all over: I couldn't look any more. And yet I was still looking: 150 yards, 100 yards. I jumped into the bottom of the hole, and with my face to the ground, I did not make a move; in a second death would come, of that I was certain . . .

Instinctively, I murmured a prayer . . . All of a sudden, a hurricane, the noise of thunder, the earth was quaking! Was this death? Was it possible? It was reinforcements. Our guns were firing! What I could hear was *our* shells!

Meanwhile, another drama was unfolding in the Boisjos yard: A German tank had taken up position beside the tower and was firing at the Canadians who were coming to our rescue. The Canadians fired at the manor, believing it to be in German hands. A medic took a sheet and, with a red curtain, placed a large cross on the sheet which he promptly exhibited at a first-floor window, facing the Canadians, which had the effect of stopping them shelling us. With the Canadian response, the German tank left the yard and went about sixty yards down the road where it came face to face with a Polish tank. Each of them fired their gun once and came to a halt on the road. The Germans were burnt to death inside their tank, whilst the Poles were taken to Boisjos, some of them in a bad way.

A soldier came to see the Grandvalet family and told them that there was very little ammunition left. Would this so long-awaited Canadian column arrive in time to save us, they wondered? Sévigny was literally asleep on his feet. "I thought everything was over. I suddenly heard something, not far away: the sound of my armor. My signaller woke me up with a start: 'Sir, I can hear our tanks!' " There was no mistaking them. They were Canadian tanks, less than half a mile away.

"What scared us was that they might start firing at us thinking we were Germans." . . ."We decided to go and meet them. They couldn't be far off. Between the Poles and the Canadians, on the hillside, there was a small thicket where the Germans were still entrenched. I assembled my men. We have to attack the enemy," Sévigny told them, "to join up with our saviors. The Polish lieutenant went ahead of me; I saw him fall after being hit by a bullet in the forehead. We came out at the bottom of the hill. Six Shermans were firing at us. We were able to identify ourselves; it was the Grenadier Guards of the Fourth Canadian Armored Division."[1]

Sévigny's description of the meeting of the Canadians and Poles was poignant:

> When we arrived at the command post, the Polish commander received us, vibrant with emotion, and I was witness to scenes of delirious joy. There was laughter, tears, embraces. The soldiers told long stories in Polish to the Canadians who couldn't understand a word, but nevertheless laughed heartily![2]

Major Ned Amy, the Grenadier Guards squadron commander, remembers one less pleasant encounter:

> While we were there they brought in a German soldier in camouflage clothing who apparently had been in a tree sniping at them for some time. He was being questioned and suddenly there was a shot and the questioning was over. Not pleasant to witness but one had to realize that they had been a defenseless shooting gallery for several days without mercy and with little hope.[3]

German prisoners were treated humanely by their Polish captors—up to the moment that they checked the German pay books, which gave the records of their military actions. In their long road home the Polish survivors had little mercy for the SS that had raped their country in 1939, and again in 1944.

Krzysztof (Chris) Szydlowski, vice president of the First Polish Armored Association of Canada, is the son of Lieutenant Colonel Szydlowski, commander of the 9th Infantry Battalion.

> My father, who finally was in command at Maczuga, told me of the feelings of the men. They were not beaten, but they were in a serious position. I have the impression that General Maczek was surprised they hung on, but they would not give up. The Polish soldiers were happy to meet the Canadians on that hill. The biggest emotion was relief and also it was pride that the cork stayed [keeping the Gap sealed]. That was the impact of the whole action. Pride overruled fear.[4]

Pride had its price. The statistics were grim for a division whose fighting strength had few resources for future reinforcements. One-third of the entire Polish force were casualties at Maczuga: 325 men died on the Maczuga hills, including 21 officers; 1,002 were wounded.[5]

Meanwhile, remnants of the German Seventh Army trapped west of the Dives were being taken prisoner in wholesale lots. One corporal said, amazed at the huge numbers, that they "looked like hedgerows . . . but were moving." Stragglers "who had been living in holes in the ground in the forest since separating from their units," were gathered up. It was not uncommon for an allied division to collect prisoners from as many as twenty different divisional units in a single day.[6]

Perhaps most rewarding of all was bagging German senior commanders. Lieutenant Colonel Roger Rowley (Stormont, Dundas, & Glengarry Regiment) and his intelligence officer Reg Dixon recall the capture of Lieutenant General Erwin Menny, commander of the 84th Division.

"When his tank was searched it was found to be well stocked with silk stockings, underwear, perfume and other French luxuries," Captain Dixon noted. "Most of it found its way eventually to wives and girlfriends of the Glens."[7] Rowley still recoils at the encounter. "He was in my command post for the next three days. A real son of a bitch. He was a senior general in the Seventh German army—a nasty bastard; he wouldn't take any food. They'd give him a can of rations and he would just kick it over."[8]

In Chambois, Captain Gutowski, now second-in-command of 10th Polish Mounted Rifles when his commander was shot, recounts the drama of the surrender of Lieutenant General Otto Elfeldt. The commander of LXXXIV Corps had originally set out on his escape with Kurt Meyer. Disagreeing with *Panzermeyer's* tactics, he then struck off on his own in the pre-dawn hours with a small combat force of two hundred men. They launched an attack near St. Lambert, but were forced to capitulate to the Poles when their ammunition gave out: "A single, powerful attack would have had more success than several smaller ones," he grumbled bitterly to his captors.

Gutowski recounts,

In the early morning of the twenty-first we were fighting like hell. The enemy came to within three hundred yards, and then we opened fire. Everywhere was covered with bodies. We had a loud-speaker and I gave orders in English and in German, "Get your hands up." They brought General Elfeldt straight to me. Still in his general's uniform, with some officers, he stopped and saluted me.

He said, "In whose hands am I, American or British?" I said, "Neither. You are a prisoner of the Polish." Then I asked if he spoke French. So from morning until late in the afternoon he sat by my tank and we were speaking French. Then another enemy attack came in. He said to me in French, "At the present moment I am your prisoner. But you know how it is in the war. Maybe in half an hour you will be my prisoner." Gutowski looked at him scornfully. "*I* do not surrender to Germans."[9]

Elfeldt remembers Captain Gutowski as "a handsome man and a gentleman [who] offered me his last cigarette."[10]

The evacuation of the German wounded went on all day. The men of 2d Battalion, US 90th Infantry Regiment, combed the area for miles around Chambois to be sure that they collected up all the wounded: "Our medical personnel attempted to make use of the many German medics [to care for] their own wounded," a staff officer recalled. This backfired. The enemy medical personnel were unable to read English and therefore did not understand instructions and dosages on bottles.[11]

A German lieutenant from the *Panzer Lehr* had an extraordinary experience on the Argentan road.

> From the direction of the American line came an ambulance driving toward us; he was obviously lost. When he noticed that he was behind the German lines, he slammed on the brakes. We went over. His face was completely white, thinking that he had seen his last hour. But we told him "Please climb back into your truck and get out of here—you're Red Cross." He quickly disappeared. About half an hour later, it happened again. Here comes another Red Cross truck! It pulls up right in front of us. The driver got out, opened the back and takes a crate out. He leaves it on the street and disappears. We remained in our places as if he had left a bomb. But nothing happened, and after a while we became curious. We went over and saw that it was filled with Chesterfield cigarettes.[12]

The Chambois scene was a turmoil of thousands of troops from five nations milling around. But the Americans welcomed one special new arrival: "At 1930 hours Major Markiewicz reported that he was called upon to deliver a baby girl to a French family in the neighborhood of our CP."[13]

In the early hours of August 21, the wretched villagers of Tournai believed that their end had come. Relentless pounding by artillery from both sides had reduced the town to rubble. Only eight of the village's sixty-six houses stood undamaged. In a cramped wine cellar, a group of twenty-three civilians, several wounded German soldiers, and their major huddled in terror. Outside, in the courtyard, lay the corpses of thirty-eight horses, piled in grotesque heaps.

Five or six hundred civilian refugees and two thousand German soldiers were clinging to whatever shelter they could find in the village. Abbé Marcel Launay approached the *Wehrmacht* officer. You must surrender, or we will all be killed, he pleaded. "To save your men, run up a white flag on the church."

The German hesitated. "Only the red one," he finally agreed, indicating the Red Cross. The padre protested that the white flag of capitulation was all that could save the survivors of the village. Finally, the major agreed, and a torn white flag knotted to a scythe was carried up to the steeple. To make it more visible, a white surplice and a large cloth were added on the end of a broomstick.

"The tower was full of soldiers," the padre recalled. "Impossible to climb up. We tried to pass up the flag, but no one would take it. A row broke out between the army and the SS under the eaves of the besieged village steeple.

"The SS refused to hang up the flag. The civilians appealed to the major. The major said the SS would not obey his orders: 'Those SS swine!'" The officers parleyed. The discussion was long and drawn out. In a rage, another officer, revolver in hand, cleared the steeple; the SS were lined up against the walls. The white flag was hoisted on the tower.

The padre's drastic appeal for help failed. The rain had grounded allied support planes. And the American and Canadian artillery, perhaps not spotting the flag amid the smoke and carnage, continued to plaster the village with shells.

Just then a German Red Cross car appeared on the scene. Two orderlies and a sergeant got out.

"*Monsieur*, are you the one that wants to sue for peace?"

"Yes, *mein Herr*. You have men here and I have civilians. This evening we shall have no one."

"*Monsieur*, be kind enough to take us to the enemy lines to sue for peace."

The Germans pleaded with the padre not to surrender to Polish troops. "No! Never! The Poles have the reputation of never taking prisoners!" The padre clambered aboard and the vehicle took off.

They headed for St. Lambert, frantically waving a white flag, but the shells continued to explode around them and the route was almost unrecognizable with wreckage and dead bodies. It was impossible to get through. Turning back to Tournai they encountered a band of twelve French soldiers who had been taken prisoner and were now escaping. One of the soldiers volunteered to accompany them back to allied lines as interpreter.

This improbable delegation—a distraught thirty-one-year-old Norman clergyman, an escaping French soldier, and a German Red Cross sergeant with his corporal frantically waving a white flag of surrender—struggled back toward St. Lambert. They approached the Canadians. The first, who had just witnessed the murder of his comrades by Germans approaching under the guise of a white flag, gave a curt refusal. Finally, one Canadian agreed to accompany them back to accept the surrender.

At 1400 hours on August 21, through the persistent efforts of the village clergyman, a single Canadian with only a submachine gun accepted the surrender of two thousand German soldiers at Tournai-sur-Dives.[14]

SS Colonel General Paul Hausser—now an army commander without an army—was leading a small Seventh Army group toward Vimoutiers. As they plodded wearily eastward a shell exploded. Hausser, who had already lost an eye in Russia, went down, his jaw shot out, his face a bloody mess. He was carried out on an armored personnel carrier by one of his senior artillery officers, Colonel Kurzbein.

"Where am I?" the army chief moaned, regaining consciousness. Kurzbein identified himself and reassured him that he was safely out of the encirclement.

"I will bring you before a court-martial," the SS general retorted, anger overcoming his pain. "How could you transport a supreme commander from the field of battle without his agreement!"[15]

General Eugen Meindl stood deep in thought on the Maczuga hills in those predawn hours of August 21. Earlier, Meindl had sent officers on bicycles back into the ring to let those inside know that there was a way out through Coudehard. The news had spread like wildfire. A stream of stragglers swept through the Gap all night. "In a short time there was a good collection of men who set some value on an orderly retreat," he remembered. Later, "the traffic had dried completely."

It was time now to waken the lads and leave—disappear before it got light. They had been so exhausted they had fallen asleep the moment they sat down. Meindl had forced himself to stay awake by running around in circles from midnight until two o'clock in the morning, afraid that he might oversleep the hour for action.

Meindl gazed at the sleeping forms. My boys might look like a pack of ragged tinkers, he mused, but their glance was bright and proud, despite their exhaustion. Not like the majority of men—even the officers—who declined to get out of the trap, believing it to be a hopeless cause.

It started to rain heavily. Good—this will favor our plans.

Eyes misting, he walked over to one young soldier and quietly woke him. "Happy birthday, my son," he said gently. "Now we must wake the others and get ready to march again." Father and son quickly roused the others. Meindl smiled inwardly: Imagine, the commanding general himself going around awakening his men![16]

At St. Lambert, the battered South Albertans were recovering from the ordeal of the past two days. "There was some shelling but it was rather sporadic," David Currie noted.

> Prisoners started rolling in, in a never-ending stream. In mid-morning, a convoy of German ambulance vehicles . . . demanded that we let them through in the name of mercy. I took a look in the ambulances and the wounded were piled like cordwood. I told the doctor that if he were really interested in saving lives, he had better go to our lines and to our hospital. He didn't have enough gas in the ambulances to go anywhere else. He finally decided that we were right and took off for our hospital.[17]

That night, David Currie slept for the first time in three days:

> I slept like the dead for about eight hours and woke up to another beautiful morning. The birds were singing and all shellfire had ceased; it was so peaceful.
> When we came to St. Lambert, it was a neat, small, quiet French village, and when we left, it was a fantastic mess. The clutter of equipment, dead horses, wounded, dying and dead Germans had turned it into a hellhole. It seems incredible that such devastation could be wrought in such a short space of time.[18]

Shortly afterward, Currie was awarded the Victoria Cross, Great Britain's highest decoration for valor.

General Eberbach estimates that of the 200,000 German troops virtually encircled by the Allies, only 20,000 escaped *after its closure*—most without weapons or armored vehicles. Thirty thousand were killed.

However, a number of enemy troops were evacuated before allied forces closed in on the gap. Von Kluge should have been honored instead of disgraced by his countrymen. In his last act before committing suicide, von Kluge had indeed been "Clever Hans." By personally ordering all noncombat units out of the encirclement without waiting for Hitler's permission, he saved approximately 30 percent of the strength of each division. These early evacuees included a sizable number of troopers without tanks and artillery men without guns, as well as soldiers only involved in administration.

In addition, General Hausser's decision to launch an attack from outside the ring prematurely moved to safety the 2d SS *Panzer* Corps with 9th SS and 2d SS *Panzer* Divisions. These boosted the numbers of Germans who escaped before the Allies tried to close the trap.

Despite this, the enemy force in Normandy had been savaged. The average combat strength of German divisions now numbered only a few hundred men.[19] The 12th SS, with a strength of twenty thousand men and 159 tanks on D-Day, now had three hundred men, ten tanks, and no artillery.[20]

British historian John Keegan described this last battle of Normandy as:

the biggest disaster to hit the German army in the course of World War II, surpassing Stalingrad, Tunisia, or the destruction of Army Group Center. Twenty-seven infantry divisions were completely destroyed and the twelve armored divisions reduced from 1800 tanks to only 120. Over half a million casualties were incurred and Germany's most lucrative vassal, France, was lost for the Reich.[21]

The allied armies took some 45,000 prisoners. The US 90th Division recorded 4,054 on August 21 alone, and there were still hundreds unprocessed. The total POWs captured by the division were 14,183.[22] The Allies' 206,703 casualties in the Normandy fighting were less than half that of the Germans.[23] But 1,100 Polish soldiers are buried in France, never to complete the long road home.

Lieutenant Colonel Rowley remembers being "just swamped" with the hundreds of prisoners. More macabre were the number of German corpses still lying in contorted piles—literally blocking the roads—and the cattle and horses, all killed by shelling, some still burning. Finally, Rowley had to get a company of engineers to clear the roads.

"What we had to do with the German dead, we had a cable with a rope at the end attached to our carriers and we were hooking it over their trousers. We took mortar bombs and blew graves. That was almost the worst part of it."[24]

The soft green hills and shaded glens of the Valley of the Dives had become a giant, five-mile-long coffin, filled with rotting corpses. As many as ten thousand German soldiers lay in obscene heaps, the pile of dead so thick that bulldozers were used to clear a passage. Eisenhower wrote, "It was literally possible to walk for hundreds of yards at a time stepping on nothing but dead and decaying flesh."[25]

There were many other victims of the bitter fighting in the battle of Normandy. Over twenty thousand civilians were killed. Out of 763 towns in the Department of Calvados, only two survived intact. Two hundred thousand buildings were destroyed. Falaise was so smashed that it was difficult to even see where the roads once led. Argentan was equally annihilated.[26]

"On the morning of Tuesday, August 22nd," French historian Eddie Florentin wrote,

> the plain was silent. Stunned and decimated, the living counted their dead, discovering corpses in the meadows, the roads, the cellars, and the trenches. The stench was so appalling that Prince Jean of Luxembourg in the cockpit of his Piper Cub flying over the Trun–Chambois road was forced to gain altitude to avoid the discomfort.
>
> People emerged from shelters, exhausted, haggard, filthy, and half-bemused. No cattle in the meadows, no leaves on the trees, the grass itself had disappeared beneath a layer of dust, no birds to gladden the sky. There was no life left.[27]

A Historian's Review of the Debate

Normandy: The Real Story is a major contribution to an important historical debate. Denis and Shelagh Whitaker have set out to restore the reputation of the allied soldier and overthrow fifty years of revisionist history on the battle of Normandy. Their previous books have challenged conventional ideas about the Dieppe Raid and the battles of the Scheldt and Rhineland, and now they are redefining our understanding of the summer of 1944.

They join historians such as Stephen Ambrose in questioning the stereotype of the cautious, ineffective allied soldier versus the resolute and skilled *panzergrenadier.* The task will not be easy; the discipline of military history in Britain, Canada, and the United States is dominated by men who insist that the Allies overcame their enemies only by the application of overwhelming "brute force" by soldiers who were no match for the *Wehrmacht* and the SS.

The revisionist consensus on the poor performance of the allied soldier developed immediately after VE day, when the British military historian Basil Liddell Hart began to cultivate the myth that the German army had revolutionized warfare with Blitzkrieg tactics learned from his books. In interviews with captured generals, Liddell Hart popularized the notion that if it were not for Hitler's interventions, the Germans might well have won the war. His admiration for the men who had organized the conquest of Europe seemed to know no bounds, while allied generals and their men were portrayed as stodgy and incompetent.[1]

Liddell Hart had an enormous influence in the United States, where his views seemed to explain the "research" reported by an officially accredited US historian-journalist, S. L. A. "Slam" Marshall, who claimed to have pioneered the technique of mass interviews of soldiers. Marshall's 1947 book *Men Against Fire* argued that, in the American army, "not more than 15 percent of the men had actually fired at enemy positions or at personnel . . . during combat. . . . The best showing . . . by the most spirited and aggressive companies was that one man in four had made at least some use of his fire power."[2]

Marshall described this phenomenon as the "ratio of fire" and claimed it provided a new way of understanding what happened when citizen soldiers gripped by "fear and inertia" enter combat. The ratio of fire and Marshall's explanation of it were readily accepted by historians who lacked any experience of combat and who were anxious to distinguish their history from mere narrative. It was not until the 1980s, when combat veterans began to retire and learned what the experts were saying, that Marshall's evidence was challenged.

When Harold Leinbaugh and John Campbell began the research for their historical memoir *The Men of Company K*[3] they encountered books like John Keegan's *The Face of Battle*,[4] which relied on Marshall's statistics to argue that poorly motivated combat soldiers avoided action. They found that Russell Weigley, an influential American military historian, accepted the validity of the ratio of fire and used it to bolster his argument that allied infantry were overcautious and could not be relied upon to attack the enemy.[5]

Harold Leinbaugh knew from experience that Marshall was wrong, and the historians who relied upon him had been misled, but it was not until Dr. Roger Spiller, founder of the Combat Studies Institute at Fort Leavenworth, Kansas, reexamined Marshall's evidence that the case for the ratio of fire fell apart. It turned out that the mass interviews of men fresh from combat had never taken place and Marshall's notebooks recording occasional interviews made no reference to how many men fired their weapons. Marshall had made it all up.[6]

There were, however, other pseudoscientific arguments for veterans to contend with. Colonel Trevor N. Dupuy interviewed seven World War II veterans "who had combat experience . . . to quantify the effects and ef-

fectiveness of weapons," then used this "historical data" on eighty-one battles between US and German forces to develop a model of combat effectiveness.[7] Dupuy ignored the detailed reports of operational research
scientists who had direct knowledge of these matters and constructed
mathematical equations based on weightings that exaggerated the effect of
allied air power and artillery while understating the advantage held by the
defender.[8]

Dupuy insisted he had proved that the Germans "consistently, if not
uniformly, outfought us on a unit-to-unit basis because of their greater professional skill."[9] Professional historians bought into this approach, and in
1983 the Israeli historian Martin Van Crevald produced a study for the
Pentagon that relied on Dupuy's statistics to establish the superiority of the
German army.[10] Van Crevald argued that their greater fighting power was
due to better "morale, elan, unit cohesion and resilience." The GI, and by
extension the British "Tommy" and "Johnny Canuck," were the "tired, the
poor, the huddled masses" commanded by officers who were "less than
mediocre."[11]

Canadian military history was strongly influenced by these ideas. C. P.
Stacey, Canadian military historian, and the author of the official history
of the campaign in Northwest Europe, espoused the view that the Allies
had won because of "numerical and material superiority" and the "para-
lyzing effects" of air power.[12] The Canadians, like their comrades in the
American and British armies, were, he suggested, "overcautious"—they
failed to maintain the momentum of the attack and were "too easily satis-
fied."[13] The army as a whole, Stacey claimed, failed to make the most of its
opportunities, especially in August, when the capture of Falaise was "long
delayed."[14]

Other historians took a different approach, blaming the allied failure
on the commanders. Martin Blumenson's *The Battle of the Generals* is
subtitled *The Untold Story of the Falaise Pocket—The Campaign that
Should Have Won the War*. It is one of a number of books that insist that
"Eisenhower, Montgomery and Bradley cared little whether the Germans
escaped" and concentrated on future plans, thus failing to "properly finish
the invasion."[15] This argument suggests that Bradley should have ignored
evidence about the threat to Patton's flank at Argentan and allowed the US
Third Army to advance north to Falaise. Other historians blame Montgomery, arguing that he should have intervened, changing the army group
boundaries to place Falaise in Bradley's sector. This kind of armchair gen-

eralship fascinates readers and historians alike because counterfactual, or "what if," history allows free rein to the imagination.

Counterfactual history can be a valuable exercise if it is used to promote clear thinking about alternative courses of action, but there is no justification for believing that different choices necessarily produce better results. If Patton had been permitted to continue north toward Falaise, his two armored divisions would surely have been engaged in a pitched battle with most of the German armor and a number of infantry divisions. Could two US and one French division have closed the Falaise Gap and kept it closed when attacked from three directions? Would all the combat and rear-echelon troops west of Falaise-Argentan have been unable to escape? The probabilities are that the German army, still an organized force with an equivalent strength of eight to ten divisions, would have fought its way east just as it did a week later at the Trun-Chambois gap. Armies surrender when their will to resist is broken, not when "encirclement" is marked on a large-scale map.

The debate over the "stop order" at Argentan is part of a larger dispute over allied generalship in Normandy. Most British and Canadian historians praise Montgomery's leadership, a view shared by few Americans then or since. Perhaps the most fulsome praise comes from C. P. Stacey, who accepts Montgomery's claim that his "master plan" called for the Germans to concentrate the bulk of their armor in the Caen sector, while the breakout was planned for the American flank of the bridgehead. "There is," Stacey wrote, "no doubt as to the credit for the Normandy victory"—it is Montgomery's. His "grip on operations was firm and effective . . . he conducted them in accordance with a pattern laid down before the landings."[16]

Few American historians would accept this view. Carlo D'Este, whose 1983 book *Decision in Normandy*[17] best encapsulates the American position, dismisses the "master plan" as a myth and argues that Montgomery lost the initiative early in the campaign and was gradually forced to accept the reality of attritional warfare. There was no decision to break out on the right until *Cobra* succeeded, and only then was it reinforced.

A great deal of the controversy about strategic decision-making in Normandy arises out of an unwillingness to admit that the German response dictated the shape of the campaign. Hitler's decision to try to contain the allied bridgehead without transferring additional infantry divisions from the north of the Seine forced Rommel to keep the *Panzer* divisions well forward in the open country around Caen. There was no role for such divisions in the *bocage* until a major operation such as the Mortain offensive was planned. So long as Montgomery kept attacking, the *Panzer* divisions could not disengage, and the battle for Normandy developed into a slugging match reminiscent of the western front in the Great War.

Denis Whitaker, like others who actually fought the Germans in Italy or Northwest Europe, agrees that in some situations specific German units were highly effective in stopping allied advances. Many German soldiers were brave and resolute in battle. But the same was true of the Allies, who had to bear the burden of constantly attacking the enemy. Like other veterans, he also wondered how historians came to emphasize failure when writing about Normandy. Denis Whitaker was one of those who attended Montgomery's famous conference at St. Paul's School in London on Good Friday, April 1944, where the assembled officers were told that by D-plus-90, September 6, the Allies hoped to occupy an area bounded by the Seine and the Loire and would then have to pause before mounting new operations to overwhelm the enemy before advancing to Germany.[18] No one even suggested that the battle of France might end in August with the total defeat of two German armies and the liberation of both France and Belgium. A victory on such a scale was beyond the wildest dreams of the men preparing to invade France.

Readers who really wish to understand what happened in Normandy and why it happened that way will want to know more about the way the Allies and their enemy fought the campaign. A good place to begin is on D-Day when the Allies stormed ashore in one of the most successful military operations in all of history. Those who have seen Steven Spielberg's twenty-minute opening segment in *Saving Private Ryan* know that it is an extraordinary cinematic achievement, but viewers are less certain about the events portrayed. Did men really land in front of such obstacles, suffer such casualties, and keep fighting until they won? The answer is yes. Similar situations developed all along Omaha and on beaches in the British and Canadian sectors.[19]

Success on D-Day depended upon soldiers like the ones portrayed by Tom Hanks and his fellow actors because virtually every part of the plan to overwhelm the German defenses with firepower failed. The Allies tried to apply "brute force," but the weather and the limitations of their weapons meant that the assault troops had to overcome most of the resistance themselves.

Careful studies by operational research teams determined that the elaborate bombing program carried out by RAF Bomber Command and the US Eighth Army Air Force caused little damage to the defenses because "most bombs fell some distance back from the beaches."[20] Heavy cloud cover limited the efforts of tactical air force fighter-bombers, and these aircraft played no role in overcoming the beach defenses. Naval fire, thought to be one of the keys to the success of the assault landing, did "no serious damage to the defences"[21] and there was little evidence that the massive fire-power directed at the beaches "had any significant neutralizing effect . . . when the infantry touched down, the enemy were able to deliver lethal fire in great quantity."[22] The Atlantic Wall of the Normandy beaches was breached by those "unaggressive, overcautious soldiers who hesitated to fire their weapons."

In the first few days after the landings, the Allies were able to link up their beachheads and establish a substantial bridgehead in Normandy. The confusion in the enemy's command structure, and *Fortitude*, the British deception scheme that persuaded the Germans that a second landing was imminent, helped the Allies, but the enemy was able to bring substantial reinforcements to Normandy before the Allies were strong enough to break out. Much has been made of the role of air power in delaying the arrival of German forces, largely because Rommel and other German commanders reported that the allied air forces made the "movement of major formations impossible, both at the front and behind it, by day and night." This and other comments on the "dreaded fighter bombers" or *Jabos* that "paralyzed every movement" have been endlessly quoted by historians unwilling to examine what actually happened in Normandy.[23]

The reality is that every German division ordered to move to the battlefront in early June reached its destination without suffering serious losses or major delays. The divisions of II Parachute Corps, stationed in Brittany, moved to the American landing area without serious difficulty and the 346th Division, transferred from the Fifteenth Army, crossed the Seine on D-plus-1 in daylight. Its lead elements cycled south joining in counterattacks against British and Canadian airborne troops within forty-eight hours of the landings. The *Panzer* divisions were delayed by Hitler's indecision, but once the order to move was given, the tactical air forces still based in Britain could do little more than harass the columns which were in position to counterattack on June 7 or 8. II SS *Panzer* Corps traveled all the way from Poland between June 11 and 28, and arrived without significant losses in transit.[24] Air power played a major role in the allied triumph in Normandy, especially in hampering German movement, but it was never the decisive factor the German generals, seeking to explain their defeat, have claimed.

Again, it is the evidence from operational research, not the self-serving testimony of German generals, that must be reviewed. Experiments with fighter-bombers in England had repeatedly demonstrated that average pilots "given a six-figure map reference were unable to spot well-camouflaged guns even when the guns were firing."[25] When practice targets were recognizable, few hits could be obtained by either fighter-bombers or rocket-equipped aircraft. The tactical air forces were best employed behind enemy lines, seeking targets of opportunity.

As reinforcements arrived, the Germans, in accordance with their doctrine that emphasized decisive action through immediate counterattacks, struck hard at the bridgehead, especially in the Canadian sector, where the 12th SS Hitler Youth Division mounted a series of attacks intended to secure a start line for an advance to the beaches. The terrain, natural and man-made, favored the Canadians, who used their artillery and antitank guns to crush the attacker. The historian of the 12th SS, Normandy veteran Hubert Meyer, noted that "the tactic of surprise, using fast mobile infantry and panzers even in small, numerically inferior *Kampfgruppen* (battle groups), had often been practiced and proven in Russia," but in Normandy "against a courageous and determined enemy who was ready for the defense and well equipped" these tactics "had not resulted in the expected success."[26]

Similar attacks upon British and American troops who had time to prepare and tie in their positions with the artillery and other support troops were equally unsuccessful, and the German commanders were forced to dig in and develop a new defensive perimeter. Rommel wanted this line to be withdrawn out of range of naval gunfire, but Hitler refused. Instead, a defense-in-depth was established, and the Germans settled in to fight a defensive battle sealing off Normandy from the rest of France.

By the middle of June, the battle had become a company commander and section leader's war. Generals on both sides talk about strategy, but reality was to be found in the hedgerows and stone-walled villages of Normandy. Men had to dig or die, and when they emerged from their slit trenches to carry out an attack they would be wounded and killed in large numbers. Since it was up to the Allies to liberate France, it was they who would have to pay the heaviest price.

Unfortunately, the Allies were equipped with weapons that were distinctly inferior to those employed by their enemy. Attacks on fortified villages such as those around Caen ought to have been carried out by battle groups built around tanks or self-propelled assault guns. Combined with medium artillery to isolate the area and field artillery to shoot the combined-arms teams onto their objectives, such tactics would have improved the effectiveness of the Allies and brought victory at a considerably reduced cost. However, the Allies did not possess armored fighting vehicles capable of carrying out such a role, and Allied battle doctrine reflected this reality. The leading operational research expert on armored warfare, Tony Sargeaunt, helped to devise the preinvasion armored doctrine, which called for indirect support of the infantry. Sargeaunt knew, from the detailed testing done in England, that allied armor was highly vulnerable at ranges well in excess of a thousand yards. Tanks could only contribute to success in an attack if they survived, and survival depended on using dead ground, offering fire support from the flank, or finding other ways of staying alive in battle.[27] When Sargeaunt carried out an investigation of allied and German tanks casualties in Normandy, he confirmed the most pessimistic views about allied armor.

The statistics were stunning. Sixty percent of allied tank losses were due to a single round from a 75mm or 88mm gun, and two-thirds of all tanks brewed up when hit. German armor-piercing shells almost always penetrated and disabled a tank; the armor offered so little protection that the only way to survive was to avoid being targeted. The contrast with German tank casualties was especially striking. Only 38 percent of hits from Sherman 75mm or antitank guns penetrated German armor, and both the Panther and Tiger often survived one or two penetrations. The sloping front armor of the Panther and the German self-propelled assault and antitank guns prevented penetration of three-quarters of all direct hits.[28]

Sargeaunt accepted anecdotal evidence that spare tank tracks welded onto the front of Shermans might deflect some shots, but the main impact was on morale. Tank crews believed it worked, and this helped sustain them in battle. Sargeaunt recommended that the army concentrate on "providing a better gun to make German tanks more vulnerable,"[29] but as the man who had supervised the testing of the seventeen-pounder he was well aware of its limitations when mounted in a Sherman. For all practical purposes the gun could only fire armor-piercing shells and was therefore only useful as an antitank weapon. The ratio of one Sherman Firefly to three Sherman 75s per troop was about right, but it frequently meant that the troop concentrated on maneuvers designed to position the Firefly for defensive fire in the event German AFVs appeared.

The Americans had not received any of the seventeen-pounder Fireflies, and tanks equipped with a 76mm gun provided only marginally better performance than the Sherman 75mm. The extent of the problems encountered in fighting German armor was indicated in a letter Eisenhower wrote to General Marshall on July 5, 1944:

> I have just returned from a visit to First Army where I found them deeply concerned over the inability of our present tank guns and anti-tank weapons to cope successfully with the German Panther and Tiger tanks. None of our present ammunition . . . can penetrate the front armor . . . and due to the restricted terrain and narrow roads in which we are fighting we are unable consistently to attack these tanks from a favorable angle. Moreover, even from the flanks our present weapons and ammunition are not adequately effective.[30]

The Americans were never able to solve this problem, nor to address the equally serious weakness in tank armor. One history of the 3d US Armored Division, titled appropriately *Death Traps*, reports that, during the European campaign, the division, which entered combat in Normandy with 232 M4 Sherman tanks, "had 648 tanks completely destroyed in combat . . . and 700 knocked out, repaired and put back into action. This was a loss rate of 580 per cent."[31] The experience of all allied armored units was similar.

Seven long, agonizing weeks were to pass before the new German defensive perimeter in Normandy could be broken. During that period, the Allies enjoyed some local success, the fall of Cherbourg on June 24 and of Caen on July 8, but the price of these and other offensive operations was high. The Allies had trained their infantry divisions to rely on the artillery to support every aspect of combat. The battle for Caen, Operation *Charnwood*, provides an illustration of this, and while the details and some of the terminology would be different in a description of the attack on Cherbourg, the principles and the problems are very similar.

The operation was based upon an elaborate fire plan that included the first attempt to use heavy bombers in direct support of an attacking army. In addition to the field regiments of four divisions, the medium guns of two Army Groups Royal Artillery (AGRAs), plus the firepower of the battleship *Rodney*, the monitor *Roberts*, and the cruisers *Belfast* and *Emerald*, were available. With 656 artillery pieces and the navy ready to assist, many thought *Charnwood* would break the defenders without too much difficulty. Instead, the operation cost the British and Canadians almost as many casualties as they suffered on D-Day.[32]

The fire plan called for the navy and the mediums to concentrate on counterbattery work and the destruction of targets beyond the defensive perimeter. A great deal of attention was paid to rear areas to prevent reinforcements from arriving. The field artillery, still employing self-propelled 105mm guns, had the primary responsibility for firing the infantry onto its objectives with a timed barrage that lifted at a fast walking pace. It would then respond to requests from forward observation officers, providing their radio sets worked, and they were still alive.

The capacity to neutralize hostile gun batteries, antitank positions, mortar, and *Nebelwerfer* sites depended on two variables: intelligence, based almost exclusively on photoreconnaissance, and the accuracy of the artillery fire brought to bear on the target area. Good photoreconnaissance could locate most of the larger enemy installations, though it was seldom possible to distinguish between dummy positions and ones that were occupied. The small mortar pits and machine-gun posts and the low-profile antitank guns camouflaged in hedges and in other infantry positions were another matter, although in the case of *Charnwood*, patrolling and observation of fire over a four-week period helped.

Once the known positions were plotted, a fire plan, based on the premise that half of the rounds would be concentrated in a "50 percent zone" that would be centered on the target, was prepared. Unfortunately, accuracy depended on a host of variables, which meant that unobserved and therefore uncorrected fire was frequently plus or minus one hundred to three hundred yards for both range and line. To achieve neutralization under such conditions required a very large number of guns firing many shells, so that the overlap would ensure that the target area was struck.

"Neutralizing the target areas" did not mean destruction. This required even larger numbers of guns and shells because the 105mm or twenty-five-pounder was not powerful enough to inflict casualties on dug-in troops or weapons unless it scored a direct hit. Tests had demonstrated that a shell had to land within three feet, six inches of a slit trench to transmit a shock wave through the earth, never mind inflict casualties. Medium guns fired a heavier shell with a slightly increased zone of lethality, but a bigger crater is only significant if it is in the right place.[33]

Operation *Charnwood* was the first major set-piece battle of the campaign, and it is clear that the gunners had a great deal to learn. The attack on July 8 by the Highland Light Infantry on Buron, the single most costly engagement of the operation, is exceptionally well documented, and it is possible to learn a good deal about what actually took place.[34]

The Germans had dug a long V-shaped antitank ditch in front of Buron. They hoped to channel the allied armor into carefully constructed killing zones. The barrage got the infantry to this obstacle easily enough, but it quickly became evident that few of the German positions had been destroyed. The infantry, assisted by the 105mm guns of the field regiment firing on the village, got into Buron and began to clean out the enemy positions. The armor, which had circled west to try to provide support from the flank, ran into a minefield, suffered losses, and was effectively out of action during the advance on the village.

The struggle to win Buron lasted until late afternoon. As enemy shelling and mortar fire took its toll, the 12th SS attempted to recapture the village, employing a battle group of Panther and Mark IV tanks. This counterattack was quickly dealt with by a self-propelled battery of the corps' antitank regiment, mounting seventeen-pounder antitank guns, which destroyed thirteen tanks at the cost of three of its own SPs.[35]

The final phase of *Charnwood* required an assault on the inner defensive ring, including the *Abbaye d'Ardenne*. That battle lasted well into the night, but as dawn broke it was evident the surviving Germans were gone.[36] Rommel was unwilling to sacrifice more men in counterattacks and ordered a withdrawal across the River Orne, abandoning the ruins of Caen to the Allies.

There were many lessons to be learned from the battle for Caen. The gunners, particularly the medium regiments, needed air ops—pilots flying light, single-engine planes to observe and correct fire—to be effective. The

RAF had bombed accurately, but fears of short bombing had led to a decision to concentrate on rear areas, including the northern part of the city, rather than risk targeting the ring of defended villages closer to Allied positions. The bombers boosted allied morale and impressed the enemy but did no damage to the defenses. The next time, the planners would take greater risks and use the bombers more effectively.

Another problem of enormous importance was the development of an effective countermortar doctrine. Everyone in the front lines knew that the enemy employed virtually unlimited amounts of mortar fire, but it was not until operational research scientists analyzed the impact of enemy mortars and *Nebelwerfers* across the battlefield that systematic action was undertaken. Michael Swann, who had carried out extensive work on mortars at Barnard Castle, the British advanced infantry training school, prepared a report that defined the extent of the problem in early July:

> The German army uses mortars and *Nebelwerfers* in large numbers. These weapons are small and difficult to detect from the air; their trajectories make it possible to conceal them completely from ground observation, particularly in close country. The small noise of discharge of the mortar and the ripple fire of the *Nebelwerfer* make sound ranging difficult, while the flash and smoke from the mortar is slight and hard to spot. In defence the casualties from mortars and *Nebelwerfers* may be considerable, while the strain of holding a position and being mortared for days on end is intense. In attack the casualties in forming up areas and on the objective may be very heavy indeed, and are often decisive in throwing back an attack. In either attack or defences, mortars can make movement in forward areas difficult.
>
> So much has long been realized. In the present campaign, however, casualties from mortars have been particularly heavy and have contributed as much as anything else to making advances slow and costly. The enemy's mortars are as much a weapon to be defeated as his tanks. This will continue as long as fighting goes on in undulating and cultivated country. Even on the plains of Picardy and Flanders, there is enough cover to conceal mortars, and although their importance may decline, they are still likely to prove a great source of trouble.[37]

Swann interviewed battalion medical officers from four different divisions and found that all agreed in placing the proportion of mortar casualties at above 70 percent of total casualties. He found that divisional countermortar staffs tended to underestimate the number of mortars and *Nebelwerfers* opposite them, noting that a German infantry division possessed as many as fifty-seven 81mm mortars plus between twelve and twenty of the 120mm type. *Panzer* divisions were equipped with about half these numbers. In Normandy, the German army had also provided a regiment composed of fifty-four six-barrel *Nebelwerfers* on the scale of one per division. Swann estimated that to bring the problem under control, divisions might need to obtain between sixty and eighty hostile mortar locations a day.

Every division in the Allied armies developed its own methods of dealing with enemy mortars. Most relied on sound bearings and flash spotting with dedicated signals equipment that permitted rapid response from howitzers or heavy mortars. The best solution, radar sets that could track the arc of the mortar bomb and provide an instant location, were not available until the fall of 1944—an oversight that was to cost many lives.[38]

Efforts to improve the accuracy of artillery and to develop better counterbattery and countermortar techniques began to pay dividends, but the war could not wait. On July 18, Montgomery and Dempsey, his army commander, launched Operation *Goodwood*, an attempt to stage an armored Blitzkrieg employing all three British armored divisions. The gently rolling countryside south of Caen, with its network of fortified villages, was the worst possible country for allied armor. It was actually flatter than the desert in that "there were few bumps or depressions where a tank could take a hull down position and provide covering fire."[39]

The planners of *Goodwood* were aware of the problems the tanks would encounter if the enemy was able to direct long-range antitank fire at them in this wide-open country, and they proposed to use heavy bombers and medium artillery to neutralize or destroy the fortified village network, which was the key to the German defenses. The plan worked in the sense that those villages that were accurately bombed were neutralized, and the armor was able to advance beyond them. The difficulty was that a number of villages were left untouched, as were the 88mm guns of the flak corps positioned on Bourguebus-Verrières ridge. The British lost more than two hundred tanks in just two days.[40]

While the British and Canadians were learning how to deal with mortars, *Nebelwerfers*, and long-range antitank guns in the Caen sector, the US army was coping with the problem of the *bocage*. It had underestimated the problems of fighting in this close, hostile terrain that gave every advantage to the defender. The Germans could take the risk of keeping their armored divisions in the Caen sector because platoon-sized battle groups, backed up by one or two self-propelled guns, were able to hold off repeated attacks. If the GIs ignored their casualties and pressed forward, the Germans could yield one enclosed field and get ready to defend the next one.

Much attention has been focused on the innovations in tactics and equipment that helped the Americans overcome the *bocage*:

> The most effective method of attack proved to be a combined action of infantry, artillery and tanks with some of the tanks equipped with dozer blades or large steel teeth in front to punch holes through the hedgerows. It was found necessary to assign frontages according to specific fields and hedgerows instead of by yardage and to reduce the distances or intervals between tactical formations.[41]

These methods certainly helped in the advance to St. Lô, but such tactics worked far better after six weeks of steady combat had worn down German resistance, reducing the fighting power of their divisions to a small fraction of their original strength. Russell Weigley, who insists that "aggressive American infantry fighting was rare," admits that the Germans found the American pressure in July "unrelenting" and called in vain for reinforcements. Weigley also recognizes that, when the Germans mounted major attacks such as *Panzer Lehr*'s thrust along the Vire River on July 11, GIs taking advantage of the terrain inflicted enormous casualties on their enemy.[42]

The US Army's steep learning curve was also evident in the changes introduced by Major General Pete Quesada's Ninth Tactical Air Force. The US Army Air Force went to war in 1944 with a system of air support adapted from the British experience in North Africa. This doctrine called for centralized control of all aircraft, with daily conferences deciding upon the missions that would be flown in direct or close support of the ground troops. These tasks, in turn, had to compete against the air force's favored roles, the maintenance of air superiority, and armed reconnaissance, both of which permitted the pilot freedom to choose his targets.

Ninth Tac modified the British system, introducing greater flexibility, but it was not until the results of air support in the battle for Cherbourg were studied that Quesada revolutionized tactical air doctrine. The first step was to arrange for pilots to be briefed by an Air Support Party Officer (ASPO) working beside the forward troops. One of the first experiments resulted in a devastating attack by Thunderbolts that broke up a German counterattack without inflicting any casualties through "friendly fire." Quesada built up ground-to-air communication capability, creating a system known as Armored Column Cover that provided a VHF radio link between an ASPO in a Sherman tank and pilots in the air over the column.[43]

The RAF were much less successful in establishing a workable close-support system, though the introduction of "Cab Rank," in which a forward controller directed aircraft onto a selected target, was an improvement on previous methods.[44] Cab Rank was, however, rarely employed in Normandy, whereas Armored Column Cover became the norm in the US Army.

Armored Column Cover could not be fully exploited until the breakout that followed Operation *Cobra* began, but that story has already been told in the preceding pages. The purpose of this epilogue is to link the events of the last month of the Normandy battle with the entire campaign, reminding the reader that it took almost two months of attritional warfare to set the stage for the breakout, encirclement, and destruction of the German armies in France—two months of fighting that fully paralleled the horrors of the Western Front in World War I.

Modern memory has a firm image of "suicide battalions" and futile battles in the Great War, but we are not accustomed to thinking of Normandy in these terms. Perhaps a single crude comparison will help to make the point. During a single 105-day period in 1917, British and Canadian soldiers fought the battle of Third Ypres, which included the struggle for Passchendaele. General Haig employed forces equivalent to those Eisenhower commanded in Normandy. When it was over, Haig's armies had suffered 244,000 casualties, or 2,121 a day. Normandy cost the Allies close to 2,500 casualties a day, 75 percent of them among the combat troops at the sharp end who had to carry the battle to the enemy. It was their valor, their endurance, and their ability to adapt that won the battle of Normandy and launched the liberation of Western Europe.

—Terry Copp
Director, Laurier Centre for Military,
Strategic and Disarmament Studies,
Sir Wilfrid Laurier University,
Waterloo, Ontario, Canada

Some Sequels to Characters in Book

Matt Urban: The Ghost of US 9th Division

Lieutenant Colonel Matt Louis Urban had to wait thirty-five postwar years to get recognition from his country for his battlefield courage. Then he was given the highest award of all: the Congressional Medal of Honor.

But on the Normandy battlefields it took the Germans just a few weeks to recognize Urban's skill and daring. In over five separate engagements from June 14 to September 3, 1944—including his outstanding leadership in Operation *Cobra*—they came to call him *The Ghost*. No matter how many times they thought they had killed him, he always came back to fight them again in another place.

Urban, a captain in Normandy, rose to command the 2d Battalion, 60th Infantry Regiment, 9th Infantry Division. He received countless wounds, the final one being a gunshot in the neck by German infantry. Army doctors gave Urban no hope for survival, but he recovered two years later with damaged vocal cords and a raspy voice.

Although Urban had received two Silver Stars for actions in Africa, his valorous actions in France and Belgium in 1944 had not been recognized with a military decoration for heroism except for a Bronze Star Medal he received for action on June 14, 1944, and seven Purple Hearts—one for each wound.

Officials discovered they mistakenly had overlooked awarding the

Congressional Medal to Urban. Because of a "bureaucratic shuffle," his records in federal government files were not unearthed until 1978. As the Army Awards Branch assembled the pieces of the puzzle, a most dramatic picture of Urban emerged. He had clearly established himself as an outstanding combat leader who was fearless and highly esteemed by his men.

The eyewitness statements, even though they were prepared many years after the fact, showed a remarkable consistency in what they describe. In each case, Urban's fearlessness is related in detail, but his concern for the welfare and safety of his men and his ability to inspire them to their best efforts are just as clearly demonstrated.

In 1980 Urban received the Congressional Medal of Honor from President Jimmy Carter, thirty-five years after he was recommended for the honor. It was discovered then that his exploits on World War II battlefields earned him more citations — twenty-nine — than the legendary Audie Murphy, whose postwar career was greatly enhanced by his wartime fame.

Anthony J. Bajdek, Associate Dean of NE University in Boston, wrote: "The flames of that controversy have been fueled by the fact that the 1989 Guinness Book of World Records identified Matt Urban as "The Most Combat-Decorated Soldier in American History" and in the June 11, 1984, issue of *PEOPLE Weekly* magazine, staff writer Michael Ryan stated in his "An American Hero" article that a "generation of Americans was taught that Audie Murphy — heroic soldier, Medal of Honor holder, later movie star — was the most decorated US fighting man of World War II. That was true — until 1980, when former Lieutenant Colonel Matt Urban received a spate of honors — including his seventh Purple Heart, a Croix de Guerre, the Legion of Merit and the Congressional Medal of Honor — all of which had been lost in a bureaucratic shuffle at the end of the War. With 29 medals in 20 months, Urban is the most decorated soldier in US history."

There has recently been a strong groundswell among the Polish-American community to have a stamp issued in Urban's honor in 2005 (the mandatory ten years after his death). Anthony Bajdek heads up the campaign to circulate a petition nationwide. The target of 150,000 signatures is required by the US Senate in order for the Postal Service to issue a commemorative stamp honoring Matt Urban.

So far, a handful of men — mainly pounding the pavement in exhaustive effort — have amassed 60,000. John Merten (formerly Mazurczyk), of

Toms River, New Jersey, undisputed East Coast pioneer and leader of the signature-gathering campaign, laboriously collected 14,000 signatures for the Matt Urban cause.

Dean Bajdek said, "It is not about being Polish; it is to recognize a genuine American hero. Even if I were an Italian-American I would still be signing." Supporters who wish to pledge signatures can reach Mr. Bajdek at: a.bajdek@neu.edu, or A.J.Bajdek@aol.com, or access the Web page: www.paceasternmass.org.

Major David Currie VC: 4th Canadian Armored Division

Two months after his fight to the finish in the hell of sweltering St. Lambert-sur-Dives, Major David Currie was again facing crack German troops in the icy polder warfare of the battle of the Scheldt. He received an order from South Alberta regimental headquarters: You are to go to London— on the double.

Still wearing his oil-stained and muddy tanker's overalls over the battle dress that he'd had on for weeks, Currie rushed across the Channel in a motor torpedo boat. A car hurried him along to Buckingham Palace. He doffed the coveralls in a palace anteroom, gulped a drink of water proffered by a court attendant, and walked along the carpeted dais to be presented to his king. George VI was about to honor him with the Victoria Cross.

The morning-coated Lord Chamberlain read the citation of David Currie's gallantry:

> There can be no doubt that the success of the attack on and stand against the enemy at St. Lambert-sur-Dives can largely be attributed to this officer's coolness, inspired leadership, and skillful use of the limited weapons at his disposal. The courage and devotion to duty shown by Major Currie during a prolonged period of heavy fighting were outstanding and had a far-reaching effect on the successful outcome of the battle.

The king picked up the Cross from a velvet cushion held by a brigadier and pinned it on Currie's battle dress tunic. His Majesty, dressed in the naval uniform of admiral of the fleet, smiled and chatted with the

Canadian major for a minute or so, then shook his hand in congratulations as the khaki-clad orchestra struck up "God Save the King."

The investiture over, Currie donned his coveralls and stepped out in the rain to the palace courtyard to face a photographic barrage by a surprised international and Canadian media. His was the first of three VCs awarded to Canada's military in the Northwest Europe campaign.

Within a few days, he was on his way home to Canada. His wife Isabel and their nine-year-old son, David Junior, were facing another bleak Christmas without her husband and his father. The family knew nothing about the award.

"There was a knock at the door, and there were some army people," said Isabel (who was recuperating from an appendectomy). "In those days we lived from day to day and feared anyone coming to the door." Then she got the great news: "Davie was coming home."

As a fitting tribute to Currie's outstanding efforts toward stopping the German army at St. Lambert, Prime Minister John Diefenbaker appointed Lieutenant Colonel David Vivian Currie, VC, as Sergeant-at-Arms of the Canadian House of Commons, a position he held for seventeen years. Known as "The Colonel," he led the parade of House of Commons officers through the Hall of Honour into the chamber during sittings, ceremoniously shouldering the heavy gold-gilded mace, the symbol of parliamentary government.

Curried died in 1986 at the age of seventy-three.[2]

Colonel Francis "Gabby" Gabreski, America's Greatest Living Ace

Thunderbolt history isn't complete without the story of the ace of all times, Francis "Gabby" Gabreski. Gabby was one of America's greatest fighter pilots, shooting down twenty-eight enemy aircraft in Europe and six and one-half in Korea.

As a trainee cadet Gabreski was a shaky pilot. He was scared to death during his first solo. "This is your last chance, so give it your best," the flight instructor said. He did—and never stopped giving his best in a career of courage and command that spanned wars in Europe and Korea.

Of proud Polish family background, Gabreski, then twenty-three years old, first flew in 1942 with six Polish Spitfire squadrons of the RAF in England. The next year he rejoined his American comrades in US Eighth Air Force 56 Fighter Group, flying P-47 Thunderbolts.

On June 6, 1944—D-Day—Gabreski led his squadron in long fighter sweeps over the beaches of Normandy. Three weeks later, he surpassed Eddie Rickenbacker's World War I record and on July 5 scored his twenty-eighth victory, making him America's leading ace—a record he held until his death in 2002.

When Gabreski's total reached 28 air victories and 193 missions, he had earned a leave back to the States. While waiting to board the plane that would fly him to the US, Gabby discovered that a mission was scheduled for that morning. He took his bags off the transport and wangled permission to "fly just one more." He met no opposition over the target, but while seeking targets of opportunity afterward he spotted enemy fighters parked on an airdrome. During his second strafing pass, his plane suddenly began to vibrate violently and crash-landed. Uninjured, he jumped to the ground and ran toward deep woods with German soldiers in pursuit. Eluding them for five days, he began to make his way toward allied lines. He encountered a Polish-speaking forced laborer whom he persuaded to bring him food and water. Eventually he was captured and interrogated by the Gestapo. Finally transferred to Stalag Luft I, a permanent prisoner of war camp holding allied air officers, he was barracked in one of the twenty-man shacks surrounded by two rows of barbed-wire fence. There he shared the bad food, hunger, and punishments. But he was proud of the men's spirits under such miserable circumstances, for they had their own clandestine radios to listen to war news, a newspaper printed under the very noses of their guards, and supervision of the simultaneous digging of as many as a hundred escape tunnels, few of which led to freedom. By March 1945, after Gabreski was given command of a newly completed prisoner compound, food was at rock bottom. But he did not lose faith. Soon he began to hear artillery to the east. When Russian soldiers arrived, it was a joyous occasion, and soon American planes evacuated the airmen to freedom.

After World War II, he spent several years in flight testing and in command of fighter units before being assigned as commander of the 51st Fighter Wing. He helped develop tactics for jet fighters and shot down six and one-half MiG-15s between July 1951 and April 1952.

After his military career, he worked in the aviation industry and later served as president of the Long Island Rail Road.

Gabreski wrote about his military career in his autobiography, "Gabby, A Fighter Pilot's Life."

A member of the National Aviation Hall of Fame, an airport in Westhampton Beach on eastern Long Island bears his name.[3]

The Spitfire Twins: Duke Mk1 and Duke Mk2

The Western Canadian Warren twins, Spitfire aces over Normandy, survived the war and returned home to Canada. Wing Commander Duke Mk2 writes: "In January 1949 my twin and I were sent overseas again as members of the Regular Royal Canadian Air Force. Duke was sent to the Test Pilot School at Farmborough and I was sent to the Fighter Leaders School at West Raynham. My career was basically as a fighter pilot. I was in charge of a group of Canadians training the new fighter arm of the re-armed Germany.

"We knew our careers were moving apart, for the RCAF at that time only planned on 12,000 personnel all ranks and we were senior F/Ls (Flight Lieutenants). They wouldn't put two senior people in the same slot. But we were pleased to have been selected for these prestigious schools.

"The trip over was wonderful, first class, but we had to pay for our wives, about 50 British pounds. England was still cold and bleak, and Melba says had we the money she would have turned around and gone home. I don't believe this, for we had only been married three years and Melba was crazy about me.

"Duke Mk1 was killed flying as a test pilot while on loan to AV Roe from the RCAF to test the CF-100 prototype. It was 5 April 1951. Never a day goes by but that I think of him. When I lecture at schools about Remembrance Day, I am doing what we both would be doing if he were alive. When I act as Padre of the Legion, I feel I am representing both of us, as we grew up in Western Canada in a small town where the Legion was important."

Duke Mk2 retired with the rank of Wing Commander, and he and his (still) adoring Melba moved back to Comax, BC.

"I started helping an ordained padre here in 1977 who was our Legion Padre. When he left, he insisted I become the Padre for Branch 160 RCL [Royal Canadian Legion] Comax. I guess I am a lay minister, now in my 20th year. I do funeral and memorial services for Legion members, as well as others who like my way of doing the service. One of my Legion comrades describes it as 'a short service, and no bible thumping.'

"When proper ministers ask me where I was ordained (a common question), I tell them I learned to pray in the cockpit of a Spitfire. Quite often they say 'that was probably better training than what I received.' "[4]

Major General Kurt Meyer, 12th SS *Hitlerjugend*

Panzermeyer was captured by Belgian partisans who found him hiding in a barn and handed him over to the Americans on September 6, 1944. He had discarded his SS uniform, but was identified later when his SS tattoo gave him away.

In 1945, in the first war crimes trial ever held in Canada, Meyer was charged with the murder of forty-one Canadians in cold blood, all prisoners of war far behind the lines. *Wehrmacht* General Heinrich Eberbach was the first witness. He was Meyer's commanding general in July and August 1944, and was with him for three months in a prisoner of war camp. General Geyr von Schweppenburg and Meyer's wife, Kate, were also character witnesses.

Meyer was found guilty and at the age of thirty-five was sentenced to death. The sentence was later commuted to life imprisonment by Canadian Major General Chris Vokes. Meyer was imprisoned in Canada, and his wife, Kate, four daughters, and ten-month-old son, Kurt, Jr., were allowed to visit him at Christmas in 1945.

After ten years in jail, the latter time spent in Germany, he was released from captivity in September 1954. One of Meyer's first jobs after his release was to work for a German brewery. "Ironically," his biographer, Howard Margolian, said, "he sold beer to Canadians at NATO headquarters, and would socialize with them in their mess after deliveries. He was very popular with Canadians."

His son, Kurt, Jr., said in a recent interview that Meyer never stopped believing in and promoting the principles of Nazism. "Long after the war, my father attended Nazi rallies with Waffen SS officers and spoke at countless meetings and gatherings, once again the *Panzermeyer*.

"He was no hero; he was a tragic figure in German history. He never distanced himself from Hitler."

In 1959 Meyer published his memoirs, as arrogant of the *Hitlerjugend* and as disdainful of his enemies as he had been during the war. Like most Nazi and *Wehrmacht* officers, he disclaimed any knowledge of the Jewish extermination camps. "In my father's case, the German excuse, 'I knew nothing because I wanted to know nothing,' was valid," Kurt Meyer, Jr., said.

In 1961, on his fifty-first birthday, Meyer died of a heart attack.[5]

Michael Gutowski: The Polish Warrior

When the war ended, Captain Michael Gutowski, one of the liberators of Chambois, was, like all of his Polish compatriots, facing the bitter fact that the country they had fought for so fervently for six years was still denied them.

Polish suffering in the war was almost unparalleled. In Warsaw, more than twenty thousand Polish soldiers were killed, as were hundreds of thousands of civilians, murdered by the Germans during the uprising or shipped to concentration camps after the garrison surrendered. The Germans destroyed most of the city during the fighting, and later burned whatever buildings were still standing.

But in the immediate postwar years, historians tended to ignore the contributions by the 1st Polish Armored Division. In the Northwest European campaign. The Sikorski Institute in London, whose aim is to fully document Poland's history, became a gathering place for Gutowski and his compatriots. They returned on a number of occasions to the battlefields and to the Polish Cemetery in Normandy to honor the eleven hundred graves of Polish soldiers. "They were all volunteers, who came from around the world to fight for the freedom of our country," he said with pride.

The freedom they had fought for so savagely still eluded them. Following Germany's defeat, Poland's borders were redefined by the Potsdam Conference of 1945, and Russia gained control of a nation that despised it. The Polish patriots who had struggled so hard to escape one tyranny now faced another. They could not go back.

Resolutely, they became new immigrants in corners of the world where freedom was still fostered. In those early days, physicians plowed fields and scientists dug ditches; it was a small price to pay to escape the

Nazis and the communists. Historian John Keegan wrote that the Poles became "the most successful immigrant community ever absorbed into British life." There isn't a country that wouldn't endorse that sentiment.

Michael Gutowski tucked his Polish war decorations—the highly respected Virtuti Militari and the American Legion of Merit—and his prewar Olympic equestrian medals into the bottom of his tack box and embarked on a new life in Canada with his wife and children.

He felt lucky to land a job so soon after his arrival in Canada, working in the sport he loved, for a horse trainer. It didn't take long for him to realize that his prewar skills as an Olympic show jumper, hired out for eighty dollars a month, would barely pay the rent. Like his countrymen in dozens of other countries, he adjusted resignedly to his new life and patiently forged ahead to establish himself all over again in his equestrian career. Ultimately, Gutowski became a renowned coach of Canada's Olympic Three-Day Event Equestrian Team.

In 1998, Captain Gutowski finally returned to Poland, with the sad mission of burying his wife of more than fifty years, as he had always promised her. To his surprise, he was met at the airport by a government official in a gleaming limousine. He learned then that he had been promoted to the rank of Brigadier General by a grateful Polish government.[6] Gutowski died in 2003.

Patton, Bradley, and Monty: The Outcome

On December 8, 1945, just two days before he was due to leave his European command and fly home, Lieutenant General George Patton was involved in a car accident. His neck was broken. He remained alive, in traction in a hospital in Heidelberg, but died of complications on December 21 and was buried in the American Cemetery at Hamm in Luxembourg.

His staunch supporter was General Omar Bradley, the man who was most outspoken in his criticism of Field Marshal Sir Bernard Montgomery, accusing him repeatedly in postwar articles and interviews for not ordering Patton to close the Falaise Gap.

When Monty died in 1976, Montgomery's PA Lieutenant Colonel Trumbull Warren was invited to the state funeral at Windsor. He recounts the moment when General Bradley—long identified as a bitter enemy of Montgomery's—laid a wreath at the coffin.

"Brad said just one word: 'Thanks.' "[7]

The 116th *Panzer* Division: The *Windhunds*

Lieutenant General Gerhard Graf von Schwerin was one of the few German generals who openly defied Hitler's orders—not once but twice—and survived to become a hero to his people.

In August 1944, von Schwerin was fired by SS General von Funck when he refused to commit his division, the 116th *Panzer*, to the Mortain counterattack. He was convinced that Hitler's attack would fail and refused to throw his good troops into the disaster. His unfortunate replacement was wounded and taken prisoner at Falaise. Shortly afterward, General Sepp Dietrich insisted on the return of General von Schwerin as commander of the 116th Division after the Seine crossing in late August.

Three months later, von Schwerin again defied the SS, who were defending Aachen, a German city of historical and architectural importance dating back to Charlemagne in A.D. 768. The SS were determined to hold out, although American artillery would have destroyed the fine old city. Von Schwerin intervened at great personal risk, ordering the city abandoned without a fight. Today, a street in Aachen is named "von Schwerin Strasse." Postwar, he was "one of the fathers of the postwar Bundeswehr."

His staff officer, Lieutenant Colonel Heinz Günther Guderian (later, Major General) was one of the last German officers to escape the Falaise Pocket on August 21, and, by his account to the authors, he was also the last German officer to escape across the Rhine ahead of the allied armies on March 10, 1945.

"As a member of the German General Staff, I was on the list of war criminals. I was sent to a special camp. Later I came into the historical camp, to help prepare a history of the war. My father [General Guderian, a famed tank commander] arrived soon after," Guderian said. "It was the first time I had seen him since October 1944, when he brought me the Iron Cross direct from Hitler.

"I was released in October 1947, but my father remained there. They let my mother and her dog go and live with him. On the sixtieth birthday of my father, he was released."[8]

Ernie Pyle: 1900–1945

Ernie Pyle was a war correspondent whose coverage of the campaigns in North Africa, Sicily, Italy, and France brought him a Pulitzer Prize for reporting in 1944, as well as several other awards.

On September 5, 1944, shortly after the end of the Normandy campaign and after two and one-half years of reporting from combat zones, Ernie Pyle returned to the US for health reasons.

In his last column, he wrote this poignant farewell to the GIs in Europe:

September 5, 1944.

PARIS: This is the last of these columns from Europe. By the time you read this, the old man will be on his way back to America. After that will come a long, long rest. And after the rest, well, you never can tell.

Undoubtedly this seems to be a funny time for a fellow to be quitting the war. It is a funny time. But I'm not leaving because of a whim, or even especially because I'm homesick. I'm leaving for one reason only—because I have just got to stop. "I've had it," as they say in the Army. I have had all I can take for a while.

I've been 29 months overseas since this war started; have written about 700,000 words about it; have totaled nearly a year in the front lines.

I do hate terribly to leave right now, but I have given out. I've been immersed in it too long. My spirit is wobbly and my mind is confused. The hurt has finally become too great.

All of a sudden it seemed to me that if I heard one more shot or saw one more dead man, I would go off my nut. And if I had to write one more column, I'd collapse. So I'm on my way.

It may be that a few months of peace will restore some vim in my spirit, and I can go war-horsing off to the Pacific. We'll see what a little New Mexico sunshine does along that line.

I cannot help but feel bad about leaving. Even hating the whole business as much as I do, you come to be a part of it. And you leave some of yourself here when you depart. Being with the American soldier has been a rich experience.

To the thousands of men that I know personally and the other hundreds of thousands for whom I have had the humble privilege of being a sort of mouthpiece, this then is to say goodbye—and good luck."

—Ernie Pyle[9]

Pyle returned to cover US forces in the Pacific on Iwo Jima. During the Okinawa campaign he visited the nearby island of le Shima, where he was killed by Japanese machine-gun fire on April 18, 1945. He was forty-four years old.

Endnotes

CHAPTER 1

1. Samuel W. Mitcham, *Hitler's Field Marshals and Their Battles* (Chelson, MI: Scarborough House, 1990), 291.
2. Walter Warlimont, *Inside Hitler's Headquarters 1939–1945* (Bristol, England: Western Printing Services, 1963), 440.
3. LCMSDS. German Army Sit Reps [situation reports], Normandy.
4. William Breuer, *Death of a Nazi Army. The Falaise Pocket* (New York: Scarborough House, 1985), 29.
5. Russell F. Weigley, *Eisenhower's Lieutenants. The Campaigns of France and Germany 1944–1945* (Bloomington: Indiana University Press, 1981), 232.
6. General Dwight D. Eisenhower, *Crusade in Europe* (New York: Doubleday, 1948), 224.
7. Michael Howard, *British Intelligence in the Second World War. Vol 5: Strategic Deception* (London: HMSO, 1990), 18.
8. Ibid., 100, 120.
9. Ibid., 121.
10. Ibid., 185.
11. Ibid.
12. NA. "Moving, Commitment and Fighting of the 116 Pz Div in France, 6 June–12 Aug/4." Box 736. MSB-017. How, J. J. *Hill 112*. London: Wm. Kimber, 1984, 42.
13. Carlo D'Este, *Decision in Normandy* (New York: Dutton, 1983), 201.
14. Breuer, 38.
15. Howard. *Strategic Deception*, 235.

CHAPTER 2

1. Eisenhower Center for American Studies, Metropolitan College, (referred to hereafter as EC), University of New Orleans. Oral history: Hans-Heinrich Dibbern.
2. B. J. Danson, *A Personal Essay: Being Hit, Normandy, August 1944*. Feb. 28, 1994. Kindly loaned to the authors.

3. Ernie Pyle with 4th Division. Encyclopedia Brittanica. Author's collection.
4. Russell F. Weigley, *Eisenhower's Lieutenants*, 186.
5. Ken Tout, *A Fine Night for Tanks. The Road to Falaise* (England: Sutton Publishing, 1988), 150.
6. Sydney Jary, *18 Platoon* (Surrey, England: Sydney Jary Ltd., 1987), 20.
7. EC. University of New Orleans. Oral history: Private Adolf Rogosch, Grenadier Regiment 942, 353 Infantry Division.
8. Ibid.
9. Gerald F. Linderman, *The World Within War. America's Combat Experience in World War II* (Cambridge, MA: Harvard University Press, 1997), 25.
10. Ibid., 102.
11. Ibid., 8.
12. Martin Blumenson, *Breakout and Pursuit* (Washington, DC: Center of Military History, 1961), 47.

CHAPTER 3
1. Eisenhower, 224, 269.
2. NA. Hospital Files. RG407 E427. ML Series. (Referred to hereafter as NA Hospital Files.) Interview with Second Lieutenant Kussman, 3d Battalion, 115 Infantry, 29th Division.
3. Eversley Belfield and H. Essame, *The Battle for Normandy* (London: Pan Books, 1967), 172.
4. Nigel Hamilton, *Monty: Master of the Battlefield 1942–1944* (New York: Hodder & Stoughton, 1983), 751.
5. Stephen E. Ambrose, *The Victors. Eisenhower and His Boys: The Men of World War II* (New York: Simon & Schuster, 1998), 210.
6. Denis Whitaker and S. Whitaker, *Tug of War. The Canadian Victory That Opened Antwerp Harbour* (Toronto: Stoddart, 1984), 256; *The Canloan Roster.* Nearly 20 percent of the Canloans were killed; total casualties including killed or wounded were 438, or 70 percent. Many won decorations, some more than once. There were forty-one MCs, one DSO, one MBE, one US Silver Star, four Croix de Guerre, and one Order of Bronze Lion. This effort, both brave and brilliant, had a significant effect on the war's outcome.
7. William B. Folkestad, *The View from the Turret. The 743rd Tank Battalion During World War II* (Burd Street Press, 1996), 29–30.
8. Stephen E. Ambrose, *Citizen Soldiers. The U.S. Army from the Normandy Beaches to the Bulge to the Surrender of Germany* (New York: Simon & Schuster), 1997, 63.
9. Martin Lindsay, *So Few Got Through* (London: Collins, 1946), 48.
10. Max Hastings, *Overlord. D-Day and the Battle for Normandy 1944* (London: Pan Books, 1985), 230.
11. Alan Moorhead, *Eclipse* (London: Hamish Hamilton, 1967), 110.
12. Hamilton, 754.
13. BLM 126/16.
14. Hamilton, 746.
15. Hastings, 358.
16. LCMSDS. WD 2nd Cdn Field Historical Section. Aug. 16/44.
17. Hastings, 344. Authors' interview with Charles Richardson, 1983.
18. Henry Maule, *Normandy Breakout* (New York: Quadrangle/New York Times Book Co., 1977), 66.
19. Ibid., 67.

CHAPTER 4

1.   EC. University of New Orleans. Oral history: Hans-Heinrich Dibbern, Second Lieutenant, Adjutant, *Panzer* Grenadier Regiment 902.

2.   John Keegan, *Six Armies in Normandy* (London: Jonathan Cape, 1982), 189.

3.   EC. University of New Orleans. Oral history: Private Herbert Meier.

4.   Craig W. H. Luther, *Blood and Honor: The History of the 12th SS Panzer Division "Hitler Youth," 1943–1945* (San Jose, CA: Bender Publishing), 1987, 13.

5.   Ibid., 18.

6.   Ibid., 84.

7.   Colonel Charles C. P. Stacey, *The Victory Campaign. The Operations in North-West Europe, 1944–1945. Vol III* (Ottawa: Queen's Printer, 1960), 221. Col. Stacey writes that Meyer did not learn of his promotion from SS Colonel to SS Major General until after he became a prisoner of war.

8.   EC. University of New Orleans. Oral history: Maj. Gerhard Lemcke, 12th SS *Panzer* Division.

9.   Harold Margolian, *Conduct Unbecoming. The Story of the Murder of Canadian Prisoners of War in Normandy* (Toronto: University of Toronto Press, 1998), 70.

10. EC. University of New Orleans. Oral history: Hans-Heinrich Dibbern.

11. EC. University of New Orleans. Oral history: Friedrich Bertenrath, Radioman/Corporal, 2d *Panzer* Division, Reconnaissance Battalion 116.

12. EC. University of New Orleans. Oral history: Wenzel Borgert, Second Lieutenant/Company Commander, Artillery Support for Antitank Battalion 228, 116th *Panzer* Division.

13. EC. University of New Orleans. Oral history: Corp. Friedrich Bertenrath.

14. EC. University of New Orleans. Oral history: Private Adolf Rogosch, Private First Class, Grenadier Regiment. 942, 353 Infantry Division.

15. Dr. Paul German, *100 Days of War for Peace* (France: Charles Corlet, 1998), 23.

16. Hastings, 327.

17. Milton Shulman, *Defeat in the West* (London: Martin Secker & Warburg Ltd., 1963), 116.

18. EC. University of New Orleans. Oral history: Wenzel Borgert.

19. EC. University of New Orleans. Oral history: Corporal Bertenrath.

20. EC. University of New Orleans. Oral history: Günter Materne, Battery Officer, Artillery Regiment 363.

21. EC. University of New Orleans. Oral history: Lt. Walter Padberg, 957th Grenadier Regiment.

22. EC. University of New Orleans. Oral history: Maj. Helmut Ritgen, Commander, 2d Battalion, *Panzer Lehr* Division 130.

23. EC. University of New Orleans. Oral history: Maj. Gerhard Lemcke.

24. EC. University of New Orleans. Oral history: Herbert Meier.

25. EC. University of New Orleans. Oral history: Günter Materne.

CHAPTER 5

1.   *Linderman*, 55.

2.   Authors' interview with Padre Jock Anderson MC & Bar, Highland Light Infantry. July 28, 1998.

3.   John Colby, *War from the Ground Up: The 90th Division in WWII* (Austin, TX: Nortex, 1991), 213.

4.   Authors' interview with Dr. Art Stevenson, RCAMC, July 20, 1998.

5.   W. R. Feasby, *Official History of the Canadian Medical Services* (Ottawa: Queen's Printer, 1953); 211.

6.   NAC. The War Diary of 11th Canadian Field Ambulance.

7.   Denis Whitaker and S. Whitaker, *Tug of War.* 251–2. Authors' interview with Corporal Wes Burrows, 1983.

8.   Harold P. Leinbaugh and J. D. Campbell, *The Men of Company K* (New York: Bantam, 1987), 225–6.

9.   Captain Cliff Chadderton, Royal Winnpeg Rifles, *Caen to Calais. July–August–September 1944.* Letter to the authors from Captain Cliff Chadderton, Oct. 20, 1998.

10.   Stacey, 257.

11.   Authors' interview with Flight Lieutenant Cecil Brown, July 16, 1998.

12.   Authors' interview with Padre Jock Anderson.

13.   Ken Tout, *Tanks, Advance! Normandy to the Netherlands, 1944* (London: Grafton Books, 1987), 93.

14.   Colby, 211.

15.   Authors' interview with Dr. Art Stevenson, RCAMC.

16.   Statement by John Redden as dictated to his son, Feb. 7, 1996. Steven Campbell collection.

17.   Colonel G. W. L. Nicholson, C.D. *Seventy Years of Service (A History of a Royal Canadian Army Medical Corps)* (Ottawa: Borealis Press, 1977), 226.

18.   Authors' interview with Dr. Don Campbell.

19.   J. B. Hillsman, *Eleven Men and a Scalpel* (Winnipeg: Columbia Press, 1948), 7.

20.   Tout, *A Fine Night for Tanks*, 85.

21.   Authors' interview with B. J. Danson.

22.   Ambrose, *Citizen Soldiers*, 322–3.

23.   Brenda McBryde, *A Nurse's War* (London: Chatto & Windus, 1979), 84–96.

24.   Hillsman, 76.

25.   Feasby, 204.

26.   Ibid.

27.   Authors' interview with Dr. Art Stevenson.

28.   Connors, Major John J. M. *The Story of an Unremarkable Canadian* (London, ON: Self-published, 1981).

29.   Feasby, 203.

30.   Ambrose, *Citizen Soldiers*, 323.

CHAPTER 6

1.   Terry Copp and B. McAndrew, *Battle Exhaustion* (Montreal & Kingston: McGill-Queen's University Press, 1990), 110.

2.   Authors' interview with Padre Jock Anderson, Highland Light Infantry, July 29, 1983.

3.   Alan Wood, *The Falaise Road* (Toronto: Macmillan, 1944), 37.

4.   David French, "Tommy Is No Soldier, Morale of Second British Army 1944," *Journal of Strategic Studies* 19/4 (December 1996): 113, 100, 171.

5.   Eversley Belfield and H. Essame, *The Battle for Normandy* (London: Pan, 1967), 184–6.

6.   EC. University of New Orleans. Oral history: Private Adolf Rogosch, Private First Class, Grenadier Regiment 942, 353 Infantry Division.

7.   Denis Whitaker and S. Whitaker, *Tug of War: The Canadian Victory that Opened Antwerp Harbour* (Toronto: Stoddart, 2nd ed., 2000), 184, 188. Authors' interview with Corporal Art Kelly, June 6, 1981.

8. Authors' interview with Captain Charles Mackay, carrier platoon, Royal Hamilton Light Infantry, Oct. 23, 1999.

9. Captain Cliff Chadderton, *Caen to Calais. July–August–September 1944.* Diary, kindly lent to the authors.

10. LCMSDS: Censorship Report for period Aug. 1–15, 1944. Canadian Army Overseas.

11. Ibid.

12. George Blackburn, *The Guns of Normandy: A Soldier's Eye View, France, 1944* (Toronto: McClelland & Stewart, 1995), 383.

13. Major D. J. Goodspeed, *Battle Royal* (Toronto: Royal Regiment of Canada Association, 1962), 22.

14. IWM 84/50/1. Trooper John M. Thorpe, 2d Fife and Forfar Yeomanry, 11th Armored Division.

15. Tout, *Tanks Advance*, 209.

16. IWM 84/50/1, Trooper John M. Thorpe, 2d Fife and Forfar Yeomanry, 11th Armored Division.

17. Chadderton.

18. Patrick Delaforce, *Churchill's Desert Rats: From Normandy to Berlin with the 7th Armoured Division* (London: Alan Sutton, 1994), 69.

19. Authors' interview with Flight Lieutenant Warren, Jan. 15, 2000.

20. Martin Blumenson (Ed.), *The Patton Papers.* (Boston: Houghton Miflin, 1972), 511.

21. Carlo D'Este, interviewed on his book *Patton: A Genius for War,* Jan. 28, 1996: http://www.booknotes.org.

22. NA, Combat Exhaustion Cases: Maj. N. L. Weintrop, 29th Division.

23. Ambrose, *Citizen Soldiers,* 329.

24. Copp and McAndrew, 127.

25. French, 171.

CHAPTER 7

1. George Blackburn, *The Guns of Normandy: A Soldier's Eye View* (France, 1944; Toronto: McClelland & Stewart, 1995), 48.

2. Dr. W. G. Grant, *Did I Ever Tell You About the War?* (Hampton, ON: Self-published, March 1990), kindly loaned to the authors, 34.

3. Andy Rooney, *My War* (New York: Random House, 1995), 200–201.

4. IWM 91/13/1. Maj. A. J. Forrest. Commander, 272d Battery, Ninetieth Middlesex HA.

5. Anderson, 98.

6. Colby, 450.

7. Sir Brian Horrocks, with Eversley Belfield and Maj. Gen. H. Essame, *Corps Commander* (Toronto: Griffin House, 1977), 33.

8. Folkestad, 48–9.

9. PAC. Censorship Report Aug. 16–31, 1944. Lance Corporal, 20th Field Company RCE 2d Canadian Infantry Division; Officer, II Canadian Corps; Private, 2d Canadian Infantry Division.

10. Authors' interview with B. J. Danson.

11. IWM 94/34/1. Lt. Col. M. Crawford, CO 8th Middlesex Regiment, 43d Division.

12. NAC, WD, Royal Regment of Canada, August 1944.

13. Jary, 71.

14. PAC. Censorship Report Aug. 16–31, 1944.

15. Grant, 38.

16. Paul Fussell, *Wartime. Understanding and Behaviour in the Second World War* (New York and Oxford: Oxford University Press, 1989), 239–41.

17. NAC. Censorship Report Aug. 16–31, 1944.

18. Private soldier from the Calgary Highlanders, 2d Canadian Infantry Division.

19. NA 02406. History 305th Engineer Combat Battalion.

20. Tout, *Tanks Advance!* 99.

21. Authors' interview with Richard Malone, Sept. 1981. Richard Malone, *A World in Flames*, 49.

22. PA. RG24. 12,330. 88/3. *Time* magazine, Sept. 4, 1944. Stephen Campbell Collection.

CHAPTER 8

1. EC. University of New Orleans. Oral history: Edward Gianelloni.

2. Eisenhower, *Crusade in Europe*, 269; Ambrose, *Citizen Soldiers*, 67.

3. Ambrose, *Citizen Soldiers*, 67, 69.

4. Ernie Pyle, *Ernie's War* (New York: Random House, 1986), 319.

5. How, *Hill 112*, 203.

6. Moorhead, 113.

7. Tout, *Tanks, Advance!* 87.

8. J. A. Womack, *Summon Up the Blood: A Unique Record of D-Day and Its Aftermath*. Ed. by Celia Wolfe. (London: Leo Cooper, 1997), 65.

9. Lindsay, 40.

10. Womack, 66.

11. Ambrose, *Citizen Soldiers*, 66, 73.

12. EC. University of New Orleans. Oral history: Lt. Walter Padberg.

13. EC. University of New Orleans. Oral history: Private Kenneth Russell.

14. Ernie Pyle with the 4th Division. Encyclopedia Brittanica. Authors' collection.

15. Michael Reynolds, *Steel Inferno: I SS Panzer Corps in Normandy* (New York: Spellmount, 1997), 208.

16. Shulman, 144.

17. EC. University of New Orleans. Oral history: Private Adolf Rogosch.

18. H. Essame, *Patton. A Study in Command* (New York: Scribner, 1974), 142.

19. Ambrose, *Citizen Soldiers*, 74.

20. Ibid.

CHAPTER 9

1. NA. RG94, Combat Interviews, 24038.96. Interview of Company "F," 119th Infantry via Bruyelles, Belgium, Sept. 5, 1944. NA. RG 94. CI 95, 30th Division.

2. Denis Whitaker and S. Whitaker. *Rhineland: The Battle to End* (Toronto: Stoddart, 1989, 2000. 2nd ed.), 350. Leinbaugh & Campbell, 153.

3. Hastings, 218.

4. Whitaker/Whitaker: *Tug of War*, 221.

5. D'Este, 385.

6. Ibid., 394.

7. D'Este, 338.

8. Hastings, 249.

9. Mansoor, 158.

10. Hastings, 246.

11. NA. RG 94. CI 95, 30th Division, July 26–28, 1944.

12. NAC. 21 Army group intelligence summary No. 154. Part One, August 10, 1944.

13. Andy Rooney, *My War* (New York: Random House, 1995), 174.

14. Ambrose, *Citizen Soldiers*, 75–6.

15. P-47 Thunderbolt, USAF Museum.

16. Ibid. Authors' collection. See USAF Museum Web site: Aces of Two Wars.

17. Ibid.

18. Ibid.

19. Ibid. (Blumer was awarded the Distinguished Service Cross, Silver Star, Distinguished Flying Cross, Purple Heart, Air Medal with 22 Oak Leaf Clusters, and the Belgian Croix de Guerre.)

20. Authors' interview with Flight Lt. Baggs, 164 Squadron, 84 Group, RAF, Oct. 11, 1998.

21. U.S. Army Center of Military History by William M. Hammond (1998–2002 www.DistantCousin.com); Rooney, 174; Mansoor, 158.

22. U.S. Army Center of Military History by William M. Hammond (1998–2002 www.DistantCousin.com).

23. Rooney, 174.

CHAPTER 10

1. Omar Bradley, *A Soldier's Story* (New York: Henry Holt, 1952), 347.

2. Ernie Pyle, *A Surge of Doom-like Sound.* (Yahoo) Encyclopedia Britannica (link to Normandy–Breakout).

3. Ibid. A. J. Liebling, *The Road from Saint-Lô.*

4. Bradley, *A Soldier's Story*, 348.

5. Hastings, 256.

6. Samuel W. Mitcham, *Hitler's Field Marshals and Their Battles* (Chelson, MI: Scarborough House, 1990), 305.

7. (Yahoo) (www.army.mil/cmh-pg/). U.S. Army Center of Military History. Medal of Honor citations. WWII recipients. Matt Urban.

8. Ibid.

9. Max Hastings, *Overlord: D-Day and the Battle for Normandy, 1944* (London: Pan, 1985), 256.

10. LC MSDS. Normandy Breakthrough. Combat Command A, 3d Armored Division.

11. LC MSDS. NA, RG 94, CI 260, Operation *Cobra.* After-action report of Combat Command "B," 3d Armored Division in Breakthrough of July 25, 1944: Interview with Maj. William Castille, S-2.

12. A. J. Liebling. *The New Yorker* War Pieces. Letter from France. "At Divisional Artillery Headquarters, August 4" (by wireless). (Yahoo) Encyclopedia Britannica (link to Normandy–Breakout).

13. NAC. 21 Army group intelligence summary No. 154. Part One, Aug. 10, 1944.

14. Authors' interview with Flight Lt. William Baggs, 164 Squadron, 84 Group, RCAF, Oct. 1, 1998.

15. NA, RG 94, CI 260, Operation *Cobra.* After-action report of Combat Command "A," (Gen. Doyle O. Hickey), 3d Armored Division.

16. Paul Carell, *Invasion, They're Coming* (New York: Bantam, 1964), 243.

CHAPTER 11

1. How, *Hill 112*, 19–20.

2. G. P. B. Roberts, *From the Desert to the Baltic* (London: William Kimber, 1987), 168.

3.　*Roberts*, 185–189.

4.　IWM 84/50/1. Diary Trooper John Thorpe, 2d Fife and Forfar Yeomanry.

5.　Ibid.

6.　J. J. How, *Normandy: The British Breakout* (London: William Kimber, 1981), 54.

7.　Roberts, 189.

8.　How, *Normandy: The British Breakout*, 54.

9.　Ibid.

10.　Roberts, 185–189.

11.　How, *Normandy: The British Breakout*, 59.

12.　Ibid., 68.

13.　Ibid., 218.

14.　Roberts, 193.

15.　How, *Normandy: The British Breakout*, 208.

16.　NAC. BLM/119, 3 Aug/44.

17.　NAC. BLM/119, 2 Aug/44.

18.　Maj. Gen. Sir Francis Guingand, KBE, CB, DSO. *Operation Victory* (London: Hodder & Stoughton, 1947), 399.

19.　BLM 94/8.

20.　Sir Brian Horrocks with Eversley Belfield and Maj. Gen. H. Essame, *Corps Commander* (Toronto: Griffin House, 1977), 28.

21.　Jary, *18 Platoon*, 22.

22.　Ibid.

23.　Tout, *A Fine Night for Tanks*, 30.

24.　Horrocks, *Corps Commander*, 28; Horrocks, *A Full Life* (London: Collins, 1960), 188.

25.　Hastings, *Overlord*, 343.

26.　Delaforce, 70.

27.　Keegan, 254.

28.　Jary, *18 Platoon*, 8.

29.　Horrocks, *Corps Commander*, 35; Horrocks, *A Full Life*. 190.

30.　Thomas J. Bates, *Normandy: The Search for Sydney*. (Berkeley, CA: Bates Books, 1999), vii. 91, 94.

31.　IWM 84/50/1. Diary Trooper John Thorpe, 2d Fife and Forfar Yeomanry.

32.　Ibid.; Delaforce, 60.

CHAPTER 12

1.　NA. German Army Sit Reps. Weekly Review, July 24–30, 1944.

2.　Heinz Gunther Guderian. *From Normandy to the Ruhr: With the 116th Panzer Division in World War II* (Bedford, PA: The Aberjona Press), 62.

3.　NA. "Moving, Commitment and Fighting of the 116 Pz Div in France, 6 June–12 Aug/44." Box 736. MSB-017NA. Army Gp Intelligence Summary #155. Part II. 15 Aug/44.

4.　NA. "Moving, Commitment and Fighting of the 116 Pz Div in France."

5.　Ibid. Alwyn Featherston, *Battle for Mortain. The 30th Infantry Division Saves the Breakout, August 7–21* (Novato, CA: Presidio, 1993), 71.

6.　NA. "Moving, Commitment and Fighting of the 116 Pz Div in France."

7.　Featherston, 71–2.

8.　NA. German Army Sit Reps. A Gp B Sitrep.

9.　F. H. Hinsley, *British Intelligence in the Second World War*, Vol. III (London: HMSO, 1981), 245–6.

10.　Mansoor, 169.

11. Featherston, 712.
12. Carell, 249.

CHAPTER 13
1. Rene Langlois, *1944: Les Douets in Torment. A Memoir.* Trans. by Joyce Carter. (Mortain: Self-published, 1996), 17.
2. Ibid.
3. NA. RG94. WWII Operations Reports. 1940–48 Combat interviews, Folders 95–97; CI 96. Activities of the 120th Regiment, 30th Infantry Division. The counterattack at Mortain, Aug. 6–12, 1944.
4. NA RG94. Combat interviews. The counterattack against the 120th Infantry Mortain. The Abbaye-Blanche Roadblock.
5. Ibid.
6. Featherston, 62.
7. Ibid., 64.
8. NA. RG44. Combat interviews. Activities of the 120th Regiment, 30th Infantry Division, Aug. 6–12, 1944.
9. Featherston, 62.
10. Langlois, 21.
11. Featherston, 74.
12. Langlois, 23.
13. Featherston, 79.
14. Breuer, 185.
15. Ibid., 113.
16. Langlois, 24.
17. NA. RG94. Combat interviews. Company A's action in the Mortain counterattack; B Company account.
18. NA. RG94. Combat interviews with Sergeants Grady and Workman. 117th Infantry at St. Barthélémy.
19. Featherston, 128.
20. NA. RG94. Combat interviews. 117th Infantry at St. Barthélémy. 24038. 96; Featherston, 105–110.

CHAPTER 14
1. Featherston, 115.
2. Chronology of the actions of 2d SS Panzer Division Das Reich at Mortain by Mark Reardon. E-mail the Webmaster, WWII Web site Association, Mark Yerger's Books, 1996–98.
3. NA. RG94. Combat interviews. The counterattack against the 120th Infantry at Mortain. The L'Abbaye-Blanche roadblock.
4. NA. RG94. Repulse of German counterattack at Avranches. Comments by Brig. Gen. James Lewis.
5. Reynolds, 218.
6. Featherston, 129–130.
7. Charles Demoulin, *Firebirds! Flying a Typhoon in Action* (Washington, DC: Smithsonian Institution Press), 186.
8. Demoulin, 186.
9. Authors' interview with Flight Lt. William Baggs, 164 Squadron, 84 Group, RAF, Oct. 1, 1998. Flight Lt. Baggs noted that while 151 Typhoon pilots were killed in Nor-

mandy, a total of 656 were killed in the course of the war. "I knew the losses were high," he wrote, "but I did not realize they were *that* high" (June 12, 1999). Baggs completed a tour of ninety-two sorties in the war.

10. Ibid.

11. Featherston, 134–5.

12. Reynolds. 220. PAC, RG24, Vol. 20518, File 981 (D117), Seventh Army.

13. NA, RG 24. File 981 (D117) Vol. 20518: Report by Gen. von Gersdorff, chief of staff, on the activities of the Seventh Army.

14. Ibid.

15. Blumenson, *Breakout and Pursuit*, 474.

16. NAC. "Moving, Commitment and Fighting of the 116 Pz Div. in France, 6 June–12 Aug."

17. Heinz Günther Guderian, *From Normandy to the Ruhr: With the 116th Panzer Division in World War II*, 71.

18. PA. "Moving, Commitment and Fighting of the 116 Pz Div. in France, 6 June–12 Aug."

19. NA. MS B840. 981SOM (D123). Eberbach: Panzer Group Eberbach and the Falaise Encirclement, Feb. 1, 1946.

20. Shulman, 148.

21. Blumenson, *Breakout and Pursuit*, 481.

22. Featherston, xi.

23. NA. RG94. Combat interviews. The counterattack against the 120th Infantry at Mortain.

24. NA. RG94. Combat interviews. The counterattack against the 120th Infantry at Mortain. The L'Abbaye-Blanche roadblock.

25. NA. RG94. Combat interviews. The counterattack against the 120th Infantry at Mortain. Featherston, 180–82.

CHAPTER 15

1. Terry Copp, "The Canadians in Normandy: A Reassessment." Unpublished paper, Wilfred Laurier University, Waterloo, ON, April 12, 1998.

2. Stacey, 206.

3. Authors' interview with Richard Malone, September 1981.

4. Tout, *A Fine Night for Tanks. The Road to Falaise*, 126.

5. NAC. RG24, 2 Br. Army Intel. Rep. No. 32 July 1, 44. Meyer, 166.

6. Stacey, 221.

7. Ibid., 214.

8. Ibid., 212–13.

9. Alan Wood, 33.

10. Col. Murray Johnston, *Canada's Craftsmen. The Story of Electrical and Mechanical Engineering in the Canadian Forces* (Bordon, ON: CFB, 1997), 88.

11. Delaforce, 68.

12. Authors' interview with Brig. J. M. Rockingham, Nov. 10, 1983.

13. Authors' interview with Maj. David Russell, 5 Black Watch, St. Andrews, Scotland, Sept. 17, 1986; Elliot Rodger, quoted by Dominick Graham in *The Price of Command. A Biography of General Guy Simonds* (Toronto: Stoddart, 1993), 148.

14. IWM. BLM 72–174.

15. Authors' interview with Maj. David Russell, 5 Black Watch, St. Andrews, Scotland, Sept. 17, 1986.

16. Denis Whitaker and S. Whitaker, *Rhineland. The Battle to End the War* (Toronto: Stoddart, 1989), 98.

17. Authors' interview with Maj. Gen. Sydney Radley-Walters, Sherbrooke Fusiliers, Sept. 7, 1998.

18. Keegan, 253. The casualty figures prove the success, as Mr. Keegan points out: four infantry battalions on foot lost sixty-eight killed; the three mounted only lost seven.

19. J. B. Salmond, *History 51st Highland Division* (Edinburgh: Blackwood, 1953), 5.

20. Shulman, 149.

21. NA. Report No. 65. Historical Section (G.S.) Army Headquarters.

22. Reynolds, 234.

23. Roman Jarymowycz, *Canadian Armor in Normandy's Operation Totalize and the Quest for Operational Maneuvre.* Unpublished doctoral dissertation, McGill University, 1997, 82.

24. Authors' interview with Maj. Gen. Radley-Walters, Sept. 7, 1998.

25. Jarymowycz, 93. Wittman's body was found in 1982 and identified by the German War Graves Commission, who examined his ID disc, fragments of a leather jacket, and his pistol. His grave was five hundred yards from Radley-Walters's position and some seventeen hundred yards from the British guns. He was finally buried with his crew in the German War Cemetery at La Cambe.

26. Michael Reynolds. *Steel Inferno: ISS Panzer Corps in Normandy.* (New York: Spellmount, 1997), 235.

27. Ernie Pyle, *In Normandy, August 8, 1944;* http://eb.com/normandy/pri/Q00237.html.

28. NAC. Monk, Maj. L. C. An Account of the battle participation of the Algonquin Regiment between Aug. 6 and Aug. 22, 1944.

29. Tout, *Tanks, Advance!* 96.

30. Ibid., 112.

31. Ibid., 95–96.

CHAPTER 16

1. Terry Copp, *The Canadians in Normandy: A Reassessment.*

2. G. L. Cassidy, *Warpath: The Story of the Algonquin Regiment, 1939–1945* (Toronto: Ryerson, 1948; Markham, ON: Paperjacks, 1980), 107–8.

3. Stacey, 228.

4. Ibid.

5. LCMSDS, "An Account of Battle Experiences of 'D' Company, Algonquin Regiment," Maj. Keith Stirling.

6. The above account is taken from authors' interviews with Captains Bob Patterson and Bill Whiteside, Argyll and Sutherland Highlanders, Oct. 14, 1989.

CHAPTER 17

1. H. Essame, *Patton. A Study in Command* (New York: Scribner, 1974), 157.

2. NA. ETHINT 67. Notes from an interview with Lt. Gen. Fritz Bayerlein. Critique of the Normandy breakthrough. *Panzer Lehr* division from St. Lô to the Ruhr, Aug. 15, 1945.

3. Bradley, 368.

4. Essame, 157.

5. www.google: USAF Museum. Republic P-47 Thunderbolt. Authors' collection.

6. Patton, *War As I Knew It* (Boston: Houghton, 1947), 105.

7. IWM. Montgomery Papers. Signal to CIGS from General Montgomery.

8. Essame, 163; Ambrose, *Citizen Soldiers,* 89.

9. Ladislas Farago, *Patton. Ordeal and Triumph* (New York: Astor-Honour, 1964), 527; Featherston, 157.

10. Omar N. Bradley and C. Blair, *A General's Life: An Autobiography by General of the Army Omar N. Bradley* (New York: Simon & Schuster, 1983), 296; Featherston, 158.

11. Maule, 132.
12. Ibid. Quote by Capt. Thomas E. Cassidy from Illinois, 3d Armored Division.
13. Robert A. Miller, *August 1944* (Novato, CA: Presidio Press, 1988), 19.
14. NA. ETHINT 67. Report by Lt. Gen. Bayerlein.
15. Ibid.
16. NA. 981SOM (D118). Lieutenant General von Gersdorff. Comments to the Seventh Army's War Diary.
17. NA. Report by Lieutenant General Bayerlein.
18. NA. 981SOM (D123-4). Report on the fighting of *Panzergruppe* West from July 3–Aug. 9, 1944, by Lieutenant General Eberbach. MS #B-840.
19. Shulman, 152.
20. NA. Report of Eberbach.
21. Patton, *War As I Knew It*, 104.
22. Eddy Florentin, *Battle of the Falaise Gap* (London: Elek Books, 1965), 107.
23. Breuer, 231.
24. Blumenson, *Breakout and Pursuit*, 504.
25. Bradley, 376.
26. Copp, *Legion Magazine*, October 1999.
27. Blumenson, *Command Decision*, 409.
28. Eisenhower, 278.
29. Bradley, 352.
30. Essame, 163.
31. Blumenson, *Breakout and Pursuit*, 509.
32. Copp, *Legion Magazine*, October 1999; Featherston, 215.
33. Blumenson, *Command Decision*, 505.
34. Patton, 510.
35. Ibid., 511.

CHAPTER 18
1. NA. National Archives microfiche. "Panzer Group Eberbach at Alençon; breakthrough and encirclement of Falaise," Report by Gen. Hans Eberbach.
2. Guderian, *From Normandy to the Ruhr*, 78–79.
3. NA. Eberbach.
4. Ibid.
5. Ibid.
6. Ibid.
7. Ibid.
8. Ibid.; Warlimont, 151.

CHAPTER 19
1. Authors' interview with Capt. William Parker, Adjutant, Royal Hamilton Light Infantry, Oct. 18, 1998.
2. D. J. Goodspeed, *Battle Royal. A History of the Royal Regiment of Canada, 1862–1962* (Toronto: Royal Regiment of Canada), 445.
3. Charles Martin with Roy Whitstead, *Battle Diary* (Toronto: Dundern Press, 1994), 31–34.
4. Authors' interview with Corp. Douglas Shaughnessy, Royal Hamilton Light Infantry, Sept. 10, 1998.
5. Brereton Greenhous, *Semper Paratus* (Hamilton, ON: The Royal Hamilton Light Infantry Historical Association, 1977), 260.

6. Authors' interview with Corporal Shaughnessy.

7. Whitaker and Whitaker, *Tug of War*, 184; quote from John Ellis, *Sharp End of War. The Fighting Men in World War II* (Newton Abbot, Devon, England: David & Charles Ltd., 1980), 46.

8. Arthur Kelly, *There's a Goddamn Bullet for Everyone* (Paris, ON: Arts and Publishing, 1979), 59.

9. Authors' interview with Col. John Williamson and Corp. Douglas Shaughnessy, Royal Hamilton Light Infantry, Nov. 10, 1999.

10. Kelly, 60.

11. Authors' interview with Lt. Colin Gibson, Royal Hamilton Light Infantry, Dec. 6, 1998.

12. NAC. WD RHLI, Aug. 12, 1944.

13. Greenhous, 260–1.

14. Authors' interview with Corporal Shaughnessy.

CHAPTER 20

1. LC MSDS. CP, Vol. 5, Memo COS to GOC-in-C regarding the report of the AOC in C Bomber Command, Aug. 28, 1944.

2. Bomber Command report, Nov. 26, 1997, kindly loaned to the authors by Wing Commander (later Lt. Gen.) A. Chester Hull. Of the volunteers who flew, almost 60 percent (over 55,000 men) were killed. It was a loss-rate comparable only to the worst slaughter of the First World War trenches.

3. Report on the bombing of our own troops during Operation *Tractable*. Air Chief Marshal Arthur Harris; CP, Vol. 5, Memo COS to GOC-in-C regarding the report of the AOC in C Bomber Command, Aug. 25, 1944. Kindly loaned by Wing Commander Hull.

4. Authors' interview with Flight Sgt. Roy Clarke, Nov. 20, 1998.

5. Authors' interview with Flight Lt. Jim Llewellen, Mooloolaba, Australia, March 15, 1998.

6. A. Brandon Conron (ed.), *The History of the First Hussars 1856–1980* (London, ON: 1981), 91; NAC. An Account of Ops by 2 Cdn Armd Bde in France, Aug. 14–16, 1944.

7. Flight log of Flying Officer Ken Fulton, Aug. 14, 1944, kindly loaned to the authors by F/O Fulton.

8. Ibid.

9. Belfield and Essame, 230.

10. Report on the Bombing of our own troops, Aug. 25, 1944, kindly loaned by Lt. Gen. A. Chester Hull.

11. Authors' interview with Flight Sgt. Roy Clarke.

12. Authors' interview with Lt. Gen. A. Chester Hull, DFC, Croix de Guerre Silver Star, CMM, Nov. 18, 1998.

13. Authors' interview with Capt. Ken Turnbull, March 23, 2000.

14. Lindsay, 52.

15. NAC. RG24, Vol. 10499, War Diary, Royal Regiment of Canada, 14/44.

16. Authors' interview with Cpl. John Angus McDonald, Stormont, Dundas, and Glenharry Highlanders, Oct. 17, 1998.

17. IWM. Diary of Padre N. J. Jones, 2 Derbyshire Yeomanry.

18. IWM. Diary of Sgt. J. G. Perry, 15th Med. Regiment, RA.

19. Terry Copp, "Allied Bombing in Normandy," *Legion Magazine*, November/December 1998.

20. Authors' interview with Flight Lt. (later Sq. Ldr.) John Turnbull, DFC, CM, Oct. 12, Nov. 2, 1998.

21. Ibid.

22.　Ibid.
23.　Authors' interview with Flying Officer Ken Fulton, DFC.
24.　IWM 95/19/1. Diary of Sgt. R. T. Greenwood, 9 Royal Tank Regiment, August 1944.
25.　Blackburn, 418.
26.　Authors' interview with Flying Officer Ken Fulton, DFC, Nov. 3, 1998.
27.　Authors' interview with Lt. Gen. A. Chester Hull.

CHAPTER 21
1.　Terry Copp, *A Canadian's Guide to the Battlefields of Normandy*. LCMSDS, 1944, 135.
2.　LCMSDS. Historical Records of the Queen's Own Cameron Highlanders, 111.
3.　EC. University of New Orleans. Oral history: Maj. Helmut Ritgen, Commander, 2d Battalion, *Panzer Lehr* Regiment 130.
4.　Authors' interview with Maj. Gen. Roger Rowley, DSO, ED, CD, GCLS, Stormont, Dundas and Glengarry Highlanders, Oct. 6, 1998.
5.　Ibid.
6.　Reynolds, 250.
7.　Ibid., 254.
8.　NAC. Operation *Tractable*. An account of Operations by the 2d Canadian Armored Brigade in France, Aug. 14–16, 1944. RG24, Vol. 10, 992, file 275C2.013(D1).
9.　NAC. RG24. W.D. First Canadian Scottish Regiment, August 15.
10.　Ibid.
11.　Stacey, 249.
12.　NAC. RG24. W.D. First Canadian Scottish Regiment, August 15.
13.　Chadderton.
14.　Tout, *Tanks Advance!*, 106.
15.　IWM. Highland Padre N. F. Jones.
16.　Ambrose, *Citizen Soldiers*, 67–8.
17.　Wilfred Smith, *Code Word Canloan* (Toronto: Dundurn Press, 1992), 46.
18.　Lindsay, 51.
19.　Authors' interview with Maj. Gen. Radley-Walters, Nov. 25, 1998.
20.　Authors' interview with Brig. Gen. Frederick Clift, Nov. 16, 1998.

CHAPTER 22
1.　Featherston, 159.
2.　Russell F. Weigley, *Eisenhower's Lieutenants: The Campaigns of France and Germany, 1944–1945* (Bloomington: Indiana University Press, 1981), 310.
3.　NA. RG94, The Gap at Chambois, Aug. 15–22, 1944.
4.　NAC. RG24, Vol. 13, 751. Lt. Gen. G. Simonds, Notes on Corps Commanders Talk, Aug. 13, 1944.
5.　IWM. Montgomery to Alanbrooke. Montgomery Papers, Aug. 15, 1944.
6.　Blumenson, *Breakout and Pursuit*, 534.
7.　NA. RG94, WWII Operations Report. 80th Infantry Division August 1944; Patton's Troubleshooters.
8.　Hastings, 247.
9.　NA. RG94, 80th Division history Argentan.
10.　Ibid.
11.　Ibid. Interview with Lt. (now retired Col.) William B. "Bull" Miller.
12.　80th Division history.
13.　Ibid.
14.　Ibid. Interview with Lt. (now retired Col.) William B. "Bull" Miller.

15. Guderian, 87.
16. Florentin, 265.

CHAPTER 23
1. Bradley, 297.
2. Colby, 146, 149.
3. Ibid., 160.
4. Ibid., 485.
5. Blumenson, *The Battle of the Generals*, 427.
6. Ibid., 484.
7. Guderian, 79.
8. Guderian, 82.
9. Ibid.
10. NA. RG94, 390-FA(915)-0.3, 47285 Box No 13373: Narrative Le Bourg–St. Léonard Chambois.
11. Ibid.
12. NA. RG94, CI 194, The Gap at Chambois, Aug. 15–22, 1944. Interview with Second Lt. Vernon W. Cross, Weapons Platoon leader, "A" Company, 359th Infantry, 90th Division.
13. NA. RG94, CI 194, 90th Infantry Division. First Battalion Action at Le Bourg–St. Léonard Chambois.
14. NA. RG94, CI 194, The Gap at Chambois, Aug. 15–22, 1944.
15. NA. RG94, 390-FA(915)-0.3, 47285 Box No. 13373: Narrative Le Bourg–St. Léonard Chambois.
16. NA. RG94, CI 194, The Gap at Chambois, Aug. 15–22, 1944. Interview with Second Lt. Vernon W. Cross, Weapons Platoon leader, "A" Company, 359th Infantry, 90th Division.
17. NA. RG94, 390-FA(915)-0.3, 47285 Box No. 13373: Narrative Le Bourg–St. Léonard Chambois.
18. NA. RG94, CI 194, The Gap at Chambois, Aug. 15–22, 1944. Interview with Second Lt. Vernon W. Cross, Weapons Platoon leader, "A" Company, 359th Infantry, 90th Division.
19. NA. RG94, CI 194, The Gap at Chambois, Aug. 15–22, 1944. Conclusions and Observations.

CHAPTER 24
1. Stacey, 256. NAC. Intelligence summary by Lt. Col. Peter Wright.
2. Christopher Evans, "The Fighter-Bomber in the Normandy Campaign. The Role of 83 Group." *Canadian Military History*, Vol. 8, Number 1, Winter, 1999, 21.
3. LCMSDS. Charles Bowyer, "The Main Role and Achievements of the Typhoon during the preparation and invasion of Europe: Summary of Losses May–August 1944." *History of the RAF*, 222.
4. www.google: USAF Museum. Republic P-47 Thunderbolt. In European Theatre with USAAF. Authors' collection.
5. Hugh Halliday, *The Tumbling Sky* (Canada's Wings), 21.
6. Hugh Halliday, *Typhoon and Tempest. The Canadian Story*, 66.
7. Authors' interview with Flight Lt. Bill Baggs, Oct. 1, 1999.
8. Authors' correspondence with Dr. Jonathan E. C. Tan (grandson), Muncaster, England. Feb. 1, 2000.
9. Ibid.
10. Authors' interview with Wing Commander Russell Bannock, DSO, DFC, Jan. 10, 2000.

11.   www.google: USAF Museum. Republic P-47 Thunderbolt.

12.   Ibid.

13.   Authors' interview and correspondence with Flight Lt. Duke Warren. Nov. 1, 1999.

14.   Ibid.

15.   Report by Flight Lt. Roy A. Crane, 182 Squadron, 124 Wing, to WWII Typhoon Pilots' Memorial, Noyers Bocage, France. This document is the result of a suggestion made in a letter from Air Commodore C. D. 'Kit' North-Lewis, DSO, DFC, and bar, Commanding Officer Flying, 124 Typhoon Wing, 83 Group, Second Tactical Air Force. He suggested: "A record should be made of all historical aspects of the Noyers Bocage Memorial for the benefit of future generations . . . before we have all gone." Personal papers of F/L Bill Baggs.

16.   Hugh Halliday, *Typhoon and Tempest. The Canadian Story.* (Toronto: CANAV, 1992), 70.

17.   Stacey, 257.

18.   Wing Commander Duke Warren, "Gemini Flight," report submitted to *Fighter Pilot Association,* Self-published, 1997, 112.

CHAPTER 25

1.   Stacey, 252.

2.   Authors' interview with Capt. (now Brig. Gen.) Michael Gutowski, Virtuti Militari, May 18, 1998. For general information on the Polish campaign see Jozef Garlinski, *Poland in the Second World War* (New York: 1985).

3.   *For Your Freedom and Ours, 1944–1994* (Toronto: Polish Combatants of Canada, 1994).

4.   Keegan, *Six Armies in Normandy,* 268–9.

5.   K. Jamar, *With the Tanks of the 1st Polish Armoured Division* (Hengelo: H. L. Smit & Son, 1946), 160.

6.   Stacey, 243, 257.

7.   Jamar, 116.

8.   Ibid.

9.   Authors' interview with Krzysztof Szydlowski, Vice President, 1st Polish Armored Division Association in Canada, July 15, 1999.

10.   Stacey, 252.

11.   Jamar, 104.

12.   Authors' interview with Krzysztof Szydlowski.

13.   Authors' interview with Capt. Ted Walewicz, 2d Polish Armored Regiment, June 7, 1999.

14.   Authors' interview with Brigadier General Gutowski.

15.   Authors' interview with Capt. Ted Walewicz.

16.   Jamar, 107; Maule, 162.

17.   Authors' interview with M. Grandvalet, June 5, 1998, Boisjos, Normandy.

18.   Authors' interview with Col. (then Capt.) Pierre Sévigny, 4th Canadian Medium Regiment, RCA, May 6, 1999.

19.   Authors' interview with Robert Chombart, June 5, 1998, Chambois, Normandy.

20.   *Boisjos: Hill 262* (Montormel Memorial Committee, 1961). Montormel video.

21.   The story of the villagers is based on Abbé Marcel Launay's book *Dans la Tourmente de la Guerre* (Normandy: Self-published, 1985); on authors' interview with Abbé Launay, June 12, 1998; on authors' interview with Col. Jacques van Dijke, June 5, 1998; and on *Florentin,* 110, 146, 171, 196.

CHAPTER 26

1. An Outline of American History (1994). Part 10: The New Deal and World War. Department of Humanities Computing, 1997.
2. Tom Brokaw, *The Greatest Generation* (New York: Random House, 1998).
3. Donald E. Graves, *South Albertas. A Canadian Regiment at War* (Toronto: Robin Brass Studio, 1998), 163.
4. Maj. David D. Currie, *Story in His Words. "After the Battle: The Battle of the Falaise Pocket,"* Number 8, Ed. by Winston G. Ramsey. (London: Battle of Britain Prints International, 1982). Stephen Campbell collection.
5. NAC, RG24, 4 CAB, Battle Log. Aug. 18, 1944.
6. Currie.
7. Hastings, 223.
8. Currie.
9. Ibid.
10. Graves, 163.
11. Currie.
12. Capt. John Redden interview, Feb. 9, 1996. Stephen Campbell collection.
13. Graves, 139.
14. Stacey, 258.
15. Currie; Graves, 164.
16. DND: *Legion Magazine.* July–August 1986.
17. Currie.

CHAPTER 27

1. Robert Fraser, *Black Yesterdays: The Argyll's War* (Hamilton, ON: Argyll Regimental Foundation, 1996), 239.
2. Donald E. Graves, *South Albertas: A Canadian Regiment at War* (Toronto: Robin Brass Studio, 1998), 144.
3. Interview of Captain Redden, Stephen Campbell collection, Feb. 9, 1996; Graves, 144.
4. Currie, "Story in his Words."
5. Stacey, 260.
6. Currie.
7. Graves, 149.
8. Lt. Arkle Dunlop, Canadian Argyll Regiment, "St. Lambert-sur-Dives, August 19–21." A memoir, c. 1980.
9. Fraser, 239.
10. Authors' interview with Private Art Bridge, Jan. 24, 2000.
11. Geoffrey Hayes, *The Lincs: A History of the Lincoln and Welland Regiment at War* (Alma, ON: Maple Leaf Route, 1986), 36–8.
12. Graves, 150.
13. Florentin, 251.
14. Fraser, 240.
15. Ibid.

CHAPTER 28

1. Florentin, 234; Montormel video, Stephen Campbell collection.
2. NA. RG94, Second Battalion action at Chambois. Interview with Maj. LC Dull, Aug. 27, 1944.
3. Authors' interview with Capt. (now Brig. Gen.) Michael Gutowski.

4. Jamar, 141.

5. NA. RG94. Second Battalion Action at Chambois.

6. Keegan, 274–5.

7. NA. RG94, The Gap at Chambois, Aug. 15–22, 1944.

8. Bernage Georges and R. McNair, *Falaise-Argentan. Le Couloir de la Mort* (Bayeux: Éditions Heimdal, 1944), 35.

9. NA. RG94, The Gap at Chambois, Aug. 15–22, 1944.

10. Authors' interview with Capt. (now Brig. Gen.) Michael Gutowski, July 15, 1998.

11. NA. RG94, Second Battalion action at Chambois. Interview with Maj. LC Dull, Aug. 27, 1944. (Information on the supplies taken from Corps G-4 report.)

12. NAC. RG24, 1st Polish Armored Division.

CHAPTER 29

1. Hubert Meyer, *The History of the 12th SS Panzer Division Hitlerjugend* (Winnipeg, Man: J. J. Fedorowicz, 1992), 197.

2. Ibid.

3. NA. RG94, 90th Division in action. US troops captured a German bearing a document showing one of the actual escape routes.

4. NA. RG94, History of 21 *Panzer* Division, Normandy Campaign. Part II; NA (Ottawa): RG24, Vol. 20,519, 981 Som (D132).

5. NAC. RG24, Vol. 20519, 98 Som (D118) Seventh Army. Interview with General von Gersdorff.

6. Ibid.

7. Ibid.

8. Ibid.

9. EC. University of New Orleans. Oral history: Lt. Col. Heinz Günther Guderian, 116th *Panzer* Division Staff Officer.

10. EC. University of New Orleans. Oral history: Walter Kaspers, Adjutant, Anti-Tank Unit 228, 11th Tank Division, 116th (Greyhound) Division.

11. NA. RG94, MS #B727, The campaign in northern France.

12. 21 Army Group Intelligence Summary. No. 154, 131.

13. NA. RG94, MS #B727, The Campaign in northern France. Vol. VI, Ch. 6. NA. The Battle of the Falaise-Argentan Pocket. General von Gersdorff, chief of staff, Seventh Army, September 1946.

14. D'Este, 438.

15. Meyer, 197.

16. Shulman, 158.

17. Ibid., 160–61.

18. NAC. RG24, Vol. 20,522, Report by Lt. Gen. Eugen Meindl, II Parachute Corps, May 3, 1946.

19. Ibid.

20. NAC. 21st Army Group Intelligence Summary. No. 154, 131.

21. Graves, 152.

CHAPTER 30

1. NAC. RG24, Vol. 20,522, Report by Gen. Eugen Meindl, May 3, 1946.

2. Ibid.

3. Ibid.

4. The above italicized and paraphrased quotations are taken from NAC. RG24, Vol. 20, 522, Report by Gen. Eugen Meindl, May 3, 1946.

5. Meyer, 198.

6. Stacey, 132–3,318; Luther, 182. (This fear was justified. According to Hubert Meyer's *History of the 12th SS-Panzerdivision,* when 12th SS *Obersturmbannführer* Max Wünsche was captured three days later, he was taken to Montgomery: "We will treat the German prisoners in accordance with the Geneva convention," General Montgomery was supposed to have said to him angrily, "but not the SS. They will be treated as what they are: political vermin, political dirt."

7. Kurt Meyer, *Grenadiers* (Winnipeg, Man: J. J. Fedorowicz, 1994), 170.

8. Belfield and Essame, 232.

9. Hubert Meyer, 199.

10. *Boisjos: Hill 262.* Montormel and Memorial Committee video, 1961. Statement by Gen. Heinz Guderian.

11. EC. University of New Orleans. Oral history: Walter Kaspers, Adjutant, Anti-Tank Unit 228, 11th Tank Division, 116th (Greyhound) Division.

12. EC. University of New Orleans. Oral history: Lt. Walter Padberg.

13. EC. University of New Orleans. Oral history: Günter Materne, Battery Officer, Artillery Regiment 363.

CHAPTER 31

1. EC. University of New Orleans. Oral history: Col. Max Anger.

2. Shulman, 160.

3. Martin Blumenson, Office of the Chief of Military History (now US Army Center of Military History), Internet Center Military History, Washington, "Examples of employment of tanks in night fighting on the European land mass during world war," June 2, 1966. (The original manuscript is on file in the Historical Manuscripts Collection (HMC) under file number 2-3.7 AC.Y.

4. NA. RG94, Army Group B, Daily Sitreps, August 20.

5. Florentin, 285.

6. NA. RG94, Combat Interview 194. The Gap at Chambois—Aug. 15–22, 1944.

7. NA. RG94, The Gap at Chambois; *Colby,* 241.

8. NA. RG94, 2d Battalion action at Chambois.

9. NA. RG24, Vol. 20510, 981 Som (D117) Seventh Army.

10. Graves, 176.

11. Graves, 155.

12. Speech given by Lt. (now Maj.) Arkle Dunlop, Royal Canadian Legion dinner, Nov. 13, 1985 (Dunlop was awarded the Croix de Guerre avec Etoile de Vermeil for this action; the footbridge was renamed "Dunlop Bridge").

13. Authors' interview with Maj. Arkle Dunlop, Aug. 4, 1998.

14. Arkle Dunlop, Royal Canadian Legion.

15. Graves, 155.

16. Ibid., 168.

17. Ibid., 162.

18. Ibid., 168.

19. Currie, *After the Battle.* Major Martin was awarded the American DSC for his bravery.

20. Graves, 162.

21. Graves, 163.

22. Major R. L. Rogers, *History of the Lincoln and Welland Regiment* (Catharines, ON: The Regiment, 1954). 1954, 158.

23. NA. RG94, CI 194.

24. Terry Copp, "Closing the Falaise Pocket," *Legion Magazine,* August 1994, 42–3.

25. NA. RG94, CI 194. Opn Rpt Aug. 1944. 390-0.3. Box 13279. LeMans to Chambois, Battle of the Pocket.

26. W. W. Barrett, *The History of the 13th Canadian Field Regiment, Royal Canadian Artillery, 1940–1945*. R. K. Mackenzie collection, 60.

27. Florentin, 277.

28. Currie, "Story in His Own Words."

29. Florentin, 27.

CHAPTER 32

1. NA. National Archives microfiche. "Panzer Group Eberbach at Alençon. Its breakthrough the encirclement of Falaise," report by Gen. Heinrich Eberbach.

2. *The Last Battle of Normandy*. Montormel videotape produced by the Montormel Memorial Committee (date unknown). Statement by Corporal E. Podyma.

3. Meyer, *The History of the 12th SS Panzer Division Hitlerjugend*, 197.

4. Authors' interview with Capt. Pierre Sévigny, 4th Canadian Medium Regiment, Nov. 12, 1999.

5. Authors' interview with Maj. Bob MacKenzie, 14th Field Regiment, 3d Canadian Division, RCA, Nov. 3, 2002. Whitaker and Whitaker, *Tug of War* (2nd Ed.), 195.

6. Jack Granatstein, *Bloody Victory*, 179.

7. Authors' interview with Capt. Ted Walewicz, June 8, 1999.

8. *Boisjos: Hill 262*. Montormel Memorial Committee, 1961. As told by Commander Czarnecki, chief of staff, Polish 10th Armored Cavalry Brigade, Captain Sévigny and Pierre Grandvalet.

9. Ibid.

10. Authors' interview with M. Pierre Grandvalet, June 5, 1998.

11. *Boisjos: Hill 262*.

12. Authors' interview with Sgt. Frank Lisowski, June 8, 1999.

13. Authors' interview with Capt. Ted Walewicz, June 8, 1999.

14. *Boisjos: Hill 262*.

15. Ibid.

CHAPTER 33

1. *Boisjos: Hill 262*. Sévigny and Grandvalet accounts.

2. *Boisjos: Hill 262*. Sévigny account.

3. Authors' interview with Brig. Gen. Ned Amy, Sept. 22, 1999.

4. Authors' interview with Krzysztof (Chris) Szydlowski, vice president of the First Polish Armored Association of Canada, Aug. 10, 1999.

5. Garlinski, 260–1.

6. Blumenson, *Breakout and Pursuit*, 554.

7. Authors' interview with Maj. Gen. Roger Rowley and Capt. R. R. Dixon, Oct. 6, 1998.

8. NAC. Account by Lt. Col. Roger Rowley OC. Stormont, Dundas, and Glengarry Highlanders, given to historical officer, Aug. 22, 1944; authors' interview with Maj. Gen. Roger Rowley, Oct. 6, 1998.

9. Authors' interview with Brigadier General Gutowski, May 12, 1998.

10. Florentin, 257.

11. NA. RG94, The Gap at Chambois. 90th Infantry Division.

12. EC. University of New Orleans. Oral history: Hans-Heinrich Dibbern, Second Lieutenant, Adjutant, *Panzer* Grenadier Regiment, 902.

13. NA. The Gap at Chambois. 90th Infantry Division.

14. Launay, 70–80.

15. Hubert Meyer, 201.
16. NAC. RG24, Vol. 20522.
17. Currie, *After the Battle.*
18. Ibid.
19. Weigley, 314.
20. Stacey, 271.
21. John Keegan. *Six Armies in Normandy: From D-Day to the Liberation of Paris, June 6th–August 25th, 1944,* 283. See Keegan Web page. Authors' collection.
22. NA. The Gap at Chambois, Aug. 15–22, 1944.
23. Stacey, 270–71.
24. Authors' interview with Maj. Gen. Roger Rowley.
25. Florentin, 320.
26. Department of Calvados tourism information bulletin.
27. Florentin, 320.

A LAST WORD

1. B. H. Liddell Hart, *The German Generals Speak* (London: Cassell, 1951).
2. S. L. A. Marshall, *Men against Fire* (New York: William Morrow, 1947), 54–7.
3. Harold P. Leinbaugh and J. D. Campbell, *The Men of Company K* (New York: William Morrow, 1985).
4. John Keegan, *Face of Battle* (London: Penguin, 1976).
5. Russell F. Weigley, *Eisenhower's Lieutenants: The Campaigns of France and Germany, 1944–1945* (Bloomington: Indiana University Press, 1981).
6. Roger S. Spiller, "S. L. A. Marshall and the Ratio of Fire," *RUSI Journal,* 133/4 Winter 1988, 68–71. For an overview see Fredric Smoler, "The Secret of the Soldier Who Didn't Shoot," *American Heritage,* March 1989, 37–45.
7. Trevor N. Dupuy, *Numbers, Predictions and War* (Fairfax, VA: Hero Books, 1979).
8. John Sloan Brown, "Colonel Trevor N. Dupuy and the Mythos of Wehrmacht Superiority: A Reconsideration," *Military Affairs,* January 1985, 16.
9. Trevor N. Dupuy, "Mythos or Verity? The Quantified Judgment Model and German Combat Effectiveness," *Military Affairs,* October 1986, 210.
10. Martin Van Crevald, *Fighting Power: German and U.S. Army Performance, 1939–1943* (London: Arms and Armour Press, 1983).
11. Ibid., 168.
12. Stacey, 271.
13. Ibid., 118–19.
14. Ibid., 276.
15. Martin Blumenson, *The Battle of the Generals* (New York: Morrow, 1993).
16. Stacey, 272–3.
17. D'Este.
18. Ibid., 82–6.
19. For an account of one Canadian's D-Day see Charles Martin with Roy Whitstead, *Battle Diary* (Toronto: Dundurn Press, 1994).
20. Headquarters, United States Strategic Air Forces in Europe, "Survey of Effectiveness of Bombing of Invasion Coast Defenses, 7 July 1944," United States Military History Institute, Carlisle: PA, 2.
21. NAC. RG24, Vol. 10673: Combined Operations Headquarters, Bulletin Y/37: Naval Fire Support in Operation Overlord, November 1944.
22. Terry Copp (Ed.), *Montgomery's Scientists: Operational Research in Northwest Europe, 1944–1945* (Waterloo, ON: LCMSDS, 2000).

23.   John Ellis, *Brute Force* (London: Viking, 1990), 364.

24.   Robert Vogel, "Tactical Air Power in Normandy: Some Thoughts on the Interdiction Plan," *Canadian Military History*, 3/1 Spring 1994, 37–47.

25.   Fighter Command Tactical Memorandum, No. 30, March 14, 1943, DND Directorate of History and Heritage Ottawa, 79/32.

26.   Hubert Meyer, 61.

27.   Terry Copp interview with Tony Sargeaunt, 1991.

28.   Copp (Ed.), *Montgomery's Scientists*, 405.

29.   Ibid.

30.   Alfred D. Chandler (Ed.), *The Papers of Dwight D. Eisenhower*, Vol. III (Baltimore: Johns Hopkins, 1970).

31.   Belton Y. Cooper, *Death Traps* (Novato, CA: Presidio, 1998), viii.

32.   L. F. Ellis, *Victory in the West* (London: HMSO, 1962), 308–16.

33.   George Blackburn, *The Guns of Normandy: A Soldier's Eye View, France, 1944* (Toronto: McClelland & Stewart, 1995) offers a nontechnical account of Canadian artillery operations in Normandy. See Copp (Ed.), *Montgomery's Scientists*, for a scientific evaluation of artillery in Normandy and northwest Europe.

34.   Allan Snowie, *Bloody Buron* (Erin, ON: Boston Mills, 1984).

35.   Tony Foulds, "In Support of the Canadians: A British Anti-tank Regiment's First Five Weeks in Normandy," *Canadian Military History*, 7/2 Spring 1998, 78.

36.   Gordon Brown, "The Attack on the Abbaye d'Ardenne," *Canadian Military History*, 4/1 Spring 1995, 91–99.

37.   Copp (Ed.), *Montgomery's Scientists*, 431.

38.   Terry Copp, "Counter Mortar and Operational Research in 21 Army Group," *Canadian Military History*, 3/2 Autumn 1994, 45–52.

39.   Terry Copp interview with Tony Sargeaunt.

40.   Stacey, 228.

41.   Weigley, 127.

42.   Ibid., 128.

43.   How, *Normandy*, 221.

44.   Copp (Ed.), *Montgomery's Scientists*, introduction and 22–23.

45.   EC. University of New Orleans. Oral history: Maj. Joachim Barth.

46.   B. Michael Bechthold, "The Development of an Unbeatable Combination: U.S. Close Air Support in Normandy," *Canadian Military History*, 8/1 Winter 1999, 15–17.

47.   Christopher Evans, "The Fighter Bomber in the Normandy Campaign: The Role of 83 Group," *Canadian Military History*, 8/1 Winter 1999, 21.

POSTSCRIPTS

1.   Authors' interviews with Anthony J. Bajdek, Oct. 18, 2002 and Nov. 19, 2003. Anthony J. Bajdek, "Completing a Final Mission for Matt Louis Urban: Primus Inter Pares: First Among Equals: Pierwszy Pomiedzy Równymi," *The Life of Polonia*, a quarterly publication of the Polish American Congress of Eastern Massachusetts, Boston, Vol. XI, No. 4(55), 2001, 1–5. National campaign to request that the United States Postal Service issue a commemorative stamp in honor of Lt. Col. Matt Louis Urban (1919–1995), the most decorated American combat soldier of World War II.

2.   The postwar account of David Currie is based on notes from Donald Graves's history *South Albertas: A Canadian Regiment at War* (Toronto: Robin Brass Studio, 1998); Maj. David D. Currie, *Story in His Own Words*; Winston G. Ramsey, (Ed.), *After the Battle: The Battle of the Falaise Pocket* (London: Battle of Britain Prints International, No. 8, 1982);

Herbert Fairlie Wood, *Encounter at St. Lambert,* The Legionary, January 1964; Arthur Bishop, *Our Bravest and Our Best: The Stories of Canada's Victoria Cross Winners* (Toronto: McGraw-Hill Ryerson, 1995).

3. Accounts from *Flight Journal,* June 2002, *A Tribute to Francis S. "Gabby" Gabreski,* and Associated Press, Feb. 2, 2002.

4. Wing Commander Duke Warren's story was based on correspondence and conversation with the authors in 1999 and 2000.

5. The Kurt Meyer story is based on the following books and documentaries: Howard Margolian, *Conduct Unbecoming: The Story of the Murder of Canadian Prisoners of War in Normandy* (Toronto: University of Toronto Press, 1998); David Paperny Films Ltd., *Murder in Normandy,* 1999; Lt. Col. B. J. S. Macdonald, *The Trial of Kurt Meyer* (Toronto: Clarke Irwin, 1954), 79.

6. For the Polish story, the authors are indebted to Capt. (now Brig. Gen.) Michael Gutowski, Virtui Militari, and to Krzysztof Szydlowski, vice-president, First Polish Armoured Division Association in Canada, for their cooperation and interest in telling the story of Polish patriots in the Second World War. Other readings included Jozef Garlinski, *Poland in the Second World War;* Polish Combatants of Canada, *For Your Freedom and Ours, 1944–1994;* John Keegan, *Six Armies in Normandy;* and K. Jamar, *With the Tanks of the 1st Polish Armoured Division.*

7. Authors' interview with Lt. Col. Trumbull Warren, September 14, 1998.

8. Notes on the General Guderian story were based on a personal interview and correspondence with the authors, 1988, and on Charles B. MacDonald, *The Mighty Endeavour: The American War in Europe* (New York: Morrow, 1969, 1986).

9. There are a number of Web sites on Ernie Pyle. His best columns can be found in "The Wartime Columns of Ernie Pyle," www.journalism.indiana.edu/news/erniepyle.

Bibliography

Ambrose, Stephen E. *Citizen Soldiers: The U.S. Army from the Normandy Beaches to the Bulge to the Surrender of Germany.* New York: Simon & Schuster, 1997.

————. *The Victors: Eisenhower and His Boys: The Men of World War II.* New York: Simon & Schuster, 1998.

Barrett, W. W. *The History of the 13th Canadian Field Regiment, Royal Canadian Artillery. 1940–1945.*

Bates, Thomas J. *Normandy: The Search for Sydney.* Berkeley, CA: Bayes, 1999.

Bechthold, B. Michael. "The Development of an Unbeatable Combination: U.S. Close Air Support in Normandy," *Canadian Military History,* 8/1 (Winter 1999).

Belfield, Eversley, and H. Essame. *The Battle for Normandy.* London: Pan, 1967.

Bercuson, David. *Battalion of Heroes: History of the Calgary Highlanders.* Calgary: Calgary Highlanders Regimental Funds Foundation, 1994.

Bernage, Georges, and Ronald McNair. *Falaise-Argentan: Le Couloir de la Mort.* Bayeux: Éditions Heimdal, 1944.

Bhenamou, Jean-Pierre. *Normandy 1944: An Illustrated Field-Guide,* June 7–August 22, 1944. Bayeux: Éditions Heimdal, 1982.

Bishop, Arthur. *Our Bravest and Our Best: The Stories of Canada's Victoria Cross Winners.* Toronto: McGraw-Hill Ryerson, 1995.

Blackburn, George. *The Guns of Normandy: A Soldier's Eye View, France, 1944.* Toronto: McClelland & Stewart, 1995.

Blumenson, Martin. *The Battle of the Generals.* New York: Morrow, 1993.

————. *Breakout and Pursuit.* Washington, DC: Center of Military History, 1961.

————. *Patton. The Man Behind the Legend.* New York: Morrow, 1985.

————, ed. *The Patton Papers.* Boston: Houghton Mifflin, 1972.

Bradley, Omar. *A Soldier's Story.* New York: Henry Holt, 1952.

Bradley, Omar N., and Blair Clay. *A General's Life: An Autobiography by General of the Army Omar N. Bradley.* New York: Simon & Schuster, 1983.

Breuer, William B. *Death of a Nazi Army: The Falaise Pocket.* New York: Scarborough House, 1985.

Brokaw, Tom. *The Greatest Generation*. New York: Random House, 1998.

Brown, Gordon. "The Attack on the Abbaye d'Ardenne," *Canadian Military History*, 4/1 (Spring 1995).

Buisson, Gilles. Mortain 44. *Objectif Avranches*. Mortain: Éditions OCEP, 1984.

Carell, Paul. *Invasion: They're Coming*. New York: Bantam, 1964.

Cassidy, G. L. *Warpath: The Story of the Algonquin Regiment, 1939–1945*. Toronto: Ryerson, 1948; Markham, ON: Paperjacks, 1980.

Chandler, Alfred D., ed. *The Papers of Dwight D. Eisenhower*, Vol. III. Baltimore: Johns Hopkins, 1970.

Colby, John. *War from the Ground Up: The 90th Division in WWII*. Austin, TX: Nortex, 1991.

Conron, A. Brandon, ed. *The History of the First Hussars 1856–1980*, London, ON: Regiment, 1981.

Cooper, Belton Y. *Death Traps*. Novato, CA: Presidio, 1998.

Copp, Terry. "Allied Bombing in Normandy," *Legion Magazine*, November/December 1998.

———. *A Canadian's Guide to the Battlefields of Normandy*. Waterloo, ON: Laurier Centre for Military Strategic and Disarmament Studies, Wilfrid Laurier University, 1994.

———. "Closing the Gap," *Legion Magazine*, October 1999.

———. "Counter Mortar and Operational Research in 21 Army Group," *Canadian Military History*, 3/2 (Autumn 1994).

———. *The Canadians in Normandy: A Reassessment*. Waterloo, ON: Wilfrid Laurier University Press, April 1998.

———. *Fields of Fire. The Canadians in Normandy*. Toronto: University of Toronto Press, 2003.

———, ed. *Montgomery's Scientists: Operational Research in Northwest Europe*. Waterloo, ON: LCMSDS, Wilfrid Laurier University, 2000.

———. "TAF Over Normandy," *Legion Magazine*, January/February 1999.

Copp, Terry, and Bill McAndrew. *Battle Exhaustion*. Montreal and Kingston: McGill-Queen's University Press, 1990.

Copp, Terry, and Robert Vogel. *Maple Leaf Route: Falaise*. Alma, ON: MLR, 1983.

Currie, Maj. David D. "Story in His Own Words," in *After the Battle: The Battle of the Falaise Pocket*, Number 8. Winston G. Ramsey, ed. *London: Battle of Britain*. Prints International, 1982.

De Guingand, Maj. Gen. Sir Francis, KBE, CB, DSO. *Operation Victory*. London: Hodder & Stoughton, 1947.

Delaforce, Patrick. *Churchill's Desert Rats: From Normandy to Berlin with the 7th Armoured Division*. London: Alan Sutton, 1994.

Demoulin, Charles. *Firebirds! Flying a Typhoon in Action*. Washington, DC: Smithsonian Institution Press, 1986.

D'Este, Carlo. *Decision in Normandy*. New York: Dutton, 1983.

Dupuy, Trevor N. "Mythos or Verity? The Quantified Judgment Model and German Combat Effectiveness," *Military Affairs*, October 1986.

———. *Numbers, Predictions and War*. Fairfax, VA: Hero Books, 1979.

Eisenhower, Gen. Dwight D. *Crusade in Europe*. New York: Doubleday, 1948.

Ellis, John. *Brute Force*. London: Viking, 1990.

———. *Sharp End of War: The Fighting Men in World War II*. Newton Abbott, Devon: David and Charles, 1980.

Ellis, L. F., CVO, CBE, DSO, MC. *History of the Second World War*. Vol. II: Victory in the West. London: HMSO, 1962.

English, Jack. *The Canadian Army and the Normandy Campaign: A Study of Failure in High Command.* New York: Praeger, 1991.

Erbes, John, MD. *Hell-on-Wheels Surgeon.* New York: Vintage, 1995.

Essame, H. *Patton: A Study in Command.* New York: Scribner's, 1974.

Evans, Christopher. "The Fighter Bomber in the Normandy Campaign: The Role of 83 Group." *Canadian Military History,* 8/1 (Winter 1999).

Farago, Ladislas. *Patton: Ordeal and Triumph.* New York: Astor-Honour, 1964.

Feasby, W. R. *Official History of the Canadian Medical Services, 1939–1945,* Vol. 1: Organization and Campaigns and Vol. 2: Clinical Subjects. Ottawa: Queen's Printer and Controller of Stationery, 1953.

Featherston, Alwyn. *Battle for Mortain: The 30th Infantry Division Saves the Breakout, August 7–21.* Novato, CA: Presidio, 1993.

Florentin, Eddy. *Battle of the Falaise Gap.* London: Elek, 1965.

Folkestad, William B. *The View from the Turret: The 743rd Tank Battalion During World War II.* Shippensburg, PA: Burd Street Press, 1996.

Foulds, Tony. "In Support of the Canadians: A British Anti-tank Regiment's First Five Weeks in Normandy," *Canadian Military History,* 7/2 (Spring 1998).

Fraser, Robert. *Black Yesterdays: The Argylls' War.* Hamilton, ON: Argyll Regimental Foundation, 1996.

French, David. "Colossal Cracks . . . Morale of Second British Army 1944," *Journal of Strategic Studies,* 19/4 (December 1996).

Fussell, Paul. *Wartime. Understanding and Behavior in the Second World War.* New York and Oxford: Oxford University Press, 1989.

Garlinski, Jozef. *Poland in the Second World War.* New York: Macmillan, 1985.

German, Dr. Paul. *One Hundred Days of War for Peace.* Condé-sur-Noireau, France: Charles Corlet, 1998.

Goodman, Eddie. *Life of the Party.* Toronto: Key Porter, 1988.

Goodspeed, Maj. D. J. *Battle Royal: A History of the Royal Regiment of Canada, 1862–1962.* Toronto: Royal Regiment of Canada, 1962.

Graham, Dominick. *The Price of Command: A Biography of General Guy Simonds.* Toronto: Stoddart, 1993.

Grant, Dr. W. G. *Did I Ever Tell You about the War?* Hampton, ON: Self-published, March 1990.

Graves, Donald E. *South Albertas: A Canadian Regiment at War.* Toronto: Robin Brass Studio, 1998.

Greenfield, Kent Roberts, ed. *Command Decisions.* Washington, DC: Office of the Chief of Military History, United States Army, 1960.

Greenhous, Brereton, Kingsley Brown, Sr., and Kingsley Brown, Jr., eds. *Semper Paratus.* Hamilton, ON: Royal Hamilton Light Infantry Historical Association, 1977.

Guderian, Heinz Günther. *From Normandy to the Ruhr: With the 116th Panzer Division in World War II.* Bedford, PA: The Aberjona Press.

Guingand, Maj. Gen. Sir Francis, KBE, CB, DSO. *Operation Victory.* London: Hodder & Stoughton, 1947.

Halliday, Hugh A. *The Tumbling Sky.* Ottawa: Canada's Wing, 1978.

———. *Typhoon and Tempest: The Canadian Story.* Toronto: CANAV, 1992.

Hamilton, Nigel. *Monty: Master of the Battlefield, 1942–1944.* New York: Hodder & Stoughton, 1983.

Hastings, Max. *Overlord: D-Day and the Battle for Normandy.* London: Pan, 1985.

Hayes, Geoffrey. *The Lincs: A History of the Lincoln and Welland Regiment at War.* Alma, ON: Maple Leaf Route, 1986.

Hillsman, J. B. *Eleven Men and a Scalpel*. Winnipeg: Columbia, 1948.

Hinsley, F. H. *British Intelligence in the Second World War*, Vol. III. London: HMSO, 1981.

Horrocks, Sir Brian, with Eversley Belfield and Maj. Gen. H. Essame. *Corps Commander*. Toronto: Griffin House, 1977.

———. *A Full Life*. London: Collins, 1960.

How, J. J., MC. *Hill 112*. London: Kimber, 1984.

———. *Normandy: The British Breakout*. London: Kimber, 1981.

Howard, Michael Eliot. *British Intelligence in the Second World War, Vol. 5: Strategic Deception*. London: HMSO, 1990.

Jamar, K. *With the Tanks of the 1st Polish Armoured Division*. Hengelo: H. L. Smit & Son, 1946.

James, F. A. *Nos Plus Longs Mois (D 1 76)*. Falaise, France: Jean James, 1994.

Jary, Sydney. *18 Platoon*. Surrey, UK: Self-published, 1987.

Jarymowycz, Roman. *Canadian Armour in Normandy's Operation Totalize and the Quest for Operational Manouevre*. Unpublished doctoral dissertation, McGill University, 1997. Canadian Military History 7, No. 2 (1998), 19–40.

Johnston, Murray, ed. *Canada's Craftsmen at 50: The Story of Electrical and Mechanical Engineers in the Canadian Forces*. Borden, ON: EME Officers' Fund, 1997.

Keegan, John. *Six Armies in Normandy*. London: Jonathan Cape, 1982.

———. *Face of Battle*. London: Penguin, 1976.

Kelly, Arthur. *There's a Goddamn Bullet for Everyone*. Paris, ON: Arts and Publishing, 1979.

Kitching, George. *Mud and Green Fields*. Vancouver: Battleline, 1986.

Langlois, René. *1944: Les Douets in Torment: A Memoir*. Trans. by Joyce Carter. Mortain: Self-published, 1996.

Launay, Abbé Marcel. *Dans la Tourmente de la Guerre*. Normandy: Self-published, 1985.

Leinbaugh, Harold P., and John D. Campbell. *The Men of Company K*. New York: William Morrow, 1985.

Liddell Hart, B. H. *The German Generals Speak*. London: Cassell, 1951.

Liebling, A. J. *The Road from Saint-Lô*. http://eb.com/normandy/pri/Q00237.html.

Linderman, Gerald F. *The World Within War: America's Combat Experience in World War II*. Cambridge, MA: Harvard University Press, 1997.

Lindsay, Martin. *So Few Got Through: The Personal Diary of Lt. Col. Martin Lindsay*. London: Collins, 1946.

Luther, Craig W. H. *Blood and Honor: The History of the 12th SS Panzer Division "Hitler Youth," 1943–1945*. San Jose, CA: Bender, 1987.

MacDonald, Charles B. *The Mighty Endeavor: The American War in Europe*. New York: Morrow, 1969, 1986.

Malone, Col. Richard Sankey, OBE. *Missing from the Record*. Toronto: Collins, 1946.

———. *A World in Flames, 1944–1945*. Toronto: Collins, 1984.

Mansoor, Peter. *The GI Offensive in Europe*. Kansas City: University Press of Kansas, 1999.

Margolian, Howard. *Conduct Unbecoming: The Story of the Murder of Canadian Prisoners of War in Normandy*. Toronto: University of Toronto Press, 1998.

Marshall, S. L. A. *Men Against Fire*. New York: William Morrow, 1947.

Martin, Charles, with Roy Whitstead. *Battle Diary*. Toronto: Dundurn Press, 1994.

Maule, Henry. *Normandy Breakout*. New York: Quadrangle/New York Times Book Co., 1977.

McBryde, Brenda. *A Nurse's War*. London: Chatto & Windus, 1979.

McKee, Alexander. *Caen: Anvil of Victory*. London: Souvenir, 1964.

McNeil, Bill, ed. *Voices of a War Remembered: An Oral History of Canadians in World War Two*. Toronto: Doubleday, 1991.

Meyer, Hubert. *The History of the 12 SS-Panzerdivision Hitlerjugend*. Winnipeg: J. J. Fedorowicz, 1992.

Meyer, Kurt. *Grenadiers*. Winnipeg: J. J. Fedorowicz, 1994.

Miller, Robert A. *August 1944*. Novato, CA: Presidio, 1988.

Milner, Marc. *Canadian Military History*. Toronto: Copp Clark Pitman, 1993.

Mitcham, Samuel W. *Hitler's Field Marshals and Their Battles*. Chelson, MI: Scarborough House, 1990.

Moorhead, Alan. *Eclipse*. London: Hamish Hamilton, 1967.

Nicholson, Col. G. W. L., C.D. *Seventy Years of Service: A History of a Royal Canadian Army Medical Corps*. Ottawa: Borealis, 1977.

Patton, George. *War As I Knew It*. Boston: Houghton Mifflin, 1947.

Peden, Murray. *A Thousand Shall Fall*. Toronto: Stoddart, 1988.

Pyle, Ernie. *Ernie's War*. New York: Random House, 1986.

Ramsey, Winston G., ed. *After the Battle: The Battle of the Falaise Pocket, Number 8*. London: Battle of Britain Prints International, 1982.

Reynolds, Michael. *Steel Inferno: 1 SS Panzer Corps in Normandy*. New York: Spellmount, 1997.

Roberts, G. P. B. *From the Desert to the Baltic*. London: Kimber, 1987.

Rogers, Maj. R. L. *History of the Lincoln and Welland Regiment*. St. Catharines, ON: The Regiment, 1954.

Rooney, Andy. *My War*. New York: Random House, 1995.

Roy, Reg. *1944: The Canadians in Normandy*. Ottawa: Canadian War Museum, 1984.

Salmond, J. B. *History of the 51st Highland Division*. Edinburgh: Blackwood, 1953.

Shaughnessy, Douglas. *Harry Green*. A personal memoir kindly loaned to the authors.

Shulman, Milton. *Defeat in the West*. London: Secker & Warburg, 1963.

Sloan Brown, John. "Colonel Trevor N. Dupuy and the Mythos of Wehrmacht Superiority: A Reconsideration," *Military Affairs*, January 1985.

Smith, Wilfred I. *Code Word Canloan*. Toronto: Dundurn, 1992.

Snowie, Allan. *Bloody Buron*. Erin, ON: Boston Mills, 1984.

Spiller, Roger S. "S. L. A. Marshall and the Ratio of Fire," *RUSI Journal*, 133/4 (Winter 1988).

Stacey, Col. Charles C. P. *The Victory Campaign: The Operations in North-West Europe, 1944–1945*. Vol III. Ottawa: Queen's Printer, 1960.

Szygowski, Ludwik J. *Seven Days and Seven Nights in Normandy*. London: Self-published, 1976.

Tout, Ken. *A Fine Night for Tanks: The Road to Falaise*. Phoenix Mill, Gloucestershire, UK: Sutton, 1988.

———. *Tanks, Advance! Normandy to the Netherlands, 1944*. London: Grafton Books, 1987.

Van Crevald, Martin. *Fighting Power: German and U.S. Army Performance, 1939–1943*. London: Arms and Armour Press, 1983.

Vogel, Robert. "Tactical Air Power in Normandy: Some Thoughts on the Interdiction Plan," *Canadian Military History*, 3/1 (Spring 1994).

Warlimont, Walter. *Inside Hitler's Headquarters, 1939–1945*. London: Weidenfeld & Nicolson, 1964.

Warner, Philip. *Horrocks: The General Who Led from the Front*. London: Hamish Hamilton, 1984.

Weigley, Russell F. *Eisenhower's Lieutenants: The Campaigns of France and Germany, 1944–1945*. Bloomington: Indiana University Press, 1981.

Whitaker, Denis, and Shelagh Whitaker. *Rhineland: The Battle to End the War*. Toronto: Stoddart, 1989, 2000.

———. *Tug of War: The Allied Victory that Opened Antwerp Harbour*. Toronto: Stoddart, 1984, 2000.

Wilmot, Chester. *The Struggle for Europe*. London: Collins, 1952.

Winterbotham, F. W., CBE. *The Ultra Secret*. New York: Harper & Row, 1974.

Womack, J. A. *Summon Up the Blood: A Unique Record of D-Day and Its Aftermath*. Ed. by Celia Wolfe. London: Leo Cooper, 1997.

Wood, Alan. *The Falaise Road*. Toronto: Macmillan, 1944.

Regimental Histories

Barrett, W. W. *The History of the 13th Canadian Field Regiment, Royal Canadian Artillery, 1940–1945*. (Collection of R. K. Mackenzie.)

History of the Corps of Royal Canadian Engineers, Vol. II. Ottawa: The Corps, 1966.

The History of the First Hussars, 1856–1980. Published by the Regiment, 1981.

The Regimental History of the Governor General's Foot Guards. Ottawa: The Regiment, 1948.

Personal Memoirs and Private Collections

Chadderton, Capt. Cliff. *Caen to Calais: July–August–September 1944*.

Connors, Maj. John J. M. *The Story of an Unremarkable Canadian*. London, ON: Self-published, 1981.

Danson, B. J. "A Personal Essay: Being Hit, Normandy, August 1944." Feb. 28, 1994. Kindly lent to the authors.

Dunlop, Lt. Arkle. "St. Lambert-sur-Dives, August 19 to 21, 1944. A memoir." Canadian Argyll Regiment (written c. 1980).

Montormel Memorial Committee, 1961. *Boisjos: Hill 262*. Polish Combatants of Canada. *For Your Freedom and Ours, 1944–1994*.

van Dijke, Jacques. *L'Effondrement du front allemand en Normandie*. Rotterdam: 1995.

Index